Juvenile Justice Reform and Restorative Justice

'This is a paradigm-shifting book. It is a lucid, systematic, principle-driven treatise that connects the theory to the practice of restorative justice. That framework is applied to a national inventory of restorative conferencing programs for youth in the US that identifies 773 of them. The results cast real light on where restorative justice is going in America.' – *John Braithwaite (Australian National University)*

'Restorative justice is the most exciting idea to come along in penal reform in a century. It fundamentally changes the conversation about law breaking and law breakers. As happens with any new idea, however, the mythology can outpace the cold, hard truth. This book is a powerful step in the direction of a grounded conceptualization of the essence of what really is restorative and how to produce it through mindful action. For people who want a survey of programs, they will find no better, more current research available today. For people who want a guidebook to action that learns from practice in the field, this is the best source now available.' – *Todd R. Clear (Distinguished Professor, John Jay College of Criminal Justice)*

'This important book significantly advances our understanding of restorative justice theory and practice. Bazemore and Schiff link restorative principles with intervention theories, practices, and outcomes for each of nine dimensions of restorative practice. This conceptual work alone is a substantial contribution to the restorative justice movement; that it is grounded in a national quantitative and qualitative study of restorative justice programs makes it all the more authoritative.' – *Daniel W. Van Ness (Director, Prison Fellowship International Centre for Justice and Reconciliation)*

'Those of us working in juvenile justice reform have been eagerly awaiting this book for years. Bazemore and Schiff are consistently among the clearest voices writing about community and restorative justice on the international scene, and the findings discussed here on restorative work with young people are hugely important. The field of juvenile justice, beaten and bruised by the longstanding debate between rehabilitation and punishment, is in desperate need of new visions. This book is the place to start.' – *Shadd Maruna (University of Cambridge)*

'In an era when governments are struggling to enact justice and communities to achieve peace, Bazemore and Schiff provide us with guiding principles for restorative decision making in a particularly troubling arena – juvenile justice. Their three principles of repairing harm, including key stakeholders, and transforming government-community relations are applied to define restorative justice. By this means, they step outside of debates about the pros and cons of specific models and instead conceptualize restorative conferencing in a way that encompasses a full range of programs. Their principles are checked against and grounded in the practices of restorative justice programs across the United States, and their analysis is enriched by its attention to historical and international developments in youth justice. They propose a vision for juvenile justice that focuses on outcomes for offending young people, victims, and their families and communities and, thus, offer a means to evaluate the extent to which a just and peaceful resolution is realized.' – *Joan Pennell (Professor and Head, Department of Social Work, North Carolina State University)*

'The work Gordon Bazemore and Mara Schiff have carried out provides crucial knowledge on how all kinds of restorative conferences are being implemented in the USA. The qualitative approach of the research provides new and deep insight into exactly what it is that makes these conferences so powerful in dealing with youth crime. Their personal commitment as front line restorative justice academics, and their concern for the quality of current practices, are complemented by an exemplary scientific rigour, essential for successfully executing this project. Though the book is about restorative conferences in the United States, its importance goes far beyond these borders. The book is a must read for all those who are interested in restorative justice developments in practice, theory and systematic research.' – *Lode Walgrave (Katholieke Universiteit Leuven, Belgium)*

Juvenile Justice Reform and Restorative Justice

Building theory and policy from practice

Gordon Bazemore and Mara Schiff

Routledge
Taylor & Francis Group

LONDON AND NEW YORK

First published by Willan Publishing 2005
This edition published by Routledge 2011
2 Park Square, Milton Park, Abingdon, Oxon OX14 4RN
711 Third Avenue, New York, NY 10017 (8th Floor)

Routledge is an imprint of the Taylor & Francis Group, an informa business

ISBN 978-1-84392-095-3 (cased)
ISBN 978-1-84392-094-6 (paper)

British Library Cataloguing-in-Publication Data

A catalogue record for this book is available from the British Library

Typeset by TW Typesetting, Plymouth, Devon, UK
Project managed by Deer Park Productions, Tavistock, Devon, UK

Contents

Acknowledgements

The authors of this volume wish to acknowledge the assistance and support of a wide range of staff, consultants, practitioners, friends, and sponsors without whom the production of this work would have not been possible. We first acknowledge the sponsors of this project, the National Institute of Justice (NIJ), and the Robert Wood Johnson Foundation (RWJF), for their generous support of research that may likely be viewed as unconventional given the mandate of these agencies. We especially appreciate the continuous encouragement, moral support and patience of our RWJF Executive and Project Manager, Dr Kate Kraft, and NIJ Project Manager, Dr Akiva Liberman.

Second, project staff and Florida Atlantic University (FAU) staff provided invaluable and persistent support and input. Research Associate Carsten Erbe provided the majority of assistance with all off-site data collection, assisted in conducting interviews and focus groups, and managed project files. Similarly, Research Assistant Colleen McLeod assisted in all these areas and was responsible for transcription of interviews, and working with Mr Erbe on focus group transcription. Our on-site researchers in Minnesota and Colorado respectively, Nancy Miller McCreight and Loree Greco performed most of the difficult work associated with observing conferences, interviewing practitioners, and arranging local focus groups and meetings during site visits of the Principal Investigators. Office staff and consultants of the Community Justice Institute, who contributed to reviewing/editing, typing, and formatting of the report included at various stages: Nancy Vaniman, Lavon Dixon, Rita Kraemer, and Desmond Clark.

Third, consultants and project advisors provided invaluable assistance in gaining access to programs and practitioners, study design and instrumentation (especially for the National Survey), and early review of drafts of various chapters. Although we are concerned that we may fail to mention some individuals and organizations who provided important assistance, we specifically wish to thank the following in-dividuals and organizations who assisted in access to agencies, programs and practitioners during one or more phases of the study: Dr Mark Umbreit, Director, and his staff at the Center for Restorative Justice and Peacemaking at the University of Minnesota; the Victim Offender Mediation Association (VOMA); Beth Rodman and Paul McCold from the RealJustice organization; The National Center for Juvenile Justice (NCJJ); Kay Pranis and Sue Stacy, Minnesota Department of Corrections; Anne Rogers and Vern Fogg, The Colorado Forum on Restorative Justice and the Colorado Department of the Court Administrator respectively. Special thanks are owed to Joe Hudson who spent many hours reviewing and editing the final manuscript. Other document reviewers who provided important feedback at various phases of the writing included: Anne Warner Roberts, David Karp, Joan Pennell, Dee Bell, Kay Pranis, John Braithwaite, and Jeanne Stinchcombe.

Fourth, and most important, we thank the practitioners who participated in the research as key informants, respondents in interviews, focus group participants, and program directors and facilitators. We thank the various judges, prosecutors, police officers, probation officers and other criminal justice staff as well as the directors and facilitators of conferencing programs. While there are too many practitioners to mention individually, and because our promise of anonymity does not permit us to identify staff of programs we studied or interviewed, we here mention only a few local practitioners who participated in interviews or focus groups, allowed us to observe them as conference facilitators, provided special guidance, and indeed, often went out of their way as key informants to help us gain access to programs or individuals. These practitioners include Dave Hines, Alice Lynch, Mary Pat Panaghetti, Susan Blackburn, Carolyn McLeod, Jesus Diaz, Leslie Young, David Mrakitsch, Kelly Prybil, Beverly Title, and Barbara Gerten.

Fifth, we thank our publisher, Brian Willan, for taking on this somewhat unconventional work and being so consistently patient and good-natured with us. We also thank his staff, including Bill Antrobus of Deer Park Productions and particularly Peter Williams, who did a masterful job combing through the manuscript and correcting many errors within a very short turnaround time.

Finally, we thank our families (Cynthia Wright, Sophia and Helena Bazemore, and Jeff and Colton Holloway) for supporting and putting up with us throughout this laborious and very time-consuming project.

Foreword

Joe Hudson and Dennis Maloney

Almost fifteen years ago in the concluding chapter of an early book on restorative justice, the eminent criminologist, John Conrad, asserted that restorative justice programming was one of the few successes in corrections, and that restorative programming efforts needed to be brought to the mainstream of criminal justice policy and practice. This need has yet to be fulfilled, but this superb book by Gordon Bazemore and Mara Schiff demonstrates how far restorative programs, practices and research have come since Conrad made his observation. Among the many contributions of this fine book is an agenda for future work to be carried out on restorative decision-making to help meet Conrad's vision, moving restorative programming to the mainstream of the justice systems.

Combining a fine balance of research and practice, Bazemore and Schiff have produced a text best seen within the context of badly needed juvenile justice reforms. To a great extent this means moving away from corrections institutions being operated as places to warehouse young people. While at the same time this important book provides badly needed alternatives to the way we have reduced probation and parole services into a cat-and-mouse paper shuffling excersize in which surveillance, not service and real accountability, becomes the primary, if not exclusive focus. We need to develop well structured and measurable community justice programs, integrate them into the deep end of the justice systems so they operate as true alternatives to incarceration, and make restorative decision-making the central focus of probation work. This book should be immensely helpful in moving toward these reform goals.

While not yet geriatric candidates, we can look back on the field from even an earlier time than Conrad, back to the 1970s when we were involved in some pioneering restorative justice programs in Minnesota and Wisconsin. The year 1972 saw the birth of the Minnesota Restitution Center, the first systematic attempt to hold face-to-face victim and offender meetings to develop plans of reparation to make good the harm caused. The three broad principles seen by Bazemore and Schiff to capture the essence of restorative decision-making – principles of repair, stake-holder participation, community/government role transformation – were systematically incorporated in the Restitution Center program. Victim repair and participation with their offenders were central to program operations, along with the key aim of stimulating interest in restructuring the roles of community and government in responding to crime. The spread of reparative and victim–offender schemes within a few years of the Minnesota Restitution Center's beginning in 1972, testifies to the influence of this pioneering program which served as a true alternative to incarceration for adult felons. Notable among the early programs developing out of the Minnesota model was the Wisconsin Restitution Initiative, along with a substantial number of similar programs funded in the 1970s through a national initiative by the Office of Juvenile Justice and Delinquency Prevention. Both the Minnesota and Wisconsin restorative justice programming efforts played an important role in stimulating interest in restorative programming, and our involvement with those early programs, along with continued participation in the field over the ensuing years, provides us with some perspective on research efforts and programming and policy developments that have taken place since then. Our views have been shaped by those early experiences and, we think, help us better appreciate the immense contribution to the field that Bazemore and Schiff have made with this superb book.

The ambitious agenda Bazemore and Schiff set themselves for this book include:

surveying current program practices and providing a comprehensive accounting of what's going on in American juvenile justice systems;

identifying and articulating the theoretical bases for restorative decision-making projects and developing testable propositions for future research, practice, and theory-building;

developing a research agenda for future program development.

To the credit of these authors this product of five years' work stands as testimony to how far the field of restorative conferencing has evolved over the past three decades, a marker for determining future progress, and a challenge to move ahead and make restorative decision-making a more accepted basis for dealing with young offenders. To a greater extent than has been the case thus far, this means avoiding the inappropriate use of conferencing approaches for minor offenses that do not require intensive human resources, while utilizing restorative decision-making in more complex and serious cases.

Growth in the number and type of restorative conferencing programs operating in the United States is clearly documented in this book, and what is particularly fascinating is both the proliferation of programs and the diversity of programming efforts. Bazemore and Schiff do an admirable job of describing this scope and variety of conferencing initiatives, and in doing so purposefully take a broad approach to restorative conferencing, leaving room for different types of programming efforts. This is important in a relatively young field, leaving open the possibilities of new and creative programming efforts yet to be developed. Rigid orthodoxy is always a temptation with true believers all too quick to dogmatically assert their views as the one true way, supporting the notion that difference is the measure of absurdity. To their credit, these authors do not fall victim to this and hold to a broad perspective, seeing promise and value in different conferencing approaches and methods, while being grounded in a strong theoretical and empirical perspective.

What we found especially impressive about this study is the way it provides an insightful account of a grounded theory approach, generating restorative theory from both quantitative and qualitative data. Using a variety of research methods, including interviews, surveys, and participant observation, Bazemore and Schiff develop theories of restorative practice. Grounded as they are in actual practice, these theories should be of immense interest to policy makers looking to set standards, policies and procedures for using restorative decision making in the justice system, as well as being helpful to practitioners in their effort to improve their program services. This book stands as a testament to the notion that there is nothing as practical as good theory. The onus is now on practitioners to demonstrate that theory can be implemented with both integrity and strength, and the propositions laid out here can be put to the test to improve practice. We simply must move beyond developing and modifying our programs on the basis of word of mouth testimonials and ad hoc programming shifts and move towards evidence-based practices using systematic procedures to monitor and document our work.

While demonstrating how far theory, research, and practice have come over the past thirty years, this book also deals with some potential pitfalls and problems confronting the field. One pressing matter is the almost inevitable process of professionalization and bureaucratization. Bazemore and Schiff raise concerns about the manner and extent to which responsibility for conferencing initiatives can be transferred or co-opted by professionals, having the effect of disengaging citizens and community groups from the justice process and in this way work against their community capacity building potential. In Christie's terms, the property of conflict settlement can be stolen again, in this version by the very people and programs ostensibly begun for the purpose of engaging citizens. This could have the effect of destroying the potential of conferencing for greater community participation and a revival of a sense of democratization of sanctioning and social control, with restorative programs becoming mundane, routinized, and rather wishy-washy efforts run by credentialed professionals insulated from the community. These authors have raised the concern and provided a road map to help restorative decision-making programs remain true to their mission, embedded in local communities.

Those leaders advocating for the broadest application of restorative justice will find this contribution to be reinforcing and yet challenging. Those committed to protecting the status quo should find this book a devastating criticism of their position. Hopefully restorative justice advocates will use this contribution to better serve the public through restorative conferencing, and the hesitant will find enough evidence to join what has become nothing less than a justice system reform movement.

Joe Hudson and Dennis Maloney, October 2004

Joe Hudson is Professor Emeritus, Faculty of Social Work, University of Calgary.

Dennis Maloney is Former Director, Deschutes County Department of Corrections and Senior Program Manager of the Balanced and Restorative Justice Project.

Introduction

In North Minneapolis, members of the Northside Community Justice committee's peace-making circle project and other invited participants meet with a 17-year-old African American male juvenile offender two months prior to his release from the state's juvenile corrections facility. He had been incarcerated following an attempted armed robbery of a white adult neighbor. Attending at this meeting are the victim, his family, other supporters of the victim, the young man's family and several other supporters – some twenty people in all. After the victim describes the trauma of the event (earlier 'healing circles' had been held for victims and family) and the subsequent sadness and confusion he felt about his place in the neighborhood where he and his family have lived for 35 years, victim advocates in the circle validate his feelings and let him know it is 'OK to be afraid' and not at all abnormal that he should be having nightmares. Both the young offender and his family express their regrets about the crime and their concern for the victim. Community members from this predominately African American neighborhood express support for both families and their hope that everyone could come together to strengthen the neighborhood. Additional information is revealed by the offender regarding his drug use and sales. He explains that the attempted robbery was motivated by his effort to recover $200 taken from him in a drug deal. This leads first to shock and anger from his dad and other family members and then becomes the catalyst for family solidarity around opposition to guns and drugs. The young man's honesty is applauded by others in the circle, and his older brother, who had spoken in eloquent terms about what it takes to grow up as a young black male, expresses disappointment but also support for his brother as do other relatives. His father expresses gratitude for the circle process that gave him new insights about his son. As the talking piece is passed around the circle for the last time, the victim again thanks the group, then looks across the room at the young offender, and says, 'when you get out of Redwing [the facility], I'd like to take you to lunch.' When the circle breaks up, the offender approaches the victim's son, a young man of about the same age, and shakes his hand. The son then rises and hugs the offender. The victim and the offender's parents also embrace.

In a large city in Northern California, neighborhood accountability board volunteers meet with a 17-year-old female recently suspended from school for being in possession of a marijuana pipe. She and her friend (who did not participate in the conference) had explained to the school resource officer who discovered them with the pipe that they had only minutes before spotted it on top of a locker and taken it down. Because the pipe contained residue of recently smoked marijuana, the officer and assistant principal concluded that the girls had likely smoked and therefore under the city's zero tolerance rules warranted immediate suspension. The case was referred to juvenile court intake, where the girl and her mother had agreed to participate in the conference. After the board chairperson explains the circumstances of the case and reads from a script that says, 'we are not here to punish this girl or determine guilt or innocence, but rather to try to repair the harm her behavior has caused,' the volunteers (based on a 'strengths-based' assessment completed earlier by one of the board members) begin to talk about the positive attributes of this young girl, an A student who has never been in trouble. Though they seem to want to believe the girl's story, they never raise the question of guilt or lack of due process or, as have some other conferencing programs, question the school's zero tolerance approach. Rather, after the strengths-based discussion, the volunteers proceed to warn against the dangers of drug abuse. They ask the girl and her mother a number of questions about whether she is doing well at home (her mother says she is) and has been in any other trouble at school (she has not). Despite the opening charge by the chair to focus on harm and repair, no harm is ever identified, and the group spends the last half hour of a 90-minute conference dutifully developing a conference diversion agreement that includes drug counseling, participation in a drug education program, community service and reading a book on drug abuse. Reminded she may face court if she does not concur with the agreement, the girl is encouraged by her mother to acquiesce. Following the girl's agreement, the mother thanks the group for giving her daughter another chance.

Judging restorative decision-making: more and less than meets the eye

In many communities in various parts of the world, citizens and juvenile justice professionals are engaged in new and distinctive encounters with young offenders, their victims, families and supporters. These encounters feature face-to-face dialogue about the impact of crimes committed by young offenders and an attempt to develop meaningful agreements for them to in some way repair, or make amends for, the harm they have caused to victims and communities. Specific approaches are referred to by a variety of names reflecting program model variations – victim–offender dialogue, family group conferencing, large group conferencing, peace-making or sentencing circles, youth panels or neighborhood accountability boards, and community conferencing, or adaptations based on place of origin or sponsorship (e.g. New Zealand family group conferencing, Wagga Wagga conferencing, Bemidji Response to Crime, Vermont Reparative Boards, Longmont Community Conferencing Program). In general, though they now have many applications in multiple contexts in justice systems and communities, these non-adversarial decision-making processes provide an alternative, or supplement to, court sanctioning or other adversarial diversion or dispositional procedures in juvenile justice systems. For reasons articulated in Chapter 1, in this volume we use the term, 'restorative group conferencing,' or simply 'conferencing,' to provide a generic designation of a wide range of process models that nonetheless share a common set of goals and an underlying a set of values.

As the brief synopsis of the armed robbery case conference in the opening paragraphs indicates, restorative conferencing can be dramatic, emotionally charged, and potentially capable of producing significant transformation of individual participants, as well as collective conflicts. For some, these encounters appear to offer a superior form of justice, and may even be capable of achieving other broad outcomes including community capacity building. On the other hand, as in the second case, they may appear to be ill-conceived and inappropriate responses to isolated, rather trivial incidents where culpability and due process concerns appear to be ignored. In a climate of 'zero tolerance' (Skiba and Peterson 1999), such efforts appear to be expanding the reach of juvenile justice systems to include behavior once addressed within schools, thus absolving educational institutions of responsibility for problem-solving and disciplinary responses. At best, such encounters may appear to waste the time of participants (in this case volunteers), though the board's work may have actually saved money and time if court processing would have actually been used in its stead. In terms of the capacity of such programs to address the larger challenges facing juvenile justice systems and communities in the socialization of young people, however, observers

3

may simply conclude that, despite the hype, there is in restorative conferencing, really 'less than meets the eye'. Like the majority of court hearings, some restorative encounters may appear mundane, predictable, and routinized (Karp, 1999), devoid of emotion and apparently incapable of accomplishing much in the way of reparation or healing.

Unlike typical court hearings and other adversarial processes, however, some of these less impressive conferences may (perhaps inadvertently) accomplish other goals, such as promoting open communication between parents and youth, or reinforcing mutual support for prosocial, consistent childrearing. In this text, we also present cases in which restorative conferencing may also accomplish 'more than meets the eye', when rather undramatic encounters for example, provide opportunities for relationship-building between family members themselves as well as other community members, developing conflict resolution skills and recognizing common shared values that support resolution of the current incident and also establish standards for future behavior. Such opportunities for dialogue are highly unlikely to occur when youth are referred individually to traditional diversion programs or processed through a court that has historically been focused on either punishment or treatment with little or no attention given to the victim or other relevant stakeholders. The pipe case notwithstanding, many restorative conferences in schools today are, for example, more likely to be used as alternatives to suspension that strengthen, rather than displace or weaken, internal social control. Other cases presented herein appear to result in participants taking initiative to deal with incidents of conflict and harm in a positive way that, like the first case, provide examples that illustrate the community building potential of restorative dialogue.

So what do we make of this? Because the majority of restorative group conferences are not easily sorted into categories of 'good' and 'bad,' how may we assess effectiveness? Clearly, the *context* in which such decision-making occurs including consideration of the lack of effectiveness of existing adversarial alternatives is of paramount importance when considering the potential pitfalls of restorative decision-making models.

Our intent in this volume is to examine a set of common standards for gauging the strength and integrity of restorative group conferencing interventions. We begin (in Chapter 1) by proposing a set of core restorative justice principles which provide general dimensions for judging the effectiveness of restorative decision-making processes in multiple contexts. We also suggest intervention theories compatible with these principles (Chapter 2) that provide logical explanations for why restorative justice *should* work when certain practices and processes are implemented according to these standards, and offer suggestions for linking initial or immediate outcomes of restorative encounters with more long term objectives.

The international popularity of restorative justice is due largely to the potential suggested by the restorative justice vision for a more holistic, more effective response to youth crime. The challenges represented at the micro level by the case examples above, and by others presented in this text, must therefore be placed in a larger systemic context. In the U.S. in particular, perhaps the greatest challenge to even the strongest and most effective restorative justice processes is in the effort to fit such intervention into a juvenile justice system whose transformation in the past decade has followed a direction that must seem less than inviting to restorative justice policy and practice. Thus, while researchers and practitioners have spent much time debating the value and effectiveness of different restorative group conferencing models (see Chapter 1), differences between these program models, and even more important differences in philosophy and theory associated with practice variations, seem trivial in comparison to differences between the restorative vision as a whole and mainstream juvenile justice priorities.

Restorative policy in the US juvenile justice context

The past few decades of justice reform have brought an increased formalization of what was once a juvenile court that granted judges almost unlimited powers to make dispositional decisions, theoretically in the 'best interests' of young people, unrestricted by procedural or other standards (Platt, 1977; Krisberg and Austin, 1978). Although never living up to the promise of individualized responses that matched needs of offenders with appropriate interventions, it was perhaps more possible to consider a range of less adversarial and bureaucratic means of addressing the needs of young people in trouble in earlier periods of the history of the juvenile court.

The challenges of a more adversarial and bureaucratic system today were made worse by a movement in the 1990s toward the adoption of a wide range of legislatively mandated restrictions on the US juvenile court's jurisdictional authority over certain categories of offenders. Specifically, between 1992 and 1996, all but ten American states legislatively excluded large categories of young offenders by type of crime, age, or some combination of both and generally made it much easier to prosecute juveniles in the criminal court. Most states mandated new ways to transfer youth to adult court by statutory exclusion or prosecutorial discretion, in addition to the more traditional reliance on judicial waiver. Additionally, formalization of court and juvenile justice systems was greatly enhanced by a range of restrictions on judicial sentencing and dispositional authority through imposition of mandatory minimum and determinate sentences, blended sentences, and other forms of mandatory extension of the court's authority beyond the age of majority (Torbet et al., 1996; Feld, 1999). While these changes have had dramatic implications for the working of the criminal justice system, the juvenile court's movement toward greater formalization may pose an ever greater threat to its continued existence as a special institution dedicated to meeting the unique needs of young offenders (Feld, 1993; Torbet et al., 1996).

Though many states explicitly adopted punishment as part of their purpose clauses for the juvenile court during this period – and expanded punishment was clearly the underlying rationale for most of the aforementioned changes (Feld, 1993, 1999; Butts and Mears, 2001) – other changes such as victims' rights statutes for juvenile courts and limits on confidentiality and openness of court proceedings in many states seemed to have been inspired by a range of motivations as part of a more general attack on the court (Torbet et al., 1996). Interestingly, and somewhat ironically, during roughly this same period, some 20 states also adopted restorative justice language into their juvenile court purpose clauses, while another 15 added restorative justice to state juvenile justice administrative codes or similar policy documents (O'Brien, 1998). For some of these states, it seems likely that this addition was a carefully considered means of affirming and distinguishing a new vision, or third way, for juvenile justice that was distinctly different from either punishment or treatment-focused models and based on thoughtful consideration of the limits of these models (see Bazemore and Umbreit, 1995; Bazemore, 1996). While such realization has apparently been enough to move toward full implementation and make both philosophical and systemic integration of restorative policy rather easy in a number of countries such as the UK (Crawford and Newborn, 2003), US policy-makers seemed to have more immediate and modest objectives in mind – notably to counterbalance the aforementioned punitive onslaught by relying on arguments that appeared different from those associated with the traditional 'best interests of the child' and the individualized treatment argument used historically to defend the juvenile court (Krisberg and Austin, 1993). For many states, the restorative legislation may also have been inspired by a sense of desperation to retain some semblance of a juvenile justice system in the face of real proposals for abolition of the juvenile court (Feld, 1999). Indeed, restorative justice language in some states, including Illinois and Pennsylvania, was passed as a part of the same juvenile justice legislation that contained more punitive provisions mandating expanded transfer to the criminal court.

The greatest obstacle to the development of useful restorative justice policy in the US is the historical absence of any national juvenile justice legislation. In fact, the US has the double disadvantage of criminal and juvenile justice decision-making authority vested in 50 independent states (and many more local jurisdictions) that also look to each other, rather than abroad, when it comes to risk-taking in the direction of juvenile and criminal justice policy. Because many state legislative bodies took additional control over local innovation by centralizing more of the authority for juvenile justice functions in the mid to late 1990s in new cabinet-level departments of juvenile justice, their general mandate to promote tougher and more centrally coordinated approaches did little to encourage local creativity in experimentation with restorative practices. This meant that these departments placed few if any 'brakes' on the implementation of what were predominately punitive and more restrictive changes. Moreover, while they allowed for some funding of restorative justice training and demonstration programs in some jurisdictions, the restorative justice code changes that were approved in legislation hardly amounted to a mandate for implementation of restorative practice. These statutes provided little or nothing, for example, in the way of directives or incentives for local justice system decision-makers to refer cases to restorative programs.

By contrast, many other countries have been able to mandate the use of restorative justice processes for significant proportions of juvenile justice cases (Morris and Maxwell, 1993). These countries require that decision-makers provide reasons for *not* referring cases to restorative programs in writing (Weitekamp, 2003), or create clear incentives for making such referrals (Crawford and Newburn, 2003). Nonetheless, the lack of strong national guidance has not stopped states such as Pennsylvania, Illinois, Colorado, and others from developing their own restorative justice visions for juvenile justice reform and supporting the development of local restorative group conferencing and other restorative practices (Balanced and Restorative Justice Newsletter, 2003). It is also possible to identify local communities and local juvenile justice systems that have developed innovative restorative group conferencing approaches independent of state guidance or financial support (Hines and Bazemore, 2003; Bazemore and O'Brien, 2003). Indeed, on the positive or optimistic side of the US experience with restorative justice, it can be said that a local emphasis may be empowering independent local decision-makers such as judges, prosecutors, police, probation officers, and community leaders to craft innovative responses that represent unique adaptations to local needs. Moreover, despite the lack of national legislation and guidance, a significant amount of training has been provided by states, federally funded programs, and private initiatives, and strong commitment on the part of some advocates has helped to create a climate of openness if not support. There are now enough 'case studies' to show that implementation of restorative group conferencing practice and policy is possible, and enough research that shows positive impact to encourage advocates wishing to expand implementation.

In this context, remaining resistance is perhaps coming more from internal decision-makers and policy-makers. For some, as we will describe in later chapters of this volume, the issue is how much decision-making discretion to grant restorative justice practitioners. There is also an issue of determining where and how restorative justice fits into an already well-stocked, if not necessarily effective, arsenal of juvenile justice policy and practice. Restorative justice, even at its best, seems to present policy-makers with a difficult fit with punitive and increasingly prescriptive and bureaucratic changes described earlier in this chapter. By 'fit,' we mean not only the location of restorative processes in organizational and inter-organizational contexts, but also the philosophical positioning of restorative principles that allows practitioners and policy-makers to activate some of the big ideas of restorative justice into organizational and systemic 'sensemaking' (Weick, 1995). It is therefore important, in the US context, to consider how restorative justice fits organizationally and philosophically within the larger scheme of juvenile justice policy frameworks.

Three policy models have in recent history competed for dominance in US juvenile justice systems, and retain some degree of influence today. While not incompatible with restorative justice (see Braithwaite, 2001: ch. 2), each model has viewed the problem of youth crime and deviance through distinctive and competing 'policy lenses' (Ingram and Schneider, 1991) each of which creates priorities that may conflict with and/or diminish the strength of commitment to the restorative goals of repair through stakeholder involvement and community empowerment.

Past and future: a brief history of juvenile justice philosophy: interventionist, libertarian, and crime control lenses

Historically, the most dominant juvenile justice policy perspective has been the one associated with the traditional mission of the juvenile court to act as substitute parent in the 'best interests' of delinquent and troublesome youth. Following in this tradition, those who view youth crime and problems of socialization through the *interventionist* lens tend to assume that deviant and delinquent behaviors are symptoms of underlying psychological disturbance or deficits (Platt, 1977; Rothman, 1980). Interventionists also assume that these causes can be effectively diagnosed through clinical assessment, and then treated through various forms of therapeutic or remedial intervention (Whitehead and Lab, 1996). Despite the increasing dominance of a 'get tough' agenda in juvenile justice systems (Butts and Mears, 2001; Torbet, 1996), and ongoing critiques of interventionist policy assumptions from a variety of perspectives (Polk and Kobrin, 1972; Bazemore and Terry, 1997; Benson, 1997), the core interventionist philosophy of individualized treatment remains ideologically intact and highly influential in the juvenile court and juvenile corrections systems.

In the 1960s and 1970s, youth advocates concluded that harsh conditions of confinement under which thousands of young people around the country were held in juvenile treatment facilities could scarcely be viewed as consistent with the 'best interests' rationale for court intervention (e.g. President's Commission on Crime and Law Enforcement, 1967; Schwartz, 1989; Miller, 1991). In response, these advocates initiated the first and most significant challenge to the interventionist policy perspective in the form of national diversion and deinstitutionalization reform policies aimed specifically at reducing the court's discretion and sphere of influence over young people in trouble (Jensen and Rojek, 1998). Through the *libertarian* lens (Guarino-Ghezzi and Loughran, 1995; see Packer, 1967), even the most benevolent programs may 'widen the net' by bringing more young people into what is perceived to be a harmful system from which it is difficult to exit (Polk, 1987). From this perspective, young people involved in minor crimes and trouble, if left alone and not stigmatized, will naturally 'grow out of' this relatively normal and generally episodic behavior (Schur, 1973; Lemert, 1971; Becker 1960). Juvenile justice libertarians therefore remain skeptical of intervention in general. Though much less potent today than in the 1960s and 1970s, libertarian policy perspectives remain part of the current juvenile justice dialogue as the primary opposition to much current policy with practice focused primarily on implementing due process and pre-adjudicatory detention reforms, as well as opposition to discriminatory policing, the expansion of court processing practices, and new forms of net-widening in school-based and other programs that seek to bring status offenders back into the juvenile court (Schwartz, 1987, 1992; Miller, 1991; Guarino-Ghezzi and Loughran, 1995; Bazemore, Leip, and Stinchcombe, 2004).

In the 1980s, advocates of a new 'get tough' focus challenged what they saw as leniency in both libertarian (as reflected in the image of diversion as an avoidance of accountability) and interventionist responses. While libertarians seemed to argue only for 'expanding community tolerance limits' in the response to youth crime (e.g. Schur, 1973) and interventionists for providing expanded treatment in the 'best interests' of the child, those who viewed delinquency and youth deviance through the *crime control* policy lens argued that these problems were a consequence of general permissiveness and the absence of a sufficiently punitive response (e.g. Regnery, 1980). Crime control advocates thus gave highest priority to suppression and deterrence policies. Moreover, strengthened by incorporation of a just deserts emphasis that seemed to give new academic legitimacy to punishment (von Hirsch, 1976; Feld, 1999), the crime control agenda by the 1990s had brought about an unprecedented increase in the incarceration of juvenile offenders (Castellano, 1986; Irwin and Austin, 1991). As it gained dominance, this agenda ushered in the structural transformation in juvenile courts noted above that today includes determinate and mandatory sentencing and a range of new policies and procedures designed to expedite the transfer of juvenile cases to the adult court (Torbet et al., 1996; Feld, 1999; Butts and Mears, 2001). Some have also suggested that the new, more formalized juvenile justice in the US has become a less 'loosely coupled' system (Weick, 1976), that features new alliances between the court, its traditional social service components (e.g. treatment programs), probation, law enforcement and prosecution. Notably, despite widespread criticisms of the court in the 1990s (Feld, 1993; Lemov, 1994; Torbet et al., 1996), these alliances have targeted troublesome, though non-criminal, behavior by young people that in previous decades had been declared off limits to court intervention (Lemert, 1981; Empey, 1982). Ironically, on the heels of a period of national concern about violent youth crime, juvenile justice agencies and programs (often with the support of new criminal justice system partners and law-makers) have begun 'reaching down' to reclaim jurisdiction over runaways, incorrigibles, curfew violators, youth experimenting with alcohol and smoking, truants, status offenders, and other non-criminal forms of deviance, trouble, and conflict once dealt with informally by families, neighbors, schools, various youth development agencies, and other non-judicial entities (Shiraldi and Soler, 1998; Bazemore, Leip, and Stinchcomb, 2004). As an approach emphasizing less formal and non-adversarial responses that maximize the involvement of community stakeholders in the response to crime and harm, restorative justice programs may find that even these low level cases have been already targeted for formal responses.

Where restorative justice fits: the promise of adaptation

Despite what appears to be a clear disconnect between restorative justice intervention and reform protocols filtered through the lenses of the three more dominant and familiar policy models, restorative justice by the mid-1990s had become surprisingly popular with administrators and policy-makers in a number of jurisdictions. The restorative justice focus on the extent to which harm is repaired, and the extent to which communities increase their capacity to respond to crime and conflict, seemed to offer a broader framework that challenges the role of punishment and treatment as the primary currencies of intervention. In doing so, the restorative agenda provided a distinctive new standard for gauging intervention success that has apparently been perceived as *neither* soft on crime, nor supportive of expanded punishment (Van Ness and Strong, 1997; Bazemore, 1998).

Is restorative justice therefore incompatible with other juvenile justice priorities? Most restorative justice proponents will likely stand with advocates of rehabilitation and treatment (interventionists) in affirming the need to actively respond to a range of problems that may be related to offending and at risk behavior with a variety of evidence-based interventions. However, they also insist that the complex problems of youth crime and deviant behavior cannot be resolved by policies based on offender-driven services and surveillance alone (Braithwaite and Mugford, 1994; Bazemore, Nissen, and Dooley, 2000). Restorative justice principles also have implications for redefining the role and boundaries of juvenile justice, and providing a new continuum for gauging the success of juvenile justice reform. And while restorative justice advocates will therefore ultimately stand with libertarians on many issues regarding limits of juvenile justice intervention and the critique of recent expansionist trends in juvenile justice (Bazemore, 1999), most acknowledge the concern of crime control advocates that youth crime and behavioral problems do not go away simply by ignoring them. The new restorative vision is not therefore anti-interventionist, and it cannot be reduced to a 'hands-off' approach. In contrast to the interventionist or expansionist view, however, intervention is not seen as a job that should be left to government alone. Instead, more consistent with a communitarian approach (Etzioni, 1996; Braithwaite, 1994), restorative justice seeks to promote a community 'hands on' agenda, and to do so in part through government action that casts justice agencies and professionals in a significantly different role.

Despite challenges, one benefit of restorative justice may therefore be its ability to also supplement other agendas in prevention, treatment, and sanctioning. As Braithwaite (2002) has effectively argued, restorative justice, as a principled response to crime rather than a program, can be used to enhance rehabilitative, deterrence, incapacitation, and regulatory strategies. Moreover, restorative justice has already shown itself to be adaptable and resilient in multiple contexts. In Chapter 1, we begin to address this adaptability and utility of group conferencing as an essential restorative practice. As discussed in this chapter, principles are fundamental in distinguishing restorative decision-making and other forms of restorative practice from intervention more consistent with other policy lenses. Principles are also essential to facilitating replication of restorative practices and for allowing policy-makers to 'know restorative practice when they see it.'

Purpose of this book

Five years ago when the authors conceptualized and initiated a preliminary study of restorative decision-making that was later supported with funding from the National Institute of Justice (NIJ) and the Robert Wood Johnson Foundation (RWJF), we thought it important to address several basic, yet unanswered questions. First, how much and what kind of programs and practices had been initiated in the US in the wake of the first introduction of new restorative group conferencing models in the early to mid-1990s? Second, in addition to this broad 'what's going on?' question, we wanted to gain an understanding of the extent to which these new programs and processes adhered to some standard of practice that could distinguish them from other diversion or community intervention programs. Specifically, we were concerned with how programs determined or gauged the 'restorativeness' of their practice, and how staff and participants in these programs engaged restorative values and principles – both in vision and in practice. At this early stage of implementation, it was unrealistic to expect that practice would be fully aligned with a restorative vision. We argued that the vision itself was nonetheless a necessary, though not sufficient, prerequisite to the implementation of restorative practice. Third, we were and remain interested not just in restorative group conferencing processes as special 'programs' or pilot initiatives, but as a core component of a larger juvenile justice system reform initiative. One key objective was therefore to examine the fit between restorative process and juvenile justice systems and organizations in various community contexts. Finally, perhaps the most important aspect of our study was to develop grounded accounts of what restorative conferencing practitioners appeared to be trying to accomplish. In other words, we wanted to learn about how they carried out their work *and why* – in other words, to document the logic or theory behind this practice.

Research objectives and the evaluation audience

In order to answer these questions, we proposed a multi-level, multi-method national case study that featured: (1) a quantitative national program inventory and survey; and (2) a qualitative study focused on interviews with a national sample of practitioners, and participant observation along with intensive, unstructured interviewing in several communities in two states active in restorative justice decision-making (Colorado and Minnesota). Our objective in this exploratory, formative and descriptive research was to increase understanding of the prevalence, structure, practices, processes, goals, and philosophical/theoretical focus of restorative conferencing for youth across the United States. One overall goal of this 'pragmatic case study' (Fishman, 1999; Yin, 1994) was to advance practice, policy, theory, and research in restorative decision-making by improving the 'fit' between these domains (Fishman, 1999). While the findings presented in this volume should in no way be viewed as a formal evaluation of restorative decision-making processes, we hoped to improve future evaluation in restorative justice, and to thereby improve practice.

As we completed the writing for this volume, we noted that much change had occurred in restorative justice evaluation and research both nationally and internationally in the five years since the beginning of this study. A number of impact evaluations begun prior to our research had been completed and had reported findings (e.g. Sherman et al., 2000; McGarrell, 2001; Maxwell and Morris, 2001; Hayes and Daly, 2003; Strang, 2003). Specifically, studies of several varieties of family group conferencing had become available (for summaries see Hudson et al., 1996; Burford and Hudson, 2001; Bazemore, 2000) that examined the effectiveness of this model as a juvenile justice intervention strategy in New Zealand (Maxwell and Morris, 1993; Morris and Maxwell, 2001), Australia (Sherman, 2000; Daly, 2001; Hayes and Daly, 2003; Strang, 2003), the United States (McCold and Wachtel, 1998; McGarrell, 2001) and the United Kingdom (Roberts and Masters, 1999; Young and Hoyle, 2002). Several of these studies (McCold and Wachtel, 1998; Maxwell and Morris, 1999; Sherman, Strang, and Woods, 2000; McGarrell, 2001) utilized experimental and/or other strong impact designs that allowed for causal inferences that greatly expanded knowledge about the impact of restorative decision-making beyond that gained from earlier studies. Process and outcome studies of peace-making circles, reparative and community boards, and other models are either in progress or in the planning stages (e.g. Coates et al., 2000; Karp et al., forthcoming).

In general, these studies have established a baseline viability for restorative justice decision-making as a non-adversarial alternative to court and other formal/legalistic procedures. In doing so, they have added breadth and depth to prior positive findings that had focused almost exclusively on victim–offender mediation (Umbreit et al., 2001; Nugent et al., 2000; Schiff, 1999). Moreover, emerging findings from meta-analyses of dozens of studies summarizing a wider range of research on restorative justice practice using an array of research designs (Bonta et al., 2003) and mediation and conferencing (Nugent et al., 2000) seem to be pointing in a positive direction, with limited though consistently positive findings about impact on satisfaction, sense of justice, and other outcomes – as well as recidivism.

While obviously not as conclusive or compelling as some bodies of evaluation literature with studies spanning more than three decades, such as the literature on effective treatment or 'what works' (Lipsey, 1993; Andrews and Bonta, 1997), taken together, these experimental and quasi-experimental studies of conferencing now provide at least an initial basis for ruling out the hypothesis that restorative justice processes have negative impacts on juvenile justice outcomes. Moreover, findings of neutral, but not harmful, impact on recidivism and other offender outcomes in themselves would be insufficient to diminish support for these programs from advocates who provide normative justification for

13

benefits of restorative justice such as crime victim satisfaction and input. Most studies, in fact, indicate some positive impact (Schneider, 1991; Schiff, 1999; Umbreit, 1999; Braithwaite, 1999; Bazemore et al., 2000), and some even suggest that restorative programs may have equal or greater impact than many treatment programs (Umbreit, 1999; Sherman, 2000).

Ultimately, when viewed in context, the limited impact of restorative interventions at this comparatively early stage of both program development and evaluation may be considered surprisingly strong and robust. Specifically, while no one should *expect* dramatic rehabilitative impacts from one-time, short-term conferencing encounters when these are contrasted with long-term, multi-modal treatment programs whose sole purpose is reducing offender recidivism (Bazemore, Nissen, and Dooley, 2000; Levrant et al., 1999), restorative justice practitioners would nonetheless likely be pleased at the magnitude of effects demonstrated in some studies.

In search of theory in restorative justice process

Despite these findings, some questions remain about the *meaning* of restorative justice research results. Some authors, for example, question the value, interpretation, and applicability of recent experimental and quasi-experimental findings that have for the most part contrasted restorative justice processes with those of the adversarial processes of the juvenile court (Kurki, 2003; Hayes and Daly, 2004). One related overriding concern is the fact that research findings demonstrating the presence of a positive impact relative to court and similar alternatives do not provide much insight into *why* these programs seem to achieve these positive outcomes. Most importantly, in the case of positive findings, there are remaining doubts about whether it is in fact the 'restorative' aspects of the encounter, or some other features of the process such as procedural justice (Tyler, 1990) that explains the positive impacts.

On the other hand, where restorative justice has apparently *failed* to produce positive impacts, as in the drunk driving component of the RISE studies (Sherman et al., 2000; Braithwaite, 2001a), there is some uncertainty about whether restorative justice or some other process accounted for this failure. In other words, the field as a whole seems to be less than certain about what theory or theories explain both negative and positive results. More pertinent to policy and practice needs, theories, and the research studies that test them, should help to specify what *aspects* of conferencing practice are most responsible for these outcomes. Yet in a cogent critique of 'service delivery criteria' (e.g. number of agreements completed, amount of restitution collected) as indicators of intermediate success in victim–offender conferencing (Brookes, 2000), one observer notes that even if these criteria were shown to be satisfied:

Such an evaluation would tell us almost nothing about the more substantive claims made for victim–offender encounters: how would we know, on the basis of service-delivery data whether a particular encounter has, indeed, 'given participants access to a higher quality of justice,' 'evoked genuine remorse in the offender,' 'enabled the victim to overcome her resentment, fear and negative identity,' 'repaired social bonds' . . . and so on . . . But until such information is forthcoming – that is in non-anecdotal form – there remains little basis for the claim that victim–offender encounters are theoretically grounded in the social and experiential reality of their participants.

(p. 4)

This state of affairs should not be viewed as surprising in a still emerging arena of practice that for the first two decades of its existence seemed primarily content to show that restorative processes (generally victim–offender mediation programs) produced greater satisfaction among participating victims and offenders than did court and other adversarial processes. Moreover, restorative justice intervention is often a complex mixture of practice components including, though not limited to, dialogue, emotional responses, developing and committing to reparative agreements, and following through with those obligations. But while practitioners probably had their own theories about why this process produced such outcomes, these have seldom been articulated, or at least documented. It is therefore often difficult to develop definitive linkages between restorative practice and a coherent restorative theory of process that can be clearly differentiated from procedural justice, substantive justice, or similar alternative theories of justice, including even theories of retributive justice (von Hirsch, 1976; Barton, 2000; Duff, 2003).

In this context, Braithwaite's reintegrative shaming theory as articulated in *Crime, Shame and Reintegration* (1989) has seemed in the past decade to fill a conceptual void in restorative practice and research while also helping the field make the critical connection between western restorative process and indigenous and non-western settlement and conflict resolution practices. However, it is primarily as a general sociological theory of informal social control that reintegrative shaming can be used to link most restorative justice practice to broader theoretical concepts. Specifically, Braithwaite's often-cited summary of reintegrative shaming, i.e. 'low crime societies are those in which community members do not mind their own business,' is an important restatement of core assumptions of classic social disorganization theory (e.g. Kornhauser, 1978; Bursik and Grasmick, 1993; Sampson, Raudenbush, and Earls, 1997) that provides an important *new* insight to both restorative justice practitioners and scholars about the potential for recreating informal social control processes at a micro level. Indeed, Braithwaite connected the response to individual crimes in restorative processes to a larger vision of social capital (Putnam, 2000) and collective efficacy (Sampson, Raudenbush, and Earls, 1997) that, conceptually at least, moved restorative practice beyond a focus on solving individual victim–offender conflict and repairing the harm of individual crimes (see Bazemore, 2000; Pranis, 2001).

However, the more direct programmatic and more individualized application of the social-psychological aspects of reintegrative shaming, via Tomkins's (1962) theories addressing the positive role of shame and emotion (see Nathanson, 1992) to specific programs – has been more or less limited to the Australian Wagga Wagga model and its North American application via the Real Justice model (McDonald et al., 1995). The connection between this approach and the mainstream practice of victim–offender mediation (VOM) in North America and Europe in particular seemed especially tenuous except at the general level of informal social control (Bazemore and Umbreit, 1995). The ideas of shaming and the 'scripted' Wagga model of family group conferences (FGCs) were not well-received, at least initially in pockets of the US where practitioners interested in family group conferencing had been schooled in VOM and principles of mediation and to some degree had begun to view those principles as those most compatible with restorative justice values (see Umbreit and Stacy, 1996).

Elsewhere Daly and Kitcher (1999) note that reintegrative shaming was never the focus of New Zealand family group conferencing (see also Morris and Maxwell, 2003). Rather, New Zealand conferencing advocates and other observers of these and other FGC approaches give greater emphasis to empathy than shame as a causal link between conferencing and reduced recidivism (Hayes and Daly, 2002; Toews-Shenk and Zehr, 2001). Nor is reintegrative shaming the dominant model in much of Australia where states such as Queensland, Victoria, South Australia, and New South Wales and others seemed to prefer New Zealand style conferencing or other adaptations (Daly and Kitcher, 1999). According to these authors, in Australia in the 1990s, it was difficult to determine what theory was in play by examining policy statements or practice guides, and there was uncertainty about 'the degree to which ideas of restorative justice, reintegrative shaming, or admixtures [of these] and other theories guide[d] practitioners . . . in their work' (1999: 18). Notably, these authors imply at least some degree of independence, or lack of a solid merger between restorative justice and reintegrative shaming. Similarly, though a variety of family group conferencing models have become popular, US practice in states where conferencing is used frequently is by no means fully grounded in reintegrative shaming theory – at least in the strict sense as articulated in practice guides (McDonald et al., 1995).

Nonetheless, reintegrative shaming theory, more than any other perspective, has informed scholarship related to restorative justice by providing testable propositions to guide empirical research that are different from those of procedural justice and other perspectives. Further, these propositions are connected to the larger normative theory of dominion (Braithwaite and Petit, 1990) as well as to other bodies of etiological theory including social psychological theories of stigma and labeling (Goffman, 1963; Becker, 1963; Scheff, 1990), theories of positive identity transformation at the interactional level (see Erickson, 1968; Maruna, 2001; Retzinger and Scheff, 1996), and as noted above, to social disorganization perspectives at the community level. Yet, as Hayes and Daly summarize, reintegrative shaming is not strictly a 'restorative justice theory,' in part because it does not encompass what these authors view as a core dimension of the restorative perspective:

> In general, reintegrative shaming focuses on how a conference may affect an offender. Restorative justice assumes a broader set of interactions between an offender and a victim (and their supporters) in which the recognition of the 'other' is expected to encourage a more empathetic orientation in the offender and a more sympathetic orientation by the victim to the offender's situation.
>
> (2003, p. 729)

Practically, few *restorative justice advocates* and practitioners would be content with a theory of practice focused only on the extent to which the offender experiences shame from those he/she cares about in a respectful encounter where participants then emphasize reintegration, no matter how much importance they attach to this occurrence. Though researchers must necessarily, as Hayes and Daly's statement suggests, attempt to measure and specify causal implications of what we observe to be the essence of the restorative encounter, some advocates might also want to include more than is implied even in this comprehensive statement. Specifically, some would insist on inclusion of the extent to which reparation of harm occurs in a context that empowers and promotes community leadership and ownership of conflict (Van Ness and Strong, 1997). The 'restorativeness' of the process would then be determined by the answers to a different, more comprehensive set of questions focused on whether participants identified the harm, determined how it might be repaired, and defined roles and responsibilities for stakeholders in this endeavor (Zehr, 1990).

These broad normative statements of the value of restorative justice intervention may therefore imply multiple theories and/or multiple dimensions of various theories at work in producing restorative outcomes. In that regard, Hayes and Daly's important emphasis on the collective movement of victim and offender toward a more empathetic view of one another may reflect a valuable theoretical orientation that distinguishes restorative intentions and outcomes from those associated with procedural justice, retributive justice, crime control, social welfare/treatment, or other perspectives.

Reintegrative shaming reflects at least one dimension of a broader normative theory that draws a clear distinction between justice as punishment and justice as dominion. While reintegrative shaming theory has become so popular that it does not *need* restorative justice, more than anything else, it has been Braithwaite's personal commitment to integrating this theory with core principles of restorative justice that has appropriately linked it with restorative justice in the minds of many researchers and practitioners. Ultimately, the North American application of reintegrative shaming at its best is represented by Braithwaite's (2001a) general idea that:

> *tolerance of crime makes things worse;* stigmatization, or disrespectful outcasting shame of crime, makes things worse still *while ... disapproval within a continuum of respect for the offender ... terminated by rituals of forgiveness, makes things better.*

(emphasis ours)

From this summative statement, we may conclude that an intervention theory focused on 'empathetic engagement' of all stakeholders who matter to the offender and victim is a relational one, where the 'collective quality of the resolve' provides the source of motivation to stop or reduce the harmful behavior (Braithwaite, 2001a: 230). Shame that may occur through the essential act of denouncing the offense and confronting the offender with the harm caused, though an essential characteristic of reintegrative shaming theory, is therefore but one step in a sequential three-stage process of collective transformation. Such a process, as Braithwaite (2001a: 228) suggests, actually begins with 'the experience of love as a key ingredient;' includes empathy (that for the offender may even be associated with the experience of shame); provides for 'redemption rituals' that assist with 'motivational transformation;' and finally, offers offenders the opportunity for 'earned redemption' (Bazemore, 1998)

The above statement places the 'stripped down' version of reintegrative shaming as operationalized in some practice manuals in a broader context that looks like a normative theory of restorative justice and reflects its multi-dimensionality. It also reflects the reality that there is almost always more than one theory at play within a given victim, offender, and community encounter – e.g. a theory of support, empathy with others, redemption, motivation, etc. Despite the highly significant, though somewhat loose, connection between reintegrative shaming and restorative practice in the US, there have been few statements of other theories of intervention that might account for the presumed relationship between restorative process, immediate and intermediate outcomes, and long-term impacts.

There are many other such theories that could indeed account for the effects of restorative intervention. Recent theoretical inventories by Braithwaite (2002) and others, as well as other statements that articulate specifically restorative theoretical models of rehabilitation (Bazemore and O'Brien, 2002), have since provided numerous and more explicit logical rationales for the presumed offender impact of restorative justice that also can be linked to causal theoretical traditions in criminology. However, like most criminological theory, these rationales have little to say about impact on victims (but see Toews-Shenk and Zehr, 2001; Strang, 2003) or communities (Pranis, 2001; Bazemore, 2001; Boyes-Watson, 2004). As a guide to developing new, testable practice models in the future, Braithwaite's (2002) work in particular provides a very useful inventory and template for developing alternative theoretical models. In addition, qualitative work such as Roche's (2003) study of how practitioners articulate and seek to achieve accountability in the restorative process has implications for theory of a different kind, and other quantitative research on how restorative logics are applied in a national initiative using a kind of 'community conferencing' model in the UK (i.e. the Youth Offender Panel) are closer to some of the emerging US models than those seen elsewhere in the world (Crawford and Newborn, 2003). Together, these add to the growing inventory of emerging theories that purport to link restorative process and outcome.

Theory to practice: policy and program goals

Despite this variation in practice and implicit theoretical diversity, research has thus far not acknowledged the wide range of theories and logical connections that may be at play in making sense of a restorative encounter – i.e. what makes it 'work' when it does, and what makes it fail, when it doesn't work. This is not a criticism of practice, scholarship, or research at this stage in their development. Indeed, one can always criticize evaluation for lack of specification of multi-dimensional measurement criteria because researchers at some point are forced to choose a more limited set of items from a potential wide array of measures – especially when contrasting restorative justice with procedural justice and other explanations for observed impacts. Even the most elaborate attempts to tease out causal impacts attributable to reintegrative shaming, remorse, procedural justice, and restorative features of the process must be limited to a relatively fixed number of items that reflect a limited set of theoretical dimensions, though most earlier research has focused only on one dimension (e.g. victim participation and empowerment, offender empathy).

Of greater concern for us at the completion of the current practice-centered study was that we continued to see, even in our focus on some of the communities most active in restorative decision-making, little connection between this theorizing and restorative conferencing practice. Despite many normative statements and strong commitments to within-program practice rules and protocols (e.g. the offender or victim must speak first; face-to-face preparation is necessary with victim and offender; only victim, offender, and their immediate family should participate), these practices seemed grounded in neither theory nor research (indeed most commitments to various protocols are normative in nature, though practitioners may strongly believe that such practice decisions are strong predictors of success). Though some practitioners seemed able to articulate the logical rationales behind these practice approaches – and these rationales had for the most part moved beyond those recommended in traditional victim–offender mediation practice – these rationales did not generally align with the logic of reintegrative shaming, or with most of the other theoretical rationales mentioned in the recent literature cited above. These practitioner 'theories-in-use' and 'espoused theories' (Argysis and Schön, 1974), like program visions, were not always consistent with actual practice and were at times not clearly articulated. We suspected, however, that these rationales had more to do with emerging, often informal variations in practice between and within programs than with what were being described elsewhere as formally differentiated program models (Bazemore and Umbreit, 2001; McCold and Wachtel, 2003). Moreover, we suspected that when analyzed and synthesized, some programs would indeed line up well with existing theories, and some might move the field toward new theory that was either more consistent with emerging research, or would raise new questions for existing theories.

The *micro* focus of our case study, like our emphasis in this volume, was therefore to first identify and more formally articulate these theories-in-use and try to determine how they guided variations in practice. While the qualitative study was in this sense an effort to discover grounded theory, and we were of course open in qualitative data collection to discovering theories that were based on completely different logics (e.g. those grounded in rehabilitative or crime control and punishment logics that would raise questions about the extent to which 'restorative' programs were merely replications of traditional diversion, treatment, or sanctioning programs), we felt that our research approach could not be totally inductive. There seemed in other words to be little value at this stage of development of restorative justice field in research that merely categorized grounded theory in a normative and theoretical vacuum.

Because we believe restorative justice to be a value and principle-based model, we began with a general set of core restorative justice principles as our guiding framework, and then focused on discovering both the extent to which practice was aligned with principles, and how practitioners addressed the normative concerns of these principles. In the qualitative study, our focus was also on resolving apparent conflicts between competing priorities suggested by these principles (e.g. balancing concern with reparative agreements and outcomes with immediate stakeholder needs in the restorative encounter). Finally, we soon became especially interested in how the 'theories-in-use' and 'espoused theories' (Argyis and Schön, 1974) were used by conferencing practitioners to justify variations in process and protocol, and in finding new theories that seemed consistent in some way with principles, but seemed to lead to new variations and adaptations in practice.

In summary, our larger rationale in this exercise in theory discovery and theory building is best stated from a practitioner/advocate perspective:

> For those of us who have observed mediation, conferencing or circles first-hand, *we know* that the claims of restorative justice ring true: for the most part, these encounters really do give participants access to 'a higher quality of justice ...' The problem is that we do not yet know how to test these sorts of claims ... (yet) what we are leaving out (in simply measuring recidivism rates, victim satisfaction and restitution payments) is essential to a truly restorative outcome. And we should acknowledge that limitation. Otherwise stakeholders may ... walk away with a profoundly distorted understanding of what counts as a successful restorative program.
>
> (Brookes, 2000: 5) (emphasis ours)

Regarding more *macro* policy and practice goals of the current national study and this volume, despite the widespread interest in restorative group conferencing in the past decade, there has been little research designed to systematically identify, locate, and describe the various types of conferencing models currently operating across the United States. There has also been little systematic examination of variation between and within types of programs, and the extent to which various forms of restorative conferencing may differ from, or converge with, each other is not well understood. Some researchers have effectively documented the national scene with regard to conferencing in some of the countries mentioned above where one conferencing model, or variations on a single model, typically dominates practice. With the exception of the ongoing efforts of Mark Umbreit and his colleagues at the University of Minnesota to track the development of victim–offender mediation/dialogue programs for the past decade (e.g. Umbreit et al., 2003), however, no efforts have been made to comprehensively describe the nature, scope, and variety of restorative conferencing programs for youthful offenders currently operating in the United States. Hence, we know little about the quantity or quality of restorative decision-making programs and there has been no effort to develop an inventory that includes the new restorative group conferencing models that emerged in the 1990s. This study seems important for that reason alone, and an added qualitative focus on simply describing variation in practice models should make a significant contribution to practice and policy development at this time.

The concern with identifying and articulating the theoretical basis underlying restorative decision-making and the alignment of such practice with core principles also has several *practical* as well as theoretical and research rationales. First, replication of empirically verified, evidence-based programs depends upon clear articulation of such underlying theories. Although clearly specified practice protocols and manuals have an important role to play in guiding program development, such tools are often context-specific and practice-oriented and tend to focus less on theoretical rationales for desired, or predicted, outcomes. Because the US restorative movement, perhaps more than such movements in other smaller and more politically and culturally integrated nations, is one struggling to become relevant to diverse community, institutional, and ethnic contexts, more general practice and implementation principles based on replicable theories would seem to be more helpful to practitioners than strict program guidelines. For example, adapting a probation or police-based family group conferencing program in a suburban community setting to a prison or residential setting, or to a housing project, would require an understanding of the dialogue process and initial outcomes sought rather than a program guide. Similarly, an urban African American community might initially struggle to adapt a peace-making circle program used successfully in remote areas of the Yukon in Canada, or a neighborhood accountability board model used successfully in Vermont. Yet both adaptations have been successfully carried out because of the broad application of general principles and theories of individual and collective transformation.

Another practical issue, at least in the US context, is an absence of theoretically grounded measurement tools and protocols that gauge the strength and integrity of the restorative process. Unfortunately, to the extent that it occurs at all, most ongoing measurement in restorative group conferencing in the US remains focused on assessing general participant satisfaction, and most ongoing assessment at the program level does not even address basic theoretical concerns with increased empathy, degree of support, accountability, and offender acceptance of responsibility. While practitioners, as well as youth, family, and victims, frequently observe aspects of a restorative process that they believe have important impacts on various stakeholders, measures of the strength of these aspects are very unusual. Measurement tools require standards based on theoretical and principle-based dimensions. To the extent that these beliefs drive practice and may account for real differences in long-term outcomes, it is important to capture the extent to which initial or immediate conferencing outcomes associated with these practice theories are in evidence.

Practically, to the extent that Osborne and Gaebler's (1992) assertion that one 'gets what one measures' is correct, it is important to note that current assessment procedures do not encourage those very practices that may indeed produce the most important restorative impacts. To the contrary, due to the failure to articulate theory and those principles associated with it, outcome measures in use today, in much of the US at least, may even diminish and routinize rather than enrich and invigorate practice (Brookes, 2000).

In summary, it is even more important, as we have suggested, that we can clearly articulate what makes the intervention we are evaluating 'restorative' rather than another example of procedural justice or some other approach. In addition, we need a standard for determining the strength of these practices based on the extent to which practice is restorative or not and to what degree. We suggest that our standards for making such assessments should begin with principles of restorative justice rather than practice-based protocols or other program- or jurisdiction-specific criteria. The theories we selected to frame this study were therefore those in which causal implications were *consistent with* these normative principles. These theories can then be examined in terms of their implications for intermediate changes participants experience in the restorative process, and for the conferencing outcomes expected to lead to these changes.

The crux of the problem we hope to address in this volume is therefore twofold: (1) the lack of clear standards that define various degrees of what may be referred to as the 'restorativeness' of practice and policies; and (2) the lack of intervention theory that can articulate *why* various approaches appear to work and why some do not. Hence one need addressed by this book is to identify and build grounded theories of restorative practice. Such theories should reflect what practitioners and participants in restorative processes actually believe to be effective and what leads them to do certain things in conferences to achieve those objectives.

Outline of this book

Chapters 1 and 2 set the context for the rest of this book. Chapter 1 defines restorative group conferencing in the context of a larger restorative justice movement and body of practice and policy. We consider alternative ways of gauging restorativeness that characterize current practice and research, and introduce three core restorative justice principles as the framework for a 'principle-based' approach to evaluation of restorative justice practice. Finally, we describe similarities and differences between restorative group conferencing models, with consideration for alternative philosophies, and differences in priority for participant involvement and facilitation.

Chapter 2 includes an inventory of the intervention theories we believe may inform practitioners' work when they seek to produce particular outcomes from restorative conferences. Each theory is presented in the context of a more elaborate discussion of one of the core restorative justice principles. Our goal is to align the value-base of restorative justice with relevant causal, practical, 'grounded' theories of intervention, and connect these theories with conference outcomes and action frameworks. We then later utilize our qualitative data to determine the degree to which practice and vision are consistent with individual principles and these theories.

Chapter 3 presents exploratory descriptive data on the prevalence of restorative conferencing in the US generally, and of various conferencing models specifically. This chapter begins to address some of the most basic questions about where and how many conferencing programs are currently operating, what types of models are being employed, who these programs are serving, and how these models/programs are distributed across states and other governmental regions. Chapter 3 also examines basic operational and conceptual facets of restorative conferencing programs and, based on our National Survey of Restorative Conferencing Programs, we address several general research questions about how conferencing programs work on a daily basis. Perhaps most importantly, we begin to investigate the consistency between program vision, restorative principles and daily practice as indicated by the extent to which programs include and feel they are meeting their own restorative goals.

Chapter 4 begins the qualitative part of this research by presenting the research design for the qualitative study, and describing primary and secondary units of analysis and the qualitative sampling protocol. This chapter provides the framework for our examination of restorative conferencing at the intermediate and micro levels, and is broadly concerned with both the *vision* and *practice* of restorative conferencing and the degree to which practitioners can maintain consistency between program vision and restorative principles which, we assert, is a necessary condition for ensuring intervention integrity. Another research goal is to examine the degree to which the theoretical premises that guide the program are evident in both their vision and practice. This section concludes with an explanation and practitioners discussion of what may be viewed as the 'architecture' of restorative conferencing and what is a key analytic framework for the qualitative study: those essential stages and phases that most conferences appear to move through before they are considered to be complete.

Chapters 5, 6, and 7 present the data for our qualitative investigation that considers how practitioners understand and apply the principles and related theories of restorative justice in these stages and phases. These chapters correspond to Van Ness and Strong's (1997) three core principles of restorative justice. Chapter 5, focused on the principle of *repairing harm,* examines how practitioners and other conferencing participants talk and think about this goal and seek to achieve specific conferencing outcomes such as 'making amends' and 'building relationships.' The principle of *stakeholder involvement* is addressed in Chapter 6 which explores how practitioners seek to include and involve victims, offenders, and other community members in the conferencing process. This chapter describes the importance attached to the roles played by each stakeholder to the success of the process in addressing objectives such as 'respectful disapproval,' empathy, and stakeholder satisfaction. Chapter 7, concerned with the principle of *transformation in community/government relationships,* first examines how conferencing interacts with U.S. juvenile justice systems and addresses changes in the role of juvenile justice professionals and the mission of their agencies. The second half of the chapter considers the potential of restorative group conferencing practice for strengthening the capacity of community groups to assume greater responsibility for the response to youth crime and provides emerging examples of how restorative justice conferencing programs may seek to enhance informal social control and social support in addressing the goal of community building.

Finally, in Chapter 8 we attempt to synthesize theories of practice and consider definitions of 'success' that relate to theories of intervention. We draw general conclusions about the current state of restorative conferencing in the United States, and about the application of theory to practice in actual conferencing experiences. Finally, we present issues, propositions, and concerns for future research, policy, and practice, develop general guiding propositions for future research, and suggest next steps.

Chapter 1

Restorative justice, restorative group conferencing, and juvenile justice

Introduction

Restorative justice is not new (Weitekamp, 1999). Though the term gained popularity in most of the western world only in the past decade (Shaw and Jane, 1998; Van Ness and Strong, 2001; Bazemore and Schiff, 2001), restorative decision-making in the form of victim–offender mediation programs has a 30-year history in the United States. This history began in 1972 with an experimental program in the Minnesota Department of Corrections using victim–offender meetings as a component of a restitution program designed for adult inmates eligible for early release (Hudson and Galaway, 1990; Hudson, personal communication, 2001). By the early 1980s, a number of community-based victim–offender mediation programs had taken hold primarily in juvenile courts and non-profit agencies. By the late 1990s, some 300 such programs had been identified (Umbreit et al., 2003).

Face-to-face restorative decision-making processes are a core feature of this broader justice paradigm that includes a potentially wide variety of practice and policy. What we will refer to in this volume as 'restorative group conferencing' is therefore viewed as one core process in a wide range of responses that share common goals and objectives.

Defining restorative justice and restorative group conferencing

There are a number of definitions of restorative justice, and even more ways of defining the dimensions by which one might determine the strength and integrity of a given restorative justice intervention. In common discussion among some restorative practitioners and advocates, 'restorative' is a term often best understood in contrast to what is viewed as its opposite – being punitive, authoritarian, or even simply mean-spirited. While the notion of 'restorative' as defining a different way of being and relating to others in a variety of contexts can be a helpful one true to the spirit of restorative justice (e.g. Boyes-Watson, 2004), so far there have been no definitions that provide any objective standard for evaluating the quality and strength of a restorative intervention.

Defining restorative justice essentially as what occurs in a restorative program or as the outcome of a restorative non-adversarial, face-to-face encounter between victim, offender, and other stakeholders in a crime (Marshall, 1996), while providing marginally greater specificity and clarity, still does not provide standards for gauging the relative strength and quality of such interventions. For example, while the assertion that 'restorative justice is any outcome reached by participants in a restorative process' (McCold and Wachtel, 2003) gives appropriate emphasis to the value of the restorative encounter as a core center of action in restorative justice, it does not specify any outcome that would distinguish a restorative process from one that seeks goals such as punishment, offender treatment, incapacitation, deterrence, or other objectives. It provides no metric for gauging the relative intensity or success of such a process and is, moreover, tautological. It defines a restorative outcome as the result of a restorative process without illuminating what might constitute a restorative process.

Other researchers and practitioners, assuming the need to actively engage victim, offender, and community as a given, have sought to draw sharper distinctions by focusing on the intensity of key stakeholder involvement. Umbreit (2001) and his colleagues, for example, have developed indices for gauging the relative intensity of victim involvement by ranking indirect or very limited victim–offender dialogue as lowest intensity, and face-to-face, direct, stakeholder needs-driven dialogue as most intensive. He and others have also suggested standards for gauging the relative success of interventions by the extent to which they attempt to address multiple victim needs (see Seymour and Bazemore, 1999; Lehman et al., 2002). As ways of gauging 'restorativeness,' such standards are, however, also one-dimensional in their implication that the strength of restorative justice interventions is limited to the extent to which only one stakeholder's needs are met (no matter how important and justifiable the emphasis on crime victims may be).

An improvement is McCold and Wachtel's three-dimensional emphasis (see Figure 1.1) that defines interventions as more or less restorative based on their presumed capacity and intent to engage all three stakeholders in restorative justice – victim, offender, and community (McCold and Wachtel, 2003). While this approach provides multiple dimensions, its

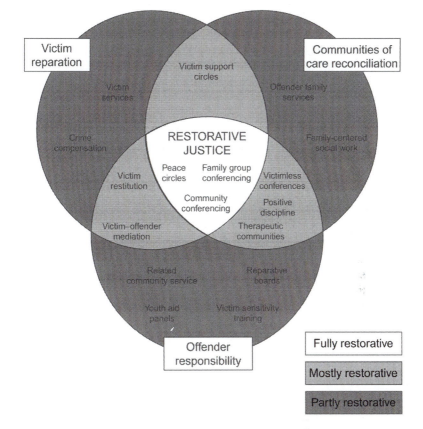

Source: In Pursuit of Paradigm: A Theory of Restorative Justice, by Paul McCold and Ted Wachtel. Paper presented at the XIII World Congress of Criminology, 10–15 August 2003, Rio de Janeiro.

Figure 1.1 McCold and Wachtel's restorative practices typology

application is limited by the use of these dimensions primarily to rate a variety of program models. Specifically, one intent of this work has been to develop a hierarchy of programs ranked as (1) 'fully restorative' (potential to engage all three stakeholders); (2) 'mostly restorative'; (3) 'partly restorative,' and by default, not restorative.

Unfortunately, this application of the three-dimensional focus only to existing program models does not allow for the possibility that any number of informal encounters *outside the context of formal programs* may fully engage all three stakeholders without following any practice model (or, for that matter, by mixing multiple models). Moreover, though this program-focused approach on the surface emphasizes key differences *between* models, it does not allow for comparison of the presence and strength of restorative intervention within a given program or a specific implementation of a restorative process (see Hayes and Daly, 2003). Similar to the focus on the presence of a face-to-face encounter alone as the measure of restorativeness (Marshall, 1994; McCold, 2003b), the program-focused, stakeholder involvement approach also appears to be concerned with stakeholder involvement only, rather than with the extent to which the 'restorative process' pursues or achieves a restorative outcome (but see also McCold and Wachtel, 2002, wherein models are compared on relative ability to accomplish certain outcomes).

The goal-focused approach is exemplified in Bazemore and Walgrave's (1999) provisional definition of restorative justice as 'every action that is primarily oriented toward doing justice by repairing the harm that has been caused by a crime' (p. 48). We view this as an appropriate general definition for the wide variety of restorative practices that may be possible in response to any crime no matter where the crime and the harm it causes is addressed in justice systems or communities, or whether or not key stakeholders (e.g. victims) are willing or able to participate directly in face-to-face dialogue. Restorative justice decision-making and restorative group conferencing is, from this perspective, part of this larger category of practices that seek to repair the harm crime causes (Bazemore and Walgrave, 1999; Van Ness and Strong, 1997). As a holistic model for responding to crime and other harms, the restorative justice framework cannot therefore be limited to one form of intervention, to certain types of offenders and victims, or to certain points in the criminal or juvenile justice process. Indeed, in the relatively short modern history of restorative justice, a wide array of restorative practices have emerged within criminal and juvenile justice systems that attempt to address harm in multiple circumstances.

As illustrated in Table 1.1, these practices address multiple objectives and range in community and justice system contexts from the point of neighborhood police or citizen encounters with troublesome behaviors or minor violations, through residential placement or incarceration, to reintegration or reentry to the community following incarceration. In addition, preventative peace-making and informal conflict resolution efforts based on restorative principles that have emerged in schools and other neighborhood settings (e.g. Karp and Breslin, 2001) that have no formal connection to juvenile or criminal justice systems may also be included in this broad definition of restorative practice.

Toward principles as standards for restorativeness

The spirit of restorative justice, and the quality and potential of the restorative justice movement, depends on its consistency with broader values. These values suggest standards that seem difficult to achieve without maximizing the direct input of the three stakeholders through a

Table 1.1 Restorative justice objectives, practice, and typical location

Objective/focus	Practice	Typical location/use
Prevention, peace-making, youth development, community building, family and school discipline	School and neighborhood conferencing, youth development circles, victim awareness education, restorative discipline, family support and discussion groups	Schools, neighborhoods, churches, civic groups
Provide decision-making alternative to formal court or other adversarial process for determining obligations for repairing harm	Victim–offender dialogue, family group conferencing, circles, neighborhood accountability boards, other restorative conferencing approaches	Police and community diversion, court diversion, dispositional/sentencing alternatives, post-dispositional planning, residential alternative discipline, conflict resolution, post-residential reentry
Victim and community input to court or formal decision-making	Written or oral impact statement to court or other entity	Court, probation, residential facilities
Provide reparative sanctions or obligation in response to crime or harmful behavior	Restitution, restorative community service, service to victims, service for surrogate victims, payment to victim service funds	Diversion, court sanction, probation condition, residential program, reentry
Offender treatment/rehabilitation/ education	Victim impact panels, victim awareness education, drunk driving panels, community service learning projects	Probation, residential facilities, diversion program, jails
Victim services and support groups	Volunteer support groups, faith community groups, counseling	Multiple settings
Reentry	Reentry conferences, support circles, restorative community service	Neighborhood and community

meaningful encounter that allows for respectful dialogue between them. Moreover, many have argued that the extent to which *repair* can be accomplished requires individual stakeholders' involvement in a process that empowers relevant communities and places system/government professionals in facilitative, rather than directive, roles (Van Ness and Strong, 1997; Bazemore and Walgrave, 1999). For this purpose, Dignan and Marsh's (2001) definition is perhaps most helpful and comprehensive in its emphasis on both a goal and process that are distinct from those of adversarial approaches and independent of any link to specific programs or process models. For these authors:

> restorative justice is not restricted to a *particular approach or program*, but is applicable to any that have the following characteristics:
> - an emphasis on the offender's personal accountability by key participants; and
> - an inclusive decision-making process that encourages participation by key participants; and
> - the goal of *putting right the harm that is caused by an offense.*
>
> (2001: 85–9; emphasis ours)

This definition includes the emphasis on a general 'inclusive decision-making process,' which – given the authors' broader statement – we take to mean victim, offender, and relevant community, without emphasizing specific programs (or the necessity of any program), and includes the goal of repairing harm caused by an offense. As such, it is consistent with our view that evaluation of restorative practice and the multi-dimensional assessment of the extent to which any intervention is restorative should be based on general principles that, while not specifying a given practice or process, provide standards for assessing the strength and integrity of such intervention in a given case.

For us, Van Ness and Strong's (1997) articulation of three broad principles – which we designate below as the principles of *repair*, *stakeholder participation*, and *community/government role transformation* – captures the essence of Dignan and Marsh's definition while adding (see Principle 3 below) the emphasis on the restructuring of the community/government role in the response to crime. Specifically, Van Ness and Strong designate:

1. *The principle of repair* – justice requires that we work to heal victims, offenders, and communities that have been injured by crime.
2. *The principle of stakeholder participation* – victims, offenders, and communities should have the opportunity for active involvement in the justice process as early and as fully as possible.

3. *The principle of transformation in community and government roles and relationships* – we must rethink the relative roles and responsibilities of government and community. In promoting justice, government is responsible for preserving a just order, and community for establishing a just peace.

These three broad principles form the basis of what we call principle-based research and evaluation and are the essence of the model we propose in this work. We use these to both ground our research and to constitute the basis by which we think 'restorativeness' in program vision and practice can be assessed. We continue by examining how and why these principles form the foundation of theory and practice in restorative conferencing.

Principles and principle-based evaluation

Like all restorative practices, restorative group conferencing approaches can be said to be generally guided by a set of principles that give priority to repairing the harm caused by crime, involving stakeholders in a decision-making process to determine how to repair this harm, and transforming the relationship between communities and justice systems while empowering the former in the response to a crime (Bazemore and Walgrave, 1999; Van Ness and Strong, 2001). It is adherence to these principles, therefore, rather than to protocols or program criteria that provide the first standard for differentiating restorative justice practices, in general and in each specific application, from other forms of intervention.

What we will refer to in this text as *principle-based process evaluation* is not unlike other efforts to establish 'program integrity,' or consistency between program intervention and guiding principles (e.g. Andrews and Bonta, 1994). To the extent that an intervention is inconsistent with restorative principles, impact evaluators are not in fact testing the effectiveness of restorative justice, regardless of the name of the program or initiative being studied. Rather, they are inadvertently testing some *other* normative theory of intervention (e.g. crime control, social welfare/ treatment), or some unspecified combination of approaches. When this is the case, neither the failure nor success of the intervention in question can be attributed to restorative justice. To the extent that a program or practice is implemented in a manner consistent with restorative principles, however, evaluators have opportunities to empirically examine the impact of restorative justice practices.

In essence, the practical rationale for general principles rather than programmatic, process, or other more specific subjective criteria as the standard for gauging restorativeness can be summarized as follows:

1. Because no practice is inherently restorative, principles help us *know restorative processes/practices when we see them*, differentiate these from practices associated with other normative perspectives, and keep practice consistent with restorative values and outcomes.
2. Principles may help practitioners *adapt* restorative justice to different contexts while maintaining the integrity of the intervention.
3. For evaluation purposes, principles provide the basis for *process and impact measures*, and should form the basis of theories that help focus practice, and test alternative restorative strategies for achieving desired outcomes.

Regarding the latter, each of the three core principles articulated by Van Ness and Strong (1997) provide the basis for independent, yet mutually reinforcing, dimensions of measurement. In Chapter 2, we link these dimensions to intervention theories that suggest, immediate, intermediate and long-term outcomes that we relate to various causal theories of crime such as reintegrative shaming (Braithwaite, 1999) and social support theory (Cullen, 1994).

As suggested in the Introduction, to understand the logic of restorative conferencing interventions, it is important to develop a better understanding of practitioner 'theories-in-use' (Agyris and Schön, 1974). Such theories provide mental 'maps' that organize action in the conferencing setting and provide the basis for logic models or *intervention theories* (Weiss, 1997; Bazemore and Stinchcomb, 2000) which link various practices to short-term program objectives and outcomes, e.g. participant satisfaction, completion of agreements, reduced fear, and stronger relationships, and then to long-term goals.

In summary, 'restorative' is not an absolute distinction to be applied mechanically to some programs or processes but not others. Hence, critical to the task of establishing intervention integrity is the development of broad principle-based dimensions and degrees of what may be called 'restorativeness.' This task is best accomplished through a critical examination of how the normative theory of restorative justice – essentially the core principles and underlying values associated with them – are applied in complex real-world encounters between offender, victim, and others aimed at achieving an overall vision of restorative justice. Our purpose in this exploratory study was not to evaluate a restorative justice conferencing program or programs, rather we were concerned with the development of a more productive framework for principle-based and theory-driven evaluation (Chen, 1990). Such a framework informs this attempt to build grounded theories of restorative practice that may guide future evaluations of restorative justice conferencing that seek to assess the quality and extent of program implementation and integrity of intervention (e.g. Patton, 1990). In addition, the framework should guide quantitative evaluation aimed at measuring restorative outcomes, and should provide opportunities to test one or more alternative intervention theories grounded in restorative justice principles.

Restorative justice, decision-making and restorative group conferencing

It is possible to use a variety of terms to emphasize distinctions between restorative practice and program models. As noted in the Introduction, we use the term 'restorative group conferencing' (or simply restorative conferencing or conferencing) in this volume as a generic way of describing and emphasizing similarities between a wide array of face-to-face non-adversarial decision-making dialogue encounters between victim, offender, and community members in response to specific crime and/or incidents of harm.

Because the term conferencing has perhaps been most directly associated with one decision-making model, *family group conferencing* (McDonald et al., 1995; McCold, 1996; but see Umbreit, 1999, 2001), such broad application of the term is viewed by some practitioners as controversial or misleading (McCold, 2000). Moreover, proponents of some restorative decision-making approaches such as peacemaking circles and neighborhood boards may not use the term 'conferencing' to describe their programs. Many others, however – including some proponents of victim–offender mediation and dialogue programs – have readily adopted the term conferencing or group conferencing (Umbreit, 2001). Employing labels such as 'victim–offender conferencing,' 'community conferencing,' and 'large group conferencing,' they – and others that do *not use* the term conferencing – often describe what appears to be a range of practice variations.

Our purpose in using the term 'conferencing' is not to minimize the importance of various practice models and programs. Yet, it is important to note that restorative justice remains an emerging national and international movement in which practice is, appropriately we think, being adapted and modified on a daily basis. Both new and long-established program models have borrowed from other models creating a number of hybrid programs. For example, VOM/D programs in the US have for some years been moving beyond the dyadic victim–offender mediation and dialogue model to include family members, and have adapted formats much like peacemaking circles such as 'large group conferencing' in order to mediate collective conflict on a broader scale (Umbreit, 2001). In the current study, we examined youth neighborhood accountability boards (NABS) in Colorado and Vermont whose processes appeared almost identical to a family group conference and bore little resemblance to the more court-like models of some other board programs. Indeed, even features of programs that may appear to be unique (and are believed by program staff to be so), as we learned in this study, are likely to have been borrowed indirectly from other models. It is therefore futile, we believe, to try to describe fixed parameters of distinctive practice models.

Common denominators

Ultimately, in this volume we hope to focus attention away from programmatic distinctions that may be rather parochial, arbitrary, and temporary. We do so in order to emphasize what we regard as more essential underlying theoretical and philosophical distinctions both within and between conferencing program models. Moreover, the nature and magnitude of these more theoretical, philosophical, and programmatic differences is an empirical question that for the most part has not been examined, but which we address using national survey data in Chapter 3 and in a different way in the qualitative portions of our study. Where there are genuine and sustained differences in value or ideological commitments, theoretical assumptions, in focal concerns and practice priorities that may indeed vary between program models, there is a need to make these differences explicit and ground them in actual data rather than program vision statements. This should not diminish the need to study variation in theory and philosophy *within* the same model type while, at the same time, identifying common themes associated with both normative and etiological theory across program models.

Many names have been given to specific adaptations of what may be viewed as generic non-adversarial responses to crime, especially when contrasted with adversarial decision-making procedures. Though it is important not to exaggerate differences between conferencing and court or other adversarial procedures in all cases, conferencing models generally share a common distinguishing characteristic: offender(s), victim(s) or a victim representative, a facilitator, and other community members sit in a face-to-face informal meeting to consider the impact of a crime or harm on victims and communities and to try to develop a plan to repair this harm that meets the needs of those most affected. The dialogue process is not about finding guilt or innocence, fixing blame, or determining punishment, and participants do not rely on formal guidelines or attorneys to come to their decisions. What makes the specific encounter and the process itself 'restorative,' as we suggested in the previous section, is *the extent to which the process adheres to a set of core principles and a focus on the overall goal of repairing the harm crime causes* (Van Ness and Strong, 1997, 2001; Bazemore and Walgrave, 1999). In addition, all restorative group conferencing models seek to in some way accomplish the following common objectives: include different points of view and give emphasis to the voice and perspective of various stakeholders; ensure honest communication between victim, offender, and others; respectfully acknowledge victims; express emotion; consider stakeholder needs; utilize a different form of accountability, empathy, and understanding; promise creative problem-solving; build relationships; and apply and develop conflict resolution and other skills.

Differences between models

Despite these essential similarities between all restorative group conferencing models – and the more important shared differences between restorative group conferencing programs and other juvenile justice programs and practices – we suggest distinguishing between four broad, relatively stable programmatic variations that have emerged in the past two decades. These include: victim–offender mediation/dialogue (VOM/D); family group conferencing (FGC); neighborhood accountability boards (NABS); and peace-making circles (circles). Variation between the four approaches is based primarily upon different priorities about: (1) which stakeholders are viewed as essential in order to conduct a conference, and which stakeholders commonly participate; (2) who facilitates the conference and how the dialogue and process is guided; (3) what structure has been adopted for ongoing maintenance of program operations beyond each individual encounter; and, (4) what dominant philosophy guides the process.

Table 1.2 contrasts the programs on these dimensions. While we caution that even on these questions, there is much overlap and borrowing between models, at the conclusion of our study, we could say that these differences remained stable between most programs representative of the four model types.

Who must attend and who normally participates?

Common mandatory participants in all group conferencing models are the facilitator and the offender. While it is possible to hold a conference with these two participants only, such an encounter would appear to lack the essential other party or parties, and there is a shared strong preference across all models for all of the stakeholders – offender, facilitator, victim and/or family – to participate. Variation between models is based on who is viewed as *necessary* or mandatory, and who constitutes the typical core group of routine participants. In VOM/D programs, with the exception of pre-meetings held separately for victims and offenders, victim and offender participation is viewed as essential. Though some programs occasionally allow for participation of a surrogate victim – usually at the request of the actual victim – the urgent and primary focus on addressing victim and offender needs *first* make these stakeholders a mandatory component. Increasingly, parents and other stakeholders may be involved with the approval of victim and offender, although these participants are not required in the VOM/D model.

Table 1.2 Restorative conferencing models administration and process

	Victim–offender mediation	Family group conferencing	Neighborhood board	Peacemaking circles
Who normally participates	Mediator, victim, offender (family)	Facilitator, offender, family (victim)	Board chair, volunteers, offender, family (victim)	Keeper, offender, volunteers, family, victim and offender supporters
Common permanent structure/staffing	Program coordinator, volunteer mediators (some paid mediators)	Program coordinator, facilitator (volunteers)	Coordinator, volunteer board chair, volunteer board members	Coordinator, volunteer circle members
Facilitation and dominant process	Victims option to speak first; mediator facilitates open-ended dialogue with minimal interference	In most programs facilitator follows script or outline in which offender speaks first, followed by victim and other participants; seeks to move process through phases	Board chair initiates member deliberation after questioning offender and parents, though some variation emerging toward circle or family group conferencing process	Keeper opens session and closes session, each person allowed to speak when talking piece is passed to them. Shared leadership and consensus decision-making
Dominant philosophy	Meeting victim and offender needs, healing dialogue as transformative	Family group as essential problem-solver. Respectful, normative disapproval with support; offender empathy and emotion key	Neighborhood social support and community norm affirmation; neighborhood problem-solving focus	Collective healing; community focus; broad problem-solving, community building focus beyond individual offense

At the other end of this continuum are neighborhood accountability boards where conferences may occur with an offender and board members when the victim chooses not to attend. Circle programs commonly hold separate circles with victim and offender (and at times a significant number of follow-up circles with offender and family), though separate meetings are generally intended as a prelude to the circle with both. In family group conferencing, family members – generally one or both parents and/or relatives – are essential players in the conference. Victims are strongly encouraged to participate, and play a vital practical and theoretical role in creating empathy and a sense of remorse for the offender, but conferences can and will be convened even when the victim or surrogate is unwilling to participate. Neighborhood boards emphasize the encounter between young offenders and neighborhood adults who care about them, but they can proceed without either victim or family present. Families are strongly encouraged to participate and victims are viewed as important by most boards, though participation rates for the latter run low in most programs.

What is the common permanent program structure?

This dimension addresses how programs accomplish the work of the conference on an ongoing basis. All programs have in common a program coordinator or administrator who may play a number of roles (including especially facilitating conferences) in addition to assuming primary responsibility for program maintenance and conference organization. While all programs include this coordinator role as a minimum staff position (programs range from half-time or less to multiple staff in this position), variation is most common around the presence and role of an ongoing group of volunteers.

At one end of this continuum, neighborhood accountability boards are essentially defined by the ongoing group of volunteer board members. NABs maintain a relatively permanent core group of volunteers recruited from the neighborhood, and a vital part of the program coordinator's job is to recruit and train these individuals and assign them to the hearing/ conference (one person serves as the board chairperson at a given encounter). US VOM/D programs typically maintain an ongoing group of volunteer mediators who generally assume most of the responsibility for facilitating and, at times, organizing conferences, pre-conferences, and follow-up activities. FGCs maintain a coordinator, a facilitator who may or may not also be the coordinator, and in some programs other paid and some volunteer staff. The latter, however, are not viewed as essential to program work as they are in boards and many VOM/D programs. Circles generally have a part-time coordinator and a core group of more loosely recruited and consolidated neighborhood volunteers. One of these core volunteers generally plays the role of circle keeper in a given encounter, and the group, though it may lose and add members over time, is considered an essential aspect of the circle's typical neighborhood focus and primary means of carrying on the circle's work.

Who facilitates and what is the dominant process?

The common element with regard to this dimension is someone in the facilitator's role and a process that gives voice to stakeholders, and encourages open, non-adversarial dialogue aimed at repairing harm. Beyond these common features, variation between the models is based on the nature of the facilitator's role and the values and expectations associated with the role. Variation is also based on the nature of the process that most typically characterizes the restorative encounter.

Because circle dialogue is maintained and controlled by use of the talking piece, the circle keeper's role is probably the least directive of the four models. While the keeper may play an important role in opening the conference so that the 'space' of the circle is safe, and even sacred, and in closing the circle in a positive way that also identifies agreements and plans for follow-up, she/he can be less concerned with guiding or controlling dialogue than in other models (though the keeper may summarize and move the group forward at various intervals and make connections between thoughts and proposed solutions).

The mediator in VOM/D is expected to initiate and maintain an open, stakeholder-driven dialogue that maximizes the exchange between victim and offender. The humanistic, non-directive, mediator style that focuses more on the dialogue than achieving agreements has become the ideal standard for restorative victim–offender mediation encounters (Umbreit, 1999, 2001). Though the mediator is expected to remain non-judgemental, in the past decade there has been greater deference to victims, e.g. allowing/encouraging them to speak first and to tell their story without interruption. This is in part to compensate for what was viewed by some as deference to offenders and the promotion of diversionary solutions based on the idea of reconciliation and even forgiveness as a primary goal.

Somewhat more directive in its focus on ensuring that the conference gets through steps or phases, FGC facilitators may also be less concerned about withholding judgement since the process values such disapproval and will ensure more structure in the dialogue by following a script or outline. The script generally calls for offenders to speak first in order to allow for the victim and other participants to hear the circumstances of the offense and ideally an apology from the offender or acknowledgement of responsibility (and if not, identify the need to change the offender's perspective). NABs have historically presumed a board chair who, as the name implies, could be quite directive in the process, asking questions of participants or calling on other board members to do so.

What is the dominant philosophy?

The common philosophical element across all models is a problem-solving, healing/reparative response to youth crime by stakeholders in a community context. Despite overlap between models in broad philosophical commitment, the first dimension of value difference between programs is around the relative importance of different stakeholders in the decision-making process. NABS provide greater emphasis on the vital role of neighbors as problem-solvers and supports for youth and families in trouble in the context of the neighborhood as the locus of decision-making. At the other extreme on this dimension, VOM provides a central focus on victim and offender as the primary parties in the crime and conflict and gives greater emphasis to problem-solving through dyadic dialogue.

FGC gives perhaps the greatest importance to the role of the family and intimates of the offender as those most capable of influencing the young person. Philosophically, FGC also appears to be more concerned than the other models with keeping the practical focus of the conference on the offense itself, and the obligations associated with it, than on the full range of offender, victim, and community needs that may be apparent. Respectful disapproval of the offender's behavior with support is at the core of the FGC philosophy, with an emphasis on the role of empathy and/or promoting a sense of shame, coupled with acceptance and support from other stakeholders. Shared leadership and consensus-based decision-making as core philosophies, as well as guides to process, are viewed as critical aspects of the transformative philosophy of circles. Collective transformation through a seamless dialogue that is the least concerned of any model with keeping the focus on the offense that brought the group together and most concerned with stakeholder and community needs characterizes circles philosophically.

Summary and conclusions

After considering various alternatives, we have made the case in this chapter for a principle-based definition of restorative justice. We have also argued for a principle-based model of evaluation. Principles provide dimensions which help us 'know restorative justice when we see it,' keep practice consistent with values, help practitioners adapt restorative processes to different contexts, and provide standards for assessing the integrity of intervention.

Although we examined what we view as key differences between four structurally different models of restorative justice, we gave emphasis to the similarities between these approaches, especially when contrasted with other justice processes. Most importantly, we suggested that philosophical and theoretical, rather than programmatic, differences most likely account for much of the variation in conferencing practice. Such practice adaptations are often shared across what are increasingly hybridized models.

In Chapter 2, we examine some of the theories that might account for this variation and may explain why restorative conferencing has its intended impacts on victim, offender and community. We also consider the alignment of these theories with core principles, conference objectives, and long-term outcomes sought by practitioners in the conferencing context. Together, these theories and principles help us organize our otherwise inductive examination of qualitative data on how practitioners accomplish their work and make sense of the impact of their decisions in various phases and stages of the restorative conferencing process.

Chapter 2

Principles to practice: intermediate outcomes, intervention theories, and conferencing tasks

Introduction

In the Introduction, we described the national case study presented in this volume as a formative effort to: (1) describe 'what's out there' in restorative group conferencing in US juvenile justice; and (2) gain a deeper understanding of the rationale and operation of these decision-making options. We noted that our study was not, however, completely inductive since both the practitioners involved in restorative group conferencing and ourselves had, to some degree, been exposed to the core principles introduced in Chapter 1 as the primary standard for gauging the integrity, or 'restorativeness' of these practices. These principles, along with related theories-in-use, may be expected to prioritize certain conferencing outcomes. Although we suspected that few programs would represent a pure application of restorative principles, and that some programs might draw upon other theories of intervention related to other justice models (e.g. deterrence, treatment/social welfare), we expected to find some commitment to core restorative principles and related intervention theories.

In this chapter, we elaborate on the implications of core restorative justice principles for the practice and evaluation of restorative group conferencing. We consider the possible intended outcomes of conferencing as these relate to core principles and to longer-term impacts on victim, offender, and community. We are especially interested in how conferencing practice is designed to achieve these outcomes. There is also a need to categorize the variety of what are essentially 'grounded logics,' applied in the conferencing environment that connect practice to the results accomplished at the end of the conference process. These results are referred to in this text as *immediate outcomes*, and these short-term objectives are connected to *intermediate*, and to some degree long-term outcomes, by intervention theories. We suggest how these logics generally relate to larger causal theories in criminology and the social sciences.

Essentially, we propose an initial framework for understanding why conferencing practitioners and participants may do what they do, and what rationales account for this variation in practice across programs, or even across individual conference encounters within the same program. We use the term 'intervention theory' to indicate what have also been referred to in the literature as evaluation 'logic models' (Weiss, 1997; Bazemore and Stinchcombe, 2000). These models provide a practical explanation for why various interventions are expected to lead to immediate outcomes, and why these outcomes are expected to lead to intermediate outcomes and long-term effects. Often this logic is not made explicit in the conferencing process. Based both on literature and observation of practice prior to this study, as well as consideration of the findings to be reported herein, this chapter attempts to clarify some of the possible objectives that conferencing programs *may* pursue, and some of the intervention theories that lead to such goals. The qualitative data chapters which follow will then provide insight into which logics seem to be articulated and followed, and how (and why) this logic may vary.

Dimensions of the vision

We begin each section of this chapter with one of the three core restorative justice principles identified in Chapter 1, focusing on several theoretical dimensions of the restorative justice vision that fit logically under that principle. Each dimension is generally concerned with addressing a particular type of harm created in the aftermath of a crime, and with certain corresponding needs and obligations that restorative interventions presumably seek to address (Zehr, 1990). Dimensions, as we use this term, essentially define the initial outcomes that may be pursued in the conference in an attempt to address these needs and obligations. Specific conferencing tasks are focused on these outcomes, which are in turn associated with a specific intervention theory that links them to longer-term objectives. Decision-making in the conferencing process may be guided by other practical logics (evident in the qualitative data to be presented in Chapters 5–7) about the best way to achieve these theory-related objectives within the conference. For example, if practitioners wish to ensure that the offender has made connections in the conference that will lead to ongoing prosocial relationships, then, following the theory of social support (Cullen, 1994), they may select participants for the conference based on who and what kinds of persons might be most likely to identify with, and reach out to the offender.

Conferencing outcomes

As Presser and Van Voorhis (2002: 163) observe, 'any one restorative justice intervention is by design composed of multiple helping and disciplinary actions.' Restorative outcomes are then typically intended to meet more than one need and may impact more than one intervention target or stakeholder. Such outcomes are therefore also *collective* in the sense that even the most basic effort to repair harm, involve stake-holders, and restructure community and government roles may result in a certain degree of mutual transformation of victim, offender, and community. For example, the simple act of 'making amends' by paying restitution can be expected to affect the victim and the community, as well as the offender (Tontodanato and Erez, 1994; Schneider, 1990). Ultimately, this holistic, even community-level, focus seems more likely to avoid the individualizing tendencies of offender-focused treatment and punishment paradigms and potentially move beyond what Sampson and Wilson (1995: 54) refer to as a 'simple "kinds of people" analysis to a focus on social characteristics of collectivities that foster violence (and crime).'

Conferencing outcomes may address long-term goals, the results to be achieved in a middle-range period of follow-up time after the conferencing encounter (intermediate objectives), and the results to be achieved at the end of the conference itself (immediate objectives). The most general *long-term outcomes* have to do with the individual well-being of victim, offender, and community (Presser and Van Voorhis, 2002). For the offender, there is likely to be a stated goal to prevent future offending, and for the victim, some sense of long-term closure and healing. For community, justice with peace and safety are often unstated but implicit long-term goals of restorative justice (e.g. Van Ness and Strong, 2001).

Although part of the conferencing vision, such long-term goals are often too far removed from immediate reality for most conferencing partici-pants to be concerned with. In any case, these long-term outcomes are the ultimate 'dependent variable' associated with various intervention the-ories. That is, these theories imply that something that happens in the conference produces *immediate outcomes* to be achieved at the conclusion of the conference. These can then be linked to *intermediate outcomes* concerned with the behavior and well-being of stakeholders in the weeks and months subsequent to the conference. These intermediate changes may then be linked theoretically to long-term reductions in offending, victim healing, and safer communities. For example, the theory of *social support* may posit that connections made between offenders and supportive community adults in the conference (immediate outcomes) may lead to ongoing caring relationships (intermediate outcomes) that ultimately have a long-term impact by creating safer and more caring communities (Cullen, 1994). Behavioral outcomes at the intermediate level might also include reductions in offender involvement in future offending or an increase in prosocial activities and victim readjustment and participation in normal routines. The linkage between these outcome levels will hopefully become evident in the discussion of intervention theories associated with each dimension.

What specific outcomes are sought in restorative conferencing? We have identified nine dimensions that appear to resonate most clearly with current US conferencing practice and are also consistent with recent theoretical and research literature. As dimensions associated with the principles of repair, stakeholder involvement, and community/government transformation respectively, these define conferencing outcomes related to the immediate and concrete completion of obligations or efforts to meet needs caused by the harm of crime (see Table 2.1), and potentially linked to outcomes related to long-term healing. These dimensions are not meant to be viewed as exhaustive, nor are the outcomes they suggest always mutually exclusive. Rather, they are meant to suggest different conferencing priorities or focal concerns that drive practice consistent with these priorities and based on different theories of what intermediate outcomes lead to long-term healing. What distinguishes these outcomes from those associated with punishment, treatment, risk management, or other agendas is the normative value base on which they are based. Table 2.1 presents the dimensions and core principles on which this analysis is based.

Table 2.1 Dimensions and core principles

Repairing harm	Stakeholder involvement	Community/government role transformation
Dimensions: • Making amends • Relationship building	*Dimensions:* • Victim–offender exchange • Respectful disapproval • Mutual transformation	*Dimensions:* • Changing system mission and professional roles • Norm affirmation/ values clarification • Collective ownership • Skill building

Intervention theories: connecting outcomes and practice

At the broadest theoretical level, what differentiates restorative justice theory from most theories of intervention is the focus on restoration. An overarching theory of restorative justice might therefore be expressed as a general proposition that practices aimed at collective healing or reparation of harms will result in safer, more peaceful communities. The assumption of restorative group conferencing is that positive outcomes are generally more likely to be achieved by participation in the conferencing process than by court or other formal proceedings.

Some of the intervention theories used in conferencing may appear to be directly or implicitly related to theories of behavior change and social well-being in various social science literatures such as criminology – e.g. labeling, differential association, control theory and social disorganization perspectives (Braithwaite and Mugford, 1994; Braithwaite, 1999; Bazemore, 1998). However, most restorative conferencing intervention theories are less formal and drawn from experience in observing conferences and talking to conferencing practitioners about how and why they make the choices they do in order to design and implement conferencing programs. These intervention theories are, in this sense, truly 'grounded.' We derive the theories presented here more from the stated *outcomes* practitioners claim to be seeking in conferencing than from the limited theoretical literature on restorative justice. Therefore we begin the explanation of each dimension with a discussion of conferencing outcomes, and then proceed to a consideration of the intervention theory relevant to those objectives. We then discuss the prioritization of certain tasks and approaches to conferencing that are necessary to achieve these outcomes.

Conferencing practice

The general tasks of a restorative conference are to: (1) identify and address one or more types of harm in the aftermath of a crime; (2) meet the needs of victims and obligations of offenders that are associated with each harm; (3) ensure that stakeholders are engaged in the process; and (4) maximize the community role in the process. However, the specific agenda of the conference may vary depending upon the type of harm that is the primary focus of attention in a given incident. Practice variation, to the extent that it is not random or based on other contingencies, is typically driven by a philosophical commitment of program staff to one or more logics of practice and to the immediate outcomes they prioritize as most important. Tasks of the conference implicitly flow logically from often unarticulated propositions about how to achieve these outcomes. These unarticulated propositions are, in fact, what link desired outcomes to theories of change and to specific conferencing tasks.

47

Part 1: Repairing harm in the conferencing environment: dimensions of repair

The principle of repair – justice requires that we work to heal victims, offenders, and communities that have been injured by crime.

(Van Ness and Strong, 1997)

Introduction

The first and most important 'big idea' of the restorative perspective is that crime is more than simply lawbreaking. If this is a valid assumption, then 'justice' cannot be achieved simply by punishing or treating the lawbreaker (Van Ness and Strong, 1997). Rather, the primary goal of intervention, the primary justice objective of the restorative approach, is that we must repair, to the greatest extent possible, the harm caused to victims, offenders, and communities who have been injured by crime. Restorative justice responses to intervention therefore begin with a focus on identifying the damage to victims and communities that has resulted from the actions of the offender. Crime may result in material and emotional damage to *individuals* – victims, offenders, and the family and acquaintances of both. It also harms the *community* surrounding the incident. Between the individual and the community, crime damages the interpersonal *relationships* of victim and offender.

Two primary dimensions are associated with the principle of repair in the conferencing context. These dimensions suggest specific restorative outcomes focused on ameliorating material and emotional harm to individuals, communities, and relationships. Harm to individual victims and to affected communities is commonly addressed by a broad dimension of reparative activity best described as *making amends.* Harm to relationships is addressed in conferences by a dimension labeled *relationship building/rebuilding.* While the general task of a restorative conference is to focus on repairing one or more of these types of harm, the following discussion of these dimensions illustrates how the specific agenda of the conference may vary depending upon the type of harm that is the primary focus of attention in a given incident and the philosophical/theoretical commitment of program staff to one of two intervention theories described below.

Dimension 1: Making amends

Making amends is typically the most common component of the reparative agreement negotiated at the conclusion of a conference, but amends may be to some extent addressed by events in the conference itself. The harm to be repaired is material and emotional damage to victims, family and friends, and the community affected by the event. The problem to be addressed is the imbalance created by the actions of the offender that has created a need or deficit for the victim and community, and an obligation for the offender to 'make things right.'

Amends and conferencing outcomes

The intermediate outcome associated with the dimension of amends-making is about repair in its most literal and practical sense: 'cleaning up one's mess,' or redressing harm through forms of reparation. As an intermediate outcome of the conference that will, for the most part, occur subsequent to the encounter during the follow-up period, amends constitutes the meeting of obligations set forward in an agreement, and may take the form of restitution, service to victims, apologies, community service, or a commitment to behavior change or a specific course of action (e.g. the victim and/or community members may request that the offender attend school or a victim sensitivity class, change certain behaviors, etc.) (Karp, 2001).

The most tangible *immediate* outcome relevant to amends in the conferencing process is the agreement itself, a conferencing product viewed almost universally as important. The quality of the agreement regarding making amends is dependent upon the extent to which conference participants have adequately answered Howard Zehr's (1990) three questions: what is the harm, how do we repair it, and who is responsible for this repair. Essentially, answering these questions most clearly differentiates amends achieved through court-ordered reparation and those resulting from the conferencing process. Offender 'accountabil-ity' from a restorative perspective is therefore defined not simply by the act of making reparation, but by a three-step process in which: (1) the offender takes responsibility, or 'ownership,' for the harm caused by his crime as defined by crime victims and affected community; (2) the offender takes action to repair the damage; and (3) relevant community members including the victim play appropriate roles in monitoring the reparative agreement and assisting the offender in its completion.

Amends and intervention theory: exchange and earned redemption

Why and how does the process of making amends influence the future well-being of victim, offender, and community, the behavior of the offender, and the interrelationship between all stakeholders? Making amends as a primary outcome is associated with exchange theory approaches which suggest that human cooperation and civil discourse is grounded in virtually universal expectations of reciprocity (Molm and Cook, 1995). Linked to a more naturalistic attitude toward crime and the offender, the obligation of offenders to 'make things right' by repairing damage resulting from their crime appears to build upon a sense of need to address the imbalance that occurs when one person harms another (Bazemore, 1998; Miller, 1993). While such imbalance is addressed in retributive justice theory via the currency of punishment, it is addressed in restorative justice by reparation. Most importantly, norms of fairness and reciprocity work against the idea that someone who has hurt another citizen should receive help or service without first taking some action to make things better. The failure to take responsibility to repair harm is therefore a barrier to meaningful offender reintegration that may also impose limits on victim healing and on the establishment of community peace and safety. However, 'by moving away from the principle of entitlement to the principle of social exchange' (Levrant et al., 1999: 22), restorative justice practices seek to engage the community and victim side of the justice equation (Herman and Wasserman, 2001).

Although exchange theory is scarcely mentioned in the restorative justice literature (e.g. Braithwaite, 2002; for exceptions see, Perry and Gorsyck, 1997; Bazemore, 2001), practitioners have used these assumptions in restorative intervention as a rationale for requiring action on the part of the offender as a first step on the road to reintegration as a type of 'earned redemption' (Bazemore, 1998). While much of this action may occur post-conference by actively working to repair the harm (e.g. by making restitution to the victims, providing service to victim and/or community), the offender is generally expected in the restorative conferencing encounter to first acknowledge responsibility for the wrong, and may also take significant reparative action in the conference itself, by for example, apologizing to the victim. Victims and affected community members will therefore be more likely to accept offenders who have demonstrated 'good faith' in this manner; said another way, *not taking* such action may be an insurmountable barrier to such acceptance.

Long-term outcomes, those linked ultimately to the well-being of victim, offender, and community and to the sense that justice has been accomplished, according to social exchange theory, flow from these amends-making actions to restore balance and the sense of reciprocity. Although there is no direct empirical evidence on community reacceptance, there are research findings relevant to the proposed connection between amends and individual transformation of victim and offender (Schneider, 1986, 1990; Tontadanato and Erez, 1994). For the victim, the receipt of a tangible repayment of loss is not only important to financial recovery in some instances, but also more often to improved psychological well-being (Tontodonato and Erez, 1994). As Presser and Van Voorhis (2002) suggest, the value of offender reparation to victims may be more about 'demonstrated willingness to pay restitution (or an effort to make things right), rather than actual completion of the reparative agreement as written.' More concretely, though the importance of victim compensation for loss should not be diminished, reparation of all kinds (money, service, meeting requests) is likely to be important to victims in part because it provides additional validation of the wrong done to them. Following the exchange theory logic, as Toews-Shenk and Zehr (2001) have argued, vindication requires reciprocity in order to allow those harmed by crime (especially direct victims) to feel that they are not somehow at fault. The *failure* to reciprocate may therefore weaken the esteem of victims (and victimized communities), who then feel a need to vindicate themselves by replacing one harm with another (Gilligan, 1996). While vindicating victims and communities by transferring their shame back to the offender through punishment merely repeats the cycle of harm, the need for reciprocity can also be met by denouncing wrongs, establishing responsibility for them, and allowing the offender to make amends.

While this dimension and the theory of earned redemption is focused primarily on the community and victim side of the equation, meeting one's obligation to victims, as Braithwaite (2001a) has observed, also has important implications for offender change. Empirical evidence suggests that the tangible act of restitution increases awareness of the need for reciprocity in the form of repairing harm (Van Voorhis, 1985; Schneider, 1990) and therefore may change offender attitudes toward obligations to others that may also lead to completion of reparative orders. Completing restitution and participating in restitution programs has also been associated with reductions in recidivism through increasing commitment to the common good (Schneider, 1990). Now in a positive 'helping' role (Riessman, 1965; Bazemore, 1999a), the offender essentially 'acts his way into better thinking' (See, 1996), or as Maruna et al. (2002: 8) put it, takes advantage of the opportunity to 'make good by doing good.'

Based on these assumptions, we suggest that when offenders accept responsibility and make credible attempts to complete their obligation to make amends to the satisfaction of victims and community members, they essentially 'earn their redemption' and are more likely to gain support for their reintegration than those who do not. Moreover, those who take an active helping role in making amends are more likely to experience positive behavioral change than those who complete reparative activities more as a routine requirement or punishment.

Amends and tasks of the conference

How does the conferencing process ensure that offenders will be more likely to complete their reparative obligations, and how does the process influence the quality of amends-making? While amends may occur as a result of a court order or other requirement and thereby lead to the outcomes discussed, conferencing has been shown to increase the likelihood of reparation (Umbreit, 2001; Braithwaite, 1999). Specific, yet variable, features of the conferencing encounter are believed to affect the likelihood of amends-making and, most importantly, the *quality* of the amends that in turn determines the extent of its impact on long-term and other intermediate outcomes. In addition to the offender's acknowledgement of responsibility and the victim's feelings as a result of this, another key immediate conferencing outcome is the provision of meaningful input into the agreement by both victim, offender, and other participants.

The conference agreement is the most concrete end result of the encounter and should reflect the specific outcomes and theoretical assumptions listed above. Specifically, conference facilitators and participants must first make the purpose of the conference clear and assess and agree upon the material and emotional harm to be addressed so that participants in the conferencing process can directly connect the obligation to repair with this harm (Karp, 2001). For example, a meaningful agreement requires an adequate assessment of the harm that is generally based upon the victim's relaying a description of the financial, emotional, relational, or other suffering as a result of the offense, in addition to added details from community members, family, and others. Conference participants will therefore need to provide time for victims and offenders to tell their stories, for offenders to acknowledge responsibility for the harm and of the choice to commit the offense, and for offender, victim, and other participants to have input into the contract. To maximize the benefits of the reparation for impacting offending behavior and to ensure that the repair has validity for the victim and community, participants will need to propose tasks that place the offender in a responsible, helping role vs. those tasks seen by everyone as sanctions or punishment. Finally, in addition to the validity, basic fairness, and practicality features of agreements, a final important conferencing outcome may be the extent to which the group takes collective ownership of the contract, is allowed discretion in developing and setting the terms of the agreement (instead of having many of the terms set by the court), and plays a role in its completion (e.g. community and family members working with the offender on community service).

Table 2.2 depicts the relationship between immediate conferencing results, theory, practice, and intermediate outcomes as described in this section.

Dimension 2: Relationship-building

Relationship-building is also frequently discussed as an important objective of conferencing (Pranis and Bazemore, 2000; Braithwaite, 1999; Bazemore, 1999a, 2001). The harm to be repaired is the damage to

Table 2.2 Restorative conferencing and repairing harm – Dimension 1: Amends-making

Theory	Immediate outcomes	Conference tasks/ priorities	Intermediate outcomes
Earned redemption /exchange theory	• Reparative agreement • Offender acceptance of responsibility • Victim and other participant input	Assess harm; victim, offender, and community input; define role of all stakeholders in the reparative agreement	Reparation in form of service, monetary restitution, apology, other

relationships caused by the crime. The problem or need to be addressed in the conference is a result of the weakening or breaking of ties of support for victims and offenders. The young offender's life situation may already be characterized by weak bonds to law-abiding peers and adults, which may have contributed to the offending in the first place (Bazemore, 1999a). The resulting lack of support is a problem to be addressed in the conference. Damage to victim relationships with significant others, and groups are also problems to be addressed in the conference.

The concern with relationship-building may emerge on a case-by-case basis if, for example, the harm in question has actually damaged a preexisting or ongoing relationship. In this case, the issue of primary concern in the conference may be about a conflict that has caused mutual harm, or about ancillary harm caused to family and friends, as well as, or rather than, a victim per se. Alternatively, relationship-building may be a focus of a conference that seeks to strategically address the preexisting harm of a lack of prosocial relationships between the offender and law-abiding adults. Addressing relational harm may be strategized in preparation for conferences by seeking to ensure that those connected to the offender and victim are part of the encounter and that others that may *need to be* connected as resource persons are also present.

Relationship-building and conferencing outcomes

Relationship-building is less observable, and therefore less easily measurable than amends-making and many other reparative outcomes. However, some practitioners argue that they can gauge success in achieving relational outcomes using rather simple indicators. Pranis, for example, suggests measuring effectiveness by the extent to which a specific conferencing encounter or conferencing program has created new positive relationships or strengthened existing ones, and created informal support systems or 'safety nets' for victims and offenders (Pranis and Bazemore, 2000). An immediate outcome of the conference itself may simply be making a connection, as when a victim or other participant offers to help the offender in some way or when someone does the same for a victim. The intermediate objective of relationship-building in the conference is indeed to create a bond to one or more persons and groups that can provide affective and instrumental support as needed on a more long-term basis (Bazemore, Nissen, and Dooley, 2000). Such relationships may then lead to other connections, which provide access to other sources of support.

Relationship-building and intervention theory: social support

The rationale/explanation linking relationship-building outcomes to subsequent offender behavior and to the long-term well-being of both offender and victim is grounded in the general theory of *social support* (Cullen, 1994; Bazemore, 2001). This theory suggests that positive connections with citizens and community groups can provide ongoing guidance and assistance to support healing and adjustment in the aftermath of a crime. Following the conference, these 'natural helpers' may function in the reintegration process as 'community guides' (McKnight, 1995), acting as bridge and buffer between the offender or victim and the community. For the victim, because the most devastating consequence of crime is often the inability to relate to family, friends, and co-workers, these individual supporters and support groups provide new connections that can help to rebuild existing relationships; such assistance is of course a fundamental part of the healing process (Achilles and Zehr, 2001).

For the offender, the more specific theory of *relational rehabilitation* attaches greatest importance to the social relationship with other law-abiding individuals and groups as a primary factor in desistance from crime (Cullen, 1994; Bazemore, Nissen, and Dooley, 2000). The linkage between these informal social relationships and the *future* behavior of offenders is through support and guidance in the form of capable guardianship and reinforcement of law-abiding behavior as well as informal support and access to roles that present opportunities for productive activities (Polk and Kobrin, 1972; Bazemore, Nissen, and Dooley, 2000). Based on this framework, we would therefore expect that offenders in such roles and in ongoing relationships of informal support will be more likely to develop a legitimate identity, commit to law-abiding behavior, and be less likely to reoffend. Similarly, victims in ongoing relationships of informal support will be more likely to move forward with a healing process than those who do not have access to such relationships (Zehr, 2001).

Relationship-building and tasks of the conference

The task of rebuilding, or building, relationships in conferencing requires critical examination of the extent to which the process is able to mobilize and engage those individuals and groups who can provide social support. The focus of the conference regarding the relationship-building outcome is on connecting or reconnecting, *as appropriate*: victim and offender, offender and community, and/or victim and community. Though relationship-building generally emerges organically, it seems more likely to occur in the conference if the facilitator and participants envision it as a primary goal and are open to allowing/encouraging discussion that facilitates connections. In addition, practically speaking, the likelihood that the conference will develop the connections that lead to supportive relationships for victim and offender would seem to increase as the number of participants in the conference increases (to a point). However, the theory suggests that connections are more likely to be made when participants include community mentors who are either important in the lives or the offender or bring special resources to the agenda. Finally, relationship-building can be implicitly built into the follow-up stage of the conference by assigning participants roles in the contract, e.g. working with the offender on service projects, attending a support group with the victim, monitoring restitution payments or providing a job that will provide funds for the offender to make payments. When participants are assigned a specific role to work with the offender and others in carrying out and monitoring the reparative agreement, relationship-building and social support is more likely.

Table 2.3 (page 56) summarizes the relationship between the theory of social support, immediate outcomes, requisite intervention practice, and intermediate outcomes.

Part 2: Stakeholder involvement in the conferencing environment: dimensions of participation and process

> *The principle of stakeholder involvement* – victims, offenders, and communities should have the opportunity for active participation in the justice process as early and as fully as possible.
>
> (Van Ness and Strong, 1997)

Introduction

The core principle of stakeholder involvement is focused on the goal of maximizing victim, offender, and community involvement in decision-making related to the response to crime. Some repair of harm to victims

Table 2.3 Restorative conferencing and repairing harm – Dimension 2: Relationship-building

Theory	Immediate outcomes	Conference tasks/ priorities	Intermediate outcomes
Social support	Connections made between offender, victim, and other participants toward new relationships or strengthening existing relationships	• Ensure participants include those willing and able to provide support including intimates of victim and offender and resource persons • Encourage discussion of support for victim and offender and assign participants and other citizens' roles to assist victim and offender in follow-up period	Ongoing relationship of support, assistance and guardianship with individual citizens and community groups; support systems for victim, offender, family

and communities, and some stakeholder input into the decision-making process, can be achieved in the court and other formal justice settings, e.g. by ordering restitution, through victim impact statements. However, from a restorative justice perspective, to address these needs requires not more courts or professional programs of any kind, but rather more open dialogue processes that, in Christie's (1977) terms, give the conflict that has been stolen by the state back to the victim and offender. Conferencing therefore seeks to provide a more 'user-friendly' forum for informal decision-making that gives consideration to the needs of victim, offender, and community, and their roles in this process (Morris and Maxwell, 2001). Its most practical value is in allowing those harmed to articulate how the crime has affected them in a way that should allow for more effective and meaningful repair. Stakeholder involvement in decision-making is, however, complex, and it is important beyond its ability to facilitate completion of the reparative agreement.

The ultimate goal of such participation is to promote stakeholder ownership of the problem presented by crime and its solution. Stakeholder involvement is primarily about the process of the conference and its three core components – inclusion, communication, and role-taking – as important process indicators of the extent to which any decision-making encounter was being conducted in a manner consistent with restorative principles. Some have argued that the quality of inclusion is in part a function of three factors: the nature of the *invitation* offered, the extent of acknowledgement of *stakeholder (vs. system) interests* in the conferencing process, and the *acceptance of alternative approaches* – essentially the flexibility and provision of a range of choices and options for participation (Van Ness and Strong, 2001). The role played by victim and offender in defining the nature of harm will of course determine the quality of the process and the resulting agreement. The roles of supporters and community members in broadening the context beyond the conflict between victim and offender may also be salient. Focused on the quality, completeness, and validity of the narrative presented, especially by victim and offender, inclusion is also concerned with the extent to which the process allows for safe expression of emotion, as well as with the extent of understanding achieved from the dialogue between participants (Van Ness, 2001).

If the process of participation in a more open informal decision process is believed to have its own intrinsic value, what outcomes are sought for the conferencing encounter? In this section, we focus specifically on what may be called the process outcomes of conferencing and the intervention theories linked to these outcomes. In doing so, we consider three primary dimensions that suggest immediate process-related outcomes of the conference. Three intervention theories focus primary attention on one or another of these outcomes and logically link them to intermediate objectives, and in turn to long-term goals associated with the behavior and well-being of victim, offender, and community. As in the case of theories associated with repairing harm, these logical frameworks set different priorities for the conference. Two of these intervention theories seem to have emerged from evolving practice in conferencing in the past three decades (especially practice initially focused on mediation-based models), while the third theory, reintegrative shaming, actually shaped the practice associated with family group conferencing and has now had influence on other models.

Dimension 1: Victim/offender exchange

An essential commitment in the tradition of restorative justice philosophy and decision-making practice is to the needs of offender and victim as primary stakeholders (Zehr, 1990; Christie, 1977). According to this view, healing or moving toward a greater sense of well-being in the aftermath of crime more than anything else requires that victims and offenders communicate with each other whenever possible in a safe and relatively unrestricted face-to-face process. The harm to be repaired must not be defined by professionals but by individual victims and offenders, and may be highly intangible and difficult to articulate (e.g. feelings of helplessness, estrangement, loss of control). The immediate need is often to get information about the offense from the perspective of the other person(s) directly involved to provide input and tell their stories, to express emotions, and to decide what alternatives are available to address needs.

Victim/offender exchange and conferencing outcomes

Victim and offender satisfaction with the process has been a mainstay of day-to-day evaluation of restorative decision-making process evaluations. Yet, while satisfaction is by far the most widely measured outcome in all restorative conferences, there has not been conclusive evidence that satisfaction results directly from the distinctly restorative features of the conference. Without some sense of the underlying components of satisfaction, there is little to ensure that this initial satisfaction is not a temporary Hawthorne effect outcome or artificial result of other aspects of the process. Such aspects may not be associated with the restorative features of the conference at all, but rather with a sense of fairness, sense of justice, or elements more associated with procedural justice (Tyler, 1999).

It is possible, based on examination of practice and the logic of victim–offender exchange, to view the satisfaction dimension as one consisting of multiple components that have theoretical importance in their own right. Some of these are likely to be primarily about procedural justice but are linked to other aspects of non-adversarial processes (e.g. giving voice to victims).[1] Other outcomes that have been linked in research and theoretical literature to the long-term well-being of victim and offender include other components of satisfaction unlikely to be achieved by court or other alternative adversarial or quasi-formal process (e.g. drug courts, teen courts), or through informal processes different from that provided by restorative conferencing (e.g. arbitration, other forms of alternative dispute resolution (ADR)). Though arguably not unique to restorative justice practice, such immediate outcomes may include: reductions in victim fear and concern about safety in the future (in particular less fear of revictimization by this offender); a sense of closure for the offender and perhaps relief that the victim and community are not out to get him; a sense of vindication on the part of the victim (having hopefully heard the offender's acknowledgement of responsibility); increased empathy or appreciation of both offender and victim interests and motivations (Hayes and Daly, 2003); and, finally, working with others to develop a positive solution that meets individual and mutual stakeholder needs – all seem to have become common features of the restorative justice encounter. Most importantly, each of these outcomes seem directly tied to the victim/offender (V/O) exchange and to relatively uninterrupted dialogue (Umbreit, 2001; Zehr, 2000).

V/O exchange and *intervention theory: healing dialogue*

A theory of *healing dialogue* suggests that the knowledge victim and offender gain from each other in open dialogue with few restrictions is the best indicator of initial 'success' in a justice decision-making process. Satisfaction with the opportunity to tell their stories, and to hear and respond to the other person's account, provides the most valid evidence of the extent to which stakeholder needs have been addressed (see Van Ness and Schiff, 2001; Umbreit et al., 2003). The value judgement that the outcome of a restorative conference should be in the hands of the key participants is difficult to dispute. From a customer service perspective, the underlying reasons for satisfaction may be unimportant (and difficult to identify), and satisfied victims and offenders are certainly consistent with core restorative justice values (Van Ness and Schiff, 2001).

The theory of healing dialogue suggests that open, relatively unrestricted dialogue leads to better intermediate and long-term results regarding the well-being and behavior of offenders and victims. While the theory suggesting a causal link between this underlying focus on stakeholder satisfaction and long-term well-being and behavior has not been well articulated, it is reasonable to suggest that it does so through its impact on reduced fear of revictimization, reduced apprehension, the offender's sense of completing a difficult task, the victim's vindication by the conferencing process, and potentially, an increase in victim and offender understanding of one another. In addition to positive feelings about working with others to develop a plan for meeting needs and obligations in the aftermath of the crime, these may all lead to long-term outcomes regarding behavior change, healing, and well-being.

V/O exchange and the tasks of the conference

How then do conferences achieve the objective of maximizing the integrity of the victim–offender exchange? First, though input into the agreement or contract is expected to be satisfying to offender and victim, the theory of healing dialogue gives less importance to the agreement or contract itself than other theories of intervention discussed so far. While no program we have encountered would neglect the agreement and its components, the theory of healing dialogue is less concerned with the material and tangible outcomes of the conference than with the quality of the dialogue and the process itself. Rather, practitioners focused on this would encourage a process that allows maximum time and discretion to victim and offender to pursue their own needs, express what they need to say, and get their questions answered as they define them, with minimal interference on the part of the facilitator. This may mean less emphasis on the agreement or no agreement at all.[2]

A challenge presented by this approach is to guard against dominance of the process by one stakeholder who may wish to control the dialogue, a problem that creates special concerns when there is a preexisting power imbalance (e.g. adults vs. youth). Because the dialogue itself, almost regardless of its content, is viewed by advocates of this theory as essential to fear reduction, the sense of safety and order, and victim vindication, facilitators must also maximize their own silence, minimize interference with the discussion between victim and offender, and avoid at all costs a rush to get to the agreement (Umbreit, 1999, 2001). Table 2.4 summarizes the relationship between immediate outcomes, the theory of healing dialogue, conferencing practice, and longer-term outcomes.

Table 2.4 Restorative conferencing and stakeholder involvement – Dimension 1: Victim–offender exchange

Theory	Immediate outcomes	Conference tasks/ priorities	Intermediate outcomes
Healing dialogue	Reduced fear; sense of relief; victim vindication; offender empathy for victim; remorse	Ensure free flow of victim–offender communication; minimize facilitator direction; provide opportunity for input and asking questions; use of silence; avoid rush to agreement	Victim and offender well-being; sense of fairness; victim movement toward healing; offender increase in general empathy

Dimension 2: Respectful disapproval

Many have noted that modernity is characterized by a lack of informal sanctioning of other people's children (Bazemore, 2000; Sampson, Raudenbush, and Earls, 1997). In addition, some have demonstrated empirically that where these informal processes are in place, youth crime is lower (Bursik and Grasmick, 1993; Sampson, Raudenbush, and Earls, 1997). According to this view, when a crime occurs, a firm response that communicates community norms and disapproval coupled with support for the offender and the possibility of reintegration is required. The need to be addressed is the lack of offender recognition of the impact of his/her behavior. There is, correspondingly, a lack of opportunity in daily life or in the juvenile justice process to communicate this in a respectful way.

Respectful disapproval and conferencing outcomes

In recent years, a number of conferencing programs have been concerned that the offender receive a clear message of disapproval from those whose opinions matter to him. Developed from Braithwaite's (1989) study of high and low crime societies, this process of informal shaming, coupled with expressions of support for the offender, formed one core of the theoretical basis for one popular variety of family group conferencing programs (Braithwaite, 1989).

From this perspective, shame is a natural, healthy emotion that may motivate all of us to either positive or negative action (Nathanson, 1992). As an immediate outcome of the conference, the emotional reaction desired is not based on the 'stigmatizing shame' that occurs in the formal justice context (and is applauded by some advocates of retributive justice, e.g. Kahan, 1996). Rather, it is a reaction to a caring disapproval that gives equal emphasis to the offender's positive attributes, in effect denouncing the harmful behavior while providing support for the person (Retzinger and Scheff, 1996). Such disapproval by friends and family, rather than judges or other criminal justice professionals, provides the external source of shame which, as a conferencing outcome, is believed to motivate behavioral change in the young offender who is threatened more with disgrace at the prospect of reoffending and disappointing others than with official punishment (McDonald et al., 1995).

A caution is to ensure that the intensive focus on encouraging feelings of shame and reintegrating the offender does not pass over the victim's voice (and the victim's needs). If disrespectful, disintegrative shaming is to be avoided, so to it would seem that the premature expression of unlimited support for the offender in the absence of consideration of the harm and the victim's needs is not desirable as an immediate conferencing outcome. Nonetheless, Braithwaite's concern is to promote an intervention theory focused on assertive and demonstrative 'empathetic engagement' of the offender and victim and all stakeholders who matter to them. In such a relational theory, rather than one based solely on shame or any individual psychology of motivation, the 'collective quality of the resolve' provides the source of motivation to begin the difficult task of stopping or reducing the harmful behavior in question (Braithwaite, 2001a: 230).

Given this need for respectful disapproval as an immediate outcome of the conference, the caution against stigmatizing shame, and the desire for support and reintegration as a primary intermediate outcome, it is possible to theoretically connect such supportive disapproval of the offense to intermediate and long-term offender reintegration outcomes specifically focused on recidivism. We would suggest, for example, that reintegrative shame is more likely to impact reoffending when the offender is concerned that loss of status and affection will result from continuation of such behavior, when it is clear that the behavior is strongly disapproved of by those who matter to the offender, and when the offender experiences empathetic engagement, support, and a collective resolve to stop the harmful behavior (Braithwaite and Mugford, 1994; Cullen, 1994; Braithwaite, 2001b).

Respectful disapproval and intervention theory: reintegrative shaming

The theory of reintegrative shaming is discussed in some detail in the Introduction to this book as the leading theory associated with restorative justice. As an *intervention theory*, reintegrative shaming is focused primarily on social psychological processes through which the offender experiences disapproval of his behavior from those whose opinions matter to him. This disapproval of the behavior is meant to distinguish offense from offender by emphasizing the positive aspects of the latter, while expressing intolerance of the offense and disappointment that this young person could have done such a thing. Hence, following the theory that shame is an important stage in a larger process, conference participants may seek to ensure that the offender feels shame as a result of hearing about how his/her behavior has affected others. In doing so, they seek to achieve what McDonald et al. (1995) refer to as the larger goal of 'building conscience' as gauged by emotional indicators of shame, remorse, and then, possibly, expressions of empathy.

While some practitioners have placed emphasis on the 'shaming' outcomes of conferences, more recently, other restorative justice advocates have expressed concerns about the negative implications of 'shaming' as a process done *to* individuals (see Toews-Shenk and Zehr, 2001).[3] These practitioners give less emphasis to shame and far more emphasis to the role of social support (see Cullen, 1994) and the importance of a general, firm yet affirming presentation of how the offender's behavior has affected others. For example, as Braithwaite and Roche (2001) observe:

> The testimony of the victims and the apologies (when they occur, as they often do) are sufficient to accomplish the necessary shaming of the evil of violence. But there can *never be enough* citizens active in the *reintegration* part of reintegrative shaming.
>
> (p. 72, emphasis ours)

We would also underscore the importance of the testimony of victims as *necessary* rather than merely 'sufficient' to achieve reintegrative shame as an outcome (see Braithwate, 2001b: 241, concerning his theoretical explanation for the weakness of impact of reintegrative shaming in the response to drunk driving offenses due in part to the fact that no victim was present in these encounters).

Respectful disapproval and tasks of the conference

To ensure that outcomes associated with reintegrative shaming are pursued (rather than those aimed at humiliation or those focused solely on the offender's needs), the conference facilitator may encourage participants to make positive comments about the offender as a person while ensuring that victims and others clearly address the harm he/she has caused. Participants may pay special attention to emotional signs of shame or remorse and try to more actively steer the group to phases of the conference where victims, offenders, and others appear to connect, and where there are positive signs of offender readiness for change (McDonald et al., 1995).

Given this understanding of the goal of the conference regarding outcomes associated with reintegrative shame, it is important that the victim's voice be heard, that support for the offender be encouraged along with denunciations of the offense, and that those whose opinions matter to the offender be present in the conference. Moreover, reintegrative shame is more likely to impact behavior when the discussion of the victim's story, the discussion of the harm caused by the offender's behavior, and disapproval of the behavior *precede* and are not diminished by expressions of support for the offender. It is also important that the offender has understood the harm caused and can articulate and express his feelings about this.

Table 2.5 (on page 64) summarizes the relationship between immediate outcomes, conferencing practice, the theory of reintegrative shaming, and longer-term outcomes.

Dimension 3: Mutual transformation

Court processes are based on the assumption that the interests of victim, offender, and community are mutually exclusive. Such processes therefore tend to separate these parties to the greatest extent possible. While victim, offender, and community clearly have many independent interests that do not overlap, restorative processes seek to discover that small area of overlapping interests between two or more stakeholders. This 'common ground' is viewed as the space that provides the most fertile soil for solutions that meet mutual needs (see Figure 2.1, page 64). The harm to be repaired is the harm to victim, offender, and their supporters pushed further apart by a lack of communication in which each fails to appreciate the situation and thought process of the others.[4]

The focus on mutual transformation may be more common as a response to incidents where there is a problem of an ongoing conflict between parties, such as student fighting, neighborhood disputes, and workplace conflict (Moore and McDonald, 2000). In this case, the harm to

Table 2.5 Restorative conferencing and stakeholder involvement – Dimension 2: Respectful disapproval

Theory	Immediate outcomes	Conference tasks/ priorities	Intermediate outcomes
Reintegrative shaming	Offender experiences disapproval/ shame; group expresses support for offender	Ensure that conference participants include those whose views and opinions are important to the offender; ensure that respectful disapproval is *combined with* positive comments; support of offender and victim; watch for emotional expressions as signs of empathy, shame, and as a transition point in the conference	Offender moves from shame to behavior change in order to avoid future disapproval; participants work to reintegrate offender

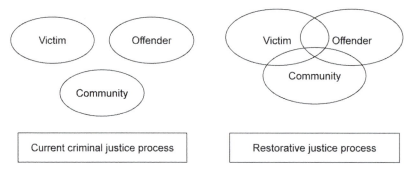

Figure 2.1 Stakeholder interests and common ground: objectives of alternative decision-making processes

be repaired may result from several recurrent incidents of unresolved conflict, with both parties in the role of victim and offender at different times. However, as a core dimension of stakeholder involvement, the search for overlapping interests is applicable in some form in the response to all crimes (e.g. Stuart, 1996, 2001).

Mutual transformation and conferencing outcomes

Conferencing programs seeking to discover the overlap in stakeholder interests seek a somewhat distinctive kind of process outcome that takes the form of a collective transformation in multiple stakeholders (Stuart, 1996, 2001). The immediate outcome sought in the conference may simply be a slight change in the position of victim, offender, and/or community relative to the position of the other parties. As an immediate objective, the dimension of collective transformation is addressed in part by the extent to which the conferencing process leads to increased understanding between the relative positions of victim, offender, and others (Daly, 2000; Hayes and Daly, 2003), and the transformation of conflict (see Moore and McDonald, 2000).

Implications for long-term and intermediate outcomes based on collective transformation would suggest that offenders and victims who have the experience of gaining a shared understanding of the harm and of the views of others will become more empathetic to one another. In addition, offenders and victims who have opportunities to give active input into an agreement should be more likely to honor these agreements. Those participants who have opportunities for reinforcement of the experience of finding common ground, to practise skills in conflict resolution/ transformation, and who have support from conference participants which reinforces commitment to agreements may also be more likely to avoid confrontations and encounters that lead to crime in the future. Finally, community groups who practise consensus decision-making in the form of shared leadership in the pursuit of common ground should become more effective in resolving conflict and addressing harm and conflict.

Mutual transformation intervention theory: common ground

In general, restorative processes are based on the assumption that the best solutions for each individual stakeholder cannot be achieved without consideration for the needs and interests of the other two. Although not usually articulated in this way, many conferencing program participants speak of a kind of collective transformation that can begin when victim, offender, and their supporters gain a basic understanding of and/or move toward the other's position (Hayes and Daly, 2003). In so doing, they follow the logic of what may be described as a theory of *common ground* (Stuart, 1996). For the offender, a theory of common ground would provide a foundation for empathy leading to a reduction in offense behavior. Indeed, this important connection is partly borne out in empirical research, which suggests that restorative conferences produce greater empathy in offenders than courts (Ahmed et al., 2001), *and* that

65

empathy seems to be related to changes in the behavior of offenders (Maxwell and Morris, 1999; Hayes and Daly, 2003).

The theory of *common ground* for the victim may mean coming to terms with the offense and the reasons behind it – even to the point of developing some empathy for an offender in difficult family situations or other challenging life circumstances. Supporters and other community members in conferences may similarly find shared agreement even with those they initially doubted – e.g. supporters of the offender might empathize and/or concur with the victim on some issues (and vice versa for victim supporters in the case of the offender). Similarly, a neutral community member may find a 'small plot' of common ground in the form of a connection with either offender or victim which provides enough leverage to turn a difficult conference around – even in the case where there seems little or no basis for shared understanding between victim and offender (see Figure 2.1).

More broadly, the theory of common ground, similar to what some have called 'transformative justice' (McDonald and Moore, 2001), can also apply to a model of consensus decision-making used most commonly in peacemaking circles where the idea of 'shared leadership' is operationalized (Pranis and Stuart, 2000). This consensus model requires finding the greatest area of overlap among multiple diverse interests based on an agreement to 'live with' group consensus even when the solution is seen by most participants as less than ideal. Most importantly, the model seeks to maximize inclusion. It is grounded in an assumption that true inclusion will always involve conflict, but that such conflict is the wellspring of effective resolution. The more intermediate, or long-term, objective achieved here is the adaptation by participants to new situations of conflict, through the development of conflict resolution capacity and skill in community entities committed to democratic decision-making (Braithwaite, 1998, 1999).

Mutual transformation and tasks of the conference

While the idea of shared understanding of the problem presented by a crime or conflict and movement towards the position of the other is a core idea in restorative justice, there has been relatively little consideration of what factors bring about this transformation. A key task is to find one or more points of agreement, understanding, or mutual interest around the incident. When this is accomplished, a meaningful and mutually satisfying resolution in the form of affirmative efforts to repair damage to the victim, families, and everyone else, and/or avoid conflict in the future becomes possible.

To achieve objectives associated with finding common ground, conferences must allow for interchanges between victim and offender after ensuring that the story presented by each is complete and consistent.

Though observers have sometimes described the emergence of such collective insight as 'magic,' some facilitators attribute this transformation to moments of silence that promote active listening, or an alert sense of when to build on 'bridging comments.' Such comments require that the facilitator and other participants make time and space for clarification of victim and offender stories, and victim/offender acknowledgement of the validity, or invalidity, of each other's stories.

Conferences using the theory of common ground to move toward mutual transformation may also be more 'scripted' and focus on phases of the conference, especially when these phases indicate transition to emotional states that lead closer to mutual transformation (McDonald and Moore, 2001). We may suggest that conferences more likely to achieve common ground will be those in which the facilitator and others build upon small points of common understanding after carefully listening to and clarifying victim and offender stories. They may also encourage peers and/or supporters of victim and offender to reframe and reinforce areas of mutual understanding, and delay movement toward agreement until there are signs from the group of some shared ownership of the conflict and collective commitment to its resolution (Moore and McDonald, 2000). Table 2.6 summarizes the relationship between immediate outcomes, the theory of common ground, conferencing practice, and intermediate, longer-term outcomes.

Table 2.6 Restorative conferencing and stakeholder involvement – Dimension 2: Mutual transformation

Theory	Immediate outcomes	Conference tasks/ priorities	Intermediate outcomes
Common ground	Victim, offender, and other participants gain shared understanding of the problem, empathy and understanding of the other's position, motive, etc.	Build on bridging statements and comments indicating increased understanding of offender and victim perspective; give attention to stakeholder acknowledgement of each other and emotional cues as signals to move to next phase of the conference	Skills learned in completing agreement become basis for future conflict resolution; peaceful relationships; increased empathy leads to decrease in recidivism

Part 3: Community/government role transformation in the conferencing environment: dimensions of system change and community-building

The principle of transformation in community and government roles and relationships – we must rethink the relative roles and responsibilities of government and community. In promoting justice, government is responsible for preserving a just order, and community for establishing a just peace.

(Van Ness and Strong, 1997).

Introduction

The third 'big idea' in restorative justice stems from the conviction that there are limitations on the role of criminal and juvenile justice systems in responding to crime. Communities therefore have an essential part to play in this response. Indeed, if we wish to repair the harm of crime by utilizing an inclusive decision-making process, we must change the role of justice professionals and the mandate of the justice system to ensure that communities are encouraged to assume greater responsibility. The core principle of transformation in community/government roles includes two related goals or agendas. The first, *systemic reform*, is concerned with providing a structure to support restorative decision-making processes by changing the role of criminal justice professionals and the mandate or mission of justice systems and agencies to support maximum community participation in the justice process. The second, *community-building*, is concerned with using conferencing programs to strengthen community capacity to respond effectively to youth crime by relying extensively on the informal resources of communities.

Broadly, the goal of the systemic reform agenda requires *change in the mission and mandate of criminal/juvenile justice agencies*, and *change in the role of the justice professional.* Specifically, the extent to which restorative group conferencing will thrive and maximize its impact is dependent in part upon the extent to which this mission and role change occurs. While restorative justice programs have at times been initiated through direct pressure from community groups outside the juvenile justice system, in the US juvenile justice professionals – police, prosecutors, judges, probation officers, and others – have played key roles in program development, funding, and most importantly, ensuring case referral. Juvenile justice professionals have themselves at times become primary conferencing staff, and we are also interested in the role of conferencing staff *as juvenile justice professionals* who may experience some conflict in their allegiance to system goals vs. the needs of victims, offenders, and communities engaged in the restorative process.

The related community-building goal and agenda has three primary dimensions, which we label: (1) *norm affirmation/values clarification*; (2) *collective ownership*; and (3) *skill-building*. Dimension 1 is concerned with how relationships, and then networks of relationships, may be built through community-based dialogue about the response to youth crimes, i.e. restorative conferences. It is concerned with the extent to which neighborhoods and other 'micro communities,' e.g. schools, housing projects, youth programs, and conferencing programs, establish shared norms and values as the basis for relationships that provide social capital (Putnam, 2000) for mobilizing informal social control and social support. It is specifically concerned with the extent to which conferencing becomes a forum for this type of dialogue. Dimension 2, *collective ownership*, is concerned with the extent to which stakeholders in a conference take ownership of the problem and mobilize to address the needs of stakeholders in the conference and the extent to which conferences promote such collective ownership.

Dimension 3, *skill-building*, is concerned with the extent to which conference participants build on shared norms and values and the sense of collective ownership of the problem of youth crime to develop and exercise skills of informal control, social support, and informal sanctioning – essentially collective efficacy (Sampson, Raudenbush, and Earls, 1997). In the process of bringing community members into an informal decision-making process about what is to be done in response to various incidents of crime, these programs may deliberately, or inadvertently, build trust, identify common values, and reinforce reciprocity at the collective level (in a way similar to the idea of individual reciprocity associated with making amends through reparation) (see Putnam, 2000: 20–2). They do so by promoting stakeholder ownership of the problems and needs associated with youth crime, and may then help to develop community group and individual problem-solving skills as vital forms of building social capital in the response to youth crime.

In this section we first discuss the systemic reform dimension and its implications for conferencing. We are broadly guided by general intervention theory focused on professional role change in a juvenile justice system and organizational reform context that suggest immediate and intermediate outcomes associated with this dimension. We then consider the three community-building dimensions, the immediate and intermediate conferencing outcomes they suggest, and three theories of intervention that logically connect these outcomes with conferencing practice.

Professional role change

The objectives of changing the mission and management approach of juvenile justice agencies and systems, and the role of juvenile justice professionals to support restorative justice practice and policy (Carey, 2001; Bazemore and Washington, 1995), are of course bigger than the conferencing context. Restorative justice decision-making in the form of conferencing provides one unique vehicle for shifting some authority and discretion over the response to youth crime to the level of the community. Indeed, the sustainability of conferencing depends as much on the development of new roles for these traditional professionals and on a change in system priorities as it does on a change in the role of those professionals directly assigned to conferencing work.

Conferencing programs, however, may provide a context for modeling a new role for juvenile justice professionals as facilitators, and in doing so encourage representatives of the formal system to view community members as resources for solving problems. Inside the conference, the facilitator must develop a professional identity distinct from that of a traditional juvenile justice or service agency employee.

Dimension 1: Changing professional roles

Role change for juvenile justice professionals is first reflected in new job descriptions that include responsibilities to community and victim as well as offender (Dooley, 1998). Essentially, to support citizen engagement in decision-making, intervention professional responsibility for individual case management and other traditional functions must be reduced (Dooley, 1998; Pranis, 1998). The role of the conference facilitator can also be defined and incentivized in such a way as to promote primary allegiance to the system agency to which it is attached (e.g. police department, probation), *or* it can be defined in a way to promote allegiance to one or more community groups e.g. neighborhoods.

Conferencing outcomes

At the more macro-system level, judges, prosecutors, and other formal decision-makers must be willing to allow greater numbers of cases, and more serious cases, to be resolved in conferences. While police, prosecutors, and judges would retain their law enforcement, charging, and adjudicatory functions, the new role would require that these professionals cede ever greater authority over resolution, disposition, and sanctioning to community groups engaged in conferencing (Bazemore, 1999b). At the same time, another important intermediate outcome of the effort to reform and transform professional roles would be that system professionals would begin to provide guidance and leadership as partners with community members to ultimately support the empowerment of citizens and community groups in justice decision-making.

At the micro level, the effort to restructure professional roles to support conferencing would involve conferencing practitioners themselves turning over ever-greater responsibility and authority to community stakeholders. Doing so is a necessary intermediate outcome if these practitioners are to avoid simply replicating intervention efforts that expand the professional expertise of the system and possibly further weaken community capacity. The new role for juvenile justice professionals must focus less on *program-building* and more on community-building (Rojek, 1982; Bazemore and McLeod, 2002). As we will explore in the discussion of community-building later in this section, the new role for conferencing professionals is at least as much about building community capacity as it is about program management and providing an effective response to the needs of individual victims and offenders.

Intervention theory

The challenge of such professional role change is best understood with reference to applied organizational theories that take account of the incentives and restraints on job performance of 'street-level bureaucrats,' especially in the program implementation context (Knot and Miller, 1987; Lipsky, 1980; Bazemore and Day, 1996).[5] Specifically, when assigned tasks are inconsistent with incentives, resources, or time allocation and/or demand risks that staff consider unacceptable, they will adapt job expectations downward from those articulated in mission statements.

Hence, according to the theory of *street-level bureaucracy* (Lipsky, 1980), new missions and visions not supported by organizational realignment of incentives are therefore likely to fail at the ground level of implementation (Pressman and Wildavsky, 1973; Anderson, 1984). Ultimately, system and organizational performance outcomes also drive practice because value statements have little practical meaning when incentives for performance are not consistent with these values. The dictum 'you are what you measure' (Osbourne and Gaebler, 1992) has been supported in numerous case studies of, for example, community policing when mission and vision statements that encourage community-building and problem-solving contradict incentive structures that continue to reward arrests and responsiveness to 911 calls (Sparrow et al., 1990). Changing incentives and performance measures consistent with changes in system and program mandate and mission are central to moving forward with reform at the level of juvenile and criminal justice professionals. Similarly, conferencing facilitators and program directors whose performance evaluations are based solely on the number of cases conferenced, without regard to the nature and quality of the process as defined by restorative principles, may be expected to simply replicate court and other adversarial processes (Umbreit, 1999).

As we will illustrate in the discussion of community-building which follows, restorative conferencing has the potential to provide a forum for citizens and community groups to practice decision-making skills that strengthen conflict resolution and capacities to exercise social control and social support. Although both mission and professional role change objectives have for the most part not yet been achieved despite the proliferation of conferencing programs in the US (Schiff, Bazemore, and Erbe, 2002), there are existing models for such change (Dooley, 1998; Maloney, Bazemore, and Hudson, 2001). Despite structural barriers, some agencies may also be able to realign incentives and job descriptions in a way that allows system professionals to support conferencing efforts.

Moreover, as our qualitative findings reveal, personal appeals to system professionals as community members and parents, while not a part of the more incentive-focused instrumental models of organizational change and policy implementation mentioned above, also offer hope in winning greater system support and empowering professional leadership in the cause of restorative justice reform. Such affective appeals, we suggest, will require new opportunities for direct experience in conferencing programs that allow system professionals to gain experiential knowledge about the unique aspects of these decision-making approaches. Indeed, an emerging theory in some restorative conferencing circles is that system professionals, if they are to become true allies of these processes, need to directly participate in one or more conferencing encounters (Boyes-Watson, 2004).

Conferencing practitioners should be expected to provide role models for other juvenile justice professionals for the new empowering, facilitative leadership style. In contrast to the more directive style witnessed in ADR, arbitration, older mediation programs, and other quasi-formal settlement processes (Umbreit, 2001), conferencing facilitators are expected to place ever increasing authority and power in the hands of participants (Pranis, 1998). Yet, there is tension within programs with regard to the competing goals of completing greater numbers of cases vs. emphasizing the quality of the experience for participants. While we can and will raise questions about what Umbreit (1999) calls 'fast-food' or 'McDonaldized' restorative justice, efficiency cannot be totally ignored for programs connected to most juvenile justice systems. Moreover, many debates in the field about the value of extensive preparation are not confirmed by empirical research, and some beliefs about what works in restorative justice are even disconfirmed by research (e.g. Hayes and Daly, 2003). Mainstream system professionals supporting restorative justice decision-making must also ensure that incentives for these conferencing staff are aligned in such a way that they encourage such power-sharing and do not reward program-building at the expense of community capacity building (see Table 2.7).

Community-building and conferencing

Chapter 3 of this volume shows that community-building is not ranked as highly as a priority of conferencing programs relative to other principle-

Table 2.7 Restorative conferencing and systemic reform – Dimension 1: Changing professional roles

Theory	Immediate outcomes	Conference tasks/ priorities	Intermediate outcomes
Organizational and role change; 'street-level' bureaucracy	System professionals support and participate occasionally in the conferencing process; change in incentive structures; conference professionals maximize community involvement	Empowering community stakeholders in decision-making	Change in professional role from 'expert' provider to facilitator of community problem-solving

focused goals such as repairing harm, engaging crime victims, and so on. It may, however, also be the most important objective for ensuring the long-term success and sustainability of restorative conferencing. Community-building is also closely connected to other restorative goals and principles. Repairing harm caused by crime in a way that engages citizens, including victim and offender, in the decision-making process is, for example, ultimately more likely when communities in some way own and sponsor this dialogue. Decisions that are in some way a product of the community deliberation, rather than of system mandate, are also more likely to have credibility and potential for implementation and follow-up.

Community-building can take many forms. As we illustrate in Chapter 7, these can include macro-level changes in large communities or municipalities and very micro-level responses that look like the relationship-building and social support interventions discussed as a dimension of making amends earlier in this chapter. Community-building can also include a variety of interventions that strengthen capacity in various neighborhood groups and organizational entities such as schools and workplaces. First, we suggest a general framework for thinking about, observing and analyzing community-building. Then, we consider three specific but closely related dimensions of community-building that we believe define critical components of community capacity needed for an effective informal response to youth crime. These in turn suggest immediate and intermediate outcomes for the community-building goal of conferencing.

A general framework

The larger question is how any small-scale decision-making intervention such as conferencing can be expected to build individual and collective capacity in participants and community groups. In addition, how and to what extent are such competencies then translated into social capital in the form of networks of relationships that develop skills in community members and groups that yield informal social control and social support at the community level (Putnam, 2000; Cullen, 1994; Bazemore, 2001)?[6]

The connection between restorative conferencing as a decision-making process and community-building is not necessarily a natural or straight-forward one. Nor has conferencing, as it is most typically conceptualized in the literature (Morris and Maxwell, 2001; Daly, 2001; Umbreit, 2001; McCold, 2000), been routinely linked to community-building. Moreover, in the literature of community development and even the community justice literature on capacity-building (Chavis, 1998; Clear and Karp, 1999; Skogan, 1990; Rosenbaum et al., 1998), conferencing is generally not discussed as a technique. Despite interest in and use of conferencing in policing (McCold, 2000; McGarrell, 2001), the community policing litera-ture has also generally not included conferencing in various strategy discussions pertinent to the efforts of community police officers to build community (Bazemore and Griffiths, 2003).

On the other hand, some have offered useful descriptions of the kinds of common community-level deficits in addressing crime and conflict that conferencing seems ideally suited to address (Moore, 1994; Clear and Karp, 1999). David Moore, for example, suggests that formal, adversarial responses to crime

deprive people of opportunities to practice skills of apology and forgiveness, of reconciliation, restitution, and reparation. In assuming responsibility for social regulation when a citizen breaches a law and thereby challenges the moral order, the modern state appears to have deprived civil society of opportunities to learn important political and social skills.

(1994: 8)

Other advocates of restorative decision-making such as Stuart (1996, 2001) claim that at least some forms of conferencing, notably circles, definitely teach these skills and therefore make participants more capable of resolving conflict. Conferencing may also provide a kind of added value in the form of feelings of belonging and efficacy that comes from helping others (Riessman, 1965; Bazemore, Nissen, and Dooley, 2000). As Joe Hudson and his colleagues have observed in their work with conferencing in both youth justice and child welfare sectors, the greatest benefit of conferencing is often not to victim and offender:

Conferences can also be seen as an educational tool, a forum for teaching and practicing problem-solving skills. Family members can learn and practice these skills and learn about the strengths of family members and the resources available to them; young offenders can learn that their actions have real consequences for victims and that they are able to make amends.

(Hudson et al., 1996: 3)

Braithwaite (1994) argues that conferencing teaches the deliberative skills of democratic citizenship. His link from this experience to a macro impact on community, and the polity, is through: 'initiatives to foster community organization in schools, neighborhoods, ethnic communities, and churches, and through professions and other non-governmental organizations that can deploy restorative justice in their self-regulatory practices' (Braithwaite, 1998: 331). Included at this level are any other activities that mobilize informal social controls as well as social support mechanisms and serve also as educational tools through which the various entities of 'community' can function essentially as 'learning organizations' (Senge, 1990; Stuart, 1996; Bazemore, 2000).

Finally, some advocates of restorative conferencing have argued that conferencing can promote a kind of 'democratization of social control' whereby a kind of 'bubbling up' becomes possible as social justice issues are increasingly aired in community justice forums linked intentionally to a 'vibrant social movement politics' (Braithwaite, 1994; Braithwaite and Parker, 1999: 33). As Pranis (2001) suggests in her discussion of the possibilities inherent in circle sentencing and other conferencing approaches for addressing such social justice issues, the response to crime may create an occasion for breaking down barriers:

The problem of crime is generating opportunities to understand and practice democracy in the community in new ways. It has become clear that creating safe communities requires active citizen involvement. This calls for a reengagement of all citizens in the process of determining shared norms, holding one another accountable to those norms and determining how best to resolve breaches of the norms in a way that does not increase risk in the community.

(p. 3).

In the practical response to youth crime, the most important community-building task for conferencing would seem to be tapping into and strengthening informal sources of social control and social support (Rose and Clear, 1998; Bazemore, 2001; Cullen, 1994). As we have argued earlier, what Hunter (1985) has called *public social controls* have been greatly expanded in recent decades in the response to youth crime (see also Cohen, 1985; Bazemore, 1999). The challenge of conferencing, however, is to build upon and enhance *private* forms of informal control – those exercised by extended family and friends – and *parochial* controls – those exercised by neighborhoods and community collectivities (e.g. youth groups, schools, neighborhood associations, churches). Such an impact would go beyond the immediate effects of conferencing on participants in the response to a given case. The most challenging problem, according to some commentators assessing the at times disappointing results of the community-building efforts of community policing, is *connecting* private, parochial, and public controls (Duffee et al., 2001; Skogan, 1990).

Can conferencing do this? Programs that involve family and community members, as well as victim and offender, in decision-making seem well positioned to enhance family-level controls and supports by tapping into neighborhood groups, and linking both of these to justice system and social service resources to the extent necessary. It is also not impossible for programs that focus primarily on victim and offender to exercise some community-building impact, for example as a 'spillover' effect of the work of volunteer facilitators who share skills gained in conferencing in other contexts. In presenting our qualitative data on the community-building impacts of conferencing (Chapter 7), we will provide a number of examples of what appear to have been inadvertent impacts of conferencing on community capacity. However, in part because of the challenge of mobilizing and connecting the three forms of social control (and support) in a helpful way, we suggest that community-building impacts will be rare unless they are an explicit part of conferencing strategies that flow from a shared vision of the program's mission.

In general, we suggest that programs that continue to solve problems as independent incidents on a case-by-case basis focusing only or primarily on the victim and offender's needs will be much less likely to produce community-level impacts. In a parallel example that illustrates some of the perceived failures of community policing to build community, Bennett (1994) argues that police actions to reduce neighborhood disorder had little or no impact on neighborhood efficacy (and in some neighborhoods had a negative impact). Instead, long-term impacts on community-building were more likely to be more a function of 'the ways in which police interact with neighborhood groups' (Bennett, 1994) rather than the perhaps more aggressive, yet incident-based, efforts to reduce neighborhood disorder by removing disorderly people, or even resolving incident-based conflicts (see Sampson and Raudenbush, 2001).

Similarly, for conferencing, effectiveness in helping offenders repair harm to individual victims and resolve interpersonal conflict, as important as this is, may not directly affect the capacity of neighborhoods and other units of community to accomplish these goals. While we discuss ways that it *could* later in this volume, this hypothesis suggests that it may be the ancillary work in support of conferencing that has the most impact.

What may be most important is program staff devoting substantial work to getting to know families and community groups in the neighborhoods where they plan to work prior to taking cases. The work of some Aboriginal conferencing coordinators in Northern Australia, Queensland, and the state of South Australia provide examples of painstaking door-to-door work often in remote areas to get a sense of what conferencing formats and structures would be most practically and culturally acceptable to participants (seemingly minute issues such as where elders would sit in these processes, for example, became important in these discussions). By the time programs began to take cases, the coordinators had already accomplished some measure of community-building and created support for conferencing programs – without which no programs could have been successfully implemented (Conference on Restorative Justice and Family Violence, 2000).

The following discussion of three dimensions of community-building is presented to focus the qualitative data offered in Chapter 7 on the critical theoretical components of community capacity in the response to youth crime.

Dimension 1: Norm affirmation/values clarification

Norm affirmation refers to the capacity of collectives to identify and clarify shared values and set tolerance limits for behavior. In the aftermath of a crime, traditional societies found ways to denounce the behavior in question as a violation of sacred beliefs and values. Modern rituals of court processes, while sometimes effective in providing for due process and uniformity, do not generally allow for the expression of community outrage about the collective harm of crime as a violation of shared values. Some have argued that one result of the absence of such expression is that such outrage is channeled into individual diatribes on radio call-in shows and support for ballot initiatives supporting three-strike laws and legislation expanding provisions for transfer of juvenile offenders to criminal courts.

The harm of crime that needs to be repaired at the community level is a weakening of social capital as a result of a breach of community trust and the weakening of shared behavioral norms and values in the aftermath of an offense. As described in the community justice literature (Karp, 2001; Clear and Karp, 1999), the need that is unmet is the sense of connectedness, shared values, and reciprocity that allows for the collective expression of harm and disapproval of the violation of standards of conduct.

Norm affirmation/values clarification and conferencing outcomes
In terms of informal crime control and the overarching restorative justice goal of repairing harm, we suspect that norm affirmation is first related to

the success of the conference in accomplishing individual-level goals such as making amends, building relationships, and respectful disapproval (see Karp, 2001). At the level of community-building, however, norm affirmation as a conferencing outcome provides participants with a collective understanding about what behaviors are 'off limits.' It then also reinforces the values of the conference regarding the need to repair the harm and involve those affected in denouncing the behavior and developing the appropriate response.

As an intermediate outcome in the weeks and months after the conference(s), such norm affirmation may also lead to norm *clarification.* Such clarification opens the door for identifying important differences and diversity in opinion while allowing the community to make stronger commitments to a core of shared values (Pranis, 2001). This commitment may then be coupled with a willingness to tolerate behavior about which there is no strong general agreement as to its harmfulness. The connection to Dimension 2, collective ownership, and Dimension 3, collective efficacy, is that such norm affirmation and clarification about youth crime and trouble may indicate to parents the need to take responsibility for other people's children and also feel comfortable about intervening with these young people when their behavior violates accepted neighborhood standards of conduct (Sampson, Raudenbush, and Earls, 1997). Such a 'values dialogue' can also suggest ways to assist other children and families in the neighborhood.

An immediate outcome of the conference may simply be that participants experience a reduction in their anxiety that they are 'all alone' in their concerns about breaches in important standards of civility indicated by youth crime and trouble (or in adult standards of care and discipline for their children). Ideally, they may also feel more comfortable in discussions around norms and values, including dialogue with young people in cross-generational and other contexts, and about the value of airing differences of opinion and the value of conflict itself. One standard they should feel more comfortable about that is easily transported into other settings is the value of repairing harm itself and of involving community members in this process.

Norm affirmation/values clarification and intervention theory: social capital
The intervention theory most applicable to the norm affirmation objective of conferencing is derived from the focus of general social disorganization theory on the lack of shared norms of behavior and common values in transient, high-crime communities (Shaw and McKay, 1942; Bursik and Grasmick, 1993). A recent version of this theory most applicable to efforts to build capacity for informal social control and support is *social capital* theory (Coleman, 1988; Putnam, 2000). Communities in which citizens have no forum for dialogue about norms and values will often be unaware

both of differences in standards of conduct *and* of common beliefs and shared norms that could form the basis for collective action. They will therefore feel incapable of setting or reinforcing tolerance limits on behavior, become fearful of doing so and perhaps be inclined to retreat into isolation from their neighbors (Skogan, 1990; Miethe, 1995).

If such citizens experience a condition similar to what Durkheim (1961) described as *anomie*, or the sense of absence of shared standards for behavior, then conversely, members of a community where norm affirmation is a common occurrence would be expected to experience a positive sense of connection and potential to express and act on such values. At the end of the conference, community member participants, like crime victims, may also feel somewhat vindicated that their values are also upheld by others, though the goal is not to punish or cast blame on the offender and his/her family. Indeed, the hope, as articulated in the discussion of other conferencing theories and dimensions presented in this chapter is that offenders and their families will also provide further affirmation that the behavior is wrong.

Where conferences serve as a forum for clarification of shared and conflicting values and allow for norm affirmation about the harmful impacts of offense behaviors (and perhaps of prior harms), they address an important ingredient in building social capital. Essentially, social capital can be viewed here as developed through relationship-building in the conference setting (see the previous discussion of relationship-building as the second dimension of the principle of repairing harm) from which may emerge networks of relationships based on increasing levels of trust and reciprocity. As 'learning communities' (Senge, 1990), these networks – which may be represented by the conferencing program and its volunteers and supporters – can begin to develop common standards of conduct. Most importantly, conferencing can become a vehicle for identifying and then airing disagreements within communities in the practical response to real cases and real problems.

Norm affirmation/values clarification and tasks of the conference
To accomplish objectives consistent with social capital theory, conferencing programs must reinforce a comfort level both about strong affirmation of norms and discussion of values, and about listening to and tolerating differences of opinion (Pranis, 2001). Norm affirmation is more likely when conference coordinators and volunteers view it as part of their vision and mission. Specifically, the task is to view the program not simply as an opportunity for victim, offender, and supporter dialogue about an incident of harm, but also as a natural forum for expressing community norms. Another task is to increase reliance on community volunteers in the conferencing process. When conferencing programs rely heavily on volunteers from the neighborhoods where conferences take

Table 2.8 Restorative conferencing and community-building – Dimension 1: Norm affirmation/values clarification

Theory	Immediate outcomes	Conference tasks/ priorities	Intermediate outcomes
Social capital	Conference participants' feeling of relief; vindication for their values as others affirm behavioral norms; differences clarified; relationship-building	Create comfort level for open discussions of values, standards of conduct, tolerance of diversity; link dialogue on norms to conferencing task and program mission	Norm clarification; ongoing dialogue regarding shared values; increased comfort about shared values related to youth crime and trouble; network-building

place, and when they give a prominent role to such volunteers in addressing harm to the community, norm affirmation is also more likely to result.

Table 2.8 depicts the proposed linkage between these intervention theories, intermediate outcomes, and conference tasks related to the norm affirmation dimension of the community-building goal.

Dimension 2: Collective ownership

Changing system and professional roles, and building or strengthening community capacity, provide by far the greatest obstacles to the sustained success of the restorative conferencing movement. At the same time, these provide the key to unleashing the full promise of the transformative potential of this movement. Following the logic of our discussion of the repair and stakeholder involvement principles, the 'harm' to be repaired in this context is the historical expansion of system responsibility for social control, sanctioning, and social support tasks. Specifically, this expansion and the concomitant decline in the community role in social control and youth socialization have disempowered communities while enlarging state oversight and control (Black, 1976; Rose and Clear, 1998). Because the system cannot always effectively carry out its responsibility in these areas, the need to be addressed is to change the vision and mission of criminal and juvenile justice agencies and systems to one that seeks to empower community leadership and increase citizen and community ownership of the response to youth crime.

Currently criminal and juvenile justice agencies that refer cases to conferencing risk confronting agency mandates to *keep cases in* the system and retain professional decision-making discretion. When referrals are made, formal agencies such as the court and prosecution may then drastically limit the scope of discretion granted to the conferencing programs in order to protect the system's legal or administrative authority (for example by retaining the authority to set out the exact terms of disposition and compliance in a court order).

In this context, getting conferencing participants to assume increased ownership for a reparative response to crime and harm is especially challenging, but especially important to the future of restorative justice decision-making. Collective ownership of decision-making is of course a normative premise of democratic citizenship. US culture is one which, since Alexis de Toqueville's time (Toqueville, 1956/1835), has been viewed as celebrating volunteer initiative and citizen participation at all levels. Yet, US justice systems in the past half century have been at the forefront in the centralization and professionalization of justice functions. While the normative commitment to community ownership in the response to crime is explicit in the third core principle of restorative justice, there are also practical reasons behind the desire to increase citizen ownership in justice decision-making. As Dennis Maloney (1998) summarizes:

> Participation denied breeds apathy. Apathy breeds suspicion. Suspicion breeds cynicism. Cynicism prevails. Conversely, participation builds a sense of ownership and a sense of ownership builds personal responsibility. A sense of personal responsibility for the well-being of the community prevails.
>
> (p. 1)

It may also be argued that those who share a strong sense of responsibility will go to great lengths and effort to see their ideas succeed and will share a strong sense of investment in the outcome of those efforts. Rather than criticize the system, they may then become advocates.

Collective ownership and conferencing outcomes

Outcomes anticipated for this conferencing dimension are that participants in restorative processes play active roles in all phases of the conference. In doing so, each participant becomes a resource to meeting the objectives of the conference. Shared leadership allows participants, indeed asks/requires them, to take on responsibilities for meeting their own needs and those of others. For example, facilitators may rely heavily on conference participants to ensure that the victim feels comfortable telling his story, and/or that the offender is acknowledging responsibility. Community members may also speak on behalf of broader community needs, and all participants should have a role in developing the agreement. Long-term outcomes may then include: continued and increased involvement of conference participants in the conferencing program; assumption of greater community member authority in the conferencing process (e.g. as volunteer facilitators); increased willingness to participate in local prevention efforts and other juvenile justice activities; and the expansion of skills and values supportive of a greater community role in juvenile justice.

Offenders given direct input into conference decision-making may experience a greater sense of commitment to the conference agreement as well as a greater sense of responsibility and accomplishment. Hopefully, offenders experience a greater sense of justice by virtue of their role as active participants in the process. For crime victims, shared leadership outcomes can be measured by the extent and nature of their participation and sense of having contributed to the solution, their sense of efficacy in resolving conflict. Victims asked for their thoughtful input in the conference setting often propose some of the most creative alternatives, as in a case in a Minnesota conference in which the victim, at first very angry at an offender who had pointed a loaded BB rifle at his head, upon learning that the youth used the gun to hunt with his grandfather, proposed that the youth's agreement should be to simply tell his grandfather what he had done.

Collective ownership and intervention theory: civic engagement
One primary theoretical premise underlying the idea of collective ownership is Nils Christie's assertion that criminal justice systems 'steal conflict' from victims and offenders. When criminal and juvenile justice agencies take on more responsibility for community problems relating to youth crime that were once easily resolved at the community level, they invite citizens and community groups to 'dump' these problems at their doorstep. In doing so, they redefine the meaning of minor disputes, youth trouble, and neighborhood conflict as conditions requiring professional intervention and thereby encourage dependency (McKnight, 1995).

This criminalization of community conflicts and problems and professionalization of tasks and roles further undercuts community initiative, devalues citizen competencies, and denies opportunities to apply and nurture problem-solving skills of conflict resolution, reparation, and norm clarification (Christie, 1977; Moore, 1994). According to the theory of *stolen conflict*, citizens and community groups who no longer have responsibility for exercising informal social control and social support begin to lose their capacities for carrying out these tasks (Christie, 1977; Moore, 1994).[7] As Clear and Karp (1999) describe it:

> When agents of the state become the key problem solvers, they might be filling a void in community; but just as in interpersonal relation-

ships, so in community functioning, once a function is being performed by one party it becomes unnecessary for another to take it on ... parents expect police or schools to control their children; neighbors expect police to prevent late night noise from people on their street; and citizens expect the courts to resolve disputes ... informal control systems may atrophy like dormant muscles, and citizens may come to see the formal system as existing to mediate all conflicts.

(p. 38)

In contrast, a theory of civic engagement would posit that citizens and community groups have much to offer to offenders, victims, and their families that cannot be provided by professionals. To date, the term civic engagement has been used to describe a theory of offender reintegration based on the idea that offenders who become involved in activities that help others and contribute to the quality of life in their communities – including especially community service, democratic involvement, and mentoring – experience a sense of commitment to the 'common good' that is a fundamental factor in their rehabilitation (Uggen and Janicula, 1999; Uggen and Manza, 2003; Bazemore and Stinchcomb, 2004). Drawing on the theoretical and empirical work of Uggen et al. (2003) on civic reintegration, a *civic engagement* intervention model would posit and test the impact of strategies that seek to strengthen such commitments in a variety of citizenship domains. Civic engagement practice and policy would be expected to weaken barriers to prosocial identity for persons who have been under correctional supervision, change the community's image of such persons, and, most importantly, mobilize informal support and assistance. Such engagement also provides opportunities to 'try out' different roles and to learn from experience in these roles (Maruna, 2001). Strategies for changing the *public image* of offenders include strategic efforts to make productive efforts of these persons visible to various communities. Offenders engaged actively in conference decision-making may therefore benefit both from participation in the conference agreement and from taking responsibility for acknowledging harm and making things right. Notably, as discussed above, community members and crime victims may also benefit by assuming responsibility previously left to authorities as they gain skills needed for resolving conflict in everyday life.

Meeting the need created by the current lack of citizen involvement is a complex and multi-dimensional undertaking. Some argue that system professionals should simply 'get out of the way' in order to allow the community to do its work. However, given the process of 'deskilling' that has over time weakened the capacity of communities to provide informal social control and support, system agencies and professionals continue to play an essential role. Specifically, those professional agencies must provide a great deal of support, as well as education, resources, guidance, and oversight, to empower community groups and citizens to respond effectively. What is needed then is not to simply devolve responsibility to the community level (Crawford, 1997; Bazemore and Griffiths, 1997), but rather to also transform the work of juvenile and criminal justice agencies and professionals from 'expert' service providers to supporters of community and citizen-driven restorative responses (Pranis, 1998).

Collective ownership and tasks of the conference
At the micro level, tasks of the conference itself involve first of all the willingness of the facilitator to encourage collective ownership and shared leadership. The facilitator must establish both ground rules and the proper climate to empower stakeholders to take responsibility for the outcome of the conference. The careful line facilitators must walk, as illustrated by some of the case studies presented in this volume, is between allowing maximum stakeholder ownership, and what may become the dominance of one or more stakeholders. While this is never an easy task, facilitators who appear to be most effective in empowering a range of stakeholders, including especially offender and victim, appear to be those who strategize carefully prior to the conference about who will be asked to participate. Some facilitators seem particularly adept, for example, at recruiting participants who they can call on to express alternative viewpoints and even assist them in dampening the impact of an overly dominant participant.

Table 2.9 depicts the proposed linkage between outcomes, intervention theories, and practice associated with the transformation in system and justice agency mission and mandate.

Table 2.9 Restorative conferencing and community-building – Dimension 2: Collective ownership

Theory	Immediate outcomes	Conference tasks/ priorities	Intermediate outcomes
Civic engagement	Maximize use of conferencing; define leadership roles for stakeholders in process	Strategize recruitment of stakeholders to provide needed voices and empower participants; promote stakeholder input into resolution	Stakeholder sense of participation and leadership; skill-building in reparation and conflict resolution

Dimension 3: Skill-building

'Collective efficacy' is a term used generally to describe the capacity of community members and groups to exercise informal social control over the behavior of other community members. In the response to youth crime, we define collective efficacy as the extent to which neighborhood adults are able, through informal communication and other means, to limit harmful behavior of, and by, other people's children, and to provide social support for neighborhood children (Sampson, Raudenbush, and Earls, 1997; Bazemore, 2000, 2001). This definition may be broadened beyond the actions of individual community members to include networks of families and parochial groups who work together to support positive socialization of young people. We may also include in the definition of collective efficacy the efforts of *young people* as community members to provide social control and support in response to the needs of other young people. The latter expansion of the definition seems especially salient in school and residential community settings where youth have a critical role in both informal social control and support (Morrison, 2001; Riestenberg, 1999).

The harm to be repaired by interventions which promote collective efficacy is the historical loss of community skills in conflict resolution, social control, informal sanctioning, and social support. The need addressed is to strengthen the capacity of neighborhoods, schools, parochial organizations, families, and extended families to respond effectively to crime.

Skill-building and conferencing outcomes
If norm affirmation is in part about clarifying the shared standards and values underlying the response to harms in a way that builds relationships of trust as social capital (Putnam, 2000), skill-building is about mobilizing or building the capacity needed to carry out the interventions. Over time as an intermediate outcome, conferences may be expected to make citizens feel more comfortable in expressing disapproval, questioning youth about their behavior when it is inappropriate and also recognizing good behavior and providing support. Ideally, such communication would not be one-directional – from adult to youth. Rather, young people would feel free to express their views of adult values and behavior, and/or to express disapproval of the behavior of other young people while also providing support. As more conferences occur and the word spreads about the value of these events for informal sanctioning and support of young people and their families, and for resolving conflict and harm as an alternative to court, more community members would hopefully participate and thereby expand the pool of efficacious citizens and community groups.

As an immediate outcome relevant to collective efficacy, members of the conferencing group should feel at the end of the encounter that they have identified harm to *community* life, as well as to individual victims, of the offense in question. Participants as community members would be expected to feel empowered at being able to express their disapproval of the behavior in question, while supporting the offender and feeling gratified at being able to contribute to a hopefully creative and effective resolution in the form of a conferencing agreement. While these may initially seem to be small gains in efficacy, in the context of the current deficit in community member skills in responding to crime (e.g. Moore, 1994; Clear and Karp, 1999) and the lack of opportunities to apply and hone existing skills, such conferencing outcomes would be far from insignificant.

Skill-building and intervention theory: collective efficacy
As an intervention theory, collective efficacy is derived from social disorganization perspectives theory in its newer expressions focused on the crime prevention role of informal sanctioning and control (Kornhauser, 1978; Sampson and Groves, 1989) as indicated specifically by the willingness of neighbors to intervene with other people's children (Sampson, Raudenbush, and Earls, 1997; Rose and Clear, 1998). Regarding the theory, one may ask whether or not, or to what extent, conferencing tasks build capacity for citizen involvement in informal social control and social support.

In an important sense, it may be said that the two dimensions of norm affirmation and skill-building, when linked together by community level theories of social disorganization (e.g. Bursik and Grasmick, 1993), address the related problems of an absence of shared norms, values, and trust, or *social capital*, and a decline in community skills in providing informal control and social support or efficacy. When combined with the idea of 'learning organizations' or learning communities (Senge, 1990), they provide a useful framework for conferencing programs seeking to increase community cohesiveness around shared values and skills in restorative decision-making. Specifically, these components may be said also to constitute a larger theory of community justice pertinent to the exercise of social control and support in the response to youth crime (Putnam, 2000; Rose and Clear, 1998; Bazemore, 2001).

Skill-building and tasks of the conference
As previously suggested, efficacy in exercising informal social control and support is in part dependent on the ability of collectives to clarify shared values and tolerance limits. Hence, the conferencing program will be more likely to produce efficacy or skill-based outcomes if it first completes the tasks described above under the norm affirmation dimension. Second, we

suggest that programs that wish to build collective efficacy must then also consciously identify community-building as an activity that has legitimacy and receives priority alongside objectives related to the needs of individual victims, offenders, and their supporters. While community-building *may* be compatible with program-building, pragmatic tasks associated with the latter are essentially about ensuring that the conferencing projects can maintain a steady source of cases, a task that could in the worst case become a self-aggrandizing effort to promote ever increasing referrals from any available source (see Rojek, 1982). Increasing collective efficacy, on the other hand, may require devoting program resources to increasing the capacity of neighborhoods, schools, or other groups and organizations to deal with disputes and harmful behavior, rather than seeking more referrals from these entities. Ironically, conferencing programs that truly wish to build community skills may be faced with the dilemma of *giving back* cases rather than seeking to increase referrals.

Where it is most robust, collective efficacy seems to be firmly rooted in neighborhood traditions of informal social control (Sampson, Raudenbush, and Earls, 1997) and does not of course materialize overnight. Because it is therefore unlikely that any program can 'transplant' these skills anew in communities where such traditions are not in evidence (Rosenbaum, 1994), the conferencing program wishing to achieve collective efficacy outcomes should build upon the most viable and sustainable units of community where these traditions are familiar even if less active than they might be. That is to say, consistent with the example of Aboriginal communities in Australia described earlier, the program should be developed around existing processes and rituals of conflict resolution, expressions of disapproval, informal sanctioning, and mutual support.

Programs may also be most likely to achieve collective efficacy outcomes when they serve a community with clearly defined boundaries, whether these are geographic or organizational/institutional, as in the case of micro-communities such as schools, housing projects, workplaces, and residential programs. Conferencing programs that truly wish to increase the skill level of the communities they serve in restorative decision-making will need to view their responsibilities as extending beyond the response to cases referred to the program, as suggested under the norm affirmation dimension. These responsibilities might include two important kinds of tasks that educate the immediate community and essentially 'export' conferencing skills to other community entities beyond the program. Specifically, programs that devote a significant amount of time to training staff and volunteers in other settings such as schools, neighborhood organizations, and faith community groups may be expected to have broader efficacy-building impact. Programs that make staff and trained volunteers available to assist in larger disputes or community issues involving, for example, police/citizen conflict, zero tolerance

Table 2.10 Restorative conferencing and community-building – Dimension 2: Skill-building

Theory	Immediate outcomes	Conference tasks/ priorities	Intermediate outcomes
Collective efficacy	Participants express disapproval of offense and affirm harm to community life; contribute to agreement and gain skills in agreement and conflict resolution	Identify collective efficacy as a priority; devote program resorces to training in other community entities; build on existing traditions of informal control and existing community groups	Conference participants and other community members intervene with young people and provide support; more community groups and citizens gain and apply conferencing skills

policies, and so on may give much greater visibility to the conflict resolution skills intrinsic to conferencing and promote their use in broader settings.

Finally, within the conference process itself, collective efficacy can begin at a micro level through a strategic attempt to form *networks* of relationships that could be mobilized in future conferences as a resource to other participants. Such micro-level community-building may also result from a strategic effort to ensure those victims, families, teachers, employers, and others participating in a conference – as well as young offenders – gain new skills and/or insights about how to resolve conflict in the future, and whenever possible are recruited into the program as volunteers with critical experiential knowledge to reach out to others going through similar difficulties.

Table 2.10 depicts the proposed linkage between these intervention theories, intermediate outcomes, and conference tasks related to the collective efficacy dimension of community-building.

Chapter summary and transition: principles to research agendas

The purpose of this chapter has been to provide an overall framework or template for principle-based and theory driven evaluation and assessment of restorative conferencing. Figure 2.2 displays the framework which first summarizes the overall normative theory of restorative justice presented here as a set of three core principles. Each principle, in turn, is associated with overarching goals, key dimensions of variation, associated outcomes,

Normative theory of restorative justice

Values/principles	Repairing harm	Stakeholder involvement	Community/government role transformation
Goals	Repair	Stakeholder assumption of responsibility for response to crime	Change system and government roles community-building
Conferencing dimensions and outcomes	□ Amends-making □ Building/rebuilding relationships	□ Victim offender exchange □ Mutual transformation □ Respectful disapproval	□ Changing organizational mission and professional roles □ Norm affirmation/values clarification □ Collective ownership □ Skill building
Intervention theories	□ Exchange theory □ Social support □ Community healing	□ Healing dialogue □ Common ground □ Reintegrative shaming	□ 'Street-level bureaucracy' □ Social capital □ Collective efficacy □ Civic engagement
Conference practice tasks	□ Gain clarity on harm of offense □ Keep focus on repair vs. other goals □ Identify roles and responsibilities in reparative agreement □ Assess relationships and ensure support for offender and victim	□ Ensure quality of inclusion communication and role-taking □ Attend to safety issues, victim vindication and other needs □ Encourage respectful expression of disapproval of offense □ Be open to gain in mutual understanding	□ Maximize understanding, discretion □ Maximize group ownership of process □ Increase seriousness of cases heard

Figure 2.2 Conferencing and restorative justice theory: principles to practice

intervention theories, and priorities for conferencing practice. Specifically, we have argued that each principle is associated with several outcomes that receive priority in the conference by virtue of several theories tied logically to the principle, and these theories in turn give priority to different conferencing outcomes expected to lead to long-term healing for offender, victim, and community.

By way of summary, we emphasize two general points about the normative theory of restorative justice depicted in Figure 2.2. First, we believe an integrated model for restorative justice decision-making implies an inclusive focus on core principles, theories, outcomes, and practice. Second, while these principles are related and compatible, we wish to acknowledge that there are also inherent conflicts embedded in the principles themselves as they are used to guide practice.

Principle balance

We have argued that the most important concern in examining restorative decision-making should be linking core principles, theories, and composite dimensions related to them, with various intervention strategies and outcomes. However, there is the potential for conflict between what may be competing or incompatible principles, and between the various dimensions associated with each principle. The qualitative analysis and synthesis detailed in this text (Chapters 5 through 7) consider the application of each principle separately to examine how facilitators and practitioners attempt to accomplish the joint goals of restorative justice: repairing harm, stakeholder involvement and ownership, and changing the role of professionals, while strengthening the community role in the response to youth crime.

We briefly consider here what we believe to be one of the most potentially important sources of variation in each conferencing encounter: the balance between the sometimes conflicting requirements of the core principles of restorative justice in the ongoing response to each case. The separation between these principles as we have described here is, in the real world of conferencing, somewhat artificial, as practitioners must engage multiple principles and values as they come up in a practical, problem-solving context. A key general question in examining consistency of practice with principles in conferencing interventions (i.e. 'restorative-ness') is how participants negotiate, apply, and balance principles that may appear to be in conflict (Bazemore and Earle, 2002). Although these core principles are logically linked and mutually reinforcing, even cursory examination of actual restorative practice reveals that conflicts frequently arise in attempting to fully implement each principle in a specific response to each case. In weighing the practical importance of core principles to particular instances of crime and harm, genuine principle balance requires a specific fit true to the actual situation rather than literalism in adhering to general ideals.

For example, one dilemma in balancing the need to repair harm with the need to actively involve stakeholders as co-participants in the restorative decision-making process comes when stakeholders appear to be pursuing a solution that does not seem in any way focused on reparation. In the worst case, stakeholders may agree upon an offender-focused solution to simply punish or incapacitate the offender, or community members in a restorative conference may express great support for an offender and focus on addressing his/her needs without involving or adequately listening to the victim. When victims are not encouraged to speak about their own hurt or loss, participants may forget about the obligation the offender has incurred to make things right and may be insufficiently concerned about whether a victim has felt comfortable in expressing feelings and needs. On the other hand, in some conferences, facilitators and participants may give too much emphasis to ensuring that agreements are reached by proposing restitution, community service, and other requirements without giving attention to creative input from victim, offender, and community members who may need or want something very different and may want to propose a solution ideally related to victim and community needs.

A different kind of imbalance between repair and stakeholder involvement occurs when participants in a restorative process, perhaps guided by an overly dominant mediator or facilitator, rush to develop a reparative agreement without allowing sufficient time for dialogue and input. As Umbreit (1999) observes, such 'fast-food' restorative processes disempower participants, limit the flow of information to victims and victim input, and discourage expression of emotions. They also tend to result more often in generic and superficial solutions which, though they may offer some degree of repair (through restitution for example), provide little opportunity for the expression of emotions, problem-solving, healing, and relationship-building.

Though community-building aspects are harder to operationalize, we argue that these features of conferencing are in fact a kind of linchpin because they are fundamental to the distinctiveness and survival of conferencing programs. From another perspective they are essential if the conferencing enterprise is not to become simply another diversion or intervention program in juvenile justice, competing for cases with all the others. Indeed, what may ultimately best distinguish conferencing both from other informal programs and from more formal court processes is its capacity to provide a new role for citizens and community groups in the justice process that has not been seen in many years. While the back-to-community theme as expressed in the now common phrase 'it takes a village' is now driving policy discussions about youth crime and youth socialization generally (Schorr, 1988), one missing aspect of initiatives to engage citizens has been the articulation of a role in informal decision-making in response to actual incidents of crime and trouble.

As suggested in the discussion of theories of community-building, at a macro level it would be possible to integrate the various theories of conferencing within an overarching theory of social capital as applied to the response to youth crime. We do not recommend doing so at this time, however, for reasons directly related to the need to improve understanding of the conferencing process and of the relative effectiveness of the various conferencing practices. Specifically, in practice, individual facilitators and conferencing participants, individual programs, and various models may give greater priority to one or more of these intervention theories. As suggested by the variety of theories-in-use outlined above and other possible intervention theories practitioners may potentially apply, choices made in conferencing programs will often reflect differential adherence to one or another of these theories. As we believe our qualitative findings indicate, application of such theories over time in various programs can form the basis for empirical testing of various theories of decision-making. Moreover, though we believe that the three core restorative justice principles are each essential, non-negotiable, and quite robust across a range of conferencing encounters, even these principles may present practitioners with conflicting priorities in the response to various cases.

An integrated model

It important to note that the outcomes, theories, and conference practice priorities associated with the three core principles of restorative justice outlined in the above discussion should by no means be viewed as mutually exclusive. Nor is any particular program or conferencing model limited to the pursuit of one type of outcome, no specific outcomes may be addressed by more than one type of practice. An integrated restorative decision-making approach would indeed be expected to give attention at one time or another to each of the core dimensions and intermediate outcomes associated with repair, each of those associated with stakeholder involvement, and each associated with the system role change and community-building implications of the principle of transformation in community/government relationships.

In such an integrated restorative justice model, the reciprocity and social-exchange value inherent in the obligation of offenders to make amends to victim and community are viewed as directly related to the larger restorative goal of repairing the harm of crime. Such repair is considered in its broadest sense as a primary means of reintegrating victims and offenders and rebuilding communities. For example, as

Braithwaite (2001b) suggests, a reintegrative process grounded in restorative justice principles and theories of intervention for an offender involved in substance abuse might begin with a confrontation that empathetically engages the offender, affirms norms, and engages family and community support and control. Then, community forgiveness of the offender occurs through a process of 'earned redemption' (Bazemore, 1998) as the offender makes amends to those he/she has harmed. New community connections and relationships, in turn, make possible informal social support and in turn give potency and legitimacy to informal control. Community-building aspects of conferencing are of course not unrelated to the theories and practice associated with the principles of repair and stakeholder involvement. That is, relationship-building as a reparative outcome tied to a theory of social support may be linked to community-building at a more macro level. Reintegrative shaming in the conferencing setting is certainly related to skill-building and norm affirmation when neighbors 'do not mind their own business,' and feel free to discuss values and enforce norms.

Guiding research questions

The overarching research question for the qualitative part of this study was to what extent restorative conferencing programs are informed by and adhere to restorative principles. Such adherence we have argued is vital to establishing something more stable, sustainable, and replicable than can be gained from program guides and procedural manuals. While the practice objective of answering this question is to enhance replication of principles rather than techniques or program models in a variety of environments, the research goal of this effort is to gain a better understanding of the intervention theories underlying conferencing programs and how these relate to core principles. Such an understanding should provide more meaningful templates for future impact studies that can help to empirically examine the implied connection between practice, intermediate outcomes related to various dimensions of repair, and long-term indicators of intervention success.

Other general research questions of interest focus on how practitioners structure and guide the conferencing process toward repairing the harm; how practitioners engage stakeholders in various phases of the conferencing process and how inclusion and role playing are accomplished; and how conferencing practitioners seek to influence the community/system relationship and may hope to maximize their program's potential for building community capacity. Specific research questions pertinent to each of these general issues are presented in the text of each chapter of this book prior to presenting qualitative data pertinent to each of the three core restorative justice principles.

Notes

1 Braithwaite (1999) has argued, however, that it is the restorativeness of the process in such practices that in fact produces a better form of procedural justice and therefore higher participant satisfaction. He has further (2001a) suggested that the procedural justice *delivered by restorative justice* may in fact account in part for its positive results.

2 Indeed, one important standard of comparison for advocates of this approach is a dimension that contrasts processes that are truly 'dialogue-driven' with those that are more focused on the agreement, or 'settlement-driven' (e.g. Umbreit, 1999, 2001).

3 Though reintegrative shaming is an offender-focused theory in the sense of its predictions of impact, the shame concept may resonate with victims as well with regard to the earlier mentioned notion of vindication, as in part removal of victim shame in the absence of vindication (Zehr, 2000); the tendency of adult victims to assume some culpability in cases involving juvenile offenders has been frequently observed in juvenile justice practice (Seymour and Bazemore, 1999).

4 This does not imply that the victim is expected to acknowledge responsibility or a role in a shared 'conflict' as is the case in arbitration and some non-restorative forms of mediation (Umbreit, 2001). The idea of common ground, though certainly more common in a conflict where parties in dispute are viewed as relatively equal in their culpability or responsibility, is nonetheless applicable when it does not imply that victims must find common ground with offenders; rather, they may find common ground with community members, and offenders may do the same. They may also find, without any expectation or prodding, some common ground with the offender, and this notion is moreover especially appropriate in many genuine disputes between students, friends, etc. that have escalated into threats or actual outbursts of violence, and when there is indeed some joint culpability. The latter cases appear to be common in some conferencing contexts.

5 Street-level bureaucrats, according to Lipsky (1980), are those workers with whom citizens interact on a daily basis and who, by virtue of their visibility, represent government to the public. Police, teachers, child welfare caseworkers and department of motor vehicle workers are all examples of street-level bureaucrats.

6 Social support and control should be viewed as interdependent because as Cullen (1994: 545) observes: 'social support often is a precondition for effective social control ... [and] because of investments in relationships, high levels of social support provide the social capital for guardianship.'

7 Broader and more recent statements of Christie's (1977) insights have expanded the theory of usurpation of community responsibility beyond criminal justice agencies to include a wide array of service and mental health networks that today have special relevance in the professionalized social control of young people (Males, 1996; Schwartz, 1989). These networks that McKnight (1995) refers to as the 'medical/services establishment' appear to have similarly usurped control over the self-help, naturalistic support provided at the

community level. In doing so they have brought about an important transition from a view of community members as 'citizens' to a view of them as 'clients and a concomitant decline in democratic participation in a variety of issues, including the response to crime, conflict and trouble' (McKnight, 1995: 98–100).

Chapter 3

Prevalence and scope of restorative decision-making: findings from a national inventory and survey on restorative conferencing for youth

Introduction

Despite the growing interest in restorative community justice in general (Bazemore and Schiff, 2001) and restorative conferencing in particular, very little is known about how, where, and to what degree these decision-making models are operating within the United States (Schiff, 1998; Kurki, 2003). The data presented here begin to address some of the most basic questions about where and how many conferencing programs are currently operating, what types of models are being employed, who these programs are serving, and how these models/programs are distributed across states and other governmental regions. While we cannot claim to provide an exhaustive count of all conferencing programs, these findings do provide a basic, 'snapshot' summary designed to help generally estimate the prevalence of conferencing programs nationwide. Moreover, and perhaps most importantly, this information gives a baseline from which to track the growth or reduction of conferencing programs over time in the United States.

We were particularly interested in clarifying some basic issues such as the type of agency in which programs were located, their funding sources, staffing patterns, where programs are organizationally located (within or outside the 'system'), severity of cases, and referral sources. In addition, we wanted to understand the types of models being used, the extent to which staff were trained in such processes, degree of case preparation, how the process is conducted and who is present, follow-up procedures, and finally how program vision related to actual daily practice. We also wanted to comparatively examine differences in program elements across model types and assess, in a general way, perceptions of 'restorativeness' within programs based on specific criteria (e.g. repairing the harm, victim involvement, community participation, offender input) and the extent to which programs felt they were able to meet their goals in these areas.

Methodology

In this research, we utilize a very general definition of a restorative conference. This definition includes *any* non-adversarial encounter in which those affected by a specific offense or harmful behavior come together in a face-to-face dialogue, first to discuss the impact of the act, and second to determine how the harm it has caused can be repaired. This encounter would follow a finding of guilt and/or an admission of responsibility by offenders choosing to participate. In the conferencing process and subsequent reparative actions, stakeholders generally seek a resolution that meets the mutual needs of victim, offender and community *as well as* develops obligations or sanctions designed to repair the harm to the greatest extent possible (Bazemore, 2000). Although many local adaptations have arisen in response to jurisdictional concerns and resources, four basic structural and procedural models have emerged that include most restorative justice conferencing variations: victim–offender mediation and dialogue (VOM/D); family group conferencing (FGC); peace-making/sentencing circles (circles); and community and neighborhood accountability boards (NABs or boards) (Bazemore and Umbreit, 2001; Shaw and Jane, 1998). (For consistency and ease of understanding, we use the terms boards or NABs interchangeably throughout this text.) This section describes the methodology used to conduct both the national prevalence study as well as the more specific examination of restorative conferencing practices.

The national inventory

Given the absence of systematic data and general information about the presence of restorative conferencing programs, a number of data sources and data collection methodologies were utilized. This data collection effort was exploratory in nature and, in addition to using existing databases whenever possible, utilized snowball sampling and other informal techniques for identifying programs. These strategies are detailed below.

First, an extensive Internet search of restorative justice programs was conducted, focusing specifically on those including a restorative conferencing component. This included a comprehensive search through several Internet search engines of all known websites (e.g. RealJustice, Victim-Offender Mediation Association), as well as keywords applicable to this study (e.g. 'restorative', 'mediation', 'conferencing'). Although limited to those programs maintaining their own website or referred to in another's, this information provided the basis for developing a national database of current programs and contact information.

Second, juvenile justice specialists, state court administrators and other knowledgeable persons in each state were identified and contacted by telephone and/or e-mail and asked to identify restorative justice conferencing programs in their jurisdiction. Respondents in each state and Washington, DC were identified through several sources, including: (1) a previous Balanced and Restorative Justice Project (BARJ) study on restorative justice policy implementation (O'Brien, 1998); (2) the National Center for Juvenile Justice's (NCJJ) list of Juvenile Justice Specialists; and (3) State Court Administrators identified through their national organization, the National Association of State Court Administrators. Someone in each of the 51 jurisdictions was contacted using each above-mentioned source and asked whether they were aware of restorative justice programs in their jurisdiction and to provide contact information if available. If respondents were unsure about either the existence or the nature of programs in their area, we requested contact information for other individuals who might be more knowledgeable and then contacted such persons/organizations. All relevant contact information was added to the original database initiated through the Internet search. All program names and contact information was cross-referenced with information obtained from the Internet search to avoid duplication.

Third, a comprehensive national survey was disseminated in August 2000 to the above-mentioned contacts (N = 253) as well as to the following additional recipients: (1) victim–offender mediation/dialogue programs previously identified and surveyed by Dr Mark Umbreit from the Center for Restorative Justice and Peacemaking at the University of Minnesota in 1999 (N = 275); (2) members of the Victim Offender Mediation Association (VOMA) not otherwise included in the aforementioned lists (N = 172); (3) justice system practitioners trained in family group conferencing by RealJustice, the country's largest Family Group Conferencing training organization (N = 1107); and, (4) juvenile probation officers who previously reported on a National Center for Juvenile Justice survey that their departments used conferencing or mediation for juvenile probationers (N = 668).

Limitations of the inventory data

There are several important limitations to this area of the study. First, the 'snowball' approach, though necessary at this exploratory stage, is likely biased toward more established and well-marketed programs, and therefore probably undercounts newer and less well-established programs. More generally, in the context of an emerging and ever-changing movement, restorative programs as a rule are likely to be low-profile. Hence, while it is possible to overcount in instances where a program identified at one time (e.g. during our national survey) may later terminate its services, it is more likely that undercounting is a greater problem in this inventory.[1] Second, the researchers have no reliable means by which to exclude programs that do not fully meet our definition of restorative conferencing. Informants self-identified as operating a restorative conferencing program and, with the exception of the small subset of programs (i.e. those responding to the national survey), this general exploratory data collection process did not gather much information beyond basic program name, description and model type used. We are more confident that established programs such as VOM and newer forms of conferencing using a specific protocol (e.g. circles and family group conferencing) operate, in general, in a manner consistent with restorative values and principles. We are less confident about the 'restorativeness' of other models and were even less inclined to include programs such as teen courts in our count of restorative conferencing programs. Though teen courts often do include a sanctioning focus on repairing harm, many are more adversarial than restorative in both structure and process (that is, they tend to be focused on decision-making by 'attorneys' and 'judges' following a formal or quasi-formal court-like process) (Godwin, 2001; Bazemore, 2000). However, the fact that only a relative handful of teen courts (N = 23) were referred to us out of hundreds nationally suggests that this self-identification may at least reflect the intent to operate as a restorative process (Godwin, 2001).

The national survey

Survey development and dissemination

The survey was constructed between January and July 2000. In designing the survey, we sought the input of a number of researchers and practitioners to ensure we were capturing important practical and theoretical concepts in a format that could be easily understood by conferencing program directors. After initial development, the survey was previewed among known experts in the field with extensive research and/or practical experience in restorative conferencing theory and practice. The survey was then pretested among a variety of program directors from different types of conferencing programs to get feedback, assess the clarity of the questions, and determine whether the questions did in fact elicit the desired information. After a series of revisions, it was disseminated in August 2000 to the universe of all known and potential restorative conferencing programs in the United States identified through the variety of sources described above. All lists were cross-referenced to avoid duplication. A total of 2,475 surveys were disseminated.

Sampling

At the time the survey was being developed, we were simultaneously engaged in the exploratory macro-analytic part of the study intended to estimate the true population of restorative conferencing programs for youth currently operating in the US (described above). As such, the actual universe of programs that fit the criteria for inclusion in this sample was unknown during its development and dissemination, and we therefore vastly, and intentionally, oversampled the number of potential programs. Our goal was to capture as many programs as possible and, in particular, those smaller and lesser known programs that were unlikely to appear on other national lists (e.g. programs begun by RealJustice trainees in private or public agencies not yet on any other national mailing list).

We oversampled persons, programs, and organizations trained in conferencing or who might have had any connection with a conferencing program. In doing so, we knew that only some limited proportion of these were likely to actually administer a conferencing program. Only later were we able to calculate the actual number of agencies having a conferencing program and conclude that there were approximately 773 programs operating throughout the United States.

We performed extensive follow-up in order to enhance our survey response rate. First, we sent follow-up letters to all recipients encouraging the survey's prompt completion and return. Second, we called all known VOM/D programs that had received a survey and requested its completion and return. Third, we called all recipients who were either personally known to the researchers, who had been contacted at earlier stages of the research, and who either ran conferencing programs or who could be helpful in encouraging others to return the instrument. Finally, we called a sample of recipients from the RealJustice list (approximately every tenth name, or about 110 recipients) to encourage them to complete and return the survey. In addition, we attached a copy of the survey to our website for respondents to access if they had lost their original.

Because in this study we were primarily interested in four basic conferencing models – VOM/D, FGC, circles and boards – the overall program population was reduced to 738 for purposes of this survey. Upon completion of the data collection, 218 programs responded to our survey, from which 181 valid responses were derived. Responses considered invalid included those from programs that, upon further probing, clearly did not include a conferencing component (e.g. restitution or community service only programs), programs dealing with adults only, programs claiming to do restorative conferencing but that had not handled any cases during the last year, and programs that clearly did not do restorative conferencing but performed some other, related service (e.g. victim services, victim panels, family mediation, therapeutic services for offenders, etc.).

Our final response rate was about 24.5 percent among known youth conferencing programs (see Table 3.1 below). As is well-known in social science research, mail surveys typically produce the lowest response rates and a rate of over 30 percent from such surveys is rare; a rate of 25 percent is considered good (Alreck and Settle; 1995; Fowler, 1988). While this would be unacceptably low for research whose intention was to draw inferences from the sample to a general population, the intention of this research was purely exploratory and descriptive. As such, we do not suggest nor advocate that the findings presented here be considered representative of the general population of conferencing programs currently operating in the United States. However, as part of an exploratory, knowledge-building effort, these findings allow us to fill some important gaps in current understanding of restorative conferencing programs for youth in the US.

As Table 3.1 suggests, survey responses overrepresent some model types and underrepresent others. Our response rate from Family Group Conferencing programs is highest, with almost half of known programs (44.1 percent) responding to the survey. Our next best response was from circle programs where 35 percent of all known programs responded (although this only amounted to 6 programs), followed by VOM/D programs with almost 25 percent of programs responding (representing,

Table 3.1 Number and percent of programs responding to national survey compared to national prevalence rate

Type of program model	Total estimated programs	Surveys received	Percent
VOM/D	393	96	24.4
Multiple practice programs	N/A	23	N/A
Boards/panels*	227	14	6.2 (26)
Family group conferencing	93	41	44.1
Circles	17	6	35.3
Other	8	1	12.5
TOTAL	738	181 (226)	24.5 (30.6)

*Several board programs house a number of individual boards/panels. While we received 14 surveys from board programs, this in fact represented 59 actual boards.

however, the largest numerical category). In addition, based on survey responses, we constructed a category that was not known to us at the time of our original search. Programs whose dominant practice may be, for example, VOM/D but that also conduct at least 30 percent of their work using another conferencing model were considered 'multiple practice' programs. The prevalence of such 'multiple practice' programs across the country is not known, although 23 such programs are apparent in our survey results, or about 13 percent of all programs responding to the survey.

Unfortunately, our response rate among board programs was disappointing and hence our information may not reflect the majority of board practice in the field. However, the number of survey responses received from directors of board programs underrepresents the actual number of boards for which they are responsible and hence providing information about. That is, a total of 59 individual boards are in fact represented by the 14 survey responses received. This is because the administrative structure of the board programs authorizes one central program director to administer a number of separate boards operating in diverse communities in that jurisdiction. For example, as of March 2000, the Project Coordinator for the Restorative Justice Program run by the Santa Clara County Department of Corrections oversaw 7 individual neighborhood accountability boards (NABs) in different parts of that county (this number has since grown). However, only one survey was received from the program coordinator responsible for overseeing all these individual NABs. This is true for most of the other board programs as well. As a result, our information about boards may be more representative than initially apparent when considering the small number of surveys received from boards. For purposes of consistency in this report, all data have been calculated based on the 14 actual responses which represent programs with a common administrative structure, but readers should be aware that 59 individual boards are indeed represented by these responses.

Limitations of the national survey data

Given the exploratory nature of this research, there are three primary limitations to the generalizability of our findings. First, the researchers had no reliable means by which to exclude programs that did not fully meet our (or any) definition of restorative conferencing. Because informants self-identified as operating a restorative conferencing program, it is therefore possible that we have failed to exclude programs that common practice might not classify as restorative. Although no program model is inherently 'restorative,' well-established models such as VOM/D and newer forms of conferencing that use a specific protocol (e.g. circles and family group conferencing) are likely to operate, in general, in a manner consistent with restorative values and principles.

Second, from another perspective, in the context of an emerging and ever-changing movement, restorative programs as a rule are likely to be low-profile. Hence, as with the inventory data, undercounting is likely to have occurred as we may have missed some smaller, lesser known or less well-established programs which did not receive our survey. Moreover, it is possible that there were errors in how we identified the potential population of restorative conferencing programs. We used as many resources as we could identify and were available to us (e.g. previous research samples, conferencing training program databases, juvenile justice specialists in each state) in hopes of reaching the greatest possible population of current programs. In addition, we used a 'snowball' technique (asking known respondents to tell us about other potentially relevant respondents of which they are aware) to further expand the universe of potential restorative conferencing programs whenever possible. However, given the ever-changing landscape of restorative justice programs in general, and restorative conferencing in particular, it is likely that we have missed some programs.

Third, perhaps our greatest limitation is our low response rate which limits the generalizability of these findings. It is important to note that although our response rates are lower than we would have liked, the population we are attempting to describe represents a number of frequently small, marginal, and new programs that have been in operation for perhaps only a few years at best, and only a few months at worst. These programs are often decentralized, making it virtually impossible to identify, locate, and contact *all* restorative conferencing programs. Given that the universe of restorative conferencing programs is constantly shifting, and that identifying, contacting, and receiving responses from such programs has never before been undertaken by any exploratory research of this nature, we are satisfied that our survey responses offer a better representation of the 'world' of restorative conferencing in the United States than has been captured in any research to date.

Strengths of the data

Despite the limitations of this exploratory research, its strengths include the fact that multiple data sources, multiple informants and multiple data collection methodologies were used to maximize the likelihood of identifying little-known programs and obtaining the most accurate estimate of program prevalence possible. An advantage of allowing informants to self-identify as a restorative conferencing program provides an indication of the extent to which knowledge about restorative justice (a term unfamiliar to most juvenile justice professionals until five to six years ago) has spread along with a concomitant sense of desire to label programs accordingly. Moreover, extensive follow-up likely enhanced our response rate. Most importantly, findings presented in this exploratory study fill a void in basic knowledge about the availability and types of restorative conferencing available in the United States, and provide a broader picture of what informants are themselves considering 'restorative' and, in general, 'what's going on out there' with regard to restorative conferencing for youth.

Measures

Our measures were intended to help identify key aspects of program characteristics, elements of process and follow-up, and the relationship between restorative vision and its application in everyday practice. As such, we divided the survey into four sections: Respondent, agency, case type, and referral information; Type of restorative conferencing model used, charge types, and training; Case preparation and process information; and Restorative decision-making encounter goals and objectives.

This last section was, to some degree, the most important as it addressed how restorative vision matched with the day-to-day experience of the program. Specifically, we were concerned with how program vision was, (1) expressed and (2) put into practice as we suspected that programs would have difficulty ensuring that actual practice reflected program vision. Hence, we asked a series of questions designed to better understand the 'restorativeness' of the program (i.e. the extent to which restorative values and principles were articulated in program vision) and programs rated themselves on a number of restorative dimensions, such as the priority attached to victim participation, repairing harm, holding offenders accountable, and community involvement (ranging from 1, 'not at all important,' to 5, 'extremely important'). We also included several measures of goals and priorities not typically considered part of a restorative agenda to assess the extent to which programs identified other concerns, e.g. reducing court backlog, keeping offenders out of court, resolving conflict as central to their objectives. While such measures are not necessarily antithetical to a restorative platform, they are not typically considered of primary importance. We were interested to see how important programs felt these variables were to program vision. To address the extent to which respondents felt that actual practice was consistent with their vision, we asked that they rate themselves on each dimension as either 'not meeting goals,' 'meeting goals,' or 'exceeding goals' in that area.

Findings

Results of the national inventory study

Preliminary findings indicate that juvenile restorative conferencing programs are quite widespread, especially when compared with the relative paucity of programs other than victim offender mediation as recently as ten or even five years ago (Umbreit and Greenwood 1999). We found differential use of conferencing across states and across counties, a preference for some models in some states, and much greater use of some models than others.

Conferencing programs in the states

Nine out of ten states currently have some form of conferencing program in place. While this suggests that conferencing programs are generally well represented across the country, it is important to note that states vary considerably in the number and variety of programs available, as well as in the numbers of persons actually served by these programs; moreover, not all areas within a state are necessarily represented, or well represented, by such programs. Some states may have a variety of programs in several jurisdictions, while others – including some densely populated states – may have one or two small projects operating in a single locality only.

Most programs are primarily designed to serve their own county residents. Seventy-four percent of counties in the US have fewer than 50,000 people, hence examining the proportion of counties in each state served by restorative conferencing programs gives a better general sense of the proportion of state residents who might actually be served by such programs.

While almost all *states* can claim at least one restorative program, most *counties* are not served by a conferencing program. According to our count, only 13.5 percent of all counties nationally report such programs. Vermont, Alaska, Delaware, Massachusetts, and California lead the way with 50 percent or more counties reporting restorative conferencing programs; among these, Vermont and Alaska have the greatest relative number of counties with restorative conferencing programs, with 86 percent and 70 percent, respectively. In California, 50 percent of counties are served and Minnesota, despite having by far the most diverse range of programs available, actually serves less than half of its population (36 percent). In more than half of the states (N=30), only 15 percent or fewer counties claim restorative conferencing/dialogue programs.

Program models

If, in general, conferencing can be said to be relatively widespread throughout the states, not all models are equally common in each state. As the oldest type of conferencing program operating in the United States, it is not surprising that VOM/D programs are more widely represented than other, more recent restorative interventions, as they account for over one half of all programs included in this count (N=393; 51.1 percent). The second most prevalent type of restorative program, boards, represent slightly under one-third of programs identified in this study (N = 227; 29.3 percent).

Community boards may occur in a variety of forms and take on several different names, including neighborhood accountability boards (NABs) such as those in San Jose, California and various cities in Arizona; the community accountability boards (CABS) in Denver, Colorado; community restorative panels in Vermont (which account for virtually all of that state's restorative decision-making programs and are comparable to reparative boards for adults (e.g. Karp and Walther, 2001); and youth aide panels in Pennsylvania. Finally, the generally newer 93 family group and community conferencing programs represent 12 percent of restorative conferencing programs nationally, and teen courts, circles, community courts, and 'other' comprise the remaining 8 percent of programs.

State preferences and diversity in use

We also examined the distribution of programs by state. Arizona and Pennsylvania predominantly use boards, while Minnesota and Colorado have among the most diverse range of programs, including conferencing, VOM/D, boards and circles. Texas, Ohio, and Colorado have a large concentration of VOM/D programs. Interestingly, despite its geographic distance from most US states using restorative conferencing approaches, Alaska appears to be one of the more eclectic states in terms of restorative justice, boasting a variety of programs including victim–offender dialogue, circles, traditional family group and community conferences, and community courts. These programs are few in number, however, and generally spread across an expansive geographic region.

There is considerable disparity in program distribution within and between states. There does not seem to be any single or simple strategy that characterizes state implementation patterns; rather program composition may be random or reflect needs, stage of development, knowledge of, and/or resource availability within each individual state. (Detailed data confirming this hypothesis are not available from this research.)

Multiple models and hybridization

It is important to note that although most agencies or organizations employ one primary conferencing model, some practise multiple techniques and there appears to be a growing tendency for single programs to offer several types of conferencing interventions. That is, as programs gain knowledge of and training in a variety of other program models, they may be inclined to offer multiple alternatives within one organization depending, ideally, upon the needs and wishes of victims and offenders. An individual program may primarily emphasize VOM, for example, but occasionally offer peace-making circles or family group conferencing when it better suits the particular case or its participants.

Although the precise degree to which this occurs is uncertain, some preliminary information suggests a possible trend. From our sample of 181 programs responding to the national survey (representing about 24 percent of the number of programs we approximate exist nationwide), 67 percent indicated that they used one conferencing practice only, and 30 percent reported employing multiple practices (the remaining 3 percent did not respond to the question). These data suggest that using multiple practices may likely continue as organizations develop internal competence as well as better inter-program networks of communication. In addition, as restorative conferencing expertise develops, we suspect that practical distinctions between the models may blur, creating a 'hybridization' of program types and modes of service delivery. For example, a board program may change its format from the traditional model of volunteer board members who deliberate with little or no input from victim and offender, to one in which participants sit in a circle and a facilitator seeks input from victim, offender, community members, family, and supporters thus functioning more like a family group conference than a traditional board (Bazemore, 1997).

Brief summary and conclusions from the national inventory

In sum, it is clear that restorative conferencing for young offenders has become increasingly popular as a viable response to youthful offending. While the data presented here are preliminary, our national inventory suggests several important general findings:

- Almost every state is experimenting with restorative conferencing processes, and the vast majority of states (94 percent) offer at least one program.
- The current study identified 773 programs nationwide, with programs most prevalent in a few key states (e.g. California, Pennsylvania, Minnesota, Texas, Colorado, Arizona, New York, Ohio, Alaska).
- A variety of models are represented nationally, dominated by VOM and community boards.
- While specific models predominate in some states, e.g. boards in Vermont, Pennsylvania, and California, most states feature multiple conferencing practices.
- When examining program distribution at the county level, most communities are not well served by restorative conferencing programs.
- Although the previous baseline number of programs is generally unknown (except for VOM programs), a number of new programs and

program models (e.g. family group conferencing, circles) are becoming increasingly popular around the country.

- There appears to be a trend towards integrating multiple practices within one organization.
- States using conferencing are both regionally and politically diverse, suggesting that there is no tendency for restorative programs to proliferate or cluster in a particular geographic region or within a particular political environment.

Results from the national survey on restorative conferencing for youth

The survey was designed to elicit information about the location, administrative structure, process, follow-up, and 'restorativeness' of restorative conferencing programs for youth in the United States. Our findings are summarized here as responses to a series of questions intended to give an overview of how and where conferencing programs do their work.

Administrative issues: location, budget, staffing

Where are most RJ conferencing programs located?
Most conferencing programs responding to the survey say they are housed in private, community-based agencies (46 percent), followed by probation agencies (22 percent). The remaining 32 percent are distributed among courts, corrections, law enforcement, other government agencies, and/or some combination of the above. Boards are most likely to be located in probation agencies, while all other program types are most likely to be housed in private, community-based organizations.

How are restorative conferencing programs funded?
Almost 80 percent of programs responding to our survey report maintaining a separate budget for their program aside from the regular agency budget. Among the 133 valid responses to this question (excluding those with no separate budget or who did not respond), just over 8 percent of programs operate on budgets of under $5,000 and 17 percent have funding of $15,000 or less. Slightly under one-third (29.4 percent) run on budgets of $25,000 or less; 42.9 percent on budgets of $25,001–$75,000; and 27.8 percent manage on budgets of over $75,000. FGC programs are most likely to operate with lower funding levels while VOM/D and the circle programs in this study tended to run on higher budgets.

Primary funding for most restorative conferencing programs comes from government sources. A total of 73 percent of programs are funded by some combination of state, local, and/or federal agencies. Foundations, grants, individual contributions, churches, or some combination of these fund about 20 percent of programs, and the remaining 7 percent have no separate funding, but manage either using existing resources or with some other resource.

When considering where programs are organizationally located, this suggests that *the majority of programs are located in private organizations but funded with public dollars, most likely through government grants and contracts.* In fact, when examining the resources of private, community-based organizations, the data indicate that almost two-thirds of these programs (65.7 percent) are funded by government monies.

How are restorative conferencing programs staffed?
Most programs operate with less than one full-time paid or volunteer administrator dedicated to the program, suggesting that while funding may not allow for a full-time position, it may support some *portion* of an administrator's time. Survey respondents with paid administrators reported that funding might cover about 90 percent of an administrator's time, on average. For programs with volunteer administrators, the average time worked was about one-fifth that of a full-time employee.

The average number of volunteer staff for any program is 26; the average number of paid staff is about 3.5. The average number of volunteer mediators/facilitators who staffed these restorative conferencing programs was 24. The majority of programs (51 percent) operate with 10 or fewer volunteer mediators/facilitators; 76 percent have 25 or fewer such staff. Two board programs reported having 350 and 450 volunteers, respectively (the reader should remember here that one board response may represent a large number of actual board programs).

Almost 36 percent of the programs reported having no paid mediators/facilitators. The average number of paid mediators/facilitators was just under 2 and the highest number in any program was 26. The majority of programs do not maintain paid or volunteer training staff (just under 86 percent say they have no volunteer trainers and about 70 percent say they have no paid trainers). Fifty-three programs (29.3 percent) report having paid trainers on staff.

All programs report fewer paid staff than volunteers, implying that the actual work of conferencing is accomplished through the heavy use of community volunteers. Overall, this suggests that *restorative conferencing programs are maintained primarily through the efforts of volunteers with less than one full-time paid administrator responsible for overseeing the work of a large number of volunteers.*

How are restorative conferencing staff trained?
The vast majority of respondents report having been trained in multiple practices, even though they may not practice more than one model on any regular basis. For example, 30.1 percent of VOM/D programs report

having been trained in FGC, and 42.9 percent of board programs responding to the survey report having received training in FGC. There was, however, no distinction as to whether training reflected formal 'official' training in a particular practice, or if it consisted of informal, 'in-house' training for no more than a few hours. In addition, there was no indication if this was ongoing or 'one-shot' training.

More VOM/D program respondents report having received training in their dominant practice than did respondents from any other model type except circles. Specifically, over 95 percent of VOM/D or multiple practice programs say they have received training in VOM/D. In contrast, slightly over half of board respondents report having received formal training in boards. To some degree this may reflect the availability of training. All circle respondents report having received circle training.

Summary

In summary, these data suggest that most restorative conferencing programs are located in private agencies or probation departments and funded with government monies. They are staffed mostly by volunteers, with a less than full-time paid administrator. Most staff are trained in multiple practices, though they may tend to only or predominantly stick to one practice.

Getting cases: referral source and charge types

The intention here was to better understand how conferencing programs interact with the justice system and what types of cases they are most likely to accept. Our goal was to be able to characterize some of the work that occurs prior to the actual conference process itself and who is involved in this activity.

From where do most programs get their referrals?

Table 3.2 shows the percentage of programs in each model category that take referrals from various sources (law enforcement, judges, probation, etc.). The table shows the proportion of respondents within each model category that report receiving referrals from the source listed in the left-hand column (e.g. 57.5 percent of all VOM/D programs responding to the survey say they take referrals from probation). These are not mutually exclusive categories and programs might take referrals from more than one source.

Probation was the most common referral source. The least common sources of referral were from community-oriented sources, e.g. schools, community groups, victim advocates. In this sample of programs, it appears that *the formal justice system is more likely to refer cases to the program than are non-system sources.*

Table 3.2 Source of referral by type of restorative conferencing program

Referral source	Program type: VOM/D (%)	Multiple practice (%)	Circle (%)	FGC (%)	Board (%)	Total (N) (%)
Probation	57.5	63.6	50.0	30.8	66.7	52.1 (87)
Judge	46.6	52.4	66.7	23.7	33.3	41.6 (69)
Law enforcement	23.9	34.8	33.3	52.5	28.6	33.0 (58)
Prosecutor	24.4	27.3	33.3	35.0	8.3	26.5 (45)
School	14.4	23.8	16.7	45.0		21.9 (37)
Community	7.7	9.1	16.7	12.5		8.7 (15)
Victim advocate	6.6	9.1		2.5		5.2 (9)

FGC programs were more likely to accept referrals from law enforcement than from any other source and, correspondingly, were more likely to accept law enforcement referrals than were any other practice. They were also least likely to accept judicial referrals. This is not surprising given that the FGC model most commonly practised in the US derives from the Australian Wagga Wagga approach where law enforcement officers initiate and facilitate conferences before court referral. When compared to other program types, FGC programs were also most likely to report accepting referrals from prosecutors and schools, while circles and multiple practice programs reported taking referrals from judges more often than other programs.

Boards, VOM/D and multiple practice programs were most likely to take case referrals from probation. This is especially predictable for board programs which are often housed in probation or corrections departments. Though not as predictable for VOM/D, it is not surprising given that 9 out of 10 VOM/D programs report taking cases pre-court (see Table 3.4 later) and probation is often the agency that handles pre-court diversion in many jurisdictions.

What types of charges do restorative conferencing programs accept?[2]
In order to determine the types of cases conferencing programs deal with, we asked programs to tell us how many cases with different dominant charge types they took during the last year. Table 3.3 suggests that, overall, *the charge **most likely to be accepted** by restorative conferencing programs responding to the survey was minor assault, followed by property damage and personal theft charges. The charges **most likely to be excluded** from the conferencing process are those involving serious drug charges, domestic violence, and minor drug charges.* Anecdotal evidence suggests the possibility that conferencing programs may feel ill-equipped to handle the

Table 3.3 Charges accepted by type of restorative conferencing program

Charges accepted	Program type: VOM/D (%)	Multiple practice (%)	Circle (%)	FGC (%)	Board (%)	Total (N) (%)
Minor assault	79.3	81.8	100.0	67.6	91.7	78.8 (125)
Property damage	76.9	77.3	83.3	70.3	61.5	74.5 (116)
Personal theft	70.4	81.8	50.0	73.0	92.3	73.1 (116)
Business theft	51.9	59.1	33.3	73.0	76.9	59.5 (93)
B & E	41.8	86.4	66.7	45.9	61.5	51.9 (82)
Vandalism	50.0	59.1	33.3	48.6	61.5	51.6 (80)
Serious assault	40.7	45.5	66.7	29.7	23.1	38.8 (61)
Minor drug	14.6	18.2	33.3	32.4	53.8	23.6 (37)
Domestic violence	23.1	21.7	33.3	12.8	21.4	21.3 (36)
Serious drug	4.9	4.5	16.7	13.5	7.7	8.1 (12)
Other*	44.4	36.4	33.3	64.9	23.1	45.6 (73)

*Other charges include arson, harassment, loitering, alcohol, behavioral issues, auto theft, bomb threat, disorderly conduct, DUI, forgery, weapons, menacing, trespass, possession of stolen property, and various other charges as well as combinations of the above charges.

potentially complicated ancillary issues that may accompany such serious cases. It is also possible that, given the political nature of drug and drug-related cases in some areas, some conferencing programs may not be inclined to accept them, or that admission criteria imposed by justice system referral agencies may exclude certain categories of cases.

When examining which programs were more likely to accept particular charges than others, Table 3.3 suggests that circle programs were more likely than other practices to accept more severe charges, such as serious assault, drugs, and domestic violence; multiple practice programs were considerably more likely than other practices to accept referrals for breaking and entering.

In sum, programs tend to focus on generally less serious property and minor assault cases. This is likely due to several reasons, including the relative newness of many programs, both in terms of their own history as well as in their relationship to traditional justice processes. Additionally, justice system referral agencies may be reluctant to turn over more serious cases and, concomitantly, conferencing programs may be reluctant (at least initially) to deal with more complicated, serious, and politically charged cases. Anecdotal evidence suggests that there appears to be a trend towards taking increasingly serious cases, especially among more established programs with proven track records, such as VOM/D programs and some newer circle programs.

Table 3.4 Point of program referral by type of restorative conferencing

Point in process when referrals taken	Program type: VOM/D (%)	Multiple practice (%)	Circle (%)	FGC (%)	Board (%)	Total (N) (%)
Pre-court	90.1	81.8	60.0	81.6	76.9	85.2 (144)
After adjudication	53.3	54.5	40.0	28.9	23.1	45.2 (76)
After sentence	55.4	63.6	60.0	36.8	38.5	51.2 (87)

At what point in the justice process do programs generally take cases?
When examining the processing point at which cases are accepted for conferencing, Table 3.4 suggests that over four-fifths (85.2 percent) of survey respondents report taking cases prior to formal court referral.[3] Forty-five percent of programs take referrals after court adjudication and 51.2 percent after sentence (note that these are not mutually exclusive categories and programs may report accepting cases at several points in the process). This also suggests, conversely, that about 55 percent of programs *do not take* referrals after adjudication and about 49 percent *do not take* post-sentence referrals.

Overall, respondents report that, on average, 62 percent of their conference referrals occur during pre-court diversion, while on average about 13 percent are accepted after adjudication and about 23 percent occur after sentencing.

When comparing across program types, VOM/D is the most likely practice to conference cases prior to court intervention; multiple practice programs are most likely to take cases after adjudication as well as after sentencing. Of particular interest is that FGC and board programs are *considerably less likely* to take cases following adjudication or sentence than are VOM/D, multiple practice or circle programs. When examining this table in conjuction with Table 3.2, it appears that many programs take cases diverted through probation prior to court referral.

Summary
The data presented in this section suggest that referrals are most likely to come from the justice system, specifically probation, and are least likely to come from community sources. The most common charges in cases handled by restorative conferencing programs are minor assault, property damage and personal theft; the least common are drug- and domestic violence-related cases. The restorative conferencing programs responding to this survey typically take cases prior to court referral, as pre-court diversionary cases.

Table 3.5 Average number of conference participants

	Average number of people present at conference
VOM/D	5.4
Multiple practice	6.9
Board	9.2
FGC	9.5
Circle	11.8
Total average	7.1

The participants and the process

We next asked programs to report on how they manage the human part of the conference, in particular who was generally present at the conference, who speaks first, and who makes decisions about how the process will be conducted.

How many people are typically present at a conference?
Table 3.5 shows that *programs report an average of about 7 people attend a typical conference*. The largest number of participants reported by any program was 22. Volunteer facilitators or members of a coordinating committee generally comprise about 1.77 of the participants and there are typically 1.26 staffpersons present; 93 percent of programs report that there are 2 or fewer staffpersons present at the conference.

This means that *conferences have, on average, 3 additional participants present other than the victim, offender, and facilitator*. The data suggest that the average number of people present for VOM/D programs is 5.4, for multiple practice programs the number increases to 6.9, for FGC programs the number is 9.5, for boards/panels 9.2, and for circles the average is 11.8. The relatively high number of participants for VOM/D is consistent with other recent evidence suggesting that this is no longer primarily a dyadic process reserved for victims, offenders, and the mediator, but rather that there is increasing involvement of additional parties, such as family members (Umbreit and Greenwood, 1997).

Who generally speaks first at the conference?
In both training and research, there is debate about who should speak first at the conference. Table 3.6 indicates that, *in general, it is most common for the offender to speak first*. When examining who generally speaks first after the initial opening statement by the mediator/facilitator, programs report that, on average, the offender speaks first 45.4 percent of the time. The next most common occurrence is for the victim to speak first.

Table 3.6 Who typically speaks first at the conference by type of program model

Who speaks first at the conference	Program type: VOM/D (%)	Multiple practice (%)	Circle (%)	FGC (%)	Board (%)	Total (N) (%)
Offender speaks first	38.2	33.8	16.7	73.6	43.6	45.4
Victim speaks first	34.5	38.9	17.5	11.0	19.3	27.9
Who speaks first varies	24.9	27.3	49.2	10.4	22.7	22.5
Other person speaks first	1.4	—	16.7	2.5	14.4	3.0

The data suggest that FGC and boards are considerably more likely to report having the offender speak first than are other model types. In VOM/D, the offender is only slightly more likely to speak first than the victim, while multiple practice programs report that the victim is slightly more likely to speak first. The circle programs responding to this survey report that who speaks first on average varies, or that it is unpredictable who speaks first in almost 50 percent of conferences.

In what percentage of cases is there no identifiable victim?
An ongoing concern for conferencing theory and practice has been the extent to which conferences can, or should, proceed in cases where there is no identifiable victim. Just over 60 percent of programs (N = 108) report that they conference cases when there is no identifiable victim; correspondingly 38.6 percent of programs (N = 68) report that they do not conference any of their cases when there is no identifiable victim. Programs that say they will hold a conference when there is no identifiable victim report that they will do so, on average, about 25 percent of the time. In other words, it appears that *most programs are willing to conference without a clear victim, but only do so in about 25 percent of their cases.* Not surprisingly, VOM/D programs are least likely to report that they will conference a case with no identifiable victim, followed by FGCs. Boards are most likely to report that they will conference a case without an identifiable victim.

Do programs typically use a script when conducting conferences?
Another issue of debate is whether a script should be used to guide the conference process or whether it should be a more organic and less directed process. *Programs are fairly evenly split on whether or not they use set scripts when conducting conferences.* Among 176 valid responses to this question, Table 3.7 shows that 97 programs, or 55.1 percent, do not use a script while 79 programs, or 44.9 percent, report that they do use a set script in the conferencing process. Given that some of the most common

Table 3.7   Use of a standard script by type of restorative conferencing model

Is a standard script used?	Program type: VOM/D (%)	Multiple practice (%)	Circle (%)	FGC (%)	Board (%)	Total (N) (%)
No	70.2	52.4	50.0	19.5	64.3	55.1 (97)
Yes	29.8	47.6	50.0	80.5	35.7	44.9 (79)

FGC training (e.g. that provided by RealJustice) advocates using a script, it is not surprising that FGC programs are most likely to report doing so. VOM/D programs are least likely to report using scripts, followed by boards. What is perhaps most interesting is that 30 percent of VOM/D programs and almost 48 percent of multiple practice programs use scripts despite the fact that scripts have generally been discouraged in VOM/D training (Umbreit, 2001).

In what percentage of cases are offenders required to admit their involvement in the offense prior to participation in the conference? In what percentage of cases must offenders have been adjudicated guilty?
Survey data show that 138, or *78.4 percent of programs report that all offenders must admit involvement prior to participation in a conference.* Only 25 programs, or 14 percent, report that they require all offenders to be *adjudicated guilty* prior to participation. Somewhat surprisingly, 19 programs (10.8 percent) report that they do not require *any* offenders to admit involvement prior to the conference. This contradicts an important premise of restorative conferencing that the offender acknowledge responsibility prior to being accepted for conferencing.

On average, how often are victims, their families, offender's families, and other support persons typically present at the conference?
Victim presence at conferences ranges from a low of 5 percent, as reported by 3 programs, up to 100 percent, as reported by 88 programs. *Programs report the victim is present, on average, 83.8 percent of the time and the victim's family is present in an average of 51.7 percent of cases.* The highest average rate is VOM/D (89.7 percent), followed closely by multiple practice and FGC. The average percent of time when victims are present in multiple practice programs is 55.2 percent.

The least likely type of program to report victim presence is boards. Boards in this sample do not appear particularly adept at engaging support persons (which may not be a priority), but do relatively well engaging offender's family members. On average, the offender's family is present in 77.6 percent of conferences overall and when comparing across program types, the highest overall average rate of participation among victims, families, and support persons occurs within FGC programs.

Finally, the average rate of participation for other support persons is relatively low at 31.8 percent; again, this may be a reflection of the large percentage of VOM/D programs in this sample which have traditionally not been designed to include families and other support persons, or it may simply reflect the difficulty programs encounter in contacting and engaging such participants.

To what degree do parties actively participate in conferences?

Because being present at a conference is not necessarily synonymous with actively participating, we asked about the degree to which program directors perceived that participants other than the victim and offender were actually participating in the conference.

On average, programs perceived that *just over half of victims' family members present at the conference actively participate in the conference* (54.4 percent). *The offender's family is perceived to actively participate, on average, in about two-thirds of the conferences* (66.4 percent) which, as with victims, is also less than their average rate of presence. Other support persons participate actively just over one-third of the time (35.5 percent). As the FGC model depends on the participation of the victim and offender's families, it is not surprising that FGC programs report the highest levels of participation for each group. It is also not surprising that, for the same reason, circle programs responding to the survey show the next highest rate of family and supporter participation.

How often do programs use representative, surrogate, or 'stand-in' victims' when the actual victim is not present?

About half of the programs responding to the survey report that they never use surrogate victims (49.7 percent). Another 30.9 percent report using surrogate victims in up to 25 percent of their cases; the remaining 29 programs reporting using surrogate victims in more than 26 percent of their cases. The overall average percentage of time in which programs responding to the survey use surrogate victims is 17.7 percent, or in just under one-fifth of their cases. In general, this suggests that *while using surrogate victims is an acceptable practice for many programs, it is not an especially common occurrence.* Most programs that use surrogate victims do not do so in a large majority of their cases.

Summary

When considering the participants and the process, these data indicate that the average number of conference participants is about 7, which supports the notion of stakeholder involvement beyond the primary parties of victim, offender and facilitator in the conference process. It is most likely for the offender to speak first after the opening statement by the facilitator. Most programs are willing to conference cases in which there is no clearly identifiable victim, but will actually do so in only about one-fourth of their cases. Programs are about evenly split on whether or not they will use a script during the conference. Most, but not all, programs, require an admission of guilt from the offender before conferencing a case and a small number of programs require that the offender be adjudicated guilty before conferencing the case. Victims are usually present at the conference. The offender's family members are more likely to actively participate in the process than are members of the victim's family. Other support persons are least likely both to be present and to actively participate. About one-half of the respondents say they will conference cases using surrogate victims when the actual victim is unavailable, but only do so, on average, in less than one-fifth of the cases.

Conference follow-up

What does, or should, happen after a conference and who should be responsible? Conferencing process follow-up varies considerably by program type and structure. As there are various perspectives concerning the importance of follow-up, we were interested in what programs felt was most effective for following-up with victims, offenders, and community members. We were especially interested in what happened to offenders who did not complete the process, how programs followed-up with different participants in the process, and how, if at all, programs monitored reparative agreements and restitution.

What generally happens when offenders don't complete the restorative conference process?
Table 3.8 shows that the majority of respondents (60 percent) reported that offenders who did not complete the conferencing process would most likely be sent back to court. The next most common response would be for the offender to be returned to probation for action (45.4 percent) followed by return to a diversion program (22.1 percent). These are *not mutually exclusive* categories, so programs may invoke different actions in different cases, hence the total does not equal 100 percent.

These figures represent the overall percentage of programs reporting that the outcome is possible for *any* but not necessarily for *all* of their cases, and programs may invoke different responses in different circumstances when permissible by law. Overall, this suggests that *offenders are likely to be returned to a traditional justice agency if they do not complete the process, rather than being sent back to the conference or some other restorative option.*

Table 3.8 What happens when offenders do not complete the conference process

Outcome	Percentage of programs reporting outcome is possible
Offender goes to court	60.0
Offender goes to probation	45.4
Offender goes to diversion program	22.1
Some other outcome	20.0
Nothing happens	19.1
Offender goes back to conference	6.8
Offender goes to detention	1.5

How often do programs make follow-up contact with the participants?
Programs responding to the survey report doing at least some follow-up with victims, on average, in just under 70 percent of the cases. Programs report following-up with offenders in as much as 77 percent of cases and with community members in as few as 28.7 percent of cases. Circles and multiple practice programs report the highest average rates of victim follow-up, followed closely by FGC and then by VOM/D programs.

All programs report following-up with victims and offenders more often than not, although they are less likely to follow-up with community members. Given that such participants may not be perceived as key figures, it is not surprising that programs are less likely to attend to them after the conference. Given that they are not designed to include community members in the process, it is not surprising that VOM/D programs report the lowest rate of community follow-up. Concomitantly, given the community-oriented nature of the circle model, it is predictable that circles report the highest rate of community follow-up.

How often do programs monitor completion of the reparative conferencing agreement?
A concern in achieving the goal of repairing the harm is the degree to which programs monitor the completion of the reparative agreement. *Programs report following-up to check completion of conference agreement in 79.8 percent of all cases, on average.* Boards and circles report the highest average rates of follow-up, followed by FGC programs and then VOM/D and multiple practice programs. There is little variation in model types, as all report relatively high rates of agreement follow-up.

How often do programs follow-up to assure that restitution is completed?
The degree to which restitution is completed may also indicate programs' attention to repairing the harm caused by the incident. *Programs report that they follow-up to see that restitution is completed in an average of 83 percent of cases.* Again, circles and FGC programs report the highest average rates of follow-up, and VOM/D the lowest (although it should be noted that VOM/D follows up in over 80 percent of cases and, as the program representing the greatest number of survey respondents, has the most variation of any model type reported here). There is not much variation in reported average rates of reparative agreement follow-up and restitution follow-up.

Summary
The data on conference follow-up show that when offenders do not complete the conference process, they are most likely to be referred to court or to probation for action. That is, traditional justice system approaches are seen to be the most appropriate response after a failure to complete the conferencing process. Respondents say they follow-up regularly (about 70 percent or more of the time) with both victims and offenders, but less so with community members who participated in the meeting. The vast majority of programs report following up in 80 percent or more of cases on completion of the reparative agreements, as well as on any restitution agreement reached.

'Restorativeness' in conferencing model vision and philosophy

There is considerable evidence that programmatic mission and vision do not always materialize in practice (e.g. Pressman and Wildavsky, 1973). However, a restorative vision as reflected in the mission and values of programs and staff is a necessary first step in implementation. There is little available literature which examines this question in practical, empirical terms, and none for programs within the United States. For our purposes, it was first important to identify the extent to which survey respondents recognized dimensions of restorative justice principles as primary to their mission. Second, we were interested in the extent to which program respondents felt they were able to achieve those principles in actual practice.

For the purposes of this study, our primary definition of 'restorativeness' is derived from the three key principles of restorative justice identified by Van Ness and Strong (1997, 2001). These principles include: reparation of harm, stakeholder involvement, and government/community role and transformation. In addition, other characteristics have been identified by both the theoretical (Braithwaite, 1989, 2002; Van Ness and

Schiff, 2001; Bazemore and Griffiths, 1997; Bazemore, 1997) and empirical (Umbreit, 2001; Maxwell and Morris, 1993; Morris and Maxwell, 2001; Sherman, Strang, and Woods, 2000; McCold and Wachtel, 1998) literature as important to understanding 'restorativeness,' either as components of the key principles cited above (Van Ness, 2001) or as independent variables important in their own right (Umbreit, 2001; Braithwaite, 1989; Zehr, 1990; Clear and Karp, 2000). Such variables include offender accountability and reintegration, participant healing, assisting victims, and the importance of community involvement. The following data show how survey respondents view the importance of certain key program goals, and how well they believe they are meeting those goals in practice.

Perceptions of the importance of key restorative goals

In general, survey respondents were very consistent about their percep-tions of the importance of key restorative goals. Figure 3.1 shows that almost all programs responded that repairing harm was either 'very important' or 'extremely important' (96.9 percent). In addition, the overwhelming majority of programs reported that they felt victim participation (97.6 percent), victim healing (94.5 percent), and victim satisfaction (92.3 percent) were either 'very important' or 'extremely important.' With respect to offenders, programs responded that they felt offender participation (100 percent), offender reintegration (87.9 percent), and holding offenders accountable (100 percent) were either 'very important' or 'extremely important.'

To see whether, and to what extent, programs distinguished between traditionally non-restorative and restorative goals, we also asked about program perceptions of the importance of certain goals not typically associated with restorative justice, such as offender punishment, offender rehabilitation, reducing court backlog, and keeping offenders out of court. Only 25.2 percent of programs indicated that they felt offender punish-ment was 'very important' or 'extremely important.' Programs did feel that offender rehabilitation was quite important, as 85 percent felt this was very or extremely important, perhaps implying that there is either some confusion about the difference between rehabilitative and restorative goals, or that programs consider this an important goal, in addition to or irrespective of reparative goals. Only 39.5 percent of respondents felt that reducing court backlog was 'very important' or 'extremely important,' and about half (54.7 percent) felt that keeping offenders out of court was either very or extremely important. The majority of these responses support the premise that programs do distinguish between restorative and traditional justice goals and tend to base their programs on the restorative principles described above.

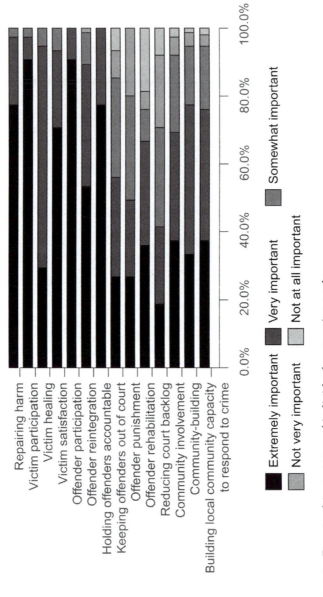

Figure 3.1 Perceived importance of individual restorative goals

The most interesting findings in this section of the survey focused on program perceptions of the importance of goals related to the community's role in restorative conferencing. Programs consistently rated community-specific goals as less important than either victim or offender-related goals. For example, only 68.1 percent of programs rated community involvement as either 'very important' or 'extremely important.' Similarly, only 75 percent of programs rated the importance of community-building and building local community capacity to respond to crime as either 'very important' or 'extremely important.'

Overall, these findings tend to support the premise that restorative conferencing programs are at least aware of, if not focused on restorative goals. They consider key goals associated with restorative justice (e.g. repairing harm) to be quite important to their programs while being less attentive to presumptive non-restorative goals (e.g. keeping offenders out of court). As suggested in other sections of this report, the relationship between vision and practice in restorative conferencing is a complicated one, and it is difficult to ensure that daily practice is always consistent with programmatic intentions. These findings indicate that restorative values are present in the vision of the restorative conferencing programs responding to this survey, though this may be difficult to consistently implement in practice. The following section addresses the degree to which programs perceive that they are able to meet these restorative goals in practice.

Perceived ability to meet restorative goals in practice

Repairing harm

Perhaps the most important indicator of 'restorativeness' is the extent to which programs focus on repairing the harm caused by the offense (Zehr, 1990). Reparation plays a key role in the mission of most programs and is arguably the primary distinction between restorative and other justice goals. Consistent with expectation, the vast majority of programs (97 percent) responded that repairing harm was either 'very important' or 'extremely important' to their program's vision, and over 90 percent report that they are either meeting or exceeding their reparative goals in actual practice. Programs that reported repairing harm to be 'extremely important' were most likely to also report exceeding their goals. However, among programs that did not meet their goals, over three-quarters also say that this goal is extremely important. There was little variation by program type, as 93 percent or more of all respondents within each model category rated repairing harm as very or extremely important. Board programs were slightly less likely than other program types to report that repairing harm was extremely, as opposed to very, important. Only one VOM/D program reported that this was not an important goal.

Key stakeholder involvement

Victims

Victim participation
According to Van Ness and Strong, the second principle of restorative justice focuses on the extent to which key stakeholders other than the offender are involved in restorative deliberation and agreement processes. This, to a large degree, differentiates restorative conferencing from traditional justice decision-making strategies. The vast majority of programs responding to the survey consider victim participation to be either 'very important' or 'extremely important' (97.1 percent) although, not surprisingly, board programs are slightly less likely than other model types to consider this to be very or extremely important. Although this is predictable, it is worth noting that while the majority of programs indicate that they are either meeting or exceeding their goals in this area, 13.2 percent acknowledge that they are not meeting this goal, a bit higher than the percentage of programs that report not meeting their goal of repairing harm. Programs that say this goal is extremely important are the most likely to report that they are exceeding their goals.

Victim healing
Some literature suggests that victim healing is an important objective of the restorative process (Umbreit, 2001; Zehr, 1990; Van Ness and Strong, 2001). Programs responding to the survey reported that this was an important characteristic and that, for the most part, they felt they were meeting their goals in this area. However, when compared with the results for victim participation, 20 percent fewer programs reported that victim healing was 'very important.' This may suggest that while programs feel victim healing is desirable, it is their participation which is the primary focus of program activities. It may also reflect the sense that since victim healing is such a personal experience, programs do not feel entitled to dictate the degree to which individual victims should undergo a healing process. Alternatively, they may feel less able to achieve this goal or, less generously, feel that the victim is important primarily because of his/her ultimate impact on the offender. Again, it is not surprising that board programs were relatively less likely than other models to report this outcome as very or extremely important.

Victim satisfaction
A final dimension often considered both theoretically and practically important to restorative programs is victim (and offender) satisfaction with the process (Umbreit, 1993, 1996, 1999, 2001; Morris and Maxwell, 2001; Van Ness and Schiff, 2001). When asked how important this was to

their program's mission and how well they thought they were meeting this goal, the majority of conferencing programs responded that it was very or extremely important, and the vast majority felt they were meeting their goals in this area (89.9 percent). Less than 8 percent felt this was somewhat or not very important and those who felt victim satisfaction was extremely important were most likely to be exceeding their goals in this area. Again, board programs were less likely to rate this variable as either very or extremely important than were other program models.

Offenders

Offender participation

When examining the role of the offender, it was more appropriate to ask about actual offender participation than it was about their mere involvement in the process, as conferencing program models cannot, by definition, proceed without the offender's involvement in some way (even if it is not in a direct, face-to-face session). As the presence of the offender does not necessarily imply his/her active and willing participation in the process itself, we were interested in identifying the degree to which programs felt that real participation by the offender was important to their program. All programs considered offender participation to be very important or extremely important (although it was unclear whether programs distinguished between offender presence and active participation when answering this question). Only 2.4 percent of programs felt they were not meeting their goals in this area while 13.5 percent felt they were exceeding them.

Offender reintegration

There are a number of other offender-related characteristics that differentiate restorative from traditional justice processes, including offender reintegration. The majority of programs considered offender reintegration to be either very important or extremely important (87.9 percent), while 12 percent considered this not at all, not very, or somewhat important. Interestingly, compared to other victim and offender-related variables, a relatively high proportion of programs (n=29, 18.4 percent), felt they were not achieving their goals in this area, while 9.5 percent felt they were exceeding them. Also of note, VOM programs were least likely to consider this variable very or extremely important, perhaps because of their long 'pre-restorative' history when this was not considered as important as some other outcomes, or because of their traditionally high attention to victim's, over offender's, needs.

Offender accountability

All programs responding to this question felt that holding offenders accountable was either very important or extremely important. The vast majority of programs felt they were meeting or exceeding their goals in this area (95.1 percent) and there was little variation between program type.

Keeping offenders out of court

We were interested in the extent to which programs felt that keeping offenders out of court was part of their restorative mission. While this is not an explicit indicator of 'restorativeness,' some programs feel this to be an important aspect of their role which may be consistent with the third key principle of developing government/community partnerships that return sanctioning discretion to the community. Just slightly over half (54.7 percent) of survey respondents thought keeping offenders out of court was either very or extremely important, with boards clearly leading the way. Among the 29 programs that felt they were not meeting their goals in this area, 15 (51.2 percent) felt this was a very or extremely important goal; slightly under one-fifth of programs overall felt they were not meeting their goals in this area. While programs clearly did not consider this to be as important as other goals to their restorative mission, the majority of programs felt they were meeting their goals in this area.

Offender punishment

As mentioned earlier, we asked several questions about goals that are not typically associated with restorative conferencing in order to identify the degree to which programs differentiated among restorative and non-restorative goals. Key among such indicators is the extent to which programs consider offender punishment as a central element in their conferencing objectives. Programs clearly felt that offender punishment was less important than most of the explicitly restorative goals, as only 25.2 percent rated it very important or extremely important. Over half of the programs felt this variable was either not at all important or not very important, the highest percentage of any variable rated. This was especially true for multiple practice programs, where 45.5 percent reported that this was not at all important. When compared to other program types, boards were most likely to say this was somewhat, very, or extremely important (although the actual numbers in these categories were very low). Not surprisingly, most programs felt they were meeting or exceeding their goals in this area (93.7 percent) .

Offender rehabilitation

Another variable not traditionally considered restorative, though often interpreted as such, is offender rehabilitation. While many conferencing programs consider this an important component of their work, it is more related to 'treating' or 'helping' the offender, a common component of rehabilitative diversion programs of some decades ago rather than of current restorative strategies. It appears that many programs still consider offender rehabilitation to be an important issue, as 85 percent consider it very or extremely important, however, 21.3 percent of programs feel they are not meeting their goals in this area, a relatively high proportion in comparison to other offender-related restorative goals. Board programs were most likely to report that this was very or extremely important, perhaps because of their focus on the back end or sanctioning phase of the justice process and because of their typical location in correctional agencies where rehabilitation has traditionally been a goal. VOM/D programs were least likely to report offender rehabilitation as very or extremely important. As suggested earlier, it is possible that programs either do not clearly distinguish between offender reintegration and rehabilitation, as the findings on each of these variables are quite similar. Moreover, it is possible that this is an important secondary goal, but that programs feel that the relatively brief encounter of the conference and the limited follow-up provided is insufficient to address rehabilitative goals.

Community

Community involvement
Another key stakeholder not traditionally involved in justice decision-making is the community. While community can have many different interpretations (Crawford and Clear, 2001; Clear and Karp, 1999), in this case we refer to the geographic community in which the event occurred. Overall, a relatively high proportion, almost one-third (31.8 percent), of programs report that community involvement is 'not at all,' 'not very,' or 'somewhat' important. Boards were most likely to report that community involvement was very or extremely important (92.8 percent) while VOM/D programs were least likely to so report (53.3 percent). Hence, it is possible that the overall proportion reflects the large proportion of survey respondents from VOM/D programs which may not consider community involvement in the conferencing process to be part of their programmatic model or intention. However, this may also be an important indicator of the degree to which programs feel they do not 'need' the community to be effective in their work. It may also indicate something about VOM/D programs not viewing volunteer community mediators as representative of 'the community' in general. Forty programs, or just over 25 percent, report that they are not meeting their goals in this area, which is high compared to the number of programs willing to admit they are not meeting their goals with either victims or offenders. In addition, only 4 programs say they are exceeding their goals in this area, which is lower than reported on other key stakeholder dimensions.

Importance of building local community capacity to respond to crime

Some restorative conferencing theorists believe it is important that conferencing build local community capacity to respond to crime (e.g. Clear and Karp, 1999, 2000, 2001). Recent literature on social capital (Putnam, 2000) and collective efficacy (Sampson, Roedenbush, and Earls, 1997; Bazemore, 2000) suggests the relevance of considering whether conferencing programs perceived this as part of their vision and how well they felt they were achieving their goals in this area. About one-fourth of programs felt this was not at all, not very, or somewhat important; the remaining 75 percent expressed that building community capacity was very or extremely important to their program's mission or vision. However, over 40 percent felt they were not achieving their goals in this area, the highest percentage for any question in this section of the survey. Again, boards were most likely to consider this variable to be very or extremely important which is not surprising given the board model's fundamental reliance on community volunteers. Initially, it might seem that the low importance, and perceived achievement, of community capacity-building could be related to the large percentage of VOM/D programs included in this survey because the VOM/D model is not designed to include community members in its conferencing approach. However, VOM/D programs *do* often use community members as volunteer mediators, a potentially important contributor to building local community capacity. We suspect that these results (high importance, low achievement) may be a reflection of the ambiguity of this factor's importance to the theory and practice of conferencing programs as there does not appear to be much consistency about whether programs believe this is, or should be, important to their mission and what to do to carry it out.

Reducing court backlog

Reducing court backlog is not generally associated with restorative programs, although this has often been considered an attribute of diversion and other informal justice decison-making models (e.g. Harrington and Merry, 1988; McGillis, 1997). As such, we were interested in the extent to which restorative programs considered this to be important to their vision and practice. We found that programs did not typically consider this important, as over 60 percent of programs felt this was somewhat, not very, or not at all important; conversely, slightly less than 40 percent considered it very or extremely important. Again, boards were most likely to consider this a very or extremely important goal. Interestingly, despite reporting that this was not an especially important goal, 20.1 percent of programs reported not meeting their goals in this area and 10.1 percent reported exceeding them. This may reflect the ambiguity with which programs view this objective which, although it may be an important justice system goal and perhaps an important 'selling point' for restorative programs, is in fact ancillary to the mission and practice of conferencing.

Summary and discussion

The national inventory

These data suggest that although some may continue to view conferencing as something of a marginal or 'trendy' innovation, our conservative estimate of 773 programs in the current study (which, by the time of this printing, will already be outdated), and the finding that all but three states have a least one program, may indicate a more firm commitment to restorative justice decision-making practices than previously documented. However, although there is generally growing familiarity with conferencing and substantial experimentation with multiple models, there is no evidence regarding the extent to which jurisdictions seek to make conferencing a real alternative for young people even in the most active states. Not surprisingly, most programs utilize the more longstanding VOM/D model. The next most frequently used model, boards, may be a holdover from a pre-restorative justice era, though there is evidence of increasing restorative focus in many board programs.

Current anecdotal evidence suggests that, in some states (e.g. Alabama, Iowa, Montana), conferencing programs may operate as small, ad hoc initiatives in community-based organizations which do not seem to have strong formal relationships to the justice system. In contrast, it appears that some states have strategies designed to encourage experimentation with various conferencing models by providing funding, training and technical assistance (e.g. Pennsylvania, Minnesota, Colorado). In so doing, these states have encouraged the creation of both formal and informal associations of conferencing programs – both regionally and statewide (e.g. The Colorado Forum on Restorative and Community Justice, The Minnesota Restorative Services Coalition).

In addition, although not specific to conferencing, it is interesting to note that informal follow-up telephone interviews conducted during the latter stages of this research suggest increasingly strong awareness of restorative justice principles and practices among juvenile justice professionals. Although several states have embarked on a restorative justice path through legislation and a commitment to a restorative mission such as Balanced and Restorative Justice (with little if any apparent commitment to conferencing (O'Brien, 1999)), knowledge and practice of conferencing mechanisms seems to be becoming more common. This may suggest that restorative decision-making practices are becoming more common despite the absence of standardized policies, procedures, and practices as well as limited mechanisms or strategies for inter-program communication.

The national survey

The intent of our national survey was to identify what characterizes the administration, process, vision, and practice of restorative conferencing programs. The data presented here describe some basic characteristics that distinguish restorative conferencing programs both from one another and from more traditional justice system initiatives. To some degree, these also reflect the emerging conceptual and empirical literature from which such programs have emanated.

What the data suggest in the context of restorative justice principles

Repairing harm

The data presented here suggest that nearly all programs responding to the survey felt that repairing harm was an important goal and the vast majority felt they were meeting or exceeding their goals in this area. If following-up with victims and offenders can be considered an element of repairing harm, these data suggest that most programs are focusing on the completion of agreements as a means of seeing that harm is repaired. On average, around three-quarters of programs reported that they were following-up with both victims and offenders, although less than one-third reported following up with community members, on average. Just under four-fifths report that they monitor completion of the reparative agreements which would support an emphasis on repairing harm. A similar percentage report following-up to ensure completion of restitution, again suggesting a focus on repairing harm.

Stakeholder involvement

Of particular importance here is the number of persons present at a conference, which ranges from about 5.5 to almost 12, and averages about 7 people per conference. This clearly suggests the presence of parties other than simply the victim and the offender, and while survey data indicate slightly lower rates of active participation among these parties, it does suggest the relatively consistent inclusion of additional parties in the process. Moreover, the vast majority of programs feel that victim and offender participation is very important or extremely important and that they are, for the most part, meeting their goals in those respects. While slightly fewer programs indicate the importance of community involvement, it remains true that almost 70 percent of programs still report that this is very or extremely important, although they appear to have somewhat more trouble meeting goals in this area. The vast majority of programs also report that victim healing is an important goal and that they are, for the most part, meeting their goals in this area.

Some insight into assessing the degree to which such additional parties are *actively* included in the process is gained by looking at who is making the key decisions about the conference process and structure. Specifically, the data indicate that the mediator/facilitator is most likely to be making decisions about where to hold the meeting, although this is perhaps more likely to be a function of experience, access to resources, and familiarity with the process than it is of exclusion or oversight. Most programs still empower the offender to speak first, although there is some debate about best practice in the field about choosing who should speak first. While some programs prefer to have the offender acknowledge and explain his/her actions before the conference goes further, others prefer that the victim be offered the opportunity to fully describe the impact of the harm and the effect it had before participants have heard from the offender. There is some concern that hearing the offender speak may dilute the impact of the victim's words as sympathy may have been generated for the offender's life, circumstances, and/or actions (for a more complete discussion, see Chapter 5).

The data also indicate that slightly over half of the programs use surrogate victims when the actual victim is unable or unwilling to participate. This is, potentially, an indication of programs' intention to be as inclusive as possible and to involve persons from the community to provide the 'voice' of the victim or represent victims and their interests whenever and however possible. However, about half the programs responding to this question said they did not use surrogate victims. While these data cannot explain program behavior in this regard, it suggests possible dispute about the benefits of this practice for conference participants who may not respond to or be affected by the stories of those whose experiences are not directly related to their own. On the other hand, it is quite possible that it simply reflects limited resources to locate and encourage victims of other crimes to participate and share their stories. This would be a valuable area for clarification in future research as the importance of this has not been studied empirically.

According to these data, most programs are staffed by volunteers and have limited paid staff. While this suggests community involvement in the program, if not in the conferences themselves, it does not necessarily suggest anything about the potential community building role of the program. Given that agencies seem to be unclear about their community building roles, this may suggest more community building than is apparent on the surface. It is also possible that the presence of community members in the program is not at all indicative of broad community participation, but rather is limited to a select few volunteers who are dedicated to the program and its work, but are not representative of the broader community nor its goals and who may, consciously or not, make it difficult for newcomers to become engaged. Moreover, the program may not be committed to increasing community involvement, but rather to keeping a small group of reliable volunteers committed to the program and the work. (The role of volunteers and other participants in bringing conferencing and restorative justice to other venues is considered in Chapters 5 and 6.)

Transforming the relationship between government and community

As most conferencing programs are housed in private agencies but funded by government, this creates an opportunity for governments to empower communities to initiate and manage processes responsive to their own needs. While these data say nothing about the extent to which this is actually occurring, it does suggest an opportunity to consciously and conscientiously choose such a relationship.

Most referrals clearly come from government sources (i.e. probation, judges, law enforcement) suggesting some form of partnership between governmental justice agencies and private, community-based organizations. However, many programs (especially family group conferencing) are housed in police and/or probation agencies, suggesting that the work has not been turned over to local non-governmental organizations. This may be tempered by the fact that many such agencies use community volunteers to perform the work as volunteer facilitators or board members.

Building local community capacity to respond to crime seems to be an ambiguous aspect of restorative conferencing programs, as there is more variation about the importance of this dimension as well as program capacity to meet it than among other, more straightforward victim and offender variables. Despite almost unanimous support for more clear-cut restorative goals of reparation and involvement, community-building showed the weakest overall commitment in both vision and practice. Programs were most likely to acknowledge being unable to meet goals in this area, which may reflect a number of causes. It is possible that this results from uncertainty regarding the relevance of this to their own program and hence it is unclear whether, and to what extent, this should be included in program mission. A competing explanation is that this is an especially difficult dimension to identify and measure, and hence programs are unsure about how to recognize it when it is indeed occurring and, subsequently, how to measure the degree of its presence. At the same time, given that there are few models for how to achieve this goal, programs may be unsure how to develop and maintain this capacity as they must 'learn as they go' to a large extent.

Conclusions

The information presented here is the only data available about conferencing programs in the United States that directly reports what program directors from a variety of conferencing models say about their practices. Until now there has been little more than anecdotal evidence from individual programs or program models (e.g. VOM/D) that uncovers the day-to-day practical world of restorative conferencing. These data offer a composite picture of 'what's going on out there' beyond the limited margins of individual program or practice.

Limitations, concluding remarks and next steps

This exploratory research provides previously unavailable macro-level information about the number, types, and distribution of restorative conferencing programs in the US. By identifying where such programs are located, target populations, and service provision strategies, it becomes increasingly possible to characterize the breadth and scope of restorative conferencing programs nationwide.

There are, however, several limitations of this research. With the national inventory, it is likely that our exploratory sampling approach resulted in underestimating the actual number of programs in use and hence may have skewed some of the findings. Moreover, the problem of respondents self-identifying their program as an example of restorative conferencing with little opportunity to confirm the degree of consistency with restorative principles leaves room for mis-characterization and inappropriate counting of programs. The fact that there are now many programs calling themselves restorative suggests a need to examine programs against some criteria for 'restorativeness' both in program vision and in reality. While the survey data enable us to better compare and contrast program characteristics and models on various dimensions of commitment to, and achievement of, restorative goals and objectives, this remains an ambiguous aspect of restorative justice theory and research.

The response rate to our national survey was somewhat lower than we had hoped for and, as a result, numbers in some of the individual reporting categories are quite small. As such, it is difficult to make broad generalizations about restorative conferencing from this group and we must qualify that these findings may not be representative of *all* restorative conferencing programs nationwide. Also, in the interest of developing the most comprehensive survey possible, some of the questions became quite complex which may have deterred some recipients from either completing the survey or, more importantly, completing it reliably. While we are concerned that this affected the response rate, we are more concerned about the quality of the information as we suspect some respondents may have been less thoughtful about their responses than we would have hoped for. Lastly, we had to eliminate some survey questions from the analysis as the data were too ambiguous to interpret with certainty which left some gaps in our analysis (e.g. pre-conferencing contact with participants). In the end, however, there is considerable reason for optimism about the results presented here.

These data help us understand the number of programs around the country and the degree to which they are emerging 'organically' or as imitations or modifications of other, related programs. While there are clearly some basic model prototypes, there are also many departures created to suit local jurisdictional needs. The extent of these variations, the purposes they serve and their effectiveness are critical questions for understanding the nature and degree of restorative innovation. Such information would be helpful to understand the extent to which existing conferencing programs tend to follow standard practice guidelines or adapt to suit individual jurisdictional and stakeholder needs. That is, while conferencing practices should be community-driven and reflect the character of their native communities, many newly initiated programs are modeled directly after programs in other communities and localities. This certainly does not indicate a problem as programs *should* learn from one another, although it does suggest that new conferencing developments are, at least initially, less likely to be organic products of the community and more likely to reflect practices and procedures initiated elsewhere. The degree to which it is possible to understand the evolution of restorative conferencing practices may make it easier to identify what practices are best suited for what types of environment.

One of the most significant contributions of this research is that it helps clarify important gaps in current knowledge and offers important guidance for future research. Specifically, it would be beneficial for subsequent research to follow-up on our survey by addressing key questions specific to principle-based evaluation in restorative justice. That is, a subsequent survey might better address principle-specific questions in the context of stages, or phases, of the conference process. While this was, to some degree, accomplished in the current survey, knowledge gained from this experience, and especially from the qualitative sections of this research, would help hone subsequent survey questions. Most importantly, research that more closely examines the critical relationship between theory of intervention and practical application could potentially revolutionize how process and outcomes connected to restorative conferencing are interrelated.

In terms of process, these data also help us understand programs' perceptions of their relationships and interactions with key stakeholders, communities, and/or between governments and communities, in the context of restorative intervention. We believe it is critical to understand and evaluate the process from the perspectives of *all* the key stakeholders, not simply conferencing practitioners, and not simply in terms of understanding the offender's behavior and then aiming to punish or fix it accordingly. This research begins to surface some of these questions in an effort to pave the way for subsequent, more in-depth research.

In the end, justifying the reallocation of government and community resources to fund new or ongoing restorative projects requires, first and foremost, basic information on the availability, structure and generalizability of such schemes. The absence of this data makes it virtually impossible to effectively coordinate resources to implement new programs or to cultivate existing ones. Reliable information about conferencing programs is vital both for identifying and supporting viable programs and for refining, redirecting, or relinquishing ineffectual ones. In general, this additional information is expected to provide a better understanding of juvenile conferencing programs nationwide, how these organizations and programs operate in practice, and the type of barriers and impediments that they collectively face. Ultimately, the overarching purpose of this information is to enable more responsive and supportive juvenile justice policy-making while at the same time facilitating community–government partnerships nationwide.

Notes

1 Moreover, in the period between when this information was gathered and its publication in this volume it is likely some new programs have emerged while others have been terminated.
2 Charge categories are not mutually exclusive and therefore add to more than 181. Programs may, and do, accept multiple charges types. Table 3.3 depicts whether the type of charge is accepted *at all*, not whether it is predominant.
3 Note that in the juvenile court the terminology is slightly different than that for adult cases processed in the criminal court. In the juvenile system, an adjudication is the stage of the process that is comparable to a conviction/ acquittal in the adult court. The disposition in juvenile court is comparable to the sentence in the adult system.

Chapter 4

Methodology for the qualitative study and description of conference stages and phases

Overview of study conceptualization

Previous evaluation research has provided a great deal of empirical evidence that conferencing yields good outcomes for offenders and victims relative to other interventions (Schiff, 1999; Umbreit, 2001; Bazemore, 2000; Braithwaite, 2002). Yet this research has not been designed to test inferences about the relative effectiveness of various competing strategies used in conferencing practice. For example, many practitioners believe strongly that face-to-face preparation of victim and offender is essential to good conferencing outcomes while others do not. Some believe that it is important to have the victim speak first in the conference while others argue equally strongly for having the offender go first. Some believe that including only the victim and offender in conferences will yield the most effective outcomes for both, while others argue strongly that either supporters of the victim and offender, or representatives of the broader community, or both, provide the most effective mix of participants. There are numerous examples of such micro-level practice variations in the restorative conferencing movement, as well as middle-range policy choices that may have significant implications for conferencing outcomes. One can find practitioners who make strong logical arguments for a specific approach based on normative preference or strong beliefs about the effectiveness of this strategy. There is, however, little if any empirical evidence to support any of these positions.

Though some researchers view such distinctions as the minutiae of practice and therefore not relevant to broader policy or theoretical concerns, many of these differences in practice priorities are interesting precisely because they are grounded in a commitment to different philosophical positions and/or theories of how to achieve stakeholder transformation. It is these theories that we believe allow researchers to address broader concerns about the role of victims, offenders, and community in non-adversarial justice decision-making.

Testing such propositions, however, is not the goal of the current study. Indeed, we suggest that such tests would be very difficult at this time because to date these practice and process distinctions and the various theories of intervention they seem to operationalize have yet to be thoroughly analyzed and catalogued. Our focus in this exploratory study is therefore to describe and categorize variation in conferencing practice protocols as they relate to various restorative justice philosophies, competing commitments to specific principals, and competing theories of intervention. In addition, though we cannot in this small, qualitative study capture the entire range of conferencing practice, we also hope to identify variations with direct implications for new intervention theory or modification of existing theories. Such theories, based on various restorative principles, can be used to develop grounded propositions for guiding future research aimed at improving practice, while also increasing our ability to generalize theory and research in restorative justice. As noted in Chapter 1, the more general focus for this study is an examination of consistency in vision and practice with restorative justice principles. This concern with 'restorativeness' – as indicated by the extent to which the 'vision' or what practitioners *say* they are trying to do, lines up with the reality of what they actually do and with restorative principles – is an overarching concern of this study.

The qualitative case study design

The findings presented in the qualitative portion of this report are based upon the results of a qualitative case study research design (Yin, 1994; Patton, 1990). More specifically, the research design is a *pragmatic case study* (Fishman, 1999), the primary aim of which is to build theory aimed at improving both practice and research. At the national level, we view this multi-method research as broadly focused on the 'case' of restorative conferencing as an innovation in informal decision-making in the response to youth crime.

The national case study also includes multiple embedded case studies (Yin, 1994) focused on specific issues and concerns addressed in various stages and phases of the conferencing process. These stages and phases help make sense out of the conference as a whole, and they are described in more detail in the final section of this chapter. The primary unit of analysis for these descriptive studies is the application of restorative principles at various stages and phases of the conference. Secondary units of analysis include the intermediate outcomes that appear to link various intervention theories applied by conferencing practitioners more or less logically to conferencing practice on the one hand and long-term outcomes on the other. Finally, though we are less interested in variation between conferencing models (Bazemore and Umbreit, 2001; McCold, 2000), we are interested in program models to the extent that they operationalize competing theories of intervention. However, given the adaptation of models and blending of various processes we have witnessed and documented in the national survey, we are also secondarily interested in individual programs as they combine model types and develop new theories of intervention to fit these hybridized practice adaptations.

While we seek a broad and inclusive approach rather than an intensive focus on one or two programs, the approach is nonetheless ethnographic in its stance toward naturalistic and appreciative, rather than evaluative, data collection and analysis (Lofland and Lofland, 1995; Patton, 1990). *Appreciative* in the ethnographic sense means we hope to gain an understanding of social action *in context* based on a non-judgemental, descriptive account of events, processes and theories of participation in the terms and frame of reference of those applying them. We are concerned for diversity in practice, initially for the sake of describing variation, but in the analysis stage for the purpose of describing how actors create meaning and develop their own theories of action in the context of restorative decision-making.

For the purposes of this study, we hope to remain open to what Braithwaite (1999) described as 'optimistic' and 'pessimistic' accounts of restorative justice while remaining skeptical of both (see also Harrington and Merry, 1988). Though we have not set out to prove that the restorative conferencing movement is simply a ploy to extend formal social control (Cohen, 1985; Abel, 1982), we are open to evidence that suggests that restorative conferencing programs may be little more than 'trivialized diversion projects' that may be widening the net of formal control. However, we remain open to the possibility that in these projects, and in the restorative justice movement, there may be 'less than meets the eye,' but also *more* (see Bazemore, 2000). We have attempted to remain open to this range of conclusions in this study by use of multiple methods including participation observation, informal and structured interviews, focus groups, and use of secondary documents, while relying on a diverse group of research participants and key informants. We also employed a multi-level and multi-dimensional sampling procedure that we believe helps to compensate for the lack of depth in this relatively brief study by providing a more inclusive and textured depiction.

Sampling

In a national study that required a focus on specific conferencing programs, it was important to make strategic sampling decisions to achieve both quality and diversity of practice in programs and individuals chosen for observation and interviews. To accomplish this, our survey strategy included three sampling 'layers' and several criteria for selection.

Practitioner telephone interviews in eight states

Based on the researchers' previous experience as well as on findings from our national inventory, we first selected eight states that could claim at least a few conferencing programs with multiple years of experience and a relatively substantial caseload. From these states, we chose practitioners that had responded to our national survey, were known to the researchers as directors of well-established programs, and/or were recommended by other restorative justice leaders as directors of exemplary programs. From this group, 15 respondents from programs representing all models of interest were identified for in-depth telephone interviews.

National focus group sample

Another group of eight program practitioners, identified in a similar way and exclusive of those from programs in our two case study sites discussed below, were chosen to participate in a national focus group. For this group of program directors we sought the most experienced practitioners representing a range of program models, and sought to the greatest extent possible to represent programs ranging in size from various regions and states.

Case study site focus group

A separate focus group was held for eight practitioners representing the programs in our two case study sites. While we used the same protocol for both groups and view both as having national implications, this group for the most part represented a more experienced group of conferencing program directors.

Case study sites

Geographic regions in two states were chosen as case sites for on-site observation and other short-term ethnographic work. Minnesota (primarily the Minneapolis/St Paul area) and Colorado (primarily the Denver/Boulder region) were chosen because of their relatively long-standing commitment to restorative justice and the diversity of programs and models represented within an accessible geographic region. Minnesota was a very early innovator in restorative decision-making practices and is one of only a handful of states experimenting actively with peace-making circles (Pranis, 1997, 2001). Colorado, as a relative newcomer, has a comparatively short but extensive history of training and funding for restorative conferencing programs. Both feature statewide and regional coalitions that sponsor training forums and numerous city and county practitioner support groups.

The program sample

Four programs were chosen for intensive observation in each site because they represented relatively established efforts (at least a year of operation and, on average, several years) and reflected the diversity of program models characteristic of each region. However, because neither program nor program model is the primary unit of analysis for the study we devote little attention in this report to detailed program description. Rather, we are more concerned with programs as a context for learning as much as possible about practice and theory variations. The important issue of programs in the larger system and community context is an exception to this rule which is addressed in Chapter 7.

In choosing program sites, we were interested in representing the diversity of models (with a special concern to profile circles), but were also interested in examining programs that varied in organizational location (part of police, court/probation, or community-based agencies). We sought out programs that, though possibly relatively new, had well-established procedures, a sound management structure, and a stable case flow (the latter became a problem when low referral rates plagued two programs in the middle of the observational period). Case study programs in Minnesota included: a police-based conferencing program; a community-based peace-making circle program in an urban African American neighborhood; a victim–offender mediation/dialogue program housed in a county probation department; a second circle only briefly observed because of its generally lower level of juvenile referral and a very recent intensive ethnographic study of this program (Coates et al., 2000); and a combination circle and family group conferencing program located in a state juvenile facility that provides reentry conferences designed to help young offenders make the transition back to their communities of residence (this program was profiled through intensive interviews and review of program materials only). Colorado programs include: a modified family group conferencing program in a non-profit organization housed in a local police department; a prosecution-based neighborhood accountability board program in the city of Denver; a police-based and operated traditional FGC program; and a probation-based community conferencing/FGC.

Data collection

To enhance our field presence and increase the number of interviews and observational time at our case study programs, we hired on-site local researchers in each region who were familiar with restorative justice programs and the juvenile justice systems serving these regions. In both intensive case study sites, these researchers were able to gain ongoing access to restorative justice program practitioners and justice system officials for a limited period of approximately two to four months in each site. In addition to interviews and other tasks such as attending pertinent practitioner meetings and training events, the researchers also observed a number of conferences. On average, three observations of each program were conducted, although a couple of programs were observed only once. In addition, the principal investigators also observed a handful of conferences in each site, though because of limited time in each jurisdiction on each visit our observations were weighted towards programs that were more easily accessible and boasted larger caseloads (two circle programs that were able to schedule circles around our visits were exceptions to the larger caseload rule).

Data analysis

Analytic techniques include thematic coding of interview and observational data. Qualitative coding involved selection of interview, focus group, and observational content consistent with one or more dimensions of each core restorative justice principle. In this way, we utilize practitioner discourse, as well as observational findings and written program material, as data indicating how staff engage each core principle in each stage and phase of the conferencing effort. We then sorted and categorized by different expressions of *vision* regarding how the principle is *operationalized* in the conferencing setting. Note that when quoting statements by individual practitioners throughout this volume, we generally do not identify those practitioners either by name or by program. This is primarily to ensure the anonymity of our practitioners in order to protect the integrity of both the practitioner and the program and to ensure that they would be as forthcoming as possible. Program intentions, staff, resources, and other things may have changed since this data collection effort, and practitioners may no longer abide by some of these references or may no longer even be associated with the same programs. We felt obligated to the practitioners and programs who were willing to participate in this effort by being as accommodating and respectful of these issues as possible.

Generalization and limitations on external validity

As a result of the program sampling difficulties noted earlier, our data on each program is not as extensive, nor as deep, as we had originally anticipated. Therefore it is certainly not possible to say whether the conferences observed here are in any way representative of typical conferences for the program in question. It is even less appropriate to conclude that case studies are representative of a particular conferencing model or that the quality of the conference is typical of a given model or the program observed.

To those familiar with the potential breakthroughs and at times astounding resolutions associated with some conferences, these conferencing descriptions may also be unsatisfying, troubling, or at best lackluster. The sometimes astounding stories of resolutions and unanticipated positive outcomes under adverse circumstances presented in media accounts and some popular literature on restorative justice are no less valid than the more mundane accounts of conferences presented here. As true stories which indicate the possibilities in restorative justice resolutions, the more dramatic accounts serve an important cultural function, acting as a counterpoint to the far more typical media horror stories of violent crimes that invite audiences to embrace extreme, fear-based responses (Pranis, 2001). While we briefly share some of these stories of dramatic impact from cases in our study sites, we focus most of our attention on cases observed in the course of this study. We present these encounters as closely as possible to the way in which they occurred and do not attempt to exaggerate their significance.

Potential contributions to theory and practice

Our observations suggest that day-to-day practice is generally more mundane, and also illustrates problems in real-world decision-making, even in the most experienced programs. Just as we cannot say that our conferences are typical, we cannot say with any certainty that the conferences observed are *atypical* (and some program directors we asked said they were not). But making such statements is not our goal.

Rather, our purpose in presenting observational data is illustrative in that we hope to create profiles of a broader set of problems and issues, as well as productive resolutions. We do not therefore treat these observations as 'samples,' but as case study examples that reveal problems and solutions that have broader generalization, as well as heuristic value. Observations therefore often illustrate an important principle or concept that can be used to make inferences to intervention theories (Yin, 1994; Patton, 1990). Finally, we also recognize that our analysis and presentation of certain conferences or parts of conferences, to some degree, takes these incidents out of context by removing them to some extent from the practical constraints on decision-making in a given encounter.

Our most general conclusion about the case studies presented is that they are complex. This is to say, it is possible that certain aspects of the encounter in a given conference (perhaps in the pre-conference or introductory phase) could be viewed by most standards as examples of sound practice, while at the same time, other elements (perhaps the conference agreement) stand as examples of bad practice. Because we are not practitioners, it is not our role in any case to critique practice. Our goal is instead to describe what we see and then generalize to broader theories about how participants 'do the business' of conference decision-making. In doing so, we also hope to portray the sense of meaning these participants attach to this work and to the theories *they* employ to make sense of it.

One conclusion from our discussion of the diverse array of possible theories-in-use in the restorative conferencing movement presented in Chapter 2 is that there are no universally agreed upon standards for conferences as a whole. At this early stage of the restorative justice conferencing movement, this is not a bad thing because such standards should hopefully be based upon empirical evidence suggesting that some practices will yield better outcomes than others. Though research cannot tell us much about practice choices at this time, to the extent that the current work spurs impact studies that contrast the relative impact of practices based on competing principles and theories of intervention, practice standards may be developed based on empirical evidence rather than simply on normative judgements.

Characteristics of programs in the qualitative case study: a profile

In the final weeks of our data collection (February and March 2002), we developed a brief descriptive profile of programs included in our case study. In addition to programs in our case study sites in Minnesota and Colorado we contacted a select group of program directors who had participated in our national focus group, and a purposive sample of the group of program directors interviewed for the national study. Of the possible 24 potential interviewees, we chose 15 programs that we knew continued to have steady case referrals and had not experienced any major disruption in program management. We sought first to maximize diversity in program model and size.

Of those selected, 13 were able to participate in follow-up interviews aimed at getting a timely profile of caseload characteristics. In addition, we were interested in profiling these programs, chosen in part because of their reputation for their sound practice on such characteristics as victim participation and the scope of program responsibility vis-à-vis formal criminal justice agencies (e.g. the court, the police). We also sought to get responses to a set of questions about the priorities of these programs that asked them to rank the importance of several outcomes. These outcomes should be viewed as primary goals to be achieved at the end of the conference and more long-term outcomes to be achieved in the months after the conference.

After sending the questions in advance to allow respondents time to compile the necessary data and also to think about their priorities for conferencing goals, we conducted telephone interviews that lasted approximately 30–45 minutes. The findings provide a descriptive profile of the current state of these programs. The data on the programs presented here was compiled by program staff for the period of time from January 2001 to January 2002. While not intended to represent a national picture (see Chapter 3), these profile data represent the programs in our qualitative study.

Rate of referrals

Overall, programs in the qualitative study served a relatively small number of clients. The average number of cases that were processed by each program on a monthly basis was 9.8. This varied greatly among the programs, with a low average of 1 case per month to a high of 35 per month. The number of cases handled depended somewhat on the type of program model utilized. Circles were the least able to handle large numbers of cases while the family group conferencing programs had the highest number of cases on average (25).

Seriousness and source of referrals

Overall, programs in our qualitative study handled predominately minor cases. First, on average, only 17 per cent of the cases conferenced in these programs in the past year were for felony offenses. Programs ranged from a high of about 35 per cent felony cases to a low of no felony cases. In fact, the mean percentage was reduced somewhat by the fact that in three of the programs in the interview sample only misdemeanor cases are eligible. However, one program discussed extensively in the qualitative findings in Chapters 5–7 whose conferencing cases include approximately 65 per cent felony offenders was not included in this volume because its director could not be scheduled for the follow-up interviews. The overall proportion of felony cases conferenced in this small sample of programs was furthered diminished by the absence of another program that has reported rates of felony cases as high as 75 per cent in recent years.

Second, another indicator of the seriousness of cases is the proportion of first offenders conferenced. On average, 68 per cent of program cases conferenced in the year 2001 were first offenders, ranging from a low of 15 per cent to a high of 100 per cent. Again, the fact that three programs were prohibited from taking offenders with priors lowered this average somewhat. Given the history of using victim–offender mediation and dialogue for more chronic (and on average more serious) offenders documented in the 1980s and 1990s (Umbreit, 1999, 2001), and more recent use of conferencing for serious offenders in other countries (Maxwell and Morris, 2001), this seems to reflect a bias toward less serious cases in this group of programs.

Finally, another possible indicator of the seriousness level of all cases from a system perspective is the proportion of conferenced offenses that were referred to the program pre-court as diversion cases. On average, conferencing programs included in this sample received 71 per cent of their cases pre-court as diversion cases. This percentage ranged from a low of 5 per cent to a high of 100 per cent, although most of the programs were in the 60–90 per cent range. This pre-court use of conferencing may indicate a willingness to deal with these cases before they progress further into the system.

Exceptions to this general trend among the programs in our qualitative samples that tend to demonstrate the capacity of conferencing for dealing with more serious and chronic offenders are discussed extensively in various chapters of this volume. However, overall it must be concluded that these programs tend to focus on less chronic and less serious offenses and cases that might not otherwise be considered for court processing. Again, this pattern does not necessarily reflect the national picture with regard to conferencing programs for juveniles (see Chapter 3). It does appear to be consistent with a recent national pattern of a general increase in the proportion of first offenders and non-felony offenders being committed to more secure programs in some states and a likely concomitant increase in lower-level cases being referred to diversion programs and probation (e.g. Fader et al., 2001; Krisberg and Patino, 2004).

Victim involvement and representation

As suggested throughout this volume, victim participation is an essential component of restorative justice conferencing. In general, programs in our qualitative sample do a good job of ensuring victim involvement. Victims participate in the conference on average 63 per cent of the time. Participation rates range from a low of 10 per cent to a high of 99 per cent (the 10 per cent case was a circle which often conducted separate 'healing circles' for victims who did not wish at that time to meet with the offender). In addition, in those cases in which victims do not directly participate in the conference, victim representation is achieved in some programs by the inclusion of surrogates in the conference who attempt to represent the victim directly or the victim's 'voice' in general. Of the programs in our small sample, surrogate victims were present in the conference in 42 per cent of the cases where the actual victim did not participate during the year 2001.

Conference roles and responsibility

Agreements

A key issue for conferencing programs once they receive a referral is how much discretion is granted them to accomplish certain tasks related to developing agreements, calculating the nature and type of restitution and community service, and monitoring these agreements. The conferencing programs we interviewed seem, for the most part, to be what might be called 'full-service' programs. With only three exceptions, conference participants in these programs are allowed to determine the amount of and schedule for restitution and community service and to determine the type and location of community service – as well as the type of service to be completed. The exceptions are programs in which the amount of restitution may be ordered by the court or other entity prior to the conference. These tend to be programs that take the majority of their referrals post-disposition.

Conferencing stages and phases: an overview and dialogue

In analyzing restorativeness, we pay special attention here to *stages and phases* of conferences. We focus on three more or less structural components, or *stages*, that appear common to all conferences: *preparation* or pre-conferencing, the *conferencing process* itself, and *follow-up*.

The existence and nature of *phases* within the conferencing process itself is more controversial than is true of the stages. In reality, practitioners may not think much about conference phases at all. Alternatively, they may have very nuanced understandings of events that need to occur within the conference before participants can move forward to another part of the conference. For most practitioners, at least one or two milestones or transitions appear to be viewed as essential to the momentum, and ultimately to the overall success of the conference. From a restorative perspective, for example, the principle of repair requires that conference participants first seek to answer the question: what is the harm and then how do we repair it, before developing an agreement and assigning responsibilities for this repair (Zehr, 1990). While we believe there is some variation between models – circles, for example, tend to separate phases into discrete meetings – training and general conferencing literature and our work thus far suggests that five basic transitions tend to characterize conferences representing a wide range of processes and models. These are described below and, following this description, a dialogue with a group of experienced practitioners in one of our focus groups illustrates how practitioners define and think about the phases, or critical steps, necessary to move successfully through the conferencing process.

Conferencing phases in use: an overview

Introduction and creating safe space

One of the most important functions of the conference facilitator is to define the purpose of the meeting, establish ground rules and expectations, and create a sense of comfort and safety. In addition to these basic requirements to promote open and meaningful communication, facilitators may also employ one or more rituals to ease tensions and help participants make the transition from the outside environment to a space for respectful dialogue and problem-solving. While victim and offender may remain anxious in anticipation of what is to come, what seems to make this phase complete is when participants have been introduced and their role clarified (e.g. victim, offender, family member, observer) and when the facilitator senses that there is comfort with and understanding of purpose, as well as a general readiness to move forward.

Telling the story

This is perhaps the most essential phase of a conference because it allows the group to take collective inventory of the harm caused by the offense. Victims must relay their story of the harm and family and community members may talk about how they were affected; the latter is especially critical in the case of a crime without a direct individual victim or when the actual victim is not present in the conference. The offender typically also relays his story of the crime, possibly addressing the issue of motive, or answering the commonly posed question, 'what were you thinking about?' If storytelling is rushed or de-emphasized, it is likely to impact the quality of an agreement, or the ability to complete an agreement at all. The group is generally ready to proceed to the next phase when the offender has given a clear account of his behavior and acknowledged some acceptable degree of responsibility, and the victim has described the impact of the incident on his/her life.

Mutual victim/offender acknowledgement and community validation and input

This phase generally constitutes a brief transition between storytelling and agreement phases. It may provide a space for more elaborate clarification of the victim's statement of harm, for developing clarity about acknowledgement of the offender's acceptance of responsibility and/or role in the offense, and for inviting other stakeholders to reflect on harm to them or to other stakeholders. If he has not already apologized, the offender may take the opportunity to do so, or otherwise indicate remorse. The victim may question why he/she was chosen by the offender, acknowledge the offender for his honesty or acceptance of responsibility or, in some cases, question the offender's honesty or sincerity. Community members may elaborate on the harm and/or validate or raise questions about victim and offender comments. Victim and offender may remain far apart in their views and need not 'bond' at any time or even completely agree in order for the conference to be judged successful. However, the conclusion of this transition phase seems to be marked by some change in the original stance of both victim and offender and an indication of increased understanding of the other's position.

Agreement

The agreement is the written contract meant to specify the obligation of the offender and to clarify the roles of other stakeholders in ensuring its completion. To proceed with this phase, stakeholders and the facilitator need to have a sense of the nature of the harm, of the needs of victim and offender, and of the offender's acceptance of responsibility. Based on this assessment of who and what has been harmed, this phase addresses the question of how to repair the harm and who is responsible. The two basic steps in developing a reparative agreement are: (1) getting victim, offender, and other group members to come up with ways to make things right that meet stakeholder needs; and (2) developing a concrete plan that defines specific roles for stakeholders in repairing the harm. The agreement is written up by the facilitator and then generally signed by participants before leaving the conference setting.

Celebration

Most conferences make time at the end of the conference itself for sharing of refreshments as an informal conclusion of the conference. Some practitioners view this time as very important because it allows an informal opportunity for participants to meet and perhaps build relationships, while facilitators may draft the formal agreement for signature.

The conferencing process: a dialogue on phases

Before discussing the application of restorative principles within the various phases of the conference itself, it is important to note that there is some debate around the importance of these phases. Practitioners may disagree somewhat about which ones must be accomplished or completed to achieve a successful result. Phases and the need to move through them raise issues of the extent to which conferencing is a linear, goal-driven process focused on a specific goal, i.e. the reparative agreement, or a more organic process-driven initiative. Use of scripts and the distinction between conferencing strategy, facilitator control, and possible 'coaching' of participants, or what may appear to be manipulation of conferencing outcomes, are also pertinent to the issue of conferencing phases.

Roles of dialogue and the facilitator's role

While many emphasize the importance of ground rules and having a sense of progression, some generally more experienced practitioners emphasize a naturalistic flow and the supreme importance of 'trusting in the process.' Commenting on the need to move forward strategically in the conference, while not being overly restrictive about prohibiting conversation in certain phases, one FGC program director reported that: 'I've had facilitators cut people off if they start to talk about restitution [in one of the earlier conference phases] and say "we will talk about that later" . . . this is not a 1-2-3 process. Human beings do not go 1-2-3.' Another coordinator of a similar program agreed, noting that: 'We have an outline – [but we] can't stop the flow – we allow questions/stories to be told when we establish a safe place.'

For a school conferencing program director, phases in a conference are most appropriately marked by the basic questions that must be addressed in the effort to repair harm: 'The most obvious break [between phases] is between Zehr's three questions: What is the harm?; How do you repair it?; Who is responsible? – in writing the agreement, you also want to reflect a wider collective understanding.'

A VOM director from Alaska supported the idea of not adhering too strictly to phases in the conference:

> . . . when I do trainings I spend a lot of time with people on having them think about becoming very comfortable within themselves with chaos, and not having to go through a particular step . . . it is important to sort of take your parties as you find them at any particular moment in the process and not be married to a process . . . we need to try to get them (facilitators) to think in a non-linear fashion.

On the other hand, the line may not be so clear between manipulation and attention to conference strategy that will help participants begin to move forward. Facilitators must be prepared to strike a balance by being willing to give up power:

> Sometimes a facilitator can *create an opening* for understandings to be reached, and if this happens the agreement phase is a breeze. As facilitators, we try to project direction . . . [but we] must be careful not to get too much of ourselves into the process (to) make sure things go along.

This same community conferencing director also noted that there may be a happy medium between strict adherence to phase protocols and unstructured dialogue with no boundaries or objectives:

> We work a little more from a script [than some other programs] . . . in the opening phase we create a safe space. In storytelling, we have to get specific about harm and effect. We do not cut people off – but we have an agenda to move people to readiness for agreement . . . the signal [for that] is spontaneous apology and acceptance.

According to the director of a NAB program, phases vary from committee to committee, but the sign for knowing when to move on is what seems to be a change in the tone and feeling of the conference: 'What they all look for is that miracle. They begin to work together and they grow.' Another agreed that the neighborhood quality of boards creates a great deal of diversity, but also noted that most boards move through phases in a more linear and methodical way. One board director justified not tampering with what she felt was an at times overly routinized approach as a way to make sure critical phases are not skipped, while a conferencing director in a comment that followed her point suggested that a script may actually help avoid the tendency to move too quickly to the more concrete agreement phase and thereby avoid important dialogue that may address emotional issues:

> . . . we use a script but never follow it word for word. [The script] certainly helps the community people because no matter how much time I spend training them, everybody wants to skip forward to the making-it-better [phase], like right away. We have a script but I don't use it except to open and close . . . It is there as a guide to make sure all the main questions are asked . . . In case someone else is there and not me doing it.

Summary and conclusions

This chapter has detailed elements of the methodology used to structure the qualitative portion of this study. In particular, we used a pragmatic case study design with multiple embedded case studies to examine variation in conferencing protocols linked with various restorative theories of intervention. Our goal was to examine the consistency of vision with practice in conferencing programs specific to the three key principles of restorative intervention (repairing harm, involving key stakeholders, transforming the community–government relationship with regard to justice processes). We described the various stages and phases of the conference, and how these informed our primary unit of analysis, the application of restorative principles at these various stages and phases.

Chapter 5

Repairing harm in the conferencing environment

The principle of repair – justice requires that we work to heal victims, offenders and communities that have been injured by crime.

(Van Ness and Strong, 1997)

Introduction

The core principle of repairing harm is about redressing material or emotional damages to individual victims and relationships. Rather than outcomes associated with treating or punishing the *offender*, repair is focused on the needs of *victim, offender, and community* in the aftermath of crime.

Of primary concern in this chapter is how conferencing practitioners think and talk about repair and what strategies they employ to engage one or more collective reparative outcomes in various phases of the conference. Do they think of the incident as a 'case' involving an offender with needs and risks, or in terms of the needs of victim, offender, and community? The primary process issue for practice and research here is the extent to which the conferencing participants focus on answering Zehr's (1990) three core restorative justice questions: what is the harm, how do we repair it, and who is responsible? What special problems arise relating to defining and assessing harm, and how are these resolved in the conference? Do participants spend time learning more about the dimensions of the harm caused by the offense from the victim, offender, and others, and do they develop plans to repair the harm that assign responsibilities and roles for stakeholders in getting it done?

Focus of this chapter

In addition to these general process questions about how repair is operationalized in the conference process, we are interested in how practitioners think about relating outcomes of conferencing to the overall goal of both individual and collective healing of those impacted by crime. We consider the extent to which the two key dimensions of repair, making amends and relationship-building, are part of the discussion of objectives or intermediate outcomes of the conference, and whether they become part of the obligation of the offender and other participants after the conference as indicated in reparative agreements. We are interested in how repair goals are articulated in each of the conference stages (preparation, conferencing, follow-up) and phases (introduction, storytelling, mutual acknowledgement) leading up to the agreement. Specifically, how are intermediate outcomes pursued, and to what extent are practitioners' actions driven by commitment to a specific theory of intervention (for a complete discussion of what we mean by immediate, intermediate and long-term goals, as well as stages and phases of the conference, please refer to Chapters 2 and 4 of this volume)? How do practitioners seek to ensure that offenders 'make amends' or 'make things right' through reparation or compensation as indicated in the exchange theory of 'earned redemption'? In addition, or as an alternative, do they seek to build or strengthen relationships around the offender based on a theory of social support in which relationships are viewed as the key to the transformation and healing of stakeholders? Finally, how are these intermediate outcomes understood to connect with long-term goals of healing, reintegration, and public safety according to these theories?

In an effort to answer these questions, we rely in this chapter on several sources of qualitative data, using references to the national survey occasionally as background for our discussion. We draw primarily on data from focus groups in which expert practitioners, selected for their experience in specific conferencing models, addressed general questions related to process dimensions. We also encouraged them to provide as much detail as possible about what actions they took in various stages and phases of conferences to achieve outcomes associated with the conference process. Structured and informal interviews with other practitioners were used to provide additional variation on process dimensions, the relationship between these and intermediate outcomes, and the priority given to various intermediate outcomes. They were then asked to speculate about how these related to what they viewed as the most important long-term outcomes. As might be expected, these theories of intervention are often loosely formulated. But though they may not match up with the theories outlined in the background discussion in Chapter 2, they are nonetheless valuable because they may reflect other important theories not yet identified. Finally, while these interviews and focus groups often reflect practice ideals and provide insight into intent and vision, we also draw upon observational data from conferences throughout in clarifying how various interactions actually occur in specific phases. In the final section of the chapter, we describe and analyze several conferencing encounters as case studies that illustrate strengths and weaknesses of implementation with regard to various dimensions of quality and consistency between practice and the pursuit of intermediate outcomes.

General findings

Do restorative conferencing programs focus on repairing harm as a primary goal? Yes, generally, at least in vision. That is to say, we did not find a single program in our sample that does not in some way acknowledge repair of harm as a primary goal. And in our survey report we note that a large majority of our respondents give highest priority to repairing harm as a conferencing goal.

The term 'repair the harm' is in fact used quite frequently in some models such as family group conferencing in which it may be included as part of the introduction to the conference in the 'script' used by facilitators to guide participants toward achieving the goals of the process. The term repair or the phrase 'repair the harm' is also used frequently in VOM and NAB programs that emphasize specific reparative objectives such as making amends or relationship-building. Some programs committed to the practice of repairing harm may often use other closely related terms, including making things right, taking responsibility, meeting victim needs, etc. For example, as one high-school principal noted, offenders in school conferences often say 'I will do anything to make it right.'

However, even using the broad multi-dimensional definition of repair presented in Chapters 1 and 2, it is clear that objectives other than repair are pursued in some conferencing programs. For those conferencing practitioners who do not seem to be in some way attempting to repair harm, what are they trying to accomplish? Some of the critical literature on restorative justice would lead one to assume that punishment is a major goal, or that a deterrence or justice model philosophy predominates. Indeed, some have implied that restorative justice is part of the new punitive wave sweeping through juvenile justice systems in the past decade (Fader et al., 2001; Moon et al., 2000). Yet we found no evidence of a punishment objective prevailing among respondents to our national survey, and it clearly is not a part of the agenda in the sample of programs in our qualitative study. Among the practitioners and community members we interviewed and observed, punishment was neither expressed nor observed as a priority in practice. And while there are examples of criminal justice professionals who seem to have been drawn to restorative justice as a way of 'getting tougher quicker,' we suspect that the vast majority of these have moved on to other causes or adopted a different perspective on accountability more consistent with the agenda and outcomes of the conference. This is not to suggest, however, that many conferences do not demand more of the offender regarding obligations than alternative approaches and programs. The point is that we find little evidence that this approach is motivated by a punitive intent.

In general, non-reparative objectives of conferencing programs seem most frequently related to offender treatment and preventative concerns. In some programs, offender rehabilitation and reintegration at times appear to be the dominant concern. Although there is little in the way of 'medical model' treatment in the conferencing experience, practitioners and volunteers often make an effort to assess problems in the home and community (as well as strengths and assets in these domains), and there is generally a spirit of caring and support for offender and victim. Programs such as older neighborhood board programs, like many diversion and early intervention-focused prevention programs, still give primary emphasis to helping young people and providing guidance or support. Proponents of peace-making circles also may seldom use the term repair, preferring other language to connote what is for some a broader focus on community-level healing outcomes and/or individual healing and support to describe their work (e.g. Pranis, 2001; Stuart, 2001). However, conferencing practitioners are likely to endorse the general focus on 'putting things right' as a primary outcome that moves beyond the goals of offender treatment and punishment.

In summary, while some conferencing programs and some models may be in fact equally committed to rehabilitation or other goals, the extent to which a focus on multiple goals diminishes the focus on repair remains an unanswered empirical question. As we will discuss in other sections of this report, conferencing programs and models may also pursue other process-focused goals such as conflict resolution, victim satisfaction and healing, offender empathy, and so on. Or they may pursue community-building and system change objectives which may nonetheless overlap with and/or reinforce practice aimed directly at reparative outcomes.

Moving toward repair in conferencing stages and phases

Stages in the conferencing process may be more or less focused on the goal of repairing harm. In conferencing and restorative justice generally, process is often viewed as most important. In this section, we primarily examine how much and in what ways the conferencing process itself is focused on repairing harm. We first consider the emphasis on repairing harm in *stages*: pre-conferencing, conferencing, and follow-up. We then devote specific attention to the five phases within the conferencing process stage: introduction/opening, storytelling, stakeholder mutual acknowledgement, agreement, and celebration.

Stage 1: Pre-conferencing

The pre-conferencing process is generally referred to as the preparation stage because its primary function is to make participants ready for the conference, while also ensuring their willingness to participate. The preparation stage generally consists of one or more separate meetings and/or contacts, such as calls, letters, or face-to-face meetings with victims, offenders, and other prospective participants that provide an opportunity to achieve several common objectives. These include: ensuring that the offender is willing to accept responsibility for the offense; discussing participant expectations or apprehensions; providing participants with more information about how the process works; discussing ground rules; and alleviating fears and apprehension. Pre-conferencing is often a time in which facilitators may begin to ask participants to think about issues directly related to repairing harm as a conference goal.

With a few notable exceptions, program staff and volunteers seem strongly committed to time spent in preparation and generally share a vision that face-to-face meetings are the most desirable approach. Actual practice regarding this vision varies widely, however, between and within model types, and the actual commitment to face-to-face preparatory meetings often depends on program resources and priorities. Though model-type is not the primary determinant, some models seem less likely than others to encourage face-to-face preparation; neighborhood accountability boards or NABS, for example, have little tradition or expectation of conducting pre-conference face-to-face meetings, while many victim–offender mediation programs and advocates strongly encourage such meetings.

The following focus group discussions with various conferencing program directors illustrates differences in the way *harm* and *repair* is addressed, and how it is addressed, in the preparation phase. These differences also reflect variation in personal styles of preparation, as well as structural differences in conferencing models. Two sets of issues received priority in our discussions with experienced practitioners about the principle of repairing harm in the preparation stage: the extent to which the pre-conference should be used to orient participants toward the reparative agreement; and what in general should be done to ensure that cases are truly appropriate for the conference and suited to the pursuit of reparative versus other objectives.

General concerns in pre-conference preparation

Culpability

In some cases, even when the offender has acknowledged responsibility for the crime (or it is established in an adjudicatory hearing), doubt may remain about the *level* of culpability (for example, when other co-offenders may be involved). When such doubts exist, perhaps the most important initial task of the pre-conferencing stage is to establish how much responsibility for the crime, if any, the offender is willing to accept. While unwillingness to accept any responsibility makes the offender ineligible for most conferencing processes, the deliberative process of some conferences can deal rather effectively with cases where offenders accept some, though less than full, responsibility for the harm caused (Braithwaite and Roche, 2001). When some basic level of culpability is not established, however, the conference may take the form of a weak (and potentially dangerous) fact-finding process. Moreover, the discussion of harm and repair in the conference itself may be thrown off course, as illustrated by this somewhat awkward beginning of a Colorado FGC:

Facilitator: 'What happened?' [directed toward the offender]

Offender: [Addressing the victim] 'In any case, I am very sorry the BB struck you. I was having a party and was shooting a BB gun into the trees . . . four or five people were shooting with me trying to hit squirrels. I wanted to shoot the gun and made sure no cars were coming. I tried to shoot the sign and missed. I was surprised someone was injured. I wondered who hit the victim.'

Facilitator: 'So you did shoot?'

Offender: 'Yes.'

Facilitator: 'What are you taking responsibility for?'

Offender: 'Negligence and carelessness,' 'shooting in public' . . . 'I was surprised someone was injured,' 'Everyone at the party was pointing the finger at me,' 'There were false statements in the police report . . . a girl said she told the police officer that she told me, 'no, no put the gun down before you get hurt' . . . she did not say that. She said that to take herself out of the process.'

[After several statements from parents]

Facilitator: 'Let's hear from our community member.'

Community Member: 'I am confused, and I need to express confusion. If he was aiming at a sign, I don't understand how someone was hit unless by ricochet. I am extremely uneasy giving time here when no one is really accountable for what happened. We don't have consensus that you committed a crime. We are on shaky ground. We are this far into the process and I am angry there is no accountability. I was shot by a BB also. My knee was severely damaged. It changes how you look at the world. It was a profound event. I don't see the responsibility. I feel a mix of emotions. This is not a valid process for this. I feel a lot of empathy for your mother.'

Offender: 'I am not saying that I didn't do anything. I was definitely responsible for carelessly shooting a gun.'

Victim: 'Which way were you shooting?'

Co-Facilitator: 'What I was hearing is the fact that there was a shooting and someone got shot.'

Community Member: 'I want to hear this particular shot hit this particular person. You don't know if your shot actually hit someone but it could have.'

In essence, whatever one may conclude about the value of a conference in this case, much of the ambiguity that caused participants to struggle around defining harm, and later developing a plan for repair, could have been resolved in a good pre-conference. The result *may* have been a finding that a conference would have been at best a waste of time, although at times the offender may take more responsibility in the actual conference than occurred in the pre-conference. (Note also the vital role of the community member participant in questioning the readiness of the group to conference in this case.)

Offender readiness and relationship
Some programs mentioned other pre-conference agendas that had little to do with the harm but were viewed as important to other overall restorative goals (e.g. connecting young offenders to positive adults). A neighborhood board program in Denver, for example, conducts a complete youth asset assessment to develop an 'asset inventory' of interests and skills board members might consider in developing recommendations for community service placements and other competency development activities that may be included in the agreement. To more directly address the issue of harm and repair, another part of the pre-conference decision-making process in this program, however, also includes a screening process to determine what might be called 'readiness for repair.' This is accomplished through use of a victim empathy survey. According to the program coordinator, based on this assessment, 'if a kid is not willing to accept responsibility, he could go back to court.'

Circles often provide a clear example of how multiple goals may be accomplished in the preparation stage, and the stage itself may be broken up into multiple meetings. Some of these other goals may be viewed as establishing the readiness and willingness of the offender to participate by ensuring that he/she has taken care of certain obligations. Some of these may be reparative in nature, e.g. some circles require community service or restitution prior to admission to the full circle process (Stuart, 1996). Other obligations are not necessarily reparative in nature but may be required in pre-circle meetings to ensure offender readiness. For example, as one circle program coordinator explained, a young offender may be required to maintain school attendance and reduce tardiness or to abide by parent rules such as curfew as evidence of stabilization before being admitted to a circle: 'We also do a social compact . . . [that addresses] what is important to be done over the next few weeks. Circle members (in a supportive role) then help the offender accomplish what is on the list.' Some circles (as well as some other conference models) also use the pre-conference meetings to allow the offender and victim to practise telling his/her story in the smaller group.

In circle programs, preparatory stages of the conference are also viewed as an opportunity to get acquainted and conduct an initial assessment of victim and offender needs and interests. As one director of a Minneapolis circle program put it:

We start at the arraignment hearing – staff explain the process, give [the offender] an application to complete. But the decision is not made there . . . we do not want to overwhelm families at that point. The interview is about 'getting to know you,' a circle with staff and a few volunteers (2–3 people) . . . then they see familiar faces when they come to the circle. We do not talk about the offense there. The first meeting of some circles, an initial circle for the offender, may also not address the offense directly.

Appropriateness of case
In other programs, including police-based FGC, much of the preparation may also be completed in multiple encounters outside of a formal pre-conference meeting. The director of a police-based conferencing program noted, for example, that: 'by the time the case gets to me, preparation has started . . . [Therefore] we don't do as much prep in person with the offender [as programs that have not had pre-conference encounters]. We probably only talk over the phone unless the facilitator thinks [a meeting is] needed. If it is a more serious case, we do it anyway.'

A preliminary concern of this program director is ensuring that other officers and volunteers make good initial decisions about the appropriateness of the case for conference. There are two problems related to this concern: '(1) the officer/facilitator pushing the case though whether appropriate or not; and, (2) the officer/facilitator vetoing things because of their own opinions – not letting participants decide.' In other words, this practitioner was concerned that officers – who are used to making quick unilateral decisions – need to be patient to ensure the willingness of offender and victim to move forward. They also need to avoid making a snap decision that an offender is inappropriate by virtue of an initially negative attitude (which may reflect what in certain stages of youth development may be considered 'cool').

Pre-conferencing as preparation for the reparative agreement

Conferencing professionals generally agree that an important goal of the conference itself is to make victim and offender stakeholders of the reparative agreement. They may disagree, however, about the relative importance of the discussion of reparative outcomes in the pre-conferencing process. Both supporters and opponents of getting victim and offender to begin thinking about the agreement in the preparation process gave several reasons for their position.

'Pros'

A police officer director of an FGC expressed strong support for prompting conferencing participants to think about the final contract:

> Our process is wide open. But I will say this: a good agreement starts in the prep phase – we hand out a written 'cheat sheet' with ideas about the kinds of things (restitution, community service) participants have proposed in the past . . . I tell them to start thinking about the agreement, directed to repair and prevention.

When asked whether or not starting at such an early point with discussion of the agreement may risk making the conference itself a 'settlement-driven' process (Umbreit, 1999), this officer responded:

> Both extremes may occur . . . [but] brainstorming does allow ideas to surface and leaves it a little more open for the offender to choose a starting point. We send everyone away with 'homework' and bring many ideas back of what could happen. The younger the juveniles, the harder it is to do restitution, therefore the homework process allows for contemplation . . . People in our society have a hard time believing they can make these decisions themselves [and therefore need some help or coaching].

On the one hand, because the conference itself may be a complex undertaking, specific preparation is therefore needed if a creative and practical contract to achieve reparative goals is to be developed. On the other hand, one may question how such an agreement can be effectively crafted without first hearing about the harm itself. Another example of using the preparation phase to get participants working towards an agreement comes from a probation-based program in which the director explained that 'at the first contact, when a juvenile comes into the probation department, we go right to the pre-conference asset interview [a tool to determine interests and skills that in this instance may be used as a guide to determining the type of community service]. The facilitator or co-facilitator explains the process and rules, and then asks them [victim and offender] to think about what they want to contribute in the . . . agreement.'

'Cons'

Because VOM best-practice protocols tend to guard against the overemphasis on the agreement as the central goal of the conference (Umbreit, 1999), it might be expected that they would also minimize its importance as a goal of pre-conferencing. While not all VOM programs are the same, in this study, a VOM/D program director said that in general, 'VOM programs follow a basic prescription *not* to discuss the agreement in the preparation stage.' Instead, volunteer mediators in this program seek to reassure victim and offender, and to answer basic questions at the preparation stage. This program director chose to address repair primarily by making sure victim and offender felt comfortable telling their stories. She expressed special concern that victims felt comfortable in relaying what she believed would provide conferencing participants with the most important means of assessing the harm to be addressed.

This VOM/D practitioner had a broader agenda for her pre-conferences aimed at presenting a menu of options for victims, *whether or not* they were willing to participate in the conference itself. While strongly tied to repair, these choices opened additional 'doors' to repairing harm, even for those who chose *not* to participate in the conference:

I call everyone first. We call all the victims (if we do not reach them in three days we accept the case anyway and assign a mediator). We are open to the idea at this point that the case could end up being a small or large group conference. But we go beyond victim–offender [face-to-face] options . . . if the victim says no (to the conference) then we just gather restitution information.

If the victim says he is interested, I assign the case [to a mediator], and send out letters to victim and mediator; then, mediators go to the homes of victim and offender (for face-to-face meetings). This meeting is *not about an agreement on repair specifically*, but rather making connection and putting everyone at ease: I ask parents of the offender to participate and meet with them. Face-to-face meetings with offenders and victims are required for pre-conferencing. The overall goal of this meeting is relationship-building.

Other choices kick in if the victim does not want to go forward or if things don't seem appropriate for a meeting: We [program staff] still follow up. We manage restitution follow-up, send out letters of apology, help them with impact statements, refer them to services or counseling and provide assistance [to victims] in other ways.

In providing this wider range of choices to the victim, the program expands its reach in terms of clients, may empower the victim in his/her decision-making, and may in the process build broader support for the program. Such support may be especially important from victims' advocates and system professionals skeptical of the value of conferencing and/or those who wish to serve victims beyond what the conference itself can accomplish (see Achilles and Zehr, 2001; Herman, 1999).

In part, the disagreement about the emphasis on the agreement, even in this preliminary stage of conferencing, seems to reflect different philosophies or theoretical understandings about what conferencing should try to accomplish. Proponents of the theory of 'healing dialogue' may see victim–offender exchange as important in reducing fear, ensuring victim vindication, and promoting offender empathy. They may view the agreement and restitution as secondary. By contrast, proponents of earned redemption, or social support theory and relationship-building outcomes might be expected to give lower priority to these goals and greater attention to the potential long-term impacts achieved through an agreement.

Stage 2: The conferencing process

The conferencing process itself generally includes five phases. We consider each phase below with regard to how participants engage issues involved in repairing harm.

Phase I: Introduction and creating safe space

The conferencing opening is one of the most important, yet potentially most variable, phases of the conferencing format. The use of cultural, group-based, and individual ritual is generally apparent in all conferences. In some models and programs, such ritual may resemble that of the courtroom, while in others it may resemble the beginning of a tribal or counter-cultural event. Independent of ritual, there are numerous differences in the content of introductions to the conference, especially from the perspective of repairing harm.

Some models, some programs, and some individual facilitators seek to maximize consistency in introductions by strict adherence to a script. Others fear that adherence to a rigid, scripted protocol may disempower victims and other key stakeholders as well as seem disingenuous or forced. While use of the script has been both discouraged (Umbreit and Stacy, 1996) and vigorously defended (McCold, 2000; McDonald et al., 1995) in literature and practice, we observed wide variation both within and between conferences using scripts and those that did not. Some introductions with scripts seemed to set a positive tone for the conference and a clear agenda, while others seemed to be ignored by participants who followed a very different protocol from the one that the script was designed to ensure. On the other hand, some introductions by facilitators that did not make use of scripts left disturbing ambiguity and confusion that persisted throughout the conference, while others seemed to set a tone of respect and openness that seemed to promote helpful dialogue and effective deliberation.

In practice, when the script is read and followed slavishly, it may make the process seem cold and 'court-like' and thereby discourage open dialogue and emotional expression about the harm caused by the crime. But it need not be used mechanically, and its advantage where the principle of repair is concerned is in ensuring that certain things about the purpose of the conference are addressed unambiguously. The script may ensure, for example, that the facilitator tells the group: 'we are here to find ways to repair the harm caused by this crime.' It may also ensure a mutual focus on both the victim and the offender. Though it is not difficult to observe in some programs a kind of lifeless reading of scripts, the following examples from a neighborhood board and family group conferencing program, respectively, illustrate how failure to use some guideline – especially in an environment characterized by a frequent influx of new facilitators and inconsistent training – can quickly move conferences away from reparative goals.

Though somewhat awkward and clearly not read verbatim, the following example from a scripted conference succinctly informs the group of the goals and objectives for the conference:

I'd like to review the process and the reason we are here. There was a crime committed with several impacts. What can the group come up with to repair the impacts of these actions?

Additional instructions asked the group to abide by the following guidelines: 'Listen respectfully;' 'Everyone will speak;' 'Use "I feel" statements;' 'We're not here to judge his character;' 'We're here to identify harms;' 'No profanity.'

This statement provides the basics and even gives guidance to participants on how they should speak and listen, while inviting dialogue with a focus on harm and repair. Whether or not it is viewed as excessively terse (and it is not necessarily typical of other conferences we observed) would depend upon the extent to which participants were carefully briefed in the pre-conference meetings or were already familiar with the process and intent of the conference. By contrast, the examples below, both from conferences where no script was utilized, indicate how the introduction can set a confusing tone when the facilitator merely improvises.

Example 1. We are here today to address the new case referred to our board. Jean has been sent to our program for the incident involving vandalism of school property. Most of you have read the case. I wanted to let you know that Jean has been having some problems in school and has recently got involved in the behavior that we are concerned with in this offense. Jean has not been in trouble like this before, but the [School Resource Officer] said that she has been having some problems with one or two teachers, and may be hanging out with some kids that may be leading her in the wrong direction. So that we can help Jean, I want us to start by asking her about some of the things she is interested in; her likes and dislikes, hobbies, etc. Then, I think we want to talk about how we get her back on track at school ... she has said she is willing to meet with the school counselor and possibly look into the anger management class.

Example 2. Tonight we are here to consider what needs to be done with this young man who was caught drinking and smoking marijuana in the park. We have been getting a lot of this type of behavior lately – this drug use in the parks. And I think – we have all agreed – we want to take a stand on this. Tonight we need to deal with how we can come up with some consequences to show Dave – and others who may do this – how serious their behavior is. Dave knows if he refuses or doesn't follow up on what we recommend – of if he does this again – he is looking at court and probably some serious punishment ... maybe some detention time. Dave, do you know how serious this is?

Neither case makes any mention of repairing harm caused by these young people. In addition, both examples begin the conference on a course that focuses total attention on the offender rather than the harm resulting from the incident. In the first example, the focus is almost completely rehabilitative, addressing how to help the offender without mention of those impacted by the crime and Jean's role and responsibility in this. In the second example, broader community concerns about disorder and drug use are raised. But these concerns are not raised in a way that describes possible harm to the community and the need to repair it, or even in a way that seeks to address past harms or strengthen relationships. Rather, this introduction seems to make Dave a scapegoat for these problems; in addition, the task of the conference is defined as one of issuing threats of future punishments to Dave and others like him.

In summary, the conference opening seems to provide perhaps the most direct opportunity to set a clear agenda for repairing harm. We observed some examples of how this task could be accomplished, both with facilitators using scripts as a basic outline, and with facilitators who apparently did not follow a script. Unfortunately, there are many other examples similar to those presented which seem to create ambiguity about the purpose of the meeting, or set it clearly on a course unrelated to the focus on harm or the goal of repair. The debate about the use of scripts may, however, miss the point about how the facilitator and other participants need to set an agenda for the conference. The broader theoretical and philosophical question may be one grounded in a debate between those who favor a more open dialogue restricted to victim and offender, those who prefer a fluid and open dialogue process involving *multiple* stakeholders, and those who seek a more clear focus on reparative outcomes.

Phase II: Storytelling

This phase of the conference is about hearing from participants how they were affected by the crime. Most especially, the storytelling phase is about hearing victim and offender (and other participants') stories in their own words. This is a time for active listening to ensure that participants understand the nature of the harm and the offender's acknowledgement of his/her responsibility in creating this harm. Harm to affected communities is an issue in some models and programs. In some instances this focus may dominate discussion, especially if the individual victim is not present.

The general question we asked in this part of our study was how storytelling focuses on harm in a way that leads to productive considerations of repair. Regarding the overall goal of repair and intermediate objectives such as making amends, two specific process concerns have been the focus of discussion and debate. These concerns are: (1) who should speak first, victim or offender; and (2) how to best appreciate the complexity of stories of harm in order to develop appropriate responses.

Sequential order of stories

The voices of both victim and offender are absolutely essential, yet who speaks first is, for some, a point of contention (Bazemore and Umbreit, 2001). Though this does not appear to be the issue of heated debate it was a few years ago, decisions about which story is heard first may have implications for both the process dynamics and outcomes of the conference. Specifically, the choice is of both practical and theoretical importance because which story is heard first may influence both the story which follows and the group response to both victim and offender. The critical question for future impact research is whether one approach is more likely to help the conference meet its objectives. Arguments for both sides of this debate are explored below.

Victim first

Advocates of having the victim speak first buttress their arguments by noting that conferences, like the juvenile justice system itself, begin with a bias towards the needs and risks of the offender. In addition to such generally persuasive normative arguments about why the victim *deserves* preferential treatment, more specific practical concerns include the fear that the right tone and focus will not be set unless participants first confront and grapple with the victim's suffering. There is therefore a concern about diluting this message by preempting the victim with the offender's story, even when that story seems likely to increase understanding of the event, and even ease the victim's fears or answer burning questions. Though a reparative agreement is important to most victims, the theory behind allowing the victim to speak first would also support erring on the side of allowing for emotional expression and honest communication of the victim's true feelings. Such communication should *not*, it is argued, be influenced by the offender's comments. One fear is that such an honest expression following the offender's often sympathetic story may give the impression to other conference participants that the victim, when it is his/her turn to speak, is being vengeful or is overreacting. If the victim senses such a reaction, he/she may limit the story by holding back on important details of the offender's behavior or his/her own feelings or experience.

Generally, some well-respected VOM programs follow the victim-first protocol (Bazemore and Umbreit, 2001). Yet we found exceptions to this rule in other VOM programs we studied, and noted from our survey that a significant number of other conferencing programs prefer the offender-first approach, or perhaps more commonly, leave this decision to the victim on a case-by-case basis. The theoretical or philosophical basis for this position is probably most closely tied to the goal of making amends and the theory of earned redemption that would imply that the details of the pain and suffering caused by the offender must first be presented before he/she can in a valid way acknowledge responsibility and take action to repair the damage. In addition, repair in the sense of rebuilding or strengthening weakened relationships would seem to require understanding of how these relationships – those of the victim in particular – have been harmed.

Offender first

With regard to the process of repairing harm, some offender-first advocates argue that the offender needs to demonstrate understanding and acknowledgment of responsibility to everyone, especially to the victim, before the group spends much time on him/her. In doing so, many practitioners also hope and anticipate that the offender's story will soften the victim's anger while building some support for him/her in the group.

This may therefore allow the conference to proceed without excessive conflict and with potential support for the offender. Advocates of this position will sacrifice some of the emotion, communication, and deference to the victim in favor of hearing from the offender first. They also argue in addition that the offender's story may provide the victim and the group with important information that may help them understand the nature of the harm. Regarding the theory of earned redemption and the need for amends-making, offender-first proponents would argue that their approach is more conducive to this objective because it allows the offender to acknowledge responsibility and take ownership *before* hearing from anyone else. Moreover, if this occurs, the goal of relationship-building – at least for the offender – is more likely to be achieved. Several training protocols insist on the offender going first in order to accomplish one or more of these goals (e.g. McDonald et al., 1995).

Perhaps the best rationale for having the offender speak first from the perspective of repairing harm came from the director of a juvenile offender reentry program that uses a conferencing model she describes as a cross between circles and FGC. This model calls for the offender to speak first based on the belief that he/she may be less authentic, and possibly less forthcoming, after hearing from the victim and other speakers:

> The offender goes first and then they all speak (victims and community members), and then it goes *back* to the offender again to respond. Otherwise, if the offender did not go first, he/she would say what *they think everyone wants to hear*. But we have them go first so they can't do that ... They may behave differently, if they knew all of the details first [emphasis ours]. The facilitator goes back to the offender after the victim then speaks in order to allow the group to determine whether or not the message of harm got through. At this point offenders may indicate surprise and be motivated to apologize for suffering he had never realized had occurred.

While it can be argued that the victim's story may also be less genuine and emotional after hearing the often sympathetic story of the offender (who in this particular model may be addressing a relatively large group of people he victimized as well as other community members), defenders of this approach – proponents of reintegrative shaming theory in particular – present a different view (McDonald et al., 1995). They suggest that the victim, after hearing the offender's less than accurate portrayal of events and/or misperception of the consequences of his actions may be equally likely or even more obliged to get the facts straight. In doing so, the victim will certainly express her/his true feelings, make certain that the group understands the harm, and seek to ensure that the offender 'owns up' to what actually occurred. Alternatively, if the offender is actually forthcoming in the opening, contrite, and willing to accept responsibility, the victim may feel vindicated and relieved.

Other theories of conferencing process such as the theory of 'common ground' might also support the idea of the offender going first when there are conflicting accounts. Such discrepancies allow the group in a larger conference to consider inaccuracies and truth in both stories and build upon those areas of common consistency. Healing dialogue proponents would seem to presume victim-first approaches to allow for vindication in the eyes of other participants and reduced fear and apprehension, but might also add that healing for the victim often comes when the offender responds positively, with acknowledgement and empathy.

In terms of theories of repair, we believe either sequence could be justified on normative or practical grounds, and as the above reentry conference account indicates, the key may well be in the opportunity for response to each other's stories and in how this exchange is processed. There is an important empirical question, however, regarding the extent to which victim or offender speaking first leads to 'better' outcomes related to amends, relationship-building, addressing past harms, etc. (this depends, of course, on some agreement as to what 'better' means).

Appreciating complexity
Crime may produce multiple harms to an individual victim and offender, and there may be multiple direct and indirect victims of any offense, as well as significant impact on community life. Such complexity is especially clear in the case of more chronic and serious offenders who seek to repair harm and return to the community after years of offending. As suggested by the comments from the reentry program director above, the context for storytelling around harm and repair may be quite distinctive in those residential and reentry settings that have begun to experiment with conferencing in recent years. For this reason, they may provide important case studies for examining how conferencing participants address the complexity of the 'harm story' likely to be associated with multiple harmful behaviors. Such behaviors may range from assaults and rule violations within the facility, to any of the offenses committed by residential wards prior to their incarceration.

In the reentry conference, when the offender is ready to move from one kind of 'community' (the residential facility) to another, it is important to bring together as many of the individuals the youth had victimized prior to his incarceration as possible, as well as likely supporters of the youth in the new community. Multiple reparative objectives in such conferences may include some amends, substantial consideration of past harms to offender and family as well as victims, and – what may be most important in the reentry context – relationship-building. Common ground, reintegrative shaming, and norm affirmation objectives also may be pursued or naturally engaged in such a complex conferencing setting. In a description that further justifies having the offender speak first, this practitioner notes that facilitators in such conferences often ask the offender prior to the conference to:

> Think about who he has hurt, and talk more specifically about things in general – his life in a nutshell, when he started getting in trouble, how that may be related to the present offense . . . It is a recap so that people who know him one way or other, who only know their piece of him, get to hear about other harm the offender has inflicted, and also experienced, in his life – so it helps to get everybody on the same page.
>
> This helps the victims to see if this is someone who has had trouble their whole life, or if they are a vicious kid who just picked them out as victim. They [offenders] also talk specifically about the offense with the victim there, so that the victim can ask questions. The victim can talk about his/her experience, what it has been like since the crime and at the [time of the] crime, and what they are thinking about now; they can say whatever they need to say, and they have their questions to raise.

This practitioner describes the storytelling process of getting clear on the harm of the offense from the perspective of the offender as follows:

> A lot of it is coming to terms with what is being said and they often say, 'Wow' and 'I'm sorry.' Sometimes occasionally, they address certain people individually, and say 'I didn't know I hurt you that badly . . .' He [the offender] really works to reassure people that he's trying to be a different person, and he doesn't want to do [that kind of thing] anymore. He answers what they're asking. And I try to guide the discussion, because they are not always well spoken or may be nervous and forget stuff. So I prompt them – ask them a question to prompt for more information or a response . . . 'a lot of times kids don't recognize the harm.'

In general, regardless of the order of presentation, practitioners want to make sure the offender is clear, as one practitioner put it, about 'who they have harmed and how' before moving on. At times, conference participants may need to go to great lengths and exercise substantial creativity to make this clear. Understanding is often best indicated in exchanges between victim and offender, or when the offender is asked to 'retell' portions of the victim's story:

> The offender explains his/her involvement in the crime [and is] encouraged to talk about any feelings he/she may have about the incident. The victim is then allowed to ask the offender for clarification about the facts. The victim then tells his/her part of the story. The offender is then asked to repeat what they think they heard. This then spills over into a freewheeling conversation.

Volunteers in a Vermont restorative panel add that cases in which tangible loss or suffering experienced by victims is not apparent are often quite difficult because the harm is so hard to define. One volunteer described a case in which a drunk driver appeared before the panel. Apparently, this offender denied that any real harm occurred. In the conversation, the panel discovered that the police had videotaped his drunk driving and asked him to view the tape. Reporting back, the young man indicated that he now understood the risk he had posed both to himself and others. He was shaken because 'he realized he could have died.'

It is of course by no means a given that the presence of a victim will mean that his/her story will be told effectively in the conference. While circles appear at times to emphasize offender needs to the exclusion of victims – and we reflect further on this and put the issue in context elsewhere in this book – the researchers observed a particularly creative incidence of a keeper drawing out the victim to provide a very powerful account of the harm she had suffered. This occurred at a point in a circle that until that time had been almost exclusively focused on the progress of the offender in meeting the goals set for him by the group. Both observers (the authors) felt that through most of the conference the victim must have felt reluctant to speak in the presence of such strong support for the offender. During a lull in this discussion, the keeper suggested to the victim that she should 'let the group in on' what she had shared with her earlier about the difficult turns her life had taken after having her car stolen by the offender. The victim first attempted to minimize this difficulty (consistent with what victim-first advocates described above believe to be the main problem with offenders speaking first), and also express her support for the offender's progress. Ultimately, she provided a very moving account of the level of chaos and disruption she had experienced with the loss of her only source of transportation, her struggles to recover the vehicle, and her difficulties in keeping her job as a result. At that point, what had been viewed by the group as a minor joyriding incident (that provided the group with an opportunity to work with a troubled youth in the community) was viewed from the perspective of a victim who had experienced a rather major trauma. Later, we discovered that this keeper had met previously with the victim on two separate occasions and had been trying to convince her to tell her story to the group.

In general, conferencing practitioners we observed and interviewed agreed that victims play an essential role in defining harm. This role becomes most apparent in programs in which victims are less likely to participate when there are clearly struggles to define harm. Though use of surrogate victims seems to be a common practice in some programs when the actual victim is unwilling or unable to participate, the director of a neighborhood board program in Colorado that has used this approach with otherwise good results reports that the focus on harm and repair is less coherent and compelling when the actual victim is not present. Other barriers to defining harm in the storytelling phase, and hence to repairing it creatively, have to do with the length of time between the conference and the offense itself. Commenting on juvenile justice boards in Vermont, or restorative panels as they are called there, this program coordinator noted that:

> The boards are less effective if it is done after six months. Six months is a long time if you are a kid and for you to deal with an offence that far in the past . . . you can hardly remember everything that you did.

Phase III: Acknowledgement of each other and community validation and input

Conference facilitators generally feel that they are ready for this phase when the offender has given a clear account of the event, acknowledged responsibility, and the victim has described the harm. Though generally brief, this transition seems to be a time when conference facilitators and participants take note of whether the group is ready to proceed to the agreement phase, or whether some aspect of the stories of victim and offender may need to be revisited. For example, perhaps more discussion is needed to determine whether the offender has appropriately acknowledged responsibility. There may be an apology by the offender, and some positive statement about the offender or insight reflected upon by the victim or other participants. This is a time when facilitators and others may begin to assess the extent of individual and collective transformation of the victim, offender, and the group. Victim and offender may acknowledge each other's positions, or a community member may make a bridging comment that spurs what some researchers believe to be a vital movement towards the other's position (Hayes and Daly, 2003). While often subtle, this acknowledgement serves as a transition to the agreement phase and is viewed as so important by one practitioner that the phase itself justifies a break, or at least a 'check-in':

> *Question*: 'So then, is the offender responding and addressing people at that point?'

Answer: 'Yep, and it opens up to a general discussion. People are generally satisfied by that point. There's usually not a lot [more] . . . Then we take a break – verbally and physically change gears. Up to that point it has been intense and I make a conscious effort to say, 'Is there anything else that you need to say right now'? Then we make this transition: "We're going to shift gears now . . . We've looked at what happened, now let's look at what's going to happen when he gets out – we can make an agreement . . ." '

Question: 'Are the positive remarks spontaneous talk, or do you talk to them beforehand?'

Answer: 'I try not to prompt their responses. I do some preparation. I talk to them about their experience with him – both good and bad – but I don't try to direct what they are going to say. I have a feeling of how the conference is going to go because of each of the conversations I have had.'

Worth noting is this facilitator's attention to detail and a careful reading of the process and subtle cues. Also worth noting is that this facilitator is the same one speaking about the need in the storytelling phase to prompt and assist the offender to tell his story effectively. In general, as we will see in subsequent chapters and some of the case studies, this is a very strategic facilitative style which, though empowering, guides the dialogue and participants through phases, leaving less to chance than promoters of a more open dialogue may approve of.

Phase IV: Agreement

The agreement phase is the construction of the written contract that is meant to specify the obligation and include a plan to repair harm (although it is possible to have a verbal agreement if that is consistent with the cultural or other needs of the participants). Based on the assessment of who and what has been harmed, how to repair the harm, and who is responsible, the agreement is the most tangible product of a conference. Indeed, the number of successful agreements negotiated is often considered an interim measure of program performance in some evaluation studies (e.g. Umbreit, 1999). Our attention to process here does not allow us to explore in depth the specifics of agreements developed in conferencing. However, we provide several examples of agreement contents as these reflect various conferencing objectives and, more importantly, explore the antecedents of these agreements.

Contents of agreement and conferencing objectives
In terms of the components of repair addressed, our research was not designed to empirically document the relative priority given to one

dimension or another, or to systematically examine apparent variation between models. However, we provide examples which illustrate alternative reparative priorities. In general, making amends is one of the most common dimensions of reparative agreements across all programs and models addressed. Issues of stakeholder safety may be included in some agreements, as well as relationship-building objectives.

Amends may take the form of written and verbal apologies to victims and other affected parties, community service, restitution, and agreements to alter one's behavior in a certain way (e.g. stopping offending, attending school). Community service, restitution, and apologies are among the most common reparative obligations. In the special case of school conferencing, however, agreements to change whatever behavior caused the altercation between students or students and teachers (name calling, disruptive classroom behavior) are common. Often incidents of harm in such settings are manifestations of an ongoing conflict. While amends-focused agreements may be less common in school settings, we may see examples of agreements that seek to reinforce 'common ground,' or find additional common ground. At a micro level, in the 'school community,' these agreements may also have community-building objectives. For example, one principal described agreements that he felt might expand conflict resolution skills in the general school population. Occasionally, making amends may involve a particular kind of service that also has elements of reintegrative shaming, such as when the offender is required to tell his story to, for example, a class of younger students. In some circles, as noted previously, participants develop a social compact as a preliminary agreement which may first involve requirements to stabilize the youth's behavior – e.g. school attendance, curfew – as well as service or other demonstrations of good faith and commitment by the offender.

Pathways to agreement
As a general rule, what leads up to the agreement is often viewed as more important than the agreement itself. Problems in the storytelling phase and other aspects of the process prior to developing the reparative plan may render an agreement irrelevant, or unlikely to be completed. Recent writing and training on VOM/D, for example, has discouraged the rush to settlement in the absence of full dialogue about feelings and emotions as an example of what Umbreit (1999) calls 'fast-food' mediation. Proponents of some other models have also gone on record regarding the importance of allowing stories to be told and emotions to be addressed (Braithwaite, 2001b; Stuart, 2001). Though there appears to be general consensus with such admonitions, not all programs and not all conferencing models are sensitive to the need to avoid rushing to agreement. The effort to avoid becoming 'settlement-driven' in the conference was

illustrated clearly by a VOM director, whose program nonetheless has a good track record at completing very tangible, reparative agreements:

> We tell the mediators to not give the parties solutions; we tell them, the volunteers, we don't *care* if you get an agreement; your process is to help the two disputants *possibly* reach an agreement but we don't want them to be pushing for a piece of paper to come out of it – even though we get our funding by producing the paper.

A successful conference, as defined by this practitioner, does not depend upon completion of an agreement, but rather simply on whether or not the conference has 'provided the space' for the parties to work toward whatever solution they wanted, or to just have a dialogue (though we may wonder about the credence and value given to the victim's story if facilitators routinely view victim and offender as 'disputants').

There is general consensus, however, that the agreement or contract should not be taken lightly, and is essential to the future of the stakeholders in the process, and to the future legitimacy of the process itself. However, there has been relatively little discussion of the conference agreement in the literature (see Karp, 1999), and some practitioners seem more careful than others about ensuring that it is consistent with long-term conferencing goals. All too common, in our view, are agreements that seem to leave everything to the offender without specifying a role for other stakeholders (e.g. family, community volunteers, system professionals), and in particular those present at the conference.

One positive sign that may help to ensure that the creativity of conference participants is not lost in what can become a rather mundane document is a conferencing group review of the core components of the agreement. In such reviews a facilitator informally asks the group a series of questions about the extent to which the agreement addresses primary objectives. In a Colorado conferencing program, for example, a co-facilitator charged with recording the conference reviews the components of the suggested agreement with the group as a whole. The facilitator then asks the group some version of the following questions: does the agreement meet the needs of the victim, the community, and the offender; is it relevant to the harm; is it achievable; is it reasonable (fair)? A slightly different version of the first question is: will the victim be satisfied with this; will the community be satisfied; will the offender be satisfied? In addition to providing a group check on the validity and overall quality of the agreement, this review allows community volunteers to again put themselves in the shoes of their fellow citizens in answering the question. The review also allows offender and victim one more chance to express disapproval or suggest amendments – in effect, solidifying group commitment to the completion of obligations. In this program, as might be expected, it is rare to find agreements that specify obligations only in terms of offender tasks. For example, as the program director explains, it is not uncommon in restitution agreements for a community volunteer or the victim to solve a problem for unemployed young offenders with restitution orders and minimal employment potential by offering them a job.

Most conferencing practitioners who talked about the agreement phase described practical challenges such as training facilitators to resist giving input into the agreement: 'counselors are the hardest to train,' said one experienced administrator of a community conferencing program, 'the hardest thing is to keep facilitators out of outcomes [agreements] . . . [I tell them] do not give suggestions for the agreement . . . it's their circle' (circle here refers to the conference seating arrangement, not a circle process). On occasion, we observed that this tendency to attempt to direct or engineer an agreement was not only a problem of facilitators asserting their power or becoming overly compulsive. Rather, facilitator input resulted in part from the fact that community members, offenders and victims in some cases turned to them for options. When this occurred, the most effective facilitators frequently threw questions back to more passive participants by asking them to apply a principle to solve a specific difficult problem. Less effective facilitators, on the other hand, may simply help the group devise a routine list of requirements, or suggest referrals to standard intervention programs.

Obligation and input
Another practical issue is the extent to which certain processes and some programs place more emphasis on offender and family input into developing the obligation than others. At one extreme, in some programs practitioners seem comfortable with the offender being generally told what his obligations will be. Some neighborhood boards in which panel members deliberate and then inform the offender of what he will be required to do provide an extreme example of minimizing stakeholder input. Such programs are not unlike arbitration and other ADR models that claim no grounding in restorative principles. In this situation, offenders may object or acquiesce, but in neither case are they given the opportunity to 'own' the obligation through full participation in decision-making.

At the other extreme are programs – not specific to model types – in which practitioners and volunteers are highly strategic in their efforts to elicit offender participation in formulating the agreement. In one community conferencing program, facilitators want to maximize the chance that the offender will provide thoughtful input into the process of crafting an obligation to be approved by the group. The practitioner explained that:

> We have enormous latitude . . . [in] the brainstorming period, we get all the ideas from the group, then say to the offender, 'What will you do?' At this point, they essentially self-sentence – they have a chance to claim it [and they have] *won the choice* around repair. Then we say to the victim, 'Will that satisfy you?' . . . there is some group negotiation after that [emphasis ours].

Similarly, in many victim–offender mediation programs, the mediator will turn first to the offender and ask him/her, 'what do you think should be done to make this right?' either before or after asking a victim the same question. Other programs and models in which participants seem open to offender input at times seem too quick to make suggestions about what should be done.

This problem of excluding stakeholders from input into decision-making regarding obligations and agreements is not limited to one conferencing model (see case examples in Chapter 6). Indeed, it is possible to observe conferences in which the offender plays a very passive role in formulating agreements even in the most ideologically and structurally inclusive conferencing models, peace-making circles, because they often include very active and vocal volunteers who at times may also fail to engage victim and offender as effectively as they might. In a recent follow-up circle for a young offender and his family, members made a number of very creative suggestions for the youth's follow-up plan, while the offender and his parent sat quietly and passively. However, this was not a case in which either the offender, or the parent, felt coerced; rather they seemed to appreciate the offers of support that went with these recommendations. Although it was impossible to determine whether or not the offender had been asked before to contribute to the agreement or the conversation about what should be done, there was simply no solicitation of input from him and he gave no input when he received the talking piece (at least not at this time). Again, great skill is often needed to 'draw out' offenders and victims, as well as family members, who may be accustomed to playing passive roles in traditional criminal justice or social service processes.

When allowed to do so, victims come up with some of the most creative ideas for reparative requirements, though we did not see them prompted to do so very often in most of the conferences we observed. Victims and other participants may well appreciate the opportunity for input into the offender's contract. In some cases – and this seems to vary between models – the victim is often asked what *they* want first. Such strategies, however they are played out, seem vital to avoiding what seems to be an all too common result of the group adding on requirements with little input from victim, offender or family. Though no one seems to know if there is evidence that one approach is better than the other, the primary issue is whether the offender and victim are given an avenue for input into the contract other than nodding agreement or expressing concerns or disapproval.

Structuring input
In between the open solicitation of ideas from the offender and the victim, and the prescriptive approach in its various forms, is an approach that provides options from which the offender may choose with input from others. For example, according to a police facilitator, in one family group conferencing program there are several steps and multiple obligations associated with the agreement (other than those tied to repair in the direct sense of the term). There are also cues in the form of suggested options to prompt offender input:

> The offender is told that everyone will agree to [the agreement] and everyone will have input into it. The offender then reads all the concerns that everyone has with his/her behavior and is then given a menu of options or sanctions for [addressing those concerns]. Then they go through some issues and some sanctions that might be appropriate for that. Finally, they go and see what sanctions the victim wants. Options for that include: restitution; volunteer work; community service; letters of apology.

The interesting issue in this discussion is not only the effort to prompt offender input, but also what seems on the surface to be the secondary priority given to repair and victim needs in the agreement phase. The emphasis on collateral behavior problems and on dealing with the offender's behavior in this agreement comes first, while the more clearly reparative work around making amends comes last. Ironically (especially given the strong emphasis on victim participation and high rates of participation in this program), the victim's input at the end of the agreement phase seems at least symbolically to diminish its value and the reparative emphasis. In defense of this approach, it can be said – and this is the argument of some circle proponents, who are, however, often dealing with more complex and serious cases than this first-offender program – that the youth's behavior is getting in the way of any effort to repair and must be brought under control first.

Some circles that require such initial behavior change utilize a 'social compact' that may be used as an entry requirement for some offenders. Various circles in different ways tend to spend time exploring the offender's strengths and interests. While this can become a routine process if this assessment is part of the agenda, the possible creativity of connecting young offenders to their community while making reparation is illustrated below:

What the circle comes up with tries to tap into what the offender is good at, so they can feel good about [reparative efforts] . . . so it's not like going to pick up trash . . . and they really get creative . . . one sanction that a circle came up with was [described as] 'something that the youth could do to make the community better.' The youth had to figure it out, tell the circle what he would do, and if they agreed, would have to go out and do it. The kid wanted to pick up the litter and plant flowers in the median where there was nothing. The youth, with one of the circle members, went to some civic organizations to get supplies . . . the final circle was held where the youth went and planted the flowers.

Stakeholder responsibility and offender support

A key feature on which agreements may vary is the extent to which they, following Zehr's (1990) third key question, determine 'who is responsible for this repair?' by specifying responsibilities and roles beyond the obligation of the offender. Where they do not, they in many ways simply replicate court orders. Where they involve others in repair, in monitoring progress, in facilitating and helping the offender, they not only build capacity and skills – as well as ownership in the group – but also provide a direct avenue for continued social support for offenders and their families (Cullen, 1994). Programs may do more or less to make this happen, and those that make extensive use of community volunteers – such as circles, boards, community conferencing, and family conferencing – may emphasize or create the necessary space for support to emerge naturally. VOM/D, for example, uses its volunteers as mediators, who are *not* encouraged to play the role of support person, though practitioners would certainly not discourage expressions of support despite the sometimes less frequent presence of outside participants in VOM/D conferences. The victim may of course offer to support the offender.

The agreement phase in the community context is often more complex and more creative. This is especially true when it involves, as in the case below, multiple victims and community members who have come together to develop a reentry agreement for a juvenile offender coming out of a facility. As described by this facilitator/program director:

They all need to agree with the conditions and then sign their name to the end of it. I give them some examples to spur their thinking. Typically the things may be on the parole plan, but I tell them they may add stuff for their personal agreement with him: get a job and go to school etc. . . . [We had] one circle where, once he [the offender] got out, they wanted him to take his mom out for lunch to make up for all the hell he had put her through. One victim requested that the offender develop 'positive influences' [in his life] . . . 'Keep his free time full' – it came out in the conference that he liked nature, so they required that he volunteer at a local nature preserve.

When an offender has already served time such agreements may also offer a great deal of support in a spirit of forgiveness that also clarifies the expectations of the community to the offender:

> Question: 'Do issues of repair come up?'
> Answer: 'They [participating victims] may need to get their restitution paid off. Typically the victims at that point don't ask for stuff for themselves, instead it is more about offering the kids [the offenders] stuff – e.g. jobs.'

Support may emerge as conference participants accept roles in helping to repair the harm. In addition concern will often be expressed about safety in the future, and the role of community members in guardianship:

> Another resident offered to assist [the offender] in coaching the kids on the basketball team. The victim's whole thing was twofold: one, he wanted the offender to do positive things in his free time, and two, he wanted to keep an eye on him. He was a next door neighbor. There are always neat dynamics coming out.

Balancing stakeholder needs
Another conference volunteer also noted that initial needs and desires of victims for full financial compensation from the offender often change due to the influence of the group. Rather than pressure to accommodate to the will of other participants, however, she views this change in victim demands as due to the support *they* receive in the circle:

> For the victim, when they go through the regular system they want money ... but when a victim [comes in] and we finally get him to go full circle, a lot of the time when they originally said 'we want this money,' they say, 'Well I would be willing to da da da.'

Another VOM director, commenting on this phenomenon noted this as a common problem related to ensuring that agreements truly reflect the wishes of victims:

> There is so much empathy in the conference – even for very serious crimes – that the victim might request just a letter of apology. This gets them in trouble with the system people [who often think more sanctions are necessary].

On the other hand, a circle director noted that:

In my experience with circles, I have never seen community people be too easy or let something slide . . . the community members there want the kid to do something that is positive, benefits the community and makes them[the offender] feel good . . . I think that one thing circles do, it just really preserves, I think, and maintains someone's dignity, it is an extremely respectful process . . . so we are not there deciding how can we punish you, and make you pay for what you did, [but rather] how can we support you so that this won't happen again.

A board director noted, on the other hand, that the urge to punish in some communities could become an obstacle to repair, though he ultimately tended not to interfere with the board's decision-making:

. . . having the six boards, the issue of consistency is important. Our response is that each community knows their needs, each neighbor-hood knows what they need to do, and what they need. I think one of the biggest dangers that we consistently espouse is the concept of punishment. If that is a goal of your committee to punish the kid, then understand that all that kid is going to learn is 'I can take punishment' and nothing is fundamentally changed. If that's what you want then understand there are already families *that do that very well* [emphasis ours].

Another issue of concern regarding repair for some circle members was the problem of young people feeling rewarded before being asked to address their obligations. In discussing this problem of what might be called 'premature support,' one circle member described how circle volunteers were often quick to express almost unconditional care and concern and offer assistance for young offenders – often prior to any meetings with victims or discussion of the crime:

For example, I took two youths to play basketball. [Some in the circle] felt it would be important for kids to see other sides of the people in the circle. Others, like me, felt kids were being rewarded before completing anything.

Phase V: Celebration

This phase is less about repairing harm and more about reinforcing human connections in an informal setting. Indeed, a key for gauging the likelihood that obligations will be completed in the post-conference phase may be that participants do not talk about the agreement at all. Other than informal talk, what is expected is perhaps further acknowledgement of each other, encouragement for offender and victim, and parents sharing supportive comments with other participants. Regarding repair, participants may also follow up on details associated with contract obligations; for example, a community member may exchange phone numbers with a parent and offender and plan to meet one or both of them at a community service work site at a specified time, a victim may make arrangements to follow up with another participant regarding counseling or provide a mailing address to the program coordinator and the offender, etc. Most importantly, many coordinators believe that much of the success of the conference can be assessed by the extent to which participants seem happy and comfortable in this phase.

Stage 3: The follow-up stage

The commitment of program resources to support follow-up is a critical determinant of the nature and amount of post-conference monitoring of reparative agreements. Other issues include the strength of collaborative agreements with other system stakeholders and the specificity of conference agreements in defining roles and responsibilities in the aftermath of the conference. Programs varied a great deal in their level of commitment to following up and monitoring the agreement and in the amount of responsibility assumed in the follow-up stage.

For this Vermont restorative panel coordinator, follow-up is simply the most important part of the conferencing effort:

> We would fail 80 per cent of the time if we didn't follow-up with the agreements . . . only 10 per cent of our kids have support mechanisms on their own that would allow them to complete their agreements. You can't just throw paper at a youth . . . they won't read it. They will throw it in the garbage and smoke another joint.

While coordinators or other program staff assume this role in many programs, in others, criminal justice professionals such as police or probation officers monitor the agreements, or volunteers are assigned this role.

A neighborhood board coordinator in Pennsylvania suggested a split responsibility model in which everyone 'shares the role in monitoring agreements: the police cover restitution, community service, etc. the members of the board monitor other stuff' (in this case a number of non-reparative requirements such as school attendance, curfew, etc.). A number of other programs described some form of shared responsibility, most often between probation and a program staffperson, although community volunteers seem to be increasingly involved. In circles, for example, volunteer circle members make phone calls to offenders, provide transportation if needed to school or work, accompany an offender to a job interview, and so on, and may also complete community service hours with the offender.

While some programs in our sample, such as a VOM/D program in Los Angeles, claimed high rates of successful completion as a result of their staff follow-up, others seemed to have little information on follow-up – especially the part they were not responsible for. Some ambiguity was also apparent in roles and responsibilities in the follow-up process. In one FGC, the person who brings the youth to the conference is responsible for the monitoring, and this is usually the parent. This is an interesting twist on conferencing follow-up, which is done apparently to reaffirm parental authority. (Yet, one may wonder if parents are capable of monitoring the contract alone if they have not been capable of monitoring the youth's behavior in the past.)

The programs most aware of follow-up success rates and who seem most committed to this stage in the conferencing process are those that operate what could essentially be described as 'full-service' reparative programs. Such programs not only prepare and conduct conferences, but are also responsible for all aspects of monitoring contracts, ensuring that restitution is paid and sent to the victim, checking on the well-being of offender and victim, and other tasks. While this work is often performed primarily by paid staff, some of the more interesting approaches include community volunteers who are involved in follow-up tasks. One of the most tightly structured follow-up efforts we encountered occurs in a neighborhood board program in Arizona. According to the program director, each board, 'makes the offender come back every three months for a check-in as a mandatory part of the contract [as an] update for the committee, a way to acknowledge the kid who is doing good. It is a good way for that connection to continue, [between] the kid, family, and community.' Moreover, this post-adjudicatory probation-based program offers an additional incentive to young people to complete obligations in a timely manner that was not mentioned by other programs:

> At the nine-month review, the committee has the option of directing the probation officer to recommend early release of the youth from probation. The probation officer has to take this recommendation to the court, and the judge decides yes or no . . . They don't need a seal of approval from the victim, but they must at least let them know . . . [and the victim can say] 'Yes, I got my payments,' or if the victim feels like it. 'No, the kid is being let off too easy,' we make that information available to the judge.

This program reports that the victim rarely says no in such cases, and if they do, it is generally because of unpaid restitution or a belief that the youth 'has not learned his lesson.' Early release from probation is a big incentive to complete restitution, both for the youth and the community. Early release usually occurs after about 14 months and the judge in such cases almost always goes along with the community's recommendation.

Summary and conclusions

The purpose of this chapter has been to address questions related to the operationalization of repair in various phases and stages of the conferencing process. Programs are, in general, strongly committed to the principle of repair as it defines core outcomes for conferences linked to making amends, rebuilding or building relationships, and repairing past harms. Conferencing programs vary in their relative commitment to these goals and the extent to which they allow other outcomes, such as meeting offender treatment or custodial needs, to become the focus of the conference.

Throughout the practitioner dialogue and case examples presented in each phase and stage of the conference, there is evidence of shared agreement on many issues regarding the vision and goal of repairing harm. There are also conflicting priorities regarding such issues as how much focus should be on the agreement vs. dialogue between victim and offender (and where this focus on agreement should begin). In the pre-conferencing stage, for example, conferencing staff and volunteers disagree about the practical and philosophical reasons why preparation work with conference participants is necessary and about what the focus of such preparation should be: for example, making contact, answering questions, and reducing anxiety vs. beginning to think about what would be desirable and fair in a reparative agreement.

Beginning with the conference opening, there are differing views about how much structure should be imposed on the conference and to what end. Some practitioners advocate use of scripts as a tool for keeping the focus on repairing harm and ensuring movement through what are viewed as critical phases, while others argue for a more free flowing dialogue. We discussed problems in both approaches when, for example, use of a script or failure to do so may limit the ability of participants to focus on the common goal of repairing the harm. Some conflict is apparent here between the core restorative principles of repairing harm and stakeholder involvement – especially as the latter implies a focus on the process itself. Moreover, theories of healing dialogue appear to conflict here with the concern with making amends in earned redemption/ exchange theory. Proponents of the latter seemed more concerned that the harm of the crime is clearly established in order to ensure the validity of, and commitment, to the reparative agreement, while advocates of the former view the dialogue as essential to achieve what is for them the ultimate objective of the conference, the stakeholder exchange fundamental to healing.

Some proponents of reintegrative shaming and healing dialogue also disagree about who should speak first in the conference, in part for different practical rationales about which approach is most likely to lead to reparation. Reintegrative shaming advocates also seek a conferencing outcome, respectful disapproval of the offender, that is not viewed as important to proponents of healing dialogue. At the agreement phase, practitioners also discussed strategies for improving the quality of agreements and reparative plans by maximizing offender, victim, and community participation in, responsibility for, and ownership of these agreements. These strategies, though not consistently employed in the conferences we observed (where too often agreements may simply be plans for what the offender must do) seem to be consistent with the expressed need to build relationships around offender and victim as suggested in the theory of social support and make amends as suggested by the theory of earned redemption.

The practitioner discussion presented and case studies based on conference observations also raise important concerns with regard to the capacity of conferences to address the overall goal of repairing harm and to achieve specific objectives related to core dimensions of repair. The attempt to blend healing and relationship-building with the practical business of developing a concrete agreement may create difficulties for conference participants. As illustrated in the case study described below, an example of this is presented when technical calculations of loss and culpability are challenging for conference participants not prepared to deal effectively with both.

A second concern evident in some conferences we observed was related to a 'routinization' of efforts to repair harm in which participants in conferences fall back on common 'going-rate' obligations for standard community service hours, apologies, and so on with little reference or linkage to the harm itself (see Karp, 2001). A third concern noted in conferences addressing extremely trivial offenses or cases in which no victim or representative is present (as illustrated in the school marijuana pipe case presented in the Introduction to this book) is the apparent 'search for harm' that does not really exist, followed by conferencing participants developing an obligatory set of requirements for the offender. We believe that these concerns, highlighted in other case studies observed in this study and described in later chapters, are shared by conferencing proponents regardless of theoretical or philosophical orientation. Moreover, strategic involvement of relevant community members in conjunction with skilled facilitation (as illustrated in the second case study presented below) may help give proper emphasis to the harm suffered by individuals and relationships rather than to other, perhaps ancillary, issues. Moreover, it may also help facilitate movement toward an effective reparative agreement. Rushing to agreement is also a concern associated largely with proponents of healing dialogue theory (e.g. Umbreit, 2001), though our observations suggest that the problem may be less one of ensuring that victim and offender engage in lengthy dialogue, than of allowing the conference to bypass critical phases that allow participants to hear the full story of the harm to victims and to consider the offender's reaction to this.

Both our issues of concern and the sometimes subtle disagreements about conferencing practice evident in practitioner discussions provide vital topics for future research. For example, despite strong commitments to such micro-practice concerns about having offenders or victims speak first, there is no empirical evidence that either approach makes a difference in terms of outcomes; nor do we have any evidence about more theoretically salient issues such as the impact of the role of other stakeholders in completion of agreements and the value of the input of multiple stakeholders into the agreement itself. Such issues of debate, we believe, can lead to clear propositions for future research with important implications for both practice and theory.

Observational case studies: issues, concerns, and resolutions

In this section, we consider problems in conferences that may diminish the likelihood that repair will occur. Such problems may influence the extent to which repair occurs either in the conference or the follow-up period. We present an example of a conference that appeared to become overwhelmed with conflicting priorities, and one that seemed to effectively resolve problems that emerged in dealing with repairing harm. The first case illustrates how the technical details of computing fair financial obligations in restitution contracts may challenge both the skill of volunteer facilitators and the capacity of the process. The challenge may be especially great when the process is oriented toward the expression of feelings in a healing dialogue that also seeks relationship-building and support and then during that session the facilitator attempts to move to an agreement that must address complex financial and equity decisions.

The second illustrates how skilled facilitation by a community-oriented volunteer facilitator (and co-facilitator) can help offender, victim, and their supporters find common ground by effectively eliciting bridging dialogue from a variety of participants.

Case 1: Addressing financial obligations

Unlike some of the circles we allude to in the previous text, in this circle, the victim plays a very different, far more assertive role. The circle raises concerns about the capacity of participants in this process to move from an effective discussion of harm and the need for understanding, support, and healing to the 'nuts and bolts' of a financial agreement. In this rather unusual circle, the victim, a 45-year-old builder/real estate agent, came prepared with photographs, medical bills, and rather extensive evidence of his expenses and physical injuries (e.g. receipts and bank statements). The injuries had resulted from being pushed by the 17-year-old defendant in an altercation in which the victim had cursed at the offender, threatened him, and put his hands on the youth's arms.

In the conference, both parties expressed respect for each other and a desire to develop a settlement that would avoid the court process. The victim acknowledged his own role in the incident (he had been charged with 'making threats' and 'use of fighting words'). Although there appeared to be mutual harm and responsibility, a conclusion was reached that the victim's loss should be addressed. The group seemed to be moving towards a solution that combined partial compensation for the victim with some community service for both parties. Apologies had been made on both sides, yet upon entering the agreement phase – by this time late in the evening – the tone and focus of the conference became more one of a civil court.

Whereas the group seemed to have assumed that the outcome would consist of a small monetary restitution agreement that could be completed by the boy from part-time job wages supplemented by loans from his mother, the victim proposed a 'discount' in full compensation for his losses (estimated at about $17,000) that amounted to an obligation of about $12,000 to cover medical bills and lost wages for the period of time when he was unable to work. When compared with the civil court and the attorney fees on both sides, this seemed to be a better outcome – for the parents of the young person who expressed fear that they could be facing a settlement of more than double that amount upon losing in court as well as a court record for their son who was on the verge of applying for and entering college, and for the uninsured victim (who apparently had based the discount on some estimate of legal fees that would offset the full compensation substantially) who risked losing everything in court.

Most members, based on their comments and concerns expressed during the agreement discussion, felt a sense of unfairness, or at least a concern that the offender and his family were being coerced without establishing culpability and the absence of precipitation on the part of the victim in this case. Moreover, there was no process suggested or attempted to establish the verocity and relevance of all of the victim's supporting documentation. Much information was brought forward in a non-adversarial dialogue about what actually happened – much of it information about the victim's role in the angry confrontation that caused his injury and his apparent acceptance of the offender's statement that there had been no intent to injure him.

Yet these facts, the apologies on both sides, acceptance of responsibility, and the circle's commitment to supporting both families, restoring peace in the community, and taking collective steps to prevent such future confrontations were ignored when it came to negotiating the settlement. And when asked by the facilitator to give input into a reasonable solution, participants (including the observing researchers in the role of community members) seemed unable or unwilling to do so. The victim's loss calculation was not something any of the dozen or so members of the circle wished to challenge, and no one had been prompted in advance to think about how a settlement should be handled.

The two and a half hours of work (not to mention extensive face-to-face preparation with both parties) that seemed initially to accomplish a great deal of healing, education, relationship-building, and open discussion of community problems that had had much to do with precipitating this conflict seemed unrelated to a monetary negotiation that could have been developed by an arbitrator or good restitution program in 20 minutes.

The most straightforward analysis of this circle agreement is simply to recognize that this apparent, generally atypical motivation for participating in a conference of this kind (to maximize financial compensation and to minimize financial obligation) produced atypical results. However, the case illustrates how conferencing processes in general, and circles specifically, may be not well equipped to handle calculation of substantial financial obligations, even while effectively engaging with the emotional harm and resolving conflict. This is especially true when the loss is highly tangible, extensive, and calculated on both sides in comparison to expectations for an adversarial process. The case also is unusual in that it featured a very strong and well-prepared victim who, while not expressing the more anticipated anger, was nonetheless motivated not so much by the need for information, vindication, input, and the increased prospect of *some* rather than *no* reparation, but by a better monetary outcome than would be likely through the court.

Though perhaps better than the court financially and emotionally for both sides, rules of judging loss and obligations, in a context which first establishes culpability (including mutual culpability) in this kind of case, seem deficient in the circle process. A possible alternative explanation is that the preparation and screening phase could have either: (1) screened this case out as inappropriate given indications of the motivations and expectations of these participants (assuming these were apparent in the preparation phase); or (2) brought in technical support, including the resources of circle members given information about the case in advance, in order to better assess actual losses and culpability, and hence develop more reasonable grounds for agreement in the preparation stage. The first option is unsatisfying because it may to fail to address the needs of real victims and offenders for a viable alternative to court, which could provide some reparation, and which could be somewhat responsive to the needs of victim, offender, and community. The second might better avoid a biased settlement, but might need to be prefaced with a requirement that the participants allow the circle to work with them to establish responsibility and mutual culpability. As an alternative, culpability should be first established in court and after that determination is made the circle can provide its multiple functions.

Case 2: Clarifying harm and repair

Effective identification of harm does not always assume a serious offense or chronic offender. As the following case illustrates, the key is rather the presence of victims and community volunteers who focus attention on how those other than the direct victim may be affected. This case also demonstrates effective facilitation guided loosely by a script tailored to the unique philosophy of this program director with the general community conferencing framework. While not obtrusive, the volunteer facilitator is active in making bridging comments that lead effectively toward the reparative goal without dominating the dialogue or limiting stakeholder stories. Both victim and offender appear to receive support from these citizens, and the latter also play an important role in clarifying harm, without over-dramatizing it, and in developing a creative appropriate response relevant to the offense and the level of impact. In this case, there was vandalism under $500, 12 total participants and 2 male juvenile offenders.

> *Facilitator*: 'I'd like to thank John and Charlie [fictitious names of the actual offenders] for coming together to let their stories be heard. One of the community members is stuck in traffic and won't be able to attend. Thanks again to everyone for having the courage to come together and to the parents of those present. [Introduction of herself (as facilitator) and the co-facilitator.] Reminder of no gum or hats. We are here to explore ways we can repair harm and reach solutions and agree on a contract that everyone can sign. This meeting is voluntary and both boys may leave at anytime. If that happens, the case will be referred back to the detective who will write a ticket. The ground rules for the conference are: listen respectfully, use I statements, talk about what 'we' did, silence is OK; we are not here to judge but to repair harm. Let's start with John.'
>
> *John (juvenile offender)*: 'It started out like, "Hey wanna throw water balloons out the window?" So I did. Then I went and talked on the phone and Charlie [co-defendant] came in and said that he hit a car. I told him "Don't do that because I got in trouble already for

that a week ago by my mom." Then the cops came and I had to work off the money. I got grounded too.'

Facilitator: 'Who's been affected?'

John: 'Everyone here. Charlie's Dad and my Dad. The police had to stop their job and come.'

Facilitator: 'Charlie?'

Charlie: 'I hit the car and didn't throw anymore after that. I broke the car windshield.'

Facilitator: 'What were you thinking?'

Charlie: 'That it was fun throwing them out the window. I wasn't really thinking of the consequences. I scared John half to death.'

Facilitator: 'How do you feel?'

Charlie: 'Bad, guilty about it for awhile.'

Facilitator: 'What happened?'

Charlie: 'I was grounded. I had to work to raise money. I affected everyone here and the officers. It made people think twice about what kind of kid I am. Others were affected and they were either mad or sad about it.'

Facilitator: 'Now for Jeff [fictitious name of the actual victim], how were you affected?'

Jeff (16-year-old): 'Well, I couldn't drive for a few days. I had to pay for it and get it replaced. I was mad and didn't know what to do. I went home to tell my mom. My mom and I went back to see who did it. I felt better once I knew what happened and knew that we would get it all figured out. It's not that big of a deal anymore. My family was mad and my friends laughed.'

Facilitator: 'It's been difficult hasn't it?'

Jeff's mom: 'It was challenging financially and it was a hindrance because I couldn't drive. My parents had to pick up and take the boys to school. Windshields are replaceable. I can replace the windshield but I can't replace my son. He could have swerved and had an accident. I'm grateful a broken windshield was the only result. I am just really happy that my son is OK. It's been scary knowing that my son is out driving. I wonder if he is driving safely. It's kind of a joke around the house to beware of UFOs. It's important to realize that we can choose our actions but not always the consequences. A rock in the pond has far reaching consequences.'

Charlie's mom: 'It's been hard knowing that my child is capable of really hurting someone else. I had a long "what if" talk with him after I got over the shock. How shocking it must have been for the victim. What if he had swerved – what if it was a mom and a small child. The consequences of his behavior are his responsibility. That's how it affected me the most.'

Charlie: 'I just got done being grounded.'

Charlie's mom: 'He needs to be responsible for himself. There is only so much that I can do. I'm not sure what to say. It's been challenging. I've got some good work out of him. It was frustrating and hurtful to see the police at my house when I got home from the grocery store. Both boys said they screwed up and were ready to do things to make things right. My son said he knew better. Now it's about how do we move forward and build on the strengths both boys showed. My son knows that I am a single mom and knows our budget. He knows the consequences of moving money around. It's been a good wake up call for me. The boys are making choices.'

Community member: 'I am concerned about the choices and how so many people were affected by them. I really want to commend them for coming forward. I'd like to find ways to help young people make better future choices.'

Facilitator: 'Now after hearing everyone, is there anything anyone would like to add?'

John: 'I am sorry.'

Charlie: 'Me too.'

Co-facilitator: 'It's obvious that you both have parents that care. You are really lucky to have the parents that you have. Water balloons are fun. I really appreciate that you said you were sorry. How much did the windshield cost?'

Jeff's Mom: '$172.89 to have it replaced and installed.'

Co-facilitator: 'Have you been paid?'

Jeff's Mom: 'No.'

John: 'I've earned enough to pay for some of it. Maybe $40.'

Charlie: 'I have more than enough to pay for the windshield. I have been working.'

Co-facilitator: 'Let's review where we are. Jeff was scared and angry about what happened and his friends laughed. It was said that things could have been much more serious but the level of impact was still felt. Jeff's mother had to make alternative transportation arrangements. Charlie's mom had a long conversation about "what ifs" and realizes that her son is growing up. The choices that her son makes affect other people. She is glad that her son came forward and stated he was responsible. She feels closer to her son because of this incident.'

Community member: 'I too am happy that the boys admitted responsibility. I feel they will make better future choices. There is a caring sense with people in this community.'

Co-facilitator: 'Let's go over the asset survey for the boys. John feels that he has support from his parents, about 20 friends, gets good grades, likes to skate and play in the snow, he's up for mowing lawns, likes science, cars, likes to be different (has blue hair), wishes for world peace, money and a house of his own. Charlie has about five close friends, likes to work on the school computer and mow lawns, likes to help others, likes to figure out how things work, likes photography, music, I work at the farmers market with my parents, wishes include food for everyone, cut down on my bad attitude and wish this didn't happen. [Charlie's mom is in tears as his strengths are read aloud.]'

Facilitator: 'Now let's work towards an agreement.'

Jeff: 'I just want my mom to be paid back and then I don't know.'

John: 'I want to pay you back. I could wash your car sometime too.'

John's mom: 'How about writing a note to their [victim's] family and the officer who responded to the call? I really appreciate the officers and was very impressed with them. They were very respectful and this was important because it was the boys' first contact.'

Jeff's mom: 'I feel it's been great to have a place to voice our frustration and I think that getting reimbursed for the windshield is enough.'

Community member: 'How were you inconvenienced?'

Jeff's mom: 'The only thing is that my son has to drive. I hated getting my parents involved because they were going out of town and had to change plans. I'm a nurse and I work terrible hours.'

Co-facilitator: 'Write a note to your grandparents about what you learned? The main thing is that victim and his mother feel repaired.'

Facilitator: 'Have the boys helped with chores?'

Jeff: 'That's nice but I can mow my own lawn. It's summer and there are better things for them to do. Mowing someone else's lawn would be a real drag.'

John's mom: 'Maybe they could do some community service like serving lunch at the OUR center. If they could find one thing during the summer as a way of saying thanks for the RJ opportunity. Find a way to give back.'

Co-facilitator: 'Let's start by paying back the money. Do you divide it down the middle? I'm not sure how you feel? Charlie?'

Charlie: 'I will pay all of it.'

John: 'But you were at my house with my balloons and I filled them.'

Charlie's mom: 'I feel that it was my son's choice to throw the balloons. Comes down to money in certain ways – the value of the experience is important too not just the money.'

John's mom: 'I don't think that Charlie should pay all of it. You do something you should take responsibility. John?'

John: 'I guess that I should pay half.'

Facilitator: 'Charlie?'

Charlie: 'I don't know, I was planning on paying for all of it.'

Community member: 'How about just putting the money available in the pot ($40 and the $172.89) and they can do what they want with it.'

Facilitator: 'Buy grandparents a gift certificate for dinner for their time and trouble.'

Charlie: 'I think that is a good idea.'

Co-facilitator: 'Letters to Jeff and his family and to his grandparents as well as police officers. Mailed to [program] first and then sent out. Jeff and his mom will get a gift certificate for dinner for the grandparents. Both moms feel that community service would be a good idea ... something they could choose and enjoy. The boys could participate in more community group conferences and affected community. The police fair is also coming up. They are looking for help at Rogers Grove for Rhythm on the River. If we are going to leave community service up to you, that's fine just get the form signed. Jeff and mom, what would you like to see?'

Jeff's mom: 'Maybe some church work, or at the SafeHouse or the OUR Center delivering food.'

John's Mom: 'There might be age requirements for community service. John is involved in church. To me it's more the idea of serving ... like the community Food Share or Meals on Wheels.'

Co-facilitator: 'So how about you try and move in that direction and we can leave the contract general. We really want the kids to succeed.'

Facilitator: 'Do we need to narrow?'

Co-facilitator: 'Pay back the money when?'

John's mom: 'I want to pay them right away.'

Charlie's mom: 'Yes, now would be a good time to pay them.'

Co-facilitator: 'OK, so what do we have? Money, letters, drop washing the car because the victims don't feel that it's necessary, community service of choice. Letters can be brought in with the money, get them out of the way. Be sure that you call the office before you come. Make sure we are here.'

Case summary

Note again the active participation of the offenders in this format, something that seems all too rare in many conferences, as well as the clear expression of the actual harm resulting from what on its face appears to be a trivial incident. The facilitator's work is to manage multiple participants and allows various stakeholder voices to be heard, prompting and raising questions when necessary. The amended reintegrative shaming theory is in effect here as the comments of anonymous community members are thrown into the mix. They add texture to the harm story, provide a sense of greater community concern, and ultimately help to resolve problems in formulating the agreement. In other conferences involving more serious cases, volunteers can be even more helpful, for example, by making bridging statements toward common ground, and more importantly by providing empathy and support for offender, victim, and parents from a place that is unexpected, the larger community.

Chapter 6

Stakeholder involvement in the conferencing environment

The principle of stakeholder participation – victims, offenders and communities should have the opportunity for active involvement in the justice process as early and as fully as possible.

(Van Ness and Strong, 1997)

Introduction

In an important sense, this entire text is focused on the principle of stakeholder involvement. Though not the only means of accomplishing the objective of inviting those most affected by crime to have a primary role in deciding what should be done in response to it, restorative group conferencing programs have as their primary rationale to provide a structured means of accomplishing this task. Given this central import-ance and the relevance of the involvement principle throughout the text, the relatively brief presentation of data and discussion in this chapter is organized around several considerations or components of variation and debate about how such involvement is to be managed.

We begin with the general question how and why (to what end) do conferencing practitioners engage victim, offender, and community in the various phases and stages of the conferencing process. While there is much consensus about the need to engage and generally empower these stakeholders in restorative dialogue, we focus in this chapter primarily on points of difference and disagreement about when and how to do so. For example, though there is little if any data to support contentions about the need for preparation, many such disagreements are of interest because they are based on strong commitments to certain principles and values, as well as theories about the conferencing process. Following Van Ness and Strong (2001), we anchor what is necessarily a wide-ranging discussion of issues raised by the practitioners we observed and interviewed with respect to three primary considerations or components of inclusion in a restorative process.

First, the quality of the *invitation* to participate is gauged by appropriate acknowledgement and engagement of various stakeholders and their interests in the conferencing process. Second, the *communication* component is concerned with the quality of the narrative or dialogue in the conference and the extent to which the victim, offender, and others affected feel that they are encouraged to tell their stories and supported in expressing their feelings and emotions (Van Ness, 2001). Third, the various *roles* stakeholders and the facilitator play in a conference are a consideration concerned with the expectations coordinators and other participants may have of each other and with how such roles are strategized and negotiated in preparation for and in the process of the conference. To what extent and how do coordinators select and prepare participants for roles in advance? In general, what is the nature of pre-conference work related to selection and preparation vis-à-vis these roles with the three stakeholders? What roles are victims and community members called on to play in conferencing programs (e.g. describing community or victim harms, supporting young people, reinforcing community norms), and how does the facilitator encourage this role-taking and ensure that various 'voices' representing different interests and perspectives emerge?

In addition to these vital concerns with the quality of inclusion of stakeholders in the process, we are interested in how practitioners think about objectives or intermediate outcomes of the conferencing process as these relate to the overall goal of getting stakeholders to assume responsibility for the response to the incident in question. What results do practitioners wish to achieve at the end of the conference, how are these intermediate outcomes pursued, and to what extent are practitioners' actions driven by commitment to a specific theory of intervention? Do practitioners seek to ensure that offenders experience respectful disapproval and show emotional signs of remorse as indicated in the theory of reintegrative shaming, or do they seek to create an open dialogue guided by the concerns of victim and offender that will lead to outcomes such as reduction in fear, vindication, and empathy as would be hypothesized in a theory of healing dialogue? Or, do they believe that what is essential is to ensure movement of victim, offender, and community to a shared general understanding as suggested in a theory of common ground?

While these process dimensions are relevant to all conferencing programs and models, qualitative data on a relative handful of programs cannot provide a complete picture of the scope of variation in how programs prioritize the concerns relevant to each dimension. We do, however, depict a range of practice priorities sufficient to allow us to raise questions for future research about what stakeholders are included and why, how communication is managed, and how roles emerge or are negotiated.

To address the above questions, we rely in this chapter on several sources of qualitative data, using references to the national survey occasionally as background for our discussion. We draw primarily on data from focus groups in which seasoned practitioners selected for their experience in specific conferencing models addressed general questions related to process dimensions. Structured interviews with other practitioners were also used to provide additional variation on process dimensions and the relative importance of various intermediate outcomes. Both groups of respondents were asked to prioritize intermediate outcomes and then to speculate about how these related to what they viewed as the most important long-term outcomes. As might be expected, these theories of intervention are often loosely formulated. But though they may not match up with the theories outlined in the background discussion in Chapter 2, they are nonetheless valuable because they drive practice decisions and may reflect other important theories not yet identified. We draw upon observational data from conferences throughout in clarifying how various practice ideals actually played out in specific conferencing phases, and at the end of the chapter present two accounts from participant observation of case studies that illustrate strengths and weaknesses of implementation with regard to dimensions of quality and the extent to which there is consistency between practice and the pursuit of intermediate outcomes.

The value of inclusion: general support for stakeholder involvement and model variation

In general, conferencing programs share a common vision of involving those most affected by the crime in decisions about what will be done in response to it. Hence, inclusion is a fundamental value and indeed must be a central part of the vision of restorative conferencing as an alternative to the traditional juvenile justice process. Despite this shared vision of inclusion, in practice programs vary in terms of the relative *urgency* of ensuring that stakeholders other than the offender participate. As we found in most other comparisons on adherence to restorative principles, variation appears wider between individual programs than between model types. However, it is in the interpretation of the value of inclusion and the principle of involvement that observers will note the most difference between models. As discussed in Chapter 1, some of this variation is structural and some appears to be built into the nature of the process of certain conferencing models (Bazemore and Umbreit, 2001).

Some is also a function of individual philosophy and a commitment to specific intervention theories.

Accounting for variation in victim participation

What is important is what programs do to ensure victim involvement and the priority given to these activities. The qualitative data do not provide complete answers, but suggest a range of variation, from primary and almost full-service efforts to include victims, to responses that appear to be an afterthought. A common low-end boundary of minimal effort at inclusion is sending a letter to victims inviting participation. Other programs go way beyond this, including letters and calls and, at the other end, face-to-face contact. In between are programs that attempt a follow-up call or try to meet victims at preliminary court hearings. Typical of many board programs we encountered, a program director in Arizona reported that staff call the victim and then send a letter. In addition, the state system, in accordance with victim's rights legislation, notifies victims of all hearings and, if the victim makes an appearance at the adjudication hearing, they are told that the board meeting will take place.[1]

Variation in victim participation rates is explained by practitioners in different ways, though neither our survey nor the qualitative study allow for systematic correlation between participation rates and independent variables including the level of seriousness of the case. Seriousness is thought by some to be positively related to participation (e.g. Karp and Walther, 2001), though some practitioners speculated that fear kept many victims away, a factor that would seem to be associated with seriousness of the offense. We identified programs with a relatively serious caseload that had very low victim participation rates (25 per cent), and also programs such as the Indianapolis FGC program that primarily accepts only first-offender and misdemeanor cases yet features a 90 per cent rate of participation for crime victims (McGarrell, 2001). Another police-based conferencing program, the Colorado FGC/community conference discussed in the previous chapter, also with a generally low-level of caseload seriousness, claims a 98 per cent victim participation rate.

Although many practitioners interviewed and observed agree that victims are the most difficult stakeholders to get to conferences, some programs do a better job of ensuring victim participation than others for reasons that are not altogether clear. Overall, the level of priority afforded to victim participation in some models and programs, whether or not the only factor, seems to play a primary role in successful victim participation. In programs where support staff or volunteers are specifically assigned to victim contact and such contact is not limited to letters or sporadic phone calls, and where conferences are held at the convenience of victims, participation rates are generally high. We note, however, that we know of no empirical research that distinguishes programs with high rates of victim participation from those with low rates.

Inclusion and other participants

As noted in Chapter 1, restorative group conferencing models vary in the relative priority given to participants other than victims. Although VOM does not generally require or actively encourage participation of other community members, it is apparent that a number of VOM programs now seem open to involving family members and perhaps other supporters in juvenile cases (Umbreit and Greenwood, 1997).

Most neighborhood boards and circles programs may also express commitment to involving victims, but some staff and volunteers feel that they can accomplish their goals of involving the community in decision-making without the victim or a surrogate. These programs may actively seek victim participation but can go forward without it by relying heavily on their volunteer members to guide a process focused on developing plans to meet the needs of offenders and their families. Circle and board programs, however, cannot function without the participation of community volunteers.

Dimensions of involvement in conference stages and phases

The three dimensions of inclusion or involvement – invitation, communication, and stakeholder roles – are discussed below in the stages and phases of the conference where they are most relevant. Not all dimensions are discussed in each phase. Invitation is associated primarily with pre-conferencing and preparation. Acknowledging interests and flexibility in terms of allowing for alternative approaches also extends through other phases and stages. Discussion of the communication dimension and its components – e.g. narrative, emotional expression, understanding – as well as participant transformation is discussed primarily in the storytelling and acknowledgement phases. We consider stakeholder roles in each phase as appropriate.

Stage 1: Preparation

In much conferencing and restorative justice practitioner training literature, preparation is the sine qua non of the conferencing experience (Umbreit, 1999; McDonald et al., 1995; Stuart, 2001). Most, though not all, of the importance of preparation has to do with the principle of stakeholder involvement. Practice guides in models such as VOM/D, for example, have long described preparation as the most important work of the conference, precisely because it is viewed as intimately related to the quality of participation and to the satisfaction of victim and offender with conferencing outcomes (Umbreit, 1999). As a general rule, conferencing practitioners wish to avoid going into a conference 'cold,' and they also wish to minimize any anxiety the victim, offender, and others may have about the structure or nature of the conference.

Invitation, victim participation, and face-to-face meetings

A key feature of the invitation to participate in a conference is the extent to which it acknowledges and emphasizes the interests of the particular stakeholder. Victims, for example, may be concerned that the meeting is actually more about recognizing and meeting the offender's needs. For the offender, it may be about facing responsibility for harm, and the opportunity for meeting an obligation. In terms of the mechanics of the invitation, most programs seem to rely on letter and phone contact, with a few strongly committed to face-to-face meetings in preparation for the conference.

A good conference is generally seen as one in which victim and offender, and ideally all other participants, have been thoroughly briefed, ideally through a face-to-face meeting. However, the reality of face-to-face preparation can be quite different. As a resource issue, preparation may compete with other goals including timeliness of conferences. In some programs, face-to-face preparation for both victim and offender is a non-negotiable requirement. Many others require face-to-face offender and or family meetings, but such meetings are optional for victims. Some practitioners insisted that the face-to-face contact is the most important variable in increasing victim participation, as asserted by this peace-making circle practitioner:

> The face-to-face work with circles is imperative. I don't think we'd ever have any circle work *if I sent out a letter* or *if I was a voice on the phone*. To increase involvement, it is important to meet with the people involved.

Challenges to face-to-face preparation

Despite their intensive, interpersonal nature, not all circles are able to achieve a high rate of victim involvement. While some may arrange multiple pre-meetings with each stakeholder, this does not always occur, and such meetings seem more likely with the offender. In their intensive study of a Minnesota circle program, for example, Coates et al. (2000) noted that although multiple circles presumably included preparatory meetings, they were relatively infrequent; only five of the 13 cases studied had more than one circle, and only two cases had face-to-face meetings prior to their circle. Circle keepers, who often conducted extensive preparation over the phone, reported that parents of victims and offenders in particular often did not want to take the time to meet prior to the circle itself. We believe, based on accounts from other programs, that victims (especially in less serious cases) may be unwilling to spend time on a pre-conference meeting, even when they agree to attend the conference itself.

Another director of a well-established VOM/D program that conducts hundreds of mediations per year in Los Angeles, but does not offer face-to-face victim preparation meetings, challenged the importance of such pre-conference contact:

> We get about a 60–70% percent [victim] participation rate. Most victim/offender mediation programs have that pre-visit. We don't because we want to handle more cases; we don't think it's either appropriate for volunteers or staff to be driving into neighborhoods that they don't know in Los Angeles, to have those pre-meetings with either the victim or offender.

The role of face-to-face pre-meeting contact, as well as other factors in improving victim and other stakeholder participation, has not been tested empirically. It may be that the ultimate value of this labor-intensive preparation process may have more to do with the success of the conference in meeting other goals of repair, effective communication, and so on, rather than increasing participation rates. For example, as one VOM/D practitioner put it, the face-to-face preparation meeting defines the standard or benchmark for later determining when the conference can be successfully terminated. When asked how he knows when a conference is complete, he noted that you know this 'when you've heard them say everything that they said in the home visit.'

Generally, not holding face-to-face pre-conference meetings is characterized as a resource issue. However, many boards and some FGC programs will meet with the offender, and at times parents prior to conference, but will call or simply write to the victim. With boards, this offender focus is in part historical, and inclusion of victims was simply never a priority until recently. Similarly, though most circles appear to make this offer to victims, face-to-face preparation with victims is not a mandate. All programs appear to respect the victim's choice *not* to meet, and some also provide other services or opportunities for input if requested by the victim.

Interestingly, the director of the aforementioned VOM/D program that claims high victim participation rates was the only practitioner in our study to make a strong philosophical and theoretical case *against* face-to-face pre-conference meetings. The argument against pre-conference meetings was based upon a concern that rehearsing victim and offender stories would limit the quality of the emotional expression in the conference:

> *We want the fireworks to happen in the meeting.* We don't want the victim to get used to telling how much pain they had, we don't want the offender apologizing to us, we want them to cry in front of the victim, in front of the parents ... so we want to save the dynamic of that meeting, because we think that's where the dynamic of the meeting takes place, and not so much in the preparation ...

The director of a combination neighborhood board and community conferencing program presented a very different rationale *for* preparatory meetings that had little to do with victim and offender. Here she describes her rather extensive face-to-face preparation process as one focused especially on getting the right mix of participants for a particular conference:

> ... we have someone go out to the house and interview everybody ... when we began going out into the community, the business community said they wanted a bigger voice – so now we have several facilitators ... I do a lot more prep than I think about. One of my tasks is deciding on which three community people are going to sit in on the process ... we don't just rotate or have the same three or have a set night or anything. It's [finding] the best mix of gender or finding the right personality, or just knowing that this kid is going to relate to this volunteer or have a shared interest or whatever ... a lot of time is spent in putting that together.

This NAB program presents an interesting case of an adaptation of a model that typically does not do a good job with victim participation. Though the above described effort is primarily about the selection and preparation of offender, family, and community members, this program also gives victims the option of a face-to-face preparation meeting conducted by a volunteer. Staff report that about half take advantage of this option, and their victim participation rate in the actual conference is relatively high for boards, at about 75 per cent when surrogate participants chosen by the victim are included.

Participants and rationales for inclusion

Who should participate in the conference? Beyond victim and offender, there are many options for involving participants and a number of considerations in determining who should be at the conference. While we encountered some controversy around whether and how to invite other stakeholders, we did not find any programs, including some traditional VOM models, that excluded or opposed having parents or other supporters of victim and offender present in the conference. One VOM program, however, allows parents to participate only after youth and victim have completed their phase of the mediation.

Perspectives on the involvement of other participants and how the decision should be made appear to be linked loosely to program model philosophies. These differences in philosophy, though not absolute, are interesting because they suggest adherence to different theories about how the conference is most likely to impact stakeholders – especially the offender. The merits of including various participants and of various methods of deciding who should be at the conference are considered below.

Letting victim and offender decide
For proponents of VOM/D, the essential stakeholders are the victim and offender. Though family and supporters may be viewed as important and, according to some accounts (Umbreit and Greenwood, 1997) often do participate, the interests of victim and offender are central to the conference, and should therefore drive this decision. In response to a question about whether or not she would want to include other supporters and community members, a VOM/D program director replied that decisions about who should participate in the conference beyond these core stakeholders were never hers to make:

> *whatever the victim and offender say* ... when we do preparation, we ask the parties who needs to be involved. Usually the victim is there – sometimes a stand in, but not often. Other people may be there ... some only to support; some want to participate.

While associated especially with victim–offender mediation, this orientation is not limited to this model. For example, a police-based family group conferencing program director noted that 'I would mirror what she said. Ask the victim and offender how they define community. These [individuals identified by victim and offenders] are the people we try to bring into the conference.' In essence, the objectives of such a conference would appear to be focused on the goals associated with victim/offender exchange, assumed to be achieved when victim and offender are given maximum discretion to create a situation in which a healing dialogue will be possible.

There is a subtle yet important difference between this perspective and the instruction provided in the practice manual of the most widely known FGC training organization in the US, RealJustice (McDonald et al., 1995). In the practice manual, the facilitator is encouraged to play the primary role in strategizing and in making the decision about which supporters of victim and offender will attend. Therefore, rather than having the young offender and the victim make the selection, the facilitator might consult with them and with others in order to identify the most appropriate participants. Where the VOM approach noted above would nonetheless generally follow the offender and the victim's recommendation of support persons [barring of course those with criminal records or those thought likely to be a disruptive influence], the FGC organizers we encountered generally take on the task of strategically locating the person or persons most influential in the young person's life. They do so first by asking the young person himself/herself, but may then go beyond the offender's choice in making the decision.

This rationale in the case of FGC is consistent with the reintegrative shaming theory in the priority given to choosing the right participants for the conference, as gauged especially in terms of their potential to exert a positive emotional impact on the offender (Braithwaite and Mugford, 1994). Specifically, those closest to and most respected by the offender are viewed as most likely to influence their behavior. In addition to supporting the offender and the victim, informal mentors or advocates such as family, extended family members, and peers are also expected in FGC to affirm the behavioral norm that was violated by denouncing the offense and the harm it caused, while reaffirming the dignity and worth of the offender (Braithwaite and Mugford, 1994; Braithwaite and Parker, 1999).

Such supporters are of course different than anonymous community members who might nonetheless speak eloquently on behalf of community norms and standards, and also show general support for the offender and other stakeholders (McDonald et al., 1995). Selection of such participants is therefore discouraged in RealJustice training, as McDonald et al. (1995: 28) recommend: 'invite only those people who have some direct involvement with the incident or who are significant people in the lives of the offenders or victims.'

Beyond victim and offender
Other programs will also use the wishes of victim and offender as a primary guide, but then go somewhat further. They begin with the requirements of the program design, and then move to recruit others based on judgements about individuals the offender or victim seem connected to. As illustrated by this NAB program director's comment, 'we are similar as well on prioritizing victim and offender choice but parents *have to be there*; [we may also include] trained secondary victims ... and we also ask about aunts, uncles, etc.'

A school-based FGC program provides a creative twist on this approach to finding the right participants by getting recommendations from the friends of the offender and victim. The principal, who founded and directs the program, goes beyond the offender to recruit participants, but nonetheless seeks to ensure that the conference will include individuals likely to have an impact on the offender and victim, and have something to say relevant to the impact of the offense on school climate. In doing so, he wants not only to reach the offender and victim, but to discuss issues of how the behavior in question may have adversely impacted the quality of life of *all students*, hence reflecting a broader concern with norm affirmation and community-building outcomes.

In another school-based conferencing program, participants may include a variety of affected community members. But for this circle keeper working in Minneapolis high schools, the choice is driven by the harm to relationships impacted by the crime and the scope of the reparative task. In making this choice to engage members of a broader community, this facilitator may have any of several unspecified theoretical purposes in mind based on consideration of addressing broader past harms, community-building, social support, or norm affirmation. The situation and specific incident may in such cases necessitate widening the circle significantly:

> In addition to kids, teachers, and other affected members of this community, [the circle] may involve having a city official, a school board member, parents, or somebody else who is related to a specific incident . . . There is no right mix of people, usually it depends on the context of the case and the dynamics of the people involved.

Letting the facilitator decide

At the other extreme from those committed only to the choices of victim and offender about participant involvement are more community-oriented practitioners who believe in selecting and including a broader range of participants. When asked why she would consider bringing in community members unknown to the offender or victim, the director of a 'community conferencing' program variation of FGC explained that:

> I found that in bringing people in that the juvenile *cannot* relate to [directly], yes, they ask, 'Who are these people?' [But we want to] get more community buy-in and participation. The energy is stronger, and we are more successful that way. We are looking for a bridge to the larger community.

In addition to the apparent goal of engaging a broader group of community members as volunteers or supporters of her program, this practitioner is also concerned with having peer or youth representation at every conference, even if such peers are usually not acquaintances of the offender:

We are hoping for one outcome – the offender will recognize them as offering a broader connection to the community . . . they get a certain kind of feedback from this: '*Look how many people care about me*' [italics ours]. In the beginning, [in choosing participants] we stuck to who was impacted directly, but learned how valuable it was to have [broader] community – who have some distance from the offender – bring a different perspective.

Originally trained in the classic FGC model which advocates sticking to a smaller group of intimates, this program director also felt a need to include members of the larger community. Citing more practical justifications, she argues that, in any case, 'it is rare for the juvenile to (identify and) bring his own support group,' a rationale validated by a number of practitioners who talked about the struggle to get the offender to identify supporters, thus leading by default to reliance on the 'voice-of- the-broader community.'

This use of general community volunteers rather than, or in addition to, family or friends is the approach of most neighborhood boards. Though board members are generally neighbors of the offender, an intimate acquaintance with an offender and his/her family (or with the crime victim) is usually an accidental rather than planned occurrence. The theory-in-use is a version of social support theory (Cullen, 1994), albeit one with a different twist focused on the role the board member plays as neighbor, and at times fellow parent. As Pranis has noted (Pranis and Bazemore, 2000), this is about bringing the 'voice of experience' of one who has lived through the experience of parent, victim, or offender into the conference. Such experience may create one of the most meaningful foundations for a relationship of support, especially because those who share such experience can empathize with the primary stakeholders, and can support parents in an effort to set limits. Indeed, volunteer board members we spoke to often talked about how they could identify with parents even though they didn't know them and, through experiences with their own children, could understand parent/child conflict and communication problems. Because these volunteers are unpaid, offender, victims, and families are believed to respect and value their input and assistance, and when they live in the same neighborhood, offender and victim may find their input more relevant.

Board directors seem to have a strong commitment to the theory that including neighbors, or other individuals who care about the event, the victim, the family, and the offender – *whether intimate with the offender or not* – is good practice. Such inclusion is thought to communicate to the offender that he or she is valuable, even to those he or she does not know. Although the connection with offender and/or victim is not generally based on intimacy, it may represent something more 'organic' by virtue of having experienced what offenders and their families are going through.

Matching and recruiting volunteers: representation and the issue of balance
In a circle program in South St Paul, Minnesota, there is also a great deal of strategizing about who should participate in order to bring community volunteers who may make an instrumental, as well as an affective, contribution as a resource to the offender or victim. Their goal is to find community members with 'similar experiences who may be mentors,' or serve 'as good resources to bring a specific perspective' on problems that are likely to be addressed. This may include an employer, an educator, a minister, a substance abuse treatment provider, or a family counselor. In a similar way, the previously mentioned director of the conferencing program who modified the reintegrative shaming theory to include the broader community points out that having a rich community volunteer base allows one to 'fit volunteers with a solution [by virtue of their skills and connections] to the problem.'

A probation-based FGC program director also reports that she calls on affected community members to play certain roles in the conference. This probation supervisor and program coordinator noted that her community members often make points about community norms and standards that would sound authoritarian if made by a law enforcement or other system professional. Other practitioners, including the director of an inner-city board program, noted the importance of conference make-up and balance to fit a demographic profile. This strategy involves recruiting ethnically and racially diverse participants for each of his boards to match up with victim and offender: 'to help with community connections . . . our boards will look very different depending on the case.'

Balancing roles
If readers are wondering by now if all or most of this pre-conference strategizing is only about making an impact on the offender, there is perhaps good reason for this concern. Though most facilitators seem attuned to the interest of the victim in other ways – e.g. emphasizing reparative needs, ensuring that victims are supported and feel comfortable telling their stories – selection of other conference participants often appears to be focused primarily on the contribution the participant can make to achieve offender outcomes. However, more experienced participants are often self-critical about this, and some are beginning to strategize about how to include victim supporters more effectively, and about what role they should play in the encounter. Indeed, time is often spent in some programs to ensure that a victim advocate and/or other victim-sensitive community members are present to support and speak on the victim's behalf.

Yet in many NAB programs where the victim focus is relatively new, and in other programs strongly committed to offender impact, there may be little discussion of strategies to engage those who can help the conference meet victim needs. Some participants may even be uncomfortable in supporting the relatively small number of victims who do show up for conferences – in part because victim participation rates are so low in some programs that facilitators or volunteers may be surprised when a victim chooses to participate. Indeed, for some practitioners, the emphasis on support and impact on the young offender is justified when the victim is a stable adult who has suffered relatively little trauma from the actions of an unstable offender who has many needs, including the need to change his behavior. The concern about imbalance in favor of the offender is illustrated in the following exchange:

> *Question (from a VOM/D Director)*: 'I am hearing an awful lot of focus on the offender in this discussion . . . what about the victim? Don't you think this needs to be more balanced?'
>
> *Answer (from a community conference director)*: 'We [speaking of staff and volunteers in her program] ask ourselves all the time about this problem . . . we hold several team meetings a year and raise that [concern] . . . we have to work at remembering. [Referring to a systemic problem about data collection] . . . unfortunately, we don't get a body of information on the victim.

In the context of the current offender-driven system that indeed collects little, if any, data on victim needs, and lacks even rudimentary theories of intervention related to victim participation and healing, this problem of a general lack of victim focus might be expected. But it also reflects the fact that even the most experienced and well-intended programs do not live up to their vision of serving three stakeholders. As this practitioner implied, however, those that move incrementally closer to providing equal services and an equal focus on victims seem to be constantly confronting resource allocation problems not necessarily of their own making. In addition, some described staff and volunteer biases toward helping the offender – coupled with some unease about working with victims.

Other practitioners note that unfortunately the offender focus feeds on itself and becomes a self-perpetuating cycle the more often the person directly victimized by the offense is not present at the conference. Even those with high victim participation rates might agree with this board coordinator who explained that: 'When we have secondary victims (e.g. security staff from department stores, community volunteers presenting the individual victim's view), we see more of an offender focus. When the real victim is there, [people are more likely] to be focused on the harm.'

Like boards, other programs such as circles that may reach out to and offer circles specifically for the victim may also miss the quality of interaction possible when both victim and offender are present. The cycle is further perpetuated when victims 'choose not to participate' in a process they may sense is really about working with an offender and his/her family.

Some suggest that part of the problem may even be an excessive concern with ensuring that young offenders are not overwhelmed by adults (see Braithwaite and Parker, 1999; Bazemore and Earle, 2002), including the victim. One police officer who directed an FGC program expressed his concern about what he viewed as a greater imbalance than those associated with one juvenile facing a variety of adults:

> Carolyn used the word 'balance.' There is a kind of tug-of-war and lots of discussion about balance. But if the offender created five victims, [she/he] needs to face all those victims. I will not try to balance that out. [On the other hand], five offenders and one victim may not be appropriate, unless the victim is OK with it. We need to err on the side of the victim to get real balance – since we start with a big imbalance . . .

According to this practitioner, to achieve such real balance, it may even be necessary to limit or even screen out certain voices in the conference:

> If someone [a peer] is coming to support the offender to continue behavior that brought them there, that is not appropriate. If the victim is stuck in revenge mode, that is not appropriate either.

Others responding to this comment argued for the value of representing diverse viewpoints, for example, to become cognizant of other influences on the offender's behavior. The suggested remedy for the problem identified is hence not exclusion of participants but rather including other strong and credible voices (e.g. other peers) to counter the negative perspective. This police officer also feels that inclusiveness in participant selection on the victim's behalf may require thinking more broadly about who has been harmed and defining victimization in a more general sense. For example, he notes that some programs also emphasize harm to parents as ancillary victims: 'If the kid has parents, they are victimized also – I do make that clear in every case.' Though not directly addressed here, the problem of a *power* imbalance between youthful offenders and adult victims is, however, a difficult one whose ramifications are clearly illustrated in one of the case studies provided at the end of this chapter.

Others suggested that the problem of balance was less about getting numerical parity between victim and offender and more about ensuring that the victim's voice is heard. One school-based practitioner who promotes 'on-the-spot,' often brief restorative encounters rather than full-blown conferences for every incident suggests that the 'quality control' needed to accomplish this goal is provided when the process follows Howard Zehr's guiding questions: what is the harm; how do we repair it; and who is responsible for this repair? Though conferences may be highly uneven in their application of these questions, this practitioner believes that they provide the vital guidance to an inclusive informal response, whether it amounts to a ten-minute meeting between two students who have an argument or a three-hour circle involving multiple participants.

In summary, inclusion strategies for the selection of participants involve complex considerations. These are based on theoretical assumptions about who can have the most impact on a successful conference generally and on the offender's behavior specifically. Who is allowed to decide and why certain participants are chosen is also related to dimensions of stakeholder involvement such as role-taking and communication, which become even more important in other phases of the conference. In the pre-conference process, such decisions may impact directly on other dimensions of process such as acknowledgement of diverse interests and openness to alternative processes (e.g. a board's capacity to move from a more structured question and answer process led by board members to a more open dialogue with offender, victim, and family).

Stage 2: The conferencing process

Phase I: Introduction and opening

The introduction to the conference must establish both expectations and ground rules for the encounter that is to follow, as well as provide a sense of comfort and security. In this opening phase, ritual is widely accepted as a means of creating the safe and somewhat shielded environment necessary to promote a dialogue that will allow participants to feel that they have been heard, *and* that they have in turn listened carefully to the stories of those harmed by the offense. Such ritual also helps participants make the transition from the world outside the conference to a space in which they feel free to 'tune out' other daily concerns and focus on the issue at hand.

In a recent training on peace-making circles, the trainer used Thomas Dryver's rationales to emphasize the importance of ritual to: (1) create order; (2) create community; and, (3) create social transformation. In circles, the use of the 'talking piece' itself is a ritual which creates order by managing dialogue in an unobtrusive way not dependent on the personality and skills of the facilitator. As the trainer in this session summed up, 'ritual marks a space to help us behave more in line with our values.' Those conducting conferences with young people in particular find that rituals, better than verbalized expressions of purpose and rules of process, communicate what is needed for conference participants to accomplish their work effectively. Though skilled facilitators may use a variety of rituals to refocus attention, resolve conflict or get through difficult times in the conference itself, the opening is believed by most to be the time to use ritual to set the proper tone for what is to come.

In some cases, the ritual of a conference may not appear to differ much from the ritual of the courts though without the legalistic overtones. In other cases, it may also reflect certain cultural and/or spiritual values as part of an effort on behalf of the facilitator to create a very different, even sacred, informal space. Though this use of such ritual may be seen as personalizing and therefore biasing the conference, it is generally not perceived this way since many conferencing facilitators – with the exception of some traditionally trained mediators – are not expected to maintain a neutral or unbiased role. As McCold (2000: 90) observes in the case of family group conferencing: 'Conferences begin with the assumption that a wrong has been done and that the offender has an obligation to repair that wrong as much as possible (hardly a neutral position).'

Circle keepers, for example, are encouraged to maintain openness, hearing all opinions, but are not expected to refrain from voicing their own opinions. Indeed, the charge for all circle members to 'speak from the heart' is not one that the circle keeper him or herself is expected to ignore, and circle keepers we encountered never seemed afraid to interject their own views. (Keepers are not, on the other hand, expected to play the role of problem solver or spiritual counselor in the manner of Navaho peace-makers who are not obliged to follow the consensus model of decision-making utilized in circles (Bluehouse and Zion, 1993).) Such personal expressions, while not discouraged, may nonetheless allow the facilitator to put their unique stamp on the flow of the conference. In the worst cases, facilitators may exercise excessive influence in the opening in a way that may limit the quality and openness of the dialogue.

The keeper or facilitator in circles, for example, is expected to 'set the tone' by bringing a talking piece and/or offering a personal reflection or story for others to think about and perhaps comment upon. In so doing, some keepers may present certain themes for discussion, ask others to reflect on a personal story, and then offer another story later in the circle. These activities need not get in the way of the business of the circle, and keepers who use such techniques may be highly inclusive, as well as effective in analyzing and synthesizing dialogue and problem-solving. Yet, through these informal processes, keepers, as well as facilitators in other conferencing models, may have the potential to subtly control the dialogue. And indeed, there are stories of dysfunctional or disbanded circles that engaged in struggles in part over who should be the circle keeper. More than anything else, however, dominance in the circle by one or more individuals is generally difficult to maintain because the dialogue process itself maximizes opportunities for everyone to speak. Additionally, shared understanding of consensus decision-making, when reinforced and nurtured by circle members, should generally prohibit such dominance (Stuart, 2001; Coates et al., 2000).

Facilitators in FGC programs may choose to play a more dominant role, though they are generally limited by the script. Because they are not encouraged to utilize unusual ritual, FGC facilitators may have to go to greater lengths if they wish to play a controlling role in the opening phase. NABs are supposed to represent the voice of the community. However, in many ways the more formal structure of the opening may be less likely to signal the importance of this mandate that should most clearly distinguish these programs from court. From the perspective of inclusion and communication, the traditional board introduction may in fact be one of the most likely to discourage stakeholder input, if not intimidate more vulnerable or less powerful participants. A more closed and formal tone may also be reinforced later in the conference in NABs where boards members in some programs deliberate outside of the presence of offender, family, and victim – or where these key stakeholders feel inhibited about speaking. We also observed numerous exceptions to this result when board chairs deliberately set an informal tone, had participants sit in a circle, and constantly encouraged dialogue and input. Regarding inclusion, the scope of authority over the process ceded to the group can range from almost none to maximum control. In contrast to the more rigid control suggested above, the facilitator can promote or negotiate shared ownership and/or 'shared leadership' as envisioned in the circle process (Stuart, 1996; Coates et al., 2000). He or she may do so by use of informal gestures, for example, strategically assigning responsibilities to various participants in the opening and then in subsequent phases of the conferences.

Phase II: Storytelling phase

If the preparation phase addresses the 'who' and 'why' of stakeholder involvement, the storytelling phase addresses the 'how.' In this phase, we examine the roles stakeholders' play, and the nature and style of communication that occurs and is intended in various programs and models. First, as previously noted, conferencing programs vary widely on their perception of the importance attached to participants other than victim and offender. A key question when other participants are present in the conference is what role, if any, they are expected to play. Second, the narrative itself is intended to be one that provides participants with information about the harm caused by the offense, answers questions about the offense, and encourages expression of emotion in a respectful way. Here we consider how competing theories of process may characterize different conferencing models (Bazemore and Umbreit, 2001) as well as different programs within single model types.

Roles and scripting of participants

VOM programs may not be very concerned about what supporters of the victim and offender do in the conference as long as they don't get in the way of the dialogue between these two primary stakeholders. FGC proponents clearly want supporters to reach the offender emotionally, as well as to provide support and encouragement. They may also want them to assist in getting offenders to experience shame and remorse, accept responsibility, and ensure that participants support and speak on behalf of the victim. Boards and community conference facilitators may hope that other participants represent the broader voice of community standards and expectations.

Typically, roles beyond those of victim, offender and facilitator emerge in the course of the storytelling phase and some facilitators try to ensure that participants take on particular roles. At the simplest level, though no one seeks to make the victim perform in any way, participants rely on the victim (or their representative) to tell of the harm he or she has experienced, and facilitators may go to great lengths to draw the victim out. Complexity is added as conferences include more participants, and the nature of the conference may vary, depending upon the extent to which role-playing is strategized in advance, is actively encouraged by the facilitator, or emerges naturally during the conference.

Community members in some programs are invited to speak in a general sense about how the crime has affected them, or they may be asked specifically as a peer or support person to describe the impact on the victim or the strengths of the offender, for example. Occasionally, the support person for the offender may 'nudge' him or her toward admitting responsibility or persuade him or her to accept an agreement. Facilitators report that this nudging typically occurs naturally in the process, without support persons being prompted to do so.

In one neighborhood board/community conferencing program, the program director describes how role-playing can be built into the conference structure. After the primary facilitator presents the ground rules and starts the dialogue:

> Another facilitator is responsible for drawing out the victim. Usually that isn't too difficult to do ... usually a volunteer is assigned that role. A facilitator that has established a relationship with the kid talks to the offender ... a friend of the offender is assigned a specific task or a role ... since there is already some sort of pre-existing relationship, and to make the juvenile and family comfortable, that person is usually assigned the task of starting the process.

Moreover, in this program the probation officer plays a rather strong prompting role in managing the dialogue:

> Typically the probation officer knows all the personalities involved on the board ... [he or she] tries not to have the strongest personality lead off because the rest follow from there ... the probation officer is aware of these dynamics and tries to exploit that.

Though VOM/D programs are less concerned about strategizing roles for citizens and supporters, they may be equally strategic in the choice of mediators, as one such program director states:

> Another big component is the facilitators and matching their personality traits to the dynamic of a case. There are a number of factors to take into consideration, gender, strong personalities, and language.

One circle coordinator provided a different view of what might be viewed as 'role scripting' expectations noting that she does not feel the need to assign roles and is somewhat uneasy with the idea: 'It is – not really applicable to the circle process – the circle keeper facilitates the process, but doesn't direct it – there is shared leadership and everyone is responsible for keeping it going.' However, other circle keepers may be as strategic as any other facilitators about asking participants to play certain roles in the conference. For example, in a school-based circle in a case involving twelve high-risk boys who 'glorified guns and violence,' the boys remained quiet even after several attempts to get them to open up. In the second circle, the keeper invited a youth who had been crippled by a stray bullet to come in and talk about his experience. The boys had 'almost instant respect for the youth and their mouths dropped open.'

In summary, role-playing, or 'role-taking,' seems to be an essential part of the conferencing environment. While some make take a pejorative view of this process as somewhat manipulative, thinking strategically about the roles participants may assume naturally in the conference seems to be a mark of well-prepared facilitators. A more problematic issue observed occasionally in conferences is when participants take on a role that seems forced, such as sometimes happens when a participant tries to represent the voice of a victim he or she does not know, or speaks in lecturing terms about harm to the community. What may be more important than such role-playing is the strategic mobilization of 'voices' that bring a life experience relevant to the issue, and relevant to the victim, offender, or other participants in the conference. Notably, bringing such a perspective into the group – as when an ex-offender is brought in to support and advise parents of the delinquent youth and/or share his experience with an offender, or when a family who has gotten through crises with their own adolescents advises and supports the offender's parents – can provide a breakthrough that appears to be less possible in the absence of such voices.

Communication
Most conferencing processes are intended to affirm community norms and express disapproval of the offender's behavior in a respectful way. However, there are competing theories of how this process occurs. Open and emotional dialogue that is less goal oriented is a characteristic of many VOM/D programs – especially those dealing with the most serious crimes in situations where the goal of the participants is likely to have little or nothing to do with getting an agreement (Umbreit, 2001). Circles may emphasize providing support and assistance for participants while simultaneously affirming community norms and values. While circles do seek reparative agreements, they are also very focused on ensuring that the process is open, inclusive, and safe for all participants. Boards, on the other hand, may be the most 'agreement-driven' conferencing process, and communication in these programs is often focused heavily on designing the reparative contract.

Regarding the narrative itself, the issue is how well the story of the offense is told and understood. The extent to which the narrative itself evokes emotions is often an important indicator that understanding has been achieved. While the discussion in Chapter 5 emphasized the role of the script in ensuring the focus on repairing harm, practitioners also talked about how the script may either detract from, or facilitate, communication.

Contrary to general training for VOM, some programs find a script important as a guide to dialogue. One Pennsylvania program director noted that the script is important because it ensures that certain things get said. 'It is followed as a guideline . . . is written out and you follow it, but it is essentially an outline to make sure that nothing is forgotten.'

From a communication perspective, the best justification to use some form of script is to ensure that enough time is spent on the dialogue itself. As one community conferencing program director put it, 'it [the script] helps the community people because no matter how much time I spend training them, everybody wants to skip forward to the making-it-better [phase], like right away.' While some view the script as promoting rigidity and limiting dialogue, in essence this program director uses the script to guard *against* a rush to agreement that might diminish the emotional content of the communication.

Boards have a natural connection to offenders and victims since the volunteers are generally neighbors, if not acquaintances. They may often attempt to affirm this connection as indicated by this description of the process in the Arizona board mentioned earlier:

The board members tell a little about themselves and they also start the discussion; go into more about the purpose and goals ... Typically they tell the family that they [the members] are your neighbors and are a part of this community ... [and they may say], 'I know I have seen you at the grocery store ... teacher at the school ...' to bring it to a personal level.

Like many other boards, those in this program are, however, somewhat constrained in their process by a tradition of board members asking questions of a young person and his family and then presenting them with their recommendations. While some boards have chosen a more informal process, communication often remains one-way. Boards aim to engage the offender, and to the extent possible include the victim's narrative when discussing the event with the offender. The most interesting and important part of the narrative is that the board members may use it to craft an agreement about what should be done that in essence seeks to communicate the will of the community to judges and the court. While the voice of the offender and victim may be less direct than in other models, the voice of the community as represented by these volunteers generally is more direct

Phase III: Mutual acknowledgement phase

This transition phase may be most critical for ensuring the quality and validity of communication. It is also important in clarifying the perception of choices for the future of the victim and offender as well as their supporters. Participants in this phase may witness some acknowledgement by victim and offenders of their mutual interests, or supporters and community members may articulate those interests. Here is where offender acknowledgement of his or her impact on others, as well as his or her indication of surprise and gratification that others care, may signal an apparent breakthrough.

Toward common ground

Though complete convergence of stakeholder interests, or 'common ground,' may be rarely or only partially achieved as an outcome, the potential for achieving it is often apparent in the transition phase as participants reflect on offender and victim narratives. The possibility of such awareness and expression of common ground is thought by some to increase as more participants are added to the conference (Moore and McDonald, 2000; Pranis, 2001). Even when one of the three stakeholders remains alienated from another stakeholder, a connection between any two – e.g. offender and community member – may be sufficient to move the conference forward in a positive way toward agreement. Comments reflecting such support between two or more participants may in turn serve as a catalyst for breaking down remaining barriers between additional stakeholders.

A somewhat different outlook on communication is provided by VOM/D practitioners in the acknowledgement phase. Though generally focused on victim and offender communication, there is also an opportunity for parents of the offender to hear things being said by their child that have not been expressed before. Describing how her process is designed to open up avenues for dialogue in the conference about harm to the *family*, one VOM/D director described the benefits of this discussion to the conference itself. 'One piece we do with parents and the offender is to always ask the parents "how this [offense] affected you".' This program director explained that when the offender 'practises' his or her story in the preparation meeting, parents are often, surprisingly, hearing it for the first time. In the conference itself, this new parental insight about their child may play an important role:

At the end we always ask parents to speak – a nice piece – beautiful things come out. When parents see the child demonstrating inner strength to face up [to their behavior] and deal with it, this is reassuring to parents.

Collective transformation

The victim and offender may remain far apart and certainly need not 'bond' for the conference to be considered a success. At a minimum, however, the two parties should increase their understanding of the other's position and feelings before moving to the next phase in which they will attempt to complete a reparative agreement. In addition, according to one VOM/D practitioner, facilitators may:

... look for some acknowledgement from the victim and some acknowledgement from the offender that they have humanized the other person, that they have gotten that essential idea out that this is not somebody I need to be afraid of, that this is not somebody who's going to do me harm, *on either side* ... We find that the youth is often the most frightened person in the room once they come to the mediation ... and just that sort of realization is two human beings talking to one another about a bad thing that happened and how to make that right ...

Not much is absolute, however, and practitioners try to be realistic about expectations. When asked what she needed to move on to the agreement phase, for example, one restorative panel coordinator noted that:

I have to see that 'personal' part happen, but it doesn't mean that you don't go forward if a kid doesn't absolutely say I'm really sorry for what I did, and I'll be sure that I won't do it again. And sometimes I even say that I'm not trying to come out of this with everybody being friends and getting each other's phone numbers. And, that makes it much safer.

The emotional indicators that some connection has been made, as suggested by another police officer who facilitates highly scripted conferences, can make an important turning point in the process:

The crowning moment is getting out what happened/how and who was affected by it. It is a very powerful part in the conference ... when you have a juvenile crying you know that you've made a point, you know that there is some reality of 'I really did harm somebody' and I really am sorry for (that) ... and for those kids, you know, you made a difference and you are not going to see them again. When you don't have that, I think that you'll see that person again in the system.

The above statement suggests a theory-in-use about *emotion* as a key to future success, and tears as one empirical indicator that an emotional transformation has occurred that may ensure success later. As the narrative involves other speakers, the communication, and no doubt the emotion, felt by conference participants intensifies. In the following account of a reentry conference for incarcerated offenders in a Minnesota facility, there is also what may appear to be an overwhelming confrontation with past behaviors and harm on the part of the offender. This awareness may, however, go hand in hand with a realization of community support and the development of profound new insights about the important role young people play in the lives of others. The coordinator of this program described a revelation by a community member that seemed to provide an offender with a remarkable amount of insight after one victim told the group, 'When Aaron is at the park all the other kids are scared':

... that resident was really struck by that because he wanted the kids to play at the park; it was a small town, he [Aaron] had stolen from the municipal store so the whole community felt the effect. The teacher said, I've always liked him, but it kills me every time he does something, it has been hard for me. His mom talked about coming down the street and seeing the police at their house – wondering whether he is in trouble or if he is dead – and she said, 'it was the longest three blocks I've ever walked.'

Phase IV: Agreement

The role of the offender in this phase may range from a very passive one, to one of active involvement in a dialogue in which he or she develops most of the ideas for the agreement to repair harm. The victim often chooses to participate actively in the agreement, but may need to be prompted and drawn out in the agreement phase – a task more familiar to participants in models where the victim's role is critical. The community may also participate actively in this phase if encouraged by the facilitator.

At the extremes of community involvement and discretion are programs, such as the Arizona NAB described earlier, in which citizens determine the entire disposition of each case and programs that allow for minimal community input. For example, programs that receive referrals for cases in which all conditions of supervision have been ordered by a judge and conference participants merely determine where community service hours will be completed appear to place little faith in the wisdom of the community. Peace-making circles will typically draw on a range of creative suggestions from community members in a process that maximizes opportunity for diverse input. Classic victim–offender mediation, on the other hand, would allow for little, if any, input by community members other than the victim, and would be less likely to have other citizens present. FGC programs would also look primarily to victim, offender, and the family while remaining open to ideas from community members who might be present, preferring to craft an agreement based on victim and offender input with the guidance of the facilitator. The community conferencing model described earlier may also look to community members for extensive input into the contract. Though these members may be extremely creative at this task, they may also feel inadequate in addressing more technical issues such as determining restitution, especially when the amount of loss and responsibility is contested.

Communication is a fundamental factor in the agreement phase as well. In at least some program models, circles in particular, the commitment to consensus decision-making is paramount (Coates et al., 2000). How stakeholders arrive at the agreement, even when all steps leading up to this phase have been followed with attention to the consensus process, however, is sometimes problematic. In many experienced programs that operate on the basis of strict adherence to the principle of consensus, what consensus means, and the actual process used to determine when it is reached, of course varies widely.

Consensus may mean a vote of NAB board members. *Or*, it may mean agreement achieved through a lengthy process of discussion in a circle in which members deliberate by passing a talking piece until participants –

including victim, offender, and their supporters – feel that they can craft a solution that is perhaps seen by all participants as less than perfect, yet something they can live with. As a member of the South St Paul (SSP), Minnesota, circle program describes their group's experience:

> It is a lesson about democracy, especially the importance of public discussion and the value of hearing diverse viewpoints and listening carefully to those who disagree with you. In SSP, there were many struggles early on and many times that participants walked away mad. What has made us successful and [what sustains us] is the commitment to 'hang in there' despite disagreements because if you just walk away, you don't accomplish very much ... This commitment to *live with* and thrive on the struggle to be inclusive has made all the difference and increased the comfort level now that it has been made explicit.

Achieving consensus appears to be a difficult endeavor in most circles, perhaps because most circles that we observed appear to take this process very seriously. Where consensus is in fact a process indicator related to mutual transformation at the group level, the theory is essentially one of 'common ground.' That is, the common ground assumptions applied to any two or three stakeholders are applied to the conference as a whole as a commitment to finding shared interests as part of a democratic decision-making process.

Phase V: Celebration

Many conferencing practitioners agree that the social gathering may provide the clearest indication of the success of a conference in ensuring meaningful stakeholder involvement. If communication has been effective, participants – including victim and offenders – will feel comfortable in talking informally. Small signs of success in achieving common ground, shared understanding and mutual transformation are perhaps no more clearly indicated than in the informal gestures that may be made between victim, offender, and their supporters in a relaxed environment with no rules for communication in effect and no expectations.

Generally, there are congratulations for the offender for having the courage to go through the process, and these may be even stronger when apologies or clear expressions of responsibility and remorse have occurred. There are also expressions of support and congratulations to the victim and for the parents. Some of the most interesting informal dialogue that occurs during this period of 'breaking bread' is often between parents of the offender and the victim and/or his or her supporters, and frequently there is empathy on the part of victim for the offender's family's troubles, along with strong apologies from the parents to the victim. As one facilitator noted:

> That is when the other staff member comes in handy. I step out of the room to write it up and I invite them to have cookies and pop before I leave. The other person can watch. Neat stuff happens, informal stuff goes on then. The victim goes up and hugs the kid. My other staff person takes note and watches what goes on – it is a good feeling. On a couple of occasions, it was tense, but normally it is good.

Stage 3: Follow-up

In general, follow-up is viewed as most important by many practitioners, yet they express less satisfaction with this stage of the process than any other. While follow-up is generally linked more directly to the principle of repair and to the government/community role and relationship (Principle 3), there are some issues directly related to stakeholder involvement. Most notably, while program staff generally have some sense of their role and the role of others in monitoring agreements, what has been less than clear is the role of stakeholders, other than the offender, in carrying out the agreement. Here, participation may range from an offender, perhaps with family support, being viewed as solely responsible for completing terms of the agreement, to the case of some circles in which community members volunteer in multiple roles to support the offender and parents in meeting their obligations.

Circles, in general, are unique in their commitment to long-term follow-up, and many continue to work with offenders and their families well beyond the terms of any typical reparative agreement. For this reason, the appropriate point of termination of the circle's involvement with a case is a point of disagreement within some circle programs, as one North Minneapolis member put it:

> Where the difference lies in the North Minneapolis circle is that we are trying to figure out when we are done with the circle process – when the file is closed. When is a case done? For example, if a youth completes community service, is attending school, has completed the plan/agreement, but still may be having some problems at home, e.g. he sneaks out of the house. Some would say that the behavior that brought him here is done; others would say we still need to hold onto him.

One important innovation in structured involvement of the community in follow-up is seen in boards such as those in the Arizona program mentioned earlier where volunteers meet at six- and nine-month intervals to determine whether the offender has met his or her obligations. Some

Vermont juvenile 'restorative panels' meet with offenders as often as monthly until the end of probation to monitor offender compliance with reparative obligations and to commend and support progress. This citizen role in follow-up, though rare, seems to complete the cycle implied in the theory of 'earned redemption' (Bazemore, 1998). This occurs when the community is allowed to witness the offender's efforts to make amends first-hand and respond positively to this successful performance. It also makes the reintegrative goals of 'reintegrative shaming' theory (Braithwaite, 1989) more concrete, even when there is some degree of relapse of the part of the offender (Braithwaite and Mugford, 1994), by allowing for continuous building upon common understandings developed between the offender and other community members to establish new connections and expand and bolster social support.

Summary and conclusions

In this chapter we examined several dimensions of stakeholder involvement as they relate to decision-making in various phases and stages of restorative conferences. We specifically focused on practitioner understandings and application of three process components of stakeholder inclusion: invitation, communication, and role-taking.

Invitation, primarily associated with the pre-conferencing stage, is directly related to the extent and quality of participant engagement and to victim and offender satisfaction with conferencing outcomes. Conferencing practitioners interviewed and observed for this part of our study share a strong commitment to the general idea of involving and maximizing the input of victim, offender and community stakeholders. Regarding the invitation component of inclusion, variation centered around strategies for recruiting the participants into the process, priorities given to efforts to ensure participation of certain stakeholders (especially crime victims), and the role and function envisioned for various participants in the primary stages and phases of the conferencing process. Victim recruitment strategies and the time and resources devoted to these, for example, varied widely among the programs represented in our study. In the pre-conferencing stage, we found that practitioners also disagreed on the extent to which they felt extensive pre-conferencing or preparation was important and to what degree it affected the quality and quantity of participation and conference outcomes. While some practitioners felt extensive face-to-face preparation was critical to achieving successful outcomes, others argued for minimizing such preparation as an impractical use of resources.

Most practitioners were open to including a range of other participants in the conference, with general consensus about the importance of victim, offender, and their families or supporters as primary, and some variation regarding the role of other community members who may not already have a relationship to offender or victim. Consistent with reintegrative shaming theory, some practitioners were less supportive of the participation of community members not a part of the family or closely attached to offender or victim; others, consistent with social support theory or civic engagement perspectives, saw value in the participation of community members who might bring other resources to the encounter. A key point of difference emerged with regard to who should determine additional participants beyond this core group. Variation ranged from the view that only victim and offender should make decisions about additional participants to the view that facilitators should make strategy-focused decisions about which participants might bring an important perspective or resource into the conferencing setting.

Communication is most important from the perspective of theoretical dimensions associated with victim–offender exchange through 'healing dialogue' (Umbreit, 2001) and 'respectful disapproval' based on reintegrative shaming theory (Braithwaite, 2001b; McDonald et al., 1995).' Regarding the process of communication, most participants in our study expressed general support for an open, not overly structured dialogue style aimed at maximizing the input of and exchange between victim, offender, and family/supporters. Programs represented by our study participants, however, demonstrated a range of communication styles from the deliberative approach used in some (but not all) NABs to the free-flowing, virtually uninterrupted dialogue between victim and offender that characterizes some VOM/D programs and is consistent with the theory of healing dialogue. Like circle practitioners, who rely primarily on the talking piece to control dialogue (and empower all participants to speak), participants who favor using a script in our sample – in a very different way – provided a middle ground between these very tightly, and very loosely directed processes.

For practitioners in our study, the script was to some degree an outline that helped them gauge when the conference was meeting fundamental objectives. Rather than forcing a rigid approach typical of some 'agreement-driven' conferences, however, these facilitators felt that structure was imposed by appropriate movement through process phases and that such movement was facilitated by attention to a script or outline. These phases are often based on the individual and collective emotions of the group and/or the sense that stakeholders had understood and acknowledged each other. Therefore, in contrast to the domineering facilitator who may rush the group or push them toward his or her own agenda, or the free-wheeling facilitator who simply allows open, uninterrupted dialogue, such facilitators make strategic comments and interventions to consolidate collective ideas in the group, or make note of progress or a particularly important insight. He or she may also call on a participant to add specific input to assist the group in moving through what are essentially process, rather than task-based, phases.

Though problems in the domineering style were often mentioned by participants in our study, possible problems in the extremely non-directive style were not generally discussed. These problems did, however, become apparent in some of the case observations – including one described at the end of this chapter in which power imbalances and loss of facilitator control appeared to detract from the restorative focus of the conference.

The communication style and preferred facilitation approach, as well as decisions about who should be invited to the conference, are no doubt influenced by practitioners' views of the roles that might be played by stakeholders in various phases of the conferencing process. For some it was apparently viewed as inappropriate or unimportant to think about the roles certain stakeholders might fill in the conference, or what they might bring to the encounter in the way of affective or instrumental resources. For others, however, a great deal of pre-conference work seems to go into strategizing about what family members might say, or what it is hoped that community members might bring in the form of an outside perspective vital to problem-solving and healing. Acknowledgement of the victim's story by as many participants as possible is viewed by some as critical to giving group validation to his or her perspective. A particularly important element of this is how key 'voices' that may empathize with the experience of the victim, offender, or other partici-pants are included in the conference. The voice of experience, of someone who can relate to participants as a parent, peer, or neighbor, for example, is one that can be brought forward to provide both direction and empathy for families and young people under pressure.

A final aspect of the conference relevant to both communication and role-taking is the agreement phase. As mentioned in the previous chapter, the quality of the agreement and buy-in to it is enhanced to the extent that the conference can elicit multiple inputs from victims, families, offenders, and community members. Because processes leading up to the agreement phase are believed to be important determinants of the quality of the agreement, theories such as those based on 'transformative justice' (Moore and McDonald, 2000) that seek collective outcomes focused on the potential for finding 'common ground' between victim, offender, and other participants may have special relevance in this context. Prior to moving to the agreement phase, many practitioners look for indicators that victim and offender stories have been told and that participants have heard these stories fully and have acknowledged each other in some way.

Also especially relevant to the agreement phase of the conference is the commitment to consensus decision-making. Though widely endorsed as a core restorative value by many conferencing practitioners, consensus is in fact a somewhat slippery concept in developing agreements. Some process models such as circles go to great lengths to get complete buy-in of the group. In reality, however, this typically means that participants will agree that, while not exactly what they wanted, they can 'live with' the agreement.

Theory and practice associated with the stakeholder involvement principle suggests a range of questions for future research. Most urgently needed are basic impact studies to determine what strategies may be most likely to increase victim participation. In addition, preferences about order of the process – e.g. which stakeholders speak first – also raised in the chapter on repair could be examined to determine if this preference is related to outcome. Different facilitation styles around the issue of communication in particular have important theoretical implications for how emotional states and stakeholder acknowledgement may lead to theoretically important outcomes such as empathy, respectful disapproval, victim vindication, and other results. Ultimately, the debate about strategic involvement of participants other than victim, offender and the family should be investigated empirically with an eye to testing theories of social support, reintegrative shaming, and common ground.

Observational case studies: problems, concerns, and resolutions

Observation of actual practice is almost guaranteed to reveal that the vision associated with various theories of conferencing may be difficult to implement in practice. Indeed, actual conferences may find practitioners struggling with competing principles in the response to actual cases, and goals and objectives associated with various theories of intervention may appear to be in conflict with each other. This is certainly the case regarding the various dimensions of stakeholder involvement, as illustrated by excerpts from victim–offender dialogue conferences presented below.

The first case illustrates a generic problem of power imbalance. Though this problem may arise in virtually any type of conferencing program, this case also raises problems that are perhaps specific to victim–offender mediation and dialogue programs – exacerbated by an institutional victim who is also an authority figure with direct power over the individual offender. VOM/D programs are guided by an approach to practice that seeks to minimize facilitator interference with victim and offender conversation, and may thus appear at times to give complete deference to stakeholders despite the failure to pursue restorative justice goals.

In presenting this example, we caution readers to view this account as a case study of a problem in the conferencing process rather than a reflection on facilitators and other participants. These participants represent otherwise very effective programs that nonetheless struggle with problems that may be related to underlying program philosophy or structure. Moreover, though this conference is presented in a critical light, we have no way of determining the actual impact on offender, victim, and other participants. Similarly, we cannot say with any certainty that conferences presented in a more positive light, including the second case, necessarily have more positive impacts on stakeholders.

Case 1: Power imbalance and institutional victim

This case involved three boys caught stealing items from a school during the summer. They also spray-painted inside and outside the school. Two of the cases were processed in another county and the boys were asked to write a letter of apology; the victim/school was not directly involved in this process. The conference described is for one of the boys, a 12-year-old. The conference was held approximately nine months from the time of the offense at a kindergarten building. Conference participants include two facilitators (husband and wife), the principal of the school where the theft occurred, the 12-year-old boy, his mother, and the participant observer. Chairs are set in a circle. Facilitators sit opposite each other, and the principal and youth are across from each other. The mother of the youth sits behind him and the observer sits behind the mother.

While waiting for the youth and mother, the facilitators review with the principal what will happen (pre-conferences had occurred). Who will go first is his choice as the victim but facilitators suggest that it might be more comfortable for the youth if he (the principal) went first (both choice of order and suggestion that the victim should go first are consistent with VOM/D protocol and philosophy). The principal is told to talk about what happened and the impact on the school. The facilitators will then ask if anyone has questions. They then showed the principal the forms used to write the restitution plan. Apparently, plans have already been made with the principal in the pre-conference for the youth to do yard work around the school (his suggested restitution) because the principal asks who will supervise him in this task (this situation seems unusual in that such agreements usually are made with the input of the offender and his parents). The facilitator then tells him that he has already told the family they have to provide supervision.

9:10 a.m. Youth and his mother arrive. Everyone sits down, and *immediately the principal begins talking.* [It is unusual to begin a conference without introductions; in this special case, with the principal in the role of victim, the conference therefore takes on a tone of a school disciplinary hearing, albeit with a kinder, more understanding focus. The facilitators provide no welcome or statement of purpose.]

Principal: 'I am delighted by this opportunity – last time I saw you, the police were there. I want to go back and re-live what happened. The custodian came to me and said kids were taking things from the building. We called the police right away – this had never happened before – very saddened by this. The two boys I talked with first denied this. This was the worst part. Do you know who owns the school? [Youth shakes head no.] All the people who live around here – it is a community school. They are very proud of the school and protect it. I got a call from a resident who saw you. I am not angry, but sad. It is hard to explain to the community. It took $365 just to repair damage from spray paint; had to throw away all of the candy, $250 worth. 4th graders had to sell candy to make up for this so they could buy more candy. It is tough because they know you and the other boys. I was thrilled when I was called about the conference and told that I would have a chance to tell you how I feel. The custodian wanted to be here but he's too busy. He said he never wanted to see you boys in this building again. What can you do to make this better for everyone? [Pauses briefly then continues.] I talked to the custodian – he needs weeds pulled near the building. This is something you can do to help pay back to the community. You do have a responsibility to fix this. Does this make sense?'

Youth: 'Yeh.'

Principal: 'I'm going to suggest you spend a day pulling weeds.' [Looks at Mother and asks if she can supervise him today.]

Mother: 'I can't today.'

Principal: 'Before we leave, we can talk about a time. [To youth] Anything you want to say?'

Youth: 'I feel really bad for what I did and I will not do it again.'

Facilitator: 'How did it happen?'

Youth: 'Said I didn't want to do it – they called me a chicken.'

Principal: 'What would you do now?'

Youth: 'Walk away.'

Principal: 'Good choice.'

Facilitator: 'Were the boys older?'

Youth: 'No.'

Principal: 'Hope you use the playground at school but you cannot come into the building during summer. Do you know why we had the doors open? We were cleaning carpets. Tell me more about what the boys said to you?'

[Above exchange is calm; principal speaks firmly but in a friendly tone. Youth looks at him and seems to listen to what is being said. He responds readily but briefly to questions.]

Facilitator: 'What kinds of toys were taken?' [To youth]

Youth: 'Game boy, yo-yos, pencils, markers.'

Principal: 'The day after, the police came and wanted me to list what was taken. The teachers were gone so I had to pay three teachers to come in and look through the classroom. Had to add up what everything was worth. Very time-consuming for me, teachers and police. Big hassle for us. Had to come in on the weekend. Had to contact the insurance person to arrange for cleaning off paint. A five-minute incident took days to clean up. Hope you have learned something. How did you feel? Did you feel funny coming into the building?'

Youth: 'Not really.'

Facilitator: 'Were you scared?'

Youth: [Pauses, then says] 'Yeh.'

Principal: 'Can I ask you, Mom, how you felt?'

Mother: 'I was shocked – very unhappy – didn't know what happened – got a phone call from the police.' [Someone adds that this was right after a school shooting somewhere.]

Principal: 'The custodian saw kids running from building – kids had taken shoes off so they would not be heard. [Looks at youth] Big deal isn't it?'

Youth: 'Yeh.'

Facilitator: [To mother] 'Do you have any questions you would like to ask?'

Mother: 'I didn't realize what all was involved in the clean up.'

Principal: 'I had not intended to involve police, but when the two boys lied to me, I knew this could not be resolved without involving the police.'

Facilitator: 'This thing about other kids teasing you – doesn't stop when you're 12 – it keeps on. Some people don't learn their lesson – can't go with the crowd. Hope you have learned yours. One thing we need to do is have a written agreement. Something you need to do to make this right; everyone has to agree and sign. We will send a copy to court. Have you done some community service hours?'

Youth: 'I've done 26 hours.'

Facilitator: 'Judge takes advice from probation. In the agreement we need to say what, who, when and where.'

Facilitator: [Pulls in table; gets agreement form. To youth:] 'What do you want to put in it?'

Youth: 'Pull weeds around school.'

Principal: 'You could probably do the entire building in about six hours or less.'

Facilitator: 'We can put estimated time in [begins writing agreement].'

Principal: 'How is later this week?'

Mother: 'We are going to the lake later this week [talks about plans to help victims of recent tornado in WI].'

Principal: 'How about tomorrow?' [Principal and mother discuss possible dates.]

Facilitator: 'Suggest you do before your court date.'

Principal: 'My dilemma is that my last day is this Friday and then there will be a new principal. [To mother.] Call me back this afternoon. Even if you had to do it in shifts, it would be better to get started.'

Mother: 'That might work – the shift thing.'

Facilitator: 'How do I write this down?'

Principal: 'Mutually agreed upon time between me and mother to be completed before July 12.'

Facilitator: [Reads agreement:] '(1) pull weeds, about 6 hrs; (2) date agreed upon by principal and Mother; (3) complete by 7/12; (4) supervision by a family member – do you want a final inspection? (5) verification of completed work by principal or custodian, and (6) write letter to school, teachers and staff.'

Principal: 'Since I am the only one here – it would be a good idea that you get a letter to the school apologizing to teachers and custodian. Make it a full page including how you felt, how it affected your mother. Not just a line saying I'm sorry. Can you bring something to pull weeds out with?'

Youth: 'Yeh.'

Mother: 'What do you need?'

Principal: 'Some weeds are big.'

Youth: 'How about a cutting thing?'

Principal: 'No, just something like a dandelion puller.'

Youth: [Now appearing more animated, relaxed] 'Yeh, we have one of those.'

Principal: 'Some weeds are prickly – you will need gloves. [To mom:] When you call, you will get my voice mail – just leave dates and times that will work.'

Facilitator: 'I am writing over the agreement – hard to get it come through all copies.'

Principal leaves for a minute. Youth looks around the room and wonders out loud if this is the room where he went to kindergarten. General talk while facilitator writes over agreement. Principal returns and he and youth talk about fishing – where they go. Agreement is completed and everyone signs.

Facilitator: (To youth:) 'Make sure you keep in touch with your PO. We will call and tell her we did this.'

Case summary

This case provides an example of what can go wrong with conference communication when there is a loss of control of dialogue by facilitators and a power imbalance between youth and adults. While the dimensions of inclusion and communication both assume relatively equal power between victim and offender and their supporters, or a strategic effort to compensate for this imbalance, neither is likely when an institutional victim is represented by an authority figure with a great deal of power over a young offender. To spur transformation consistent with the theory of healing dialogue, communication must be two-way, between stakeholders who listen actively and are open to what the other has to share, whether or not they agree with it. If communication is to lead to a reintegrative, rather than disintegrative, kind of shaming, conference participants must include supporters of the offender and victim who have an intimate relationship with these stakeholders. While finding common ground may also depend on the presence of other community members who can bridge the gap between stakeholders, the structure of the program model in this case typically does not allow for the broader stakeholder and community input that might have made a difference in this conference.

From a different perspective, many students and parents might appreciate a principal willing to meet with students and address harm in a way that allowed those responsible to make amends – *if this process had occurred without recourse to courts, school suspension, etc.* In this case, it did not. Though not the fault of the conferencing program, the youth, at the time of the conference, had been processed for a court hearing, placed on probation, and suspended from school (no discussion of these sanctions/punishments took place in the conference).

In terms of stakeholder involvement and restorative principles generally, much is disturbing here by most standards of what a restorative conference is expected to look like. While deference to stakeholders and victim empowerment are desirable in most situations, the extent of non-interference and domination by this institutional victim was inappropriate. *As a disciplinary meeting*, convened without including courts and use of suspension, this conference could be viewed as an outstanding example of a caring principal willing to give a youth another chance. *As a restorative conference*, on the other hand, most would find the encounter greatly lacking by most practice standards, for reasons including, though not limited to, the following:

1. No purpose was stated for the conference, no protocol, and no guidelines for dialogue were presented. Indeed, the principal/victim served as facilitator, presiding officer, and contract negotiator.

2. The pre-conference appears to have been used not to inform stake-holders and relieve their anxiety about the process, but to work out the details of the agreement with one party, absent input from the other, and absent any face-to-face presentation of harm (this came after the fact); giving the benefit of the doubt, at best, what occurred was shuttle mediation/arbitration – rendering the face-to-face meeting unnecessary. Oddly, this seems to violate core tenets of best practice for VOM/D professionals who are urged to place less emphasis on the agreement at least until emotional issues and harms have been addressed (see earlier dialogue in Chapter 5 in which a VOM/D practitioner argues against focus on the agreement in pre-conferencing) (Umbreit, 1999).
3. Though discussion of victim and community harm occurred, it was limited to the principal's experience in an awkward version of the role of institutional victim *and* in the more genuine role of school administrator with an overwhelming power advantage, to the exclusion of other victims more directly harmed and lack of discussion of the harm done to offender and family (e.g. through school suspension etc.). Most importantly, this harm discussion was out of sequence, and effectively irrelevant to conference outcomes, given that restitution had already been negotiated.
4. The conference discourse consisted of almost uninterrupted lecturing to the youth without the opportunity for him to digest, respond, or tell his own story.

In the larger program/system/community context discussed in more detail in our chapter focused on the principle of transformation of community/government roles, the problem in this case is not only about what occurred in the encounter between principal, youth, and parent. Certainly, there are excellent examples of school-based conferencing programs that repair harm to victims and the school community (Riestenberg, 1996, 2001), while offering the young offender opportunity for reintegration through 'earned redemption' (Bazemore, 1998) in an empowering process that brings young students, teachers and staff, and facilitators together in an open dialogue. Such a dialogue, however, usually occurs near the time of the incident, without the cost and added harm and disruption of police, a court process, and probation that occurred in the above example. In such resolutions, no outside conferencing program would have been necessary because the school would simply have resolved its problems as a community without system involvement. In this case, perhaps through no fault of its own, the VOM/D program was clearly engaged *out of context*. The conference has value only as an illustration of problems in application that render restorative conferencing of a certain type irrelevant if not harmful.

Case analysis in context

Focusing on conferencing outcomes, the example above, though em-powering the victim, failed to accomplish key process objectives of the conference. Respectful disapproval of the harmful behavior that might have been achieved with different stakeholders was not likely to have been achieved, and little if any common ground was developed or collective transformation achieved. The dialogue, moreover, did not appear to be one that provided much in the way of healing for any stakeholder.

The case is not presented to suggest that one model or philosophy is inferior to another. We do not take a position in favor of one model, and indeed have not done so in other writing (Bazemore and Umbreit, 2001; Bazemore and Schiff, 2001). Victim–offender mediation is by far the most widely implemented and most evidence-based conferencing approach; for every case of questionable value, there are thousands of cases in which VOM has yielded remarkable results, including those involving crimes of severe violence (Umbreit, 1999, 2001). By contrast, many of the newer models profiled in this report remain relatively untested. Other well-known cases not included in this study, but frequently used in training and described frequently in other commentary (Bazemore, 1998; BARJ, 2000), illustrate the great potential of VOM/D, as well as other models, to accomplish both process goals related to involvement and reparative outcomes. Finally, regarding ultimate outcomes, we do not have any information about the long-term impact, if any, of this conference, and we know little about *stakeholder perceptions* of what appeared to be chaotic and potentially harmful practice.

The following case suggests that supporters and the community can play a vital role in conferencing approaches that give them a voice. In reviewing the case, readers may wish to imagine the process and outcome of the case presented earlier had another community voice or supporter of victim and offender been present.

Case 2: Family and citizens in the mix

As described earlier in this chapter and in our survey report, neigh-borhood accountability boards (NABs) suffer more than other con-ferencing models from generally low rates of victim involvement. At times, however, this deficit is partly made up by citizens who truly empathize with the victim, and also speak to community harm. While this role in no way compares to the role of the actual victim when their story is allowed to be told, NABs may effectively bring other concerns to the table. The following case, though by no means ideal, presents something of a counterpoint to the previously discussed cases in both quality of communication and expression of harm, though ironically without the direct victim present. The case from an urban neighborhood accountability board illustrates multiple harms to several victims and the possibility of important connections between community members and young offenders.

This case, involving a charge of damaging property and disturbing the peace, is based on an offense involving scratching cars with glass. This was the first contact with the legal system for the twin 6th grade boys who live with their grandmother. Dad is in jail and mom is in drug rehab.

Facilitator: 'Thanks for attending. We will focus on the September 21st incident ... we are not here to judge the behavior of Jason, Julian and their brother [Nicholas who was involved but, not charged], but how their behavior affected others. We do not want to discuss whether the boys are "good or bad." I want everyone to remember that all three boys have admitted responsibility and are here voluntarily. With regards to confidentiality, all community members have signed the agreement and have gone through background checks. Everything that is said here is confidential especially because juveniles are involved. So, what is said in here stays here. Let's begin with Julian telling us what happened.'

Julian: 'We were walking to school; we took a different route and picked up some glass. We saw some cars and started scratching them. My brother came and he started kicking them. The meter guy came and took us up to a house and then took us to school. That's when we got the ticket.'

Facilitator: 'What were you thinking?'

Jason: 'Nothing.'

Facilitator: 'Whose idea was it?'

Julian: 'Both of us [pause] just saw the glass and picked it up.'

Facilitator: 'What have you thought about since the incident?'

Jason (prompted by grandma:) 'I can't believe that I actually did this.'

Julian: 'It was stupid. Someone threw Burger King Food all over my grandma's car. I felt bad because scratches don't wash off.'

Community Member A: 'That was your car with the food on it?'

Grandma: 'Yes, someone threw chili all over my car. It was covered. It was a lot of work but it washed off.'

Facilitator: 'The victim did not show up tonight. I am not sure why because I confirmed with him. But, he has asked that the damage to his car be paid for. I can tell you that the man who actually saw you scratching the cars felt guilty turning you in. He felt he had to turn you in because he wasn't sure how many more cars you were going to scratch. He felt bad that your grandma was going to have to pay for the damages – I told him that it didn't have to work that way.'

Community Member B: 'I can speak about being victimized because it happened to me. Someone busted out my windows. I was afraid and angry and now feel that I have to park my car way up in the driveway. It feels like a safety factor. I wonder if something else is going to happen.'

Facilitator: 'Sometimes kids don't think things through.'

Community Member C: 'I don't want to worry about my cars. I want to know how this has affected grandma.'

Julian: 'She doesn't trust us. Maybe she's worried about her car.'

Community Member C: 'Have you talked much about the worries she has? How would you feel if this happened to you?'

Julian: 'Bad.'

Community Member A: 'Do you own bicycles?'

Grandma: 'I can't afford them. They've outgrown them.'

Community Member A: 'If someone took a sledge hammer to them you'd probably feel pretty bad. Whose idea was it to scratch the cars?'

Jason: 'My brother.'

Brother of the Offenders: 'I didn't key the cars, I kicked them.'

Jason: 'I guess it was me. I did it first.'

Facilitator: 'What were you thinking? Were you mad at the guy?'

Jason: 'No, I didn't know him.'

Community Member C: 'Did you pick up the glass with the intention of scratching cars?'

Julian: 'No, just picked up the glass a couple of feet from the cars.'

Community Member D: 'How do you feel about what this is doing to grandma?'

Julian: 'She didn't do anything but now has to take us to all these meetings and court. It hurts her hands and legs [cancer]. I feel bad that she has to do this. She doesn't deserve it.'

Jason: 'She has to pay for parking and social security doesn't pay that much.'

Community Member D: 'Look at grandma. She seems pretty sad to me.'

Community Member A to Grandma: 'Do the four children live with you?'

Grandma: 'Yes, their mother is in drug rehab and tells them that they are worthless. Their Dad is in prison.'

Facilitator: 'Did you think that you were going to get caught?'

Julian: 'I felt guilty when I saw the big scratches.'

Community Member C: 'Do you know what a good paint job costs?'

Facilitator: 'Two cars need to be repaired one has been sold. There was a 94 Mustang and a 77 Chevy Impala.'

Community Member D: 'How do you think the victim feels?'

Jason: 'Angry.'

Community Member B: 'What were you thinking Nicholas? Why did you kick the car?'

Brother of the Offenders: 'I don't know.'

Community Member B: 'I guess one of the things that I want to know is how you can help each other stay out of trouble.'

Grandma: 'Their father lets them do whatever they want. He tells them that it's not their fault . . . its politics. Their mom tells them, 'You're no good.' She tells them that she is out of their life. I have them in therapy. Being identical twins the boys are really like one. I have no idea why they did this.'

Community Member D: 'How can you show you learned something?'

Jason: 'Apologize to them and pay for the cars.'

Julian: 'Grandma said that we could help them around the house.'

Brother of the Offenders: 'I took off as soon as the meter guy started walking up. I am really ashamed of myself.'

Grandma: 'The brother of the offenders is usually very quiet.'

Jason: 'We wanted to be a better brother than he was. We never mentioned our brother to the meter guy or the police. We finally got mad at him . . . He thought he was all good. I was really mad because he wanted to know what was happening. He said that he would be there for us and wasn't.'

Community Member A: 'We haven't heard from the sister of the offenders. How has this affected you?'

Sister of the Offenders: 'I feel bad. I could have been a better sister. Grandma doesn't really trust us anymore. We've all done things to mess that up.'

Community Member A: 'Grandma looks like she will trust you again. Let's talk about how to make things right.'

Facilitator: 'Any thoughts?'

Jason: 'Community service, help with house?'

Facilitator: 'We have two damaged cars. One red mustang that has a scratch as long as the door and a blue Chevy Impala that had triple gloss clear coat of a real shiny blue. A friend of the victims still has the same color of paint and will just charge for the cost of materials.'

Community Member C: 'Usually labor is around $75 an hour to paint.'

Grandma: 'I thought they could clean up trash in the park. I explained to them they would have to work but couldn't keep the money. I've asked the judge for a mentor too. They are getting facial hair and I don't know anything about shaving. Maybe doing something with big brothers or Denver Partners. I can't relate to them – they need someone who can help them do what I can't.'

Community Member A: 'I think that all three are great candidates for a big brother.'

Facilitator: 'Let's look at community service hours'

Community Member D: 'Community service and restitution are two different things.'

Community Member A: 'Do you have a Church?'

Grandma: 'Yes, I've tried also to get in touch with Baptist Church – they did have a community food share program. They could box up food. Four hours of community service per boxed meal. The minister has not called me back yet.'

Community Member D: 'The brother of the offenders feels bad. Feels sad. I heard he wants to be a part of the repair. Have you thought of what you might like to do?'

Brother of the Offenders: 'I like grandma's idea to help the guy around the house.'

Community Member D: 'Like shoveling walks?'

Offenders' Brother: 'I guess'

Facilitator: 'Let's shape this into some community service hours.'

Community Member A: 'I've always had a problem with hours, I don't know how to say what's fair.'

Facilitator: 'The court likes hours Community Member A (ha, ha).'

Grandma: 'They have been helping already.'

Community Member A: 'The president just today said that we need more active involvement in our neighborhoods.'

Grandma: 'There is another church that has a food program too.'

Community Member B: 'St John's food bank?'

Julian: 'We got help there once.'

Community Member D: 'How many hours are we talking about?'

Julian: 'I'd think 20 hours.'

Jason: 'Me too.'

Brother of the Offenders: 'I'll do 20 too.'

Sister of the Offenders: 'I want to do 20 hours too.'

Community Member A: 'What are you interested in?'

Jason: 'I want to be a Marine Biologist.'

Community Member D: 'I want to be a Zoologist.'

Sister of the Offenders: 'I want to be in the armed forces and maybe be a child psychologist.'

Community Member A: 'Well, I like the share program.'

Grandma: 'I know that there are people like me who need help. I figured if they did the community service they could just donate the hours to the bank for someone else to use. They can also clean the church.'

Facilitator: 'We've heard a number of ideas: chores, neighborhood clean-up, food bank, something done directly for the victim like an apology letter, church food banks ... did I miss anything [to co-facilitator].'

Co-facilitator: 'No.'

Community Member C: 'I like the share program and think that all 20 hours are appropriate there.'

Community Member D: 'Helping a neighbor in need if the victim doesn't want his walk shoveled could be something too. Maybe a letter to the judge about what they learned.'

Community Member A: 'The letter to the judge is a good idea.'

Facilitator: 'Everyone seems to be in agreement with the food share program for 20 hours and I see heads nodding for the letter to the judge and apology letter to the victim. OK, 4–5 months out there will be a review date. OK, while I write up the agreement for everyone to sign, help yourself to the chips and salsa. Thank you everyone.'

Case summary

Note here the quality of the dialogue and its inclusiveness. The offenders, in contrast to the previous case (and to some other NAB hearings), are active participants in the discussion and can reflect on disapproval of their behavior from not one, but many stakeholders. There is effective and apparently organic role-taking, and a creative discussion of community service. Family, extended family, and multiple community members play important roles in affirming norms, providing social support, and ensuring that the boys understand the harm of their behavior and make amends for it.

Reflecting again on the first case, the seasoned volunteers involved in this program could have also played a redirecting focus in moving this victim and the group back to the harm and insisting on a more open and inclusive dialogue process.

Note

1 When programs take the time to calculate rates of conference participation, these rates generally pertain to victim involvement. In our national program survey respondents reported what appears to be a very high rate of victim participation (cf. Umbreit, 2001) – with respondents claiming victim presence in the conference about 84 per cent of the time. This could be accounted for by the overrepresentation of VOM/D programs in our sample and the fact that VOMD conferences technically cannot occur without the victim or surrogate (the 16 per cent average rate of non-participation could refer to conferences that used a

surrogate victim, or conferences between a youth and his family, in which case the family may have been viewed as the primary victim). Variation by models is also indicated in the low rate of less than 30 per cent participation reported for NABS. In both our small qualitative sample of programs, and in the national program survey, such rates range from a low of about 5–10 per cent in some board programs to highs of 95 per cent in some VOM/D programs, or even 100 per cent if surrogate victims are counted.

Chapter 7

Community/government relationship and role transformation

The principle of transformation in community and government roles and relationships – we must rethink the relative roles and responsibilities of government and community. In promoting justice, government is responsible for preserving a just order, and community for establishing a just peace.

(Van Ness and Strong, 1997)

Introduction

The third core principle of restorative justice, transformation in community and government roles, suggests a need to restructure the relationship between justice systems and the community. It is likely self-evident to most of us that there are some things professional systems, such as criminal and juvenile justice, do relatively well, and some things they do not do well. Most will agree that many crime and justice related problems require the application of professional expertise. For example, we want our due process rights and attorneys if we are charged with a crime we did not commit, and we want police to protect us to the greatest extent possible from those who might otherwise victimize us.

While most would also recognize a role for professional expertise in the response to youth crime, young people grow up in communities – not treatment programs. It is therefore families, extended families, teachers, neighbors, ministers, and others who provide both support and guidance in the socialization process. When it comes to meeting the more complex needs of victim, offender, their supporters, and communities impacted by crime, these systems fall short because, as Judge Barry Stuart puts it:

Crime [control and prevention] should never be the sole, or even primary business of the state if *real differences* are sought in the well-being of individuals, families, and communities. The structure, procedures, and evidentiary rules of the formal criminal justice process coupled with most justice officials' lack of knowledge and connection to [the parties] affected by crime, preclude the state from acting alone to achieve transformative changes.

(Stuart, 1996: 1, emphasis in original)

With this in mind, restorative group conferencing programs may be seen as occupying a unique position. On the one hand, as a new, still somewhat marginal extension of the formal juvenile justice system in diversion, probation, court, or other administrative sectors, these programs may not be easily distinguishable from other practice designed to provide an alternative or supplement to court or diversionary sanctions. On the other hand, staff and administrators of these programs often aspire to have their conferencing programs function as vehicles for engaging and empowering community stakeholders. Restorative programs must therefore inevitably strike a delicate balance between commitments to these new constituencies in the co-production of a healing form of justice, and their system responsibilities as juvenile justice professionals. Principle Three first implies that restorative conferencing will be unlikely to achieve its goals of repairing harm and stakeholder involvement in decision-making in the absence of a systemic, structural change in the mandate of the juvenile justice system and the role of juvenile justice professionals. More specifically, the transformation in the role of the juvenile justice professional is from primary 'expert' service and surveillance provider, to facilitator of informal, problem-solving community responses to crime that will involve mobilizing community resources.

There are in fact two related overarching *goals* associated with the principle of government/community role transformation: (1) changing the role of criminal justice professionals and the mission of justice systems to support community ownership of the justice process; and, (2) increasing the capacity of citizens and community groups to address the harm of crime. Consistent with these two primary goals, this chapter is divided into two major sections: (1) mission and professional role change; and (2) community-building. Both goals are strongly interrelated in that 'government,' in this case the juvenile justice system, must allow the community to play an active and responsible role, *and* must support and seek to build its capacity to do so. Community building may also occur independent of professional systems, and even directly impact these systems (Boyes-Watson, 2004). Because of the closely connected relationship between community capacity-building and changing professional roles, our discussion within these two sections of the chapter often moves back and forth between issues relevant to the two goals.

Restorative group conferencing programs can be seen as 'modeling' a problem-solving, community-driven system response to crime that encourages increasing the amount of responsibility granted to the community. Such an increase, in turn, demands a strengthening of community capacity and willingness to respond – the *community building* goal. In Part 1, we therefore describe case examples of the often uneasy fit between the program and the system, and consider both the limits of these programs, and their general successes in demonstrating this new response. In Part 2, we focus primarily on ways in which restorative group conferencing program participants and staff envision and seek to carry out community-building practice.

Assessing mission and professional role change

The systemic reform needed in the transition to restorative justice requires change in the role of justice agencies/organizations and justice professionals. This change requires movement away from the role of expert service and surveillance provider, towards the role of facilitator and community-builder. This new role requires a partnership in which the conferencing program and the system work with and through the community rather than independently to impact the situation of victim, offender, and others affected by the crime. While conferencing programs almost by definition should adopt this role, there is the potential for replicating the 'expert' role, and thereby solving problems *for* the community rather than *with* them; similarly, there is pressure to adapt practice to fit the goals and incentive structures of the juvenile justice system rather than those associated with restorative group conferencing when the two seem incompatible.

Formal system resistance to changes that may involve sharing discretion over the response to incidents of crime is an expected feature of restorative justice reform (Carey, 2001). On the one hand, this system and professional resistance may often place the community-focused conferencing program in conflict with prosecutors, judges, police, and other system decision-makers. Hence, programs must learn to manage the tension in giving decision-making power to victims, offenders and other citizens in a context where some system professionals may be uneasy about giving up such discretion. On the other hand, some system administrators may view the program as a vehicle to accomplish their goal of empowering the community and view the mandate and role change implications of these programs as pointing the way forward for other system components and for juvenile justice professionals.

Research questions and methodological issues

These broad system changes and community-building goals also define the two basic qualitative research questions to be addressed in this chapter. The first general question is concerned with the extent to which the juvenile justice system has adapted its role to include conferencing and community involvement in the response to crime. Although efforts to change the mission of juvenile justice organizations and systems and reallocate resources are important, our system change focus is more limited to the role of individual justice professionals. Practically, our more modest, micro focus is concerned with the implications *of conferencing programs* for system change *and* efforts to redesign the roles and job descriptions of juvenile justice professionals.

We also examine how conferencing practitioners and system professionals talk about their respective roles and appear to act in a way that indicates movement towards a community-oriented facilitative role. Following the theoretical work on organizational and role transformation and its implications for juvenile justice professionals as described in Chapter 2, we note examples of resistance to restorative reforms as well as subtle shifts in mission and professional role that seem to indicate support for restorative decision-making at the organizational level. Neither these changes nor the examples of resistance are necessarily typical of all professionals or their agencies. Rather, we believe these case studies illustrate some specific forms of resistance that may occur when performance incentives are not aligned with management visions and reform objectives (Carey, 2001; Maloney, Bazemore, and Hudson, 2001). For the most part, at this early stage, these case studies of movement forward, and resistance by systems and agencies reflect tensions between the restorative vision and the practical reality of reform that seeks to challenge the expansion of system responsibility and the professionalization of the response to youth crime (McKnight, 1995; Bazemore, 1999b). In this chapter, we describe patterns in the relationship between programs, the justice systems of which they are a part, and the community, which may either encourage or limit movement toward the new role and mission.

Several important, more specific questions guided our qualitative examination of conferencing programs and their relationship both to the community and to the formal juvenile and criminal justice agencies in the jurisdictions where they operate. Specifically, where does the agency and program *fit* along a continuum in which the highest level reflects community-driven justice and where the formal system primarily provides legal authority, resources, and oversight (e.g. Pranis, 1997)? How much discretion does the program have over the cases it takes? That is, does the program have any say about what cases are admitted to the process, or does it simply take whatever the system is willing to send?

One of the most important methodological limitations surrounding observation and analysis of professional role change is the time frame involved in a study such as this one. Systemic restorative justice reform that may take months or years to complete may not be observable in a short-term case study such as this one. Therefore, other agencies and systems must be used as heuristic comparison groups in after-the-fact efforts to assess the progress in the agencies and systems examined here as they appear to be advancing along the road toward such reform. Regarding the dimensions of systemic reform focused on transformation in the professional role, we describe what are often very subtle, micro changes in role and mission that may nonetheless provide important signs of system movement towards restorative justice goals. Finally, despite the broader context of systemic reform, our primary emphasis and unit of analysis in this chapter is the restorative group conferencing program. While we also attempt to briefly profile several juvenile justice system professionals in this chapter, we focus primary attention on restorative conferencing staff, both in their role as juvenile justice professionals and as potential catalysts for change in the community/justice system relationship.

Community-building

Do conferencing programs seek to build community capacity and, if so, how do they accomplish that? At the most basic descriptive level, we first were interested in the extent to which the purposive sample of relatively more experienced restorative group conferencing programs in our qualitative study considered community-building as part of their mission. We were also interested in identifying the activities conferencing practitioners engage in to accomplish community-building goals, and what indicators, if any, they use to determine the impact of these activities. General research concerns regarding our qualitative look at community-building included:

- the extent to which conferencing practitioners define and prioritize community-building as part of their practice;
- the extent to which the conference itself appears to produce community-building outcomes;
- the forms that community-building takes given various definitions of community; and
- the extent to which there are spillover effects of conferencing programs that change the response to harm and conflict in other communities.

Based on the theoretical discussion in Chapter 2, we addressed these questions with attention to three dimensions of community-building – norm affirmation/values clarification, community ownership, and skill building – and to relevant emerging theoretical frameworks, including social capital, civic engagement, and collective efficacy. Each of these dimensions are viewed as theoretically critical features in the development of community capacity to mobilize informal social control and social support in the response to youth crime. Our primary focus on community-building was within the general context of the conferencing process. We were also concerned, however, with how the preliminary work leading up to the encounter, and the follow-up work to implement the conference agreement, might also build community capacity. Finally, we note ways in which skills and lessons learned in conferencing 'spill over' into other areas of community life.

Research questions and methodological issues

Because only a small proportion of programs in our national survey and only a few programs in the qualitative study sample think of community-building as an explicit program goal, even descriptive efforts to document these impacts are methodologically challenging. No program that we encountered in the study sought to measure or even systematically document community-building work, although some practitioners, and many conferencing volunteers, clearly devoted substantial time to these efforts. Hence the accounts of community-building activity presented in this chapter are primarily secondary descriptions drawn from practitioner and volunteer interviews and from focus groups. Typically, practitioners told us stories or gave concrete examples of the impact their conferencing program had on community-building. On occasion, field researchers in one of the two pilot jurisdictions observed first-hand and participated in community-building efforts.

As is the case with the system reform goal of Principle Three, the emerging and often subtle activity around community-building requires that our standards for assessing when and to what extent practitioners pursued community-building outcomes be less demanding than optimal. While community-building is an emerging activity within conferencing practice, it is also the case that few measurement tools are available to aid us in gauging the strength and consistency of this work, even in the literature of more widely studied fields such as community policing (Duffee et al., 2001). In addition to addressing whether and to what extent conferencing practitioners specifically directed activities to match their vision of community impact, we nonetheless felt it was important to recognize and describe instances in which 'added-value' and increased capacity appeared to grow out of conferencing experiences in communities, even if these were not designed to have such impact.

We were also open to considering what we suggest can be viewed as 'counter examples' or ways in which conferencing activity could actually diminish community capacity. That is, we considered the possibility that problems with youth crime were being taken over by programs rather than truly engaging citizens and community groups in resolving these problems. As previously suggested, our 'null hypothesis' throughout this study was that conferencing programs may simply function as trivialized diversion programs, competing with 'teen courts' and a range of other front-end programs that function not as an alternative to court and formal interventions, but rather as an alternative to other informal intervention in neighborhoods, schools, families, etc. (Bazemore, 2000). As such, they become another extension of juvenile justice systems that in essence work to relieve the community of its responsibility and in doing so widen system nets of formal control, while arguably weakening *community* nets of informal control. This pattern and a parallel community-building impact may not be mutually exclusive. However, we consider the effort to give responsibility for these problems back to the community while helping citizens develop the requisite skills for assuming this responsibility as going against the trend of juvenile justice expansion. For example, we ask what evidence there may be of the program (or system) trying to expand the conferencing process to other community-based settings, and to what extent conferencing staff train other professionals or other community members in neighborhood associations and encourage them to develop their own programs.

Part I: Vision and practice of systemic reform: mission and professional role change

General conclusions

While Chapters 5 and 6 indicate strong commitment to the core principles of repairing harm and stakeholder involvement, there seems to be more equivocal commitment to the vision of a new relationship between the juvenile justice system and the community. With a few notable exceptions, it is difficult to find local juvenile justice systems realigning missions and professional roles to provide consistent support for restorative conferencing. Concomitantly, conferencing programs vary widely in their expectation that such realignment can or needs to occur. We encountered many programs that seldom raise questions about such issues, but we describe a few that constantly expect and at times even demand such system change.

Relatively speaking, by most international standards of comparison, the majority of US conferencing programs also appear to be quite limited in the discretion and scope of authority assigned to them. Although there are exceptional programs that defy the rule, the range of seriousness of cases allowed into conferencing in the US appears to be substantially narrower than is true in other countries actively experimenting with conferencing, especially relative to overall case and offender seriousness (Morris and Maxwell, 1999; Braithwaite, 1999; Hudson et al., 1996). Some jurisdictions, such as those in Australian states and several European countries, by policy or statute send a large proportion of juvenile felony and repeat offender cases into conferencing programs, including a substantial number of personal offense cases and those involving repeat offenders. New Zealand conferences accept virtually all delinquency cases with the exception of murder and rape (Morris and Maxwell, 2001). By contrast, it is not at all uncommon to find many US programs, including some of the most well-designed and resourced efforts, that limit eligibility to misdemeanor and first-offender cases (e.g. McGarrell, 2001). In addition, the scope of authority granted to US conferencing programs also varies with regard to whether or not they are allowed to develop what becomes the core of a diversion or dispositional agreement, or simply add obligations to a list of sanctions ordered by the court or other formal juvenile justice entity.

The survey data (see Chapter 4) suggest that this scope of authority is somewhat related to program model type. Many neighborhood boards, for example, primarily take minor diversion cases, while a number of VOM and circle programs have no formal criterion that excludes more serious offenders or offenses, and some in fact receive a number of serious property offense cases and some violent offense referrals. The strong track record of victim offender mediation programs (Umbreit, 1999) and circle sentencing programs in Canada (Stuart, 1996) with such cases also suggests that this limiting of referrals by severity level is less about capacity to deal with serious and chronic offenders than about the willingness of system decision-makers to relinquish authority over both charging and sentencing, especially with serious offenses.

Moreover, by another US standard of comparison, criminal and juvenile justice systems have been very timid about referring more serious cases. Notably, the child welfare system has been much more open to using conferencing and family group decision-making with cases involving serious and chronic violence (Burford and Hudson, 2001; Pennel and Burford, 2000). According to one practitioner (Pranis, 2001), this difference may be in part about the political capital awarded to criminal and juvenile justice officials when serious crime increases and imposes a threat to communities. In criminal and juvenile justice systems where reputations are made in this way, higher rates of prosecution of serious crime can provide status to criminal justice officials who take 'get tough' stances in the fight against such crime. Most importantly, in such systems, a healed victim is not considered a success. By contrast, in child welfare, healing is viewed as the most desirable outcome, and historically there has been *no political value* in broadcasting an increase in the number of neglect or abuse cases reported.

There is another side to this apparent tendency to limit conferencing to low-level cases. The charging offense in such cases may indeed reflect only the tip of the iceberg of a multi-component problem or ongoing conflict between victim and offender and the families and acquaintances of both. In this circumstance, conferencing may be the appropriate referral, more capable of complex problem-solving regardless of the apparent lack of seriousness of the case. When the offense is indeed a trivial one with minimal problems, one may nonetheless argue by contrast that the conference is a better option than court. However, when compared to the potential of conferencing indicated by its use as a method to achieve widespread community healing in the case of chronic violence and abuse, as seen, for example, in the Hollow Water experience in Manitoba (Bushie, 1999; Ross, 2000), and in New Zealand's use of conferencing for the vast majority of chronic and violent cases, one may conclude that such use for low-level cases is, as one reviewer of this text put it, 'a waste of human capital.' At worst, we should be concerned with the previously mentioned possibilities that conferencing, like diversion program historically, displaces processes that should occur in families, schools, and neighborhoods, and even widens the net of social control (Polk, 1984).

As noted, however, there is some variation in the range of cases referred to conferencing, and especially in the scope of authority granted to these programs. Moreover, several factors appear to mitigate against the resistance to granting more discretion to the conferencing program and referring more serious cases. Length of program operation, for example, may inspire confidence in the conferencing program that allows for referrals of a more serious nature to the extent that it raises the comfort level of system professionals. This factor may predominantly account for the generally higher level of case seriousness seen in many VOM programs (Umbreit, 1999). However, in our limited sample of programs, longevity does not seem to be the primary factor in seriousness of cases referred, and any apparent relationship between longevity and seriousness may be a spurious one based on another important variable: the structural connection of the program to one or more components of the formal juvenile justice system. We suggest that *proximity to the case referral process*, in conjunction with personal *relationship to system decision-makers*, are key variables that enable the level of confidence needed to refer more cases, and more chronic and serious cases, to conferencing.

There are several case examples from our qualitative research that demonstrate support for this tentative proposition across different types of models and in different parts of the system. Below we briefly profile several examples of system 'insiders' and then consider community-based program examples with no formal ties to the system and substantial distance from case referral. Some community-based programs without formal system ties may nonetheless thrive, but in our sample of programs they do so by idiosyncratic and often informal means. Other strong programs focused on neighborhood-based referrals are vulnerable to having a viable referral process summarily disrupted by system decision-makers hostile to the program or wishing to expand their control over the referral process.

The lay of the land: structural location and system support

Conferencing models seem to be most successful when they are housed within one agency that has its own decision-making authority, and is allowed by other agencies to maximize this authority in resolving cases in the conferencing program. For example, police-based conferencing programs at the diversion level do not generally have to work with the court, and need only to convince their own officers to refer cases. Such programs also may not have to collaborate with one or more other systems to ensure referrals. While convincing one's colleagues to make referrals may be no small task, it is an internal 'sell' made easier when top leadership is in support of the program (discussed further in one of our case studies). Moreover, changing internal agency 'culture' to support conferencing is considerably easier than altering how surrounding system agencies do their business.

To push the envelope, however, police-based programs in most juvenile justice systems today still need to convince the prosecutor to relax what can be unlimited discretion over referral decisions. Because such discretion allows the prosecutor to send arrested young people into court rather than diversion, the police department must persuade the district attorney to shift some of this discretion to the program director in order to allow it to take on more cases and more serious cases.

Power-sharing: establishing system 'insiders'

Our best example of system power-sharing with the potential to keep cases out of court is the police-based conferencing program in Woodbury, Minnesota. Here, a single senior officer who, having initiated and operated a successful FGC program for several years, was allowed by the prosecutor to essentially select whatever cases seemed appropriate for conferencing. In doing so, the program in past years has maintained a balance of approximately 75 per cent felony cases since data have been collected (this dropped substantially during the year of our study due to a change in the law converting some felony offenses to aggravated misdemeanors).

Extensive training in restorative justice principles and practices – including conducting 'street-level' restorative encounters for less serious cases – for all officers has occurred since the beginning of the program. While all officers make referrals, discretion for admission lies almost exclusively in the hands of the senior officer who directs the program. Referrals are not a problem in Woodbury because officers are exposed to and educated about conferencing early on through direct experience – a form of education many practitioners agree can be critical in getting buy-in from system professionals. As program director Dave Hines puts it:

> I am the referral source primarily, along with a few other police officers. I have the final say. [Then], the facilitator has final say about what will happen in the conference. Having officers on board helps the process work well. Everyone coming into the department goes through the training process and [is] capable of doing a street diversion – [that is] built into the program. We try to get [all of the cases] into a conference as soon as possible. When they [officers] experience it, when they see it, they *get it*. That's an important part ... [That is why] we need to get people from the system to sit in.

Early on in the process, Hines, who had an informal understanding with the prosecutor that he would seek to divert as many cases as possible, gradually began keeping more serious cases at the police level. After building a record of success that included reduced recidivism rates (based on comparison with comparable current and previous diversion cases), he began sharing his results with prosecutors. Hines gradually developed a tacit understanding that allowed the county attorney to 'take credit' for the workload the cases provided while avoiding filing a petition assuming successful completion of conferencing obligations.

Though we think this arrangement is not unusual and would fit well with the agenda of community-oriented prosecution, elected officials apparently perceive that there are risks involved in giving up this discretion. Indeed, we see counter examples in neighboring Minnesota counties in which prosecutors seem unwilling to allow much police diversion (police in these counties may also be less persistent and effective in their efforts), despite a strong history of successful restorative justice programs in some of those counties. A similar, more conservative referral pattern can also be seen in jurisdictions in other states where restrictive selection criteria unfortunately were agreed upon in advance and have established a tradition of limiting referrals to low-level, first-offense cases (e.g. McGarrell, 2001).[1]

Where programs seek referrals post-adjudication or post-disposition, one would expect to find a generally higher level of seriousness of cases referred. However, this does not necessarily appear to be the case among all programs in our sample, and may be confounded somewhat by the fact that the VOM/D programs, which tend to have a longer track record in most systems, are more likely to operate at this level than other models (see Chapter 3). Our best example of an internally based, virtually institutionalized conferencing program is Washington County, Minnesota's VOM/D program, which has attained a high level of credibility and appears no longer threatening to system decision-makers, despite its firm commitment to the idea of victims, offenders, and community members as the ultimate decision-makers. The Washington County VOM/D program is now viewed as a fully institutionalized, perhaps irreplaceable, feature of the probation department and is seen by many as a preferred alternative for developing recommendations for the disposition of juvenile cases.

Another example of a probation-based program that has for some time sustained a substantial proportion of serious and chronic case referrals is Pinal County, Arizona's neighborhood board program discussed in Chapters 5 and 6 (and later in this chapter). In contrast to most neighborhood boards that are generally operated by independent agencies and/or viewed as diversion options, this program is also fully embedded in the probation department and strongly supported by the Chief Judge in this district, who is committed to maximizing the community's role in decision-making. He does so by allowing board members almost complete discretion to develop the dispositional plan, to review cases for early release from probation, and even to determine need for a residential placement – or release from such a placement.

Power-sharing: 'outsiders' and the struggle of community-based programs

A traditional working hypothesis regarding community-based programs is that they are closer to the community and therefore more capable of working with neighborhoods and residents. But 'community-based' does not necessarily mean 'community-focused,' and it does not necessarily mean that the program will be able to channel cases *away* from court and system decision-makers to the neighborhood. In contrast to the previous system-based examples, several programs in many community-based agencies in our study sample often struggled to get referrals, and unlike programs that operate within justice system agencies, more often engendered suspicion and misunderstanding from justice professionals.

Moreover, community-based programs may not aggressively seek out referrals of a higher level of seriousness, or even lobby for more discretion over what happens to these cases. Indeed, some seem powerless to influence system decision-makers and may be content to merely take referrals of whatever kind from whatever source, perhaps viewing themselves as a kind of early intervention or prevention program. Such programs may, like many other diversion programs, potentially widen the net of system control (Polk, 1984; Cohen, 1985), and may end up competing with other low-level diversion programs such as teen courts for offenses that might easily have been resolved at the school or family level.

Community-based programs that provide a clear counterpoint to such marginalization offer lessons in how the community/government relationship can be challenged from a base of citizen power – though not without ongoing struggles. Such programs are often those that have arisen from neighborhood organizations that began with the hope of playing a significant role in the disposition of cases that involve victims and offenders *from that community*. The South St Paul circle program (Coates et al., 2000) provides one example of how a strong and effective group of committed citizens with a vision can make a significant impact, but then must nonetheless struggle to develop and sustain relationships with key system decision-makers to ensure referrals. This circle initially received a wide range of referrals from the police department and from several judges (the Chief Judge for some time also sat as a member of the circle, and several system professionals occasionally participated in the circle and supported its work), including drug possession and other cases. In contrast with the case of the Woodbury FGC, however, there was no internal base for direct police referrals, which initially came directly to the circle but are now apparently tightly controlled by the County Attorney's office.

The South St Paul circle continued to receive a rather wide range of cases from police and community sources until the profile of the program was raised and system decision-makers learned about the level of seriousness of some of the cases being referred. Describing the subsequent restriction on direct referral from the police department, the coordinator of this program refers to a kind of 'pull back' on this community group's gradually increasing authority.

> We *were* getting referrals from the police department, but then money [in the form of a 'community justice' grant from the state with funding tied to prosecutor caseloads] entered the picture and different alliances were built. The police department would no longer refer cases directly but instead sent them through the county attorney. This has resulted in fewer cases and less difficult cases, and it really depends on who the prosecutor is – some will not refer any at all . . . cases we are getting now are actually not severe enough [to justify] the circle process. Now we're doing more circles for reintegration into the community, and our gears have shifted toward other neighborhood disputes.

Many other community-based programs have struggled for cases and decision-making discretion at various points in their history even when they are relatively successful in maintaining caseloads and addressing the needs of participants in the process. Though the South St Paul program remains well-respected in the community and still seeks to meet pressing neighborhood justice needs (including the need for training and support of school-based conferencing programs), it has been unable to maintain the flow of more serious and complex cases it would like to receive and, more recently, reports a decline in participation of system stakeholders.

Our final example combines some elements of a community, non-justice system location with a great deal of internal discretion over how to respond to trouble and harm. In this school-based program, a principal committed to maximizing the use of conferencing as an alternative to suspension and other zero-tolerance policies provides a unique example of how the community/government relationship can be negotiated to replace retributive responses with restorative ones.

In Stafford, Arizona, use of conferencing was made possible by virtue of a key decision-maker who assumed his organizational authority in a specific type of 'community' context. In using conferencing as a restorative decision-making model in a high school with some 700 students, the principal essentially transferred the primary responsibility for a range of incidents formerly charged as crimes and dealt with in the courts (police cars reportedly appeared at school on a daily basis) back to the community of origin. In this case the school administration is in the role of *system* decision-maker, while teachers and students in classrooms and elsewhere on school grounds constitute the *community* in question. The system decision-maker in this case chose to allow this community to address conflict and harm in *context*. By contrast, most other schools in the area appear to use zero-tolerance policies as a means of moving conflict and trouble out of the school and into the court without addressing what is typically a larger underlying problem of lack of connection and disrespect.

In between community-based solution and referral to court, conferencing programs may receive referrals to resolve conflict outside the immediately affected community, but prior to court. The counter example to the principal's internal, holistic, community-based response is the case of an outside conferencing facilitator who trains staff and/or comes in 'on call' to conference disciplinary infractions. Without buy-in from top administrators, such efforts may alleviate some stress and impact a few cases, but may never ultimately impact the flow of cases from school to court nor the conflict-resolving culture of the school as a whole.[2]

As a general hypothesis, we suggest that programs can attain more discretion over decision-making and therefore more effectively 'push the envelope' when they are internal to the system. However, the counterpoint to this argument is that it is precisely those system-based programs that are more likely to be under tight control, if not highly compromised, by system priorities. Truly community-based programs may seem more independent and we must acknowledge that community-building seems more difficult from a system rather than a community organizational base. On the other hand, when and if community-building is initiated from within a formal criminal justice agency, it may be more likely to also affect broader system impact than when it occurs in one locally based community agency.

Transforming mission and role: conferencing stages and phases

To make the discussion of system change and power-sharing with the community through the conferencing program more concrete, we turn to a consideration of specific stages and phases in the conferencing process. Because the principle of community/government role transformation is clearly less relevant to some parts of the conference enterprise than others, we focus primarily on the *preparation and follow-up stages* and the *agreement phase*. It is important to note that this principle is most concerned with the context of restorative justice beyond the confines of the conference itself, i.e. in the system and the community.

Because the transformation in professional role and agency mission is at best a vision in most jurisdictions, most of this discussion addresses the tension between programs attempting to share decision-making authority with the system on behalf of the community. There are, however, small yet important signs of professional role change and a 'loosening up' in traditional agency mandates in some cases. Notably, it is that loosening and role change, coupled with an impressive creativity and persistence on the part of some programs, that has allowed them to get referrals and assume discretion over the response to those cases.

The pre-conferencing stage

Given the discussion above regarding the system's control of cases, it can be argued that preparation may be a critical time in which signs of shifting community/government roles and relationships will be evident. Because community-based programs are dependent upon the system in this stage to get referrals, critical decision-making and negotiation may occur between the referral agency and the program. The nature of preparation may also be affected if system players overwhelm the program with referrals, and/or if the program is under-resourced. For example, we note that in a couple of jurisdictions in our extended case study of several states, conferences were being held up to eight months from the time of the offense as a result of system processing delays.

As noted earlier, establishing relationships with decision-makers in control of the screening and referral process may be one way a community-based program can ensure a smooth referral process. One such community-based program that appears to have 'co-opted' system decision-makers to funnel cases to the program is described below. Then, to demonstrate how pre-conferencing preparation may potentially influence the most positive change in the system/community relationship in a way that also builds community, we turn again to an example from the Woodbury police FGC program.

Strategies for getting referrals: 'co-opting' decision-makers
In addition to proximity to the system, internal control of the referral process, and the granting of discretion by key gatekeepers (such as prosecutors), much of the success in getting cases may well be a combination of apparently idiosyncratic factors. One such factor is personal relationships and the credibility of the program's sponsoring agency and its leader (especially if it is community-based). Another factor is whether system decision-makers have had the opportunity to directly experience the process. Indeed, a number of experienced practitioners tell a now common story about how an initially oppositional judge, prosecutor, or police officer was won over to restorative decision-making after 'sitting in the circle.' Participation at this level seems to break down fear and distrust and increase comfort that the process is valid and its community organizers are reasonable people. The director of the previously mentioned South St Paul circle describes the early experience of the program:

> Prosecutors assigned to South St Paul have come in not being supportive, but when they participate – they change their minds. [This is when we] know we're having an impact on the broader system.
>
> Q: How has the system changed in response to restorative justice?
>
> A: The County Attorneys are now promoting [circles]. After having sat in on circles, they started looking at the results and the impact they have had on the community. They started to realize being strictly punitive is not always the best-case scenario. The system people can take care of the people in the system, but the needs of the community must be met also. *The community is made up of voters* [emphasis ours].

An interesting twist on this strategy is seen in the North Minneapolis circle project operated by the Northside Community Justice Committee. Essentially, the project established an effective working relationship partly by including many criminal and juvenile justice professionals in the volunteer group itself. The credibility of these professional volunteers has no doubt influenced the level of trust among other decision-makers for this community-based group. In some cases, system professional members of the North Minneapolis Circle *are* the decision-makers. In other words, circle members who happen to be prosecutors, judges, probation officers, or public defenders sometimes bring cases from their own files or dockets for admission to the circle. More commonly, they draw upon close personal connections to other decision-makers to recruit cases. The strategy for community-based conferencing programs with no direct links to a system agency is therefore of a mild form of co-opting decision-makers into the conferencing process.

Put another way, the North Minneapolis case was about building strong professional leadership to ensure sustainability. The process by which the program initially received referrals was both ingenious and persistent. As the program coordinator describes it, a key factor was having public defenders, judges, and prosecutors active in the circle 'looking out' for cases that met program criteria. When such a case went to arraignment, these professionals tried to get the case assigned to them. This was generally accomplished by one of the professionals making a direct request to the clerk, or having the clerk refer cases to them that met the criteria. The process developed essentially by trial and error, maximizing connections within the 'court work group' that might frequently involve a judge calling someone in the county attorney's office to ensure referral. Though the circle struggles from time to time with changing judicial and prosecutorial leadership, this core group of professionals can generally advocate for the program with fellow decision-makers.

Because referral occurs often in a matter of minutes, the challenge was to create time and space for the judge to allow a program representative to conduct an interview with the youth and family. As a back-up, the public defender would explain to his or her client how the program works and offer it as an alternative. There was even what the coordinator called 'double-screening' in which a supporter in the prosecutor's office and a supporter in the public defender's office would both flag the case and follow it up with the clerk. Despite occasionally creating some delay and disruption, the process essentially circumvented the normal bureaucratic referral process.

Programs that gain support by means of this kind of 'back-door recruitment' may suffer when there is the inevitable turnover among key system decision-makers. As one circle member pointed out weeks after a change in the county attorney's office that resulted in a dramatic cut in referrals to the circle:

Q: How are things going for you now with referrals and with court and attorney relationships?

A: We *had* an excellent referral process going. The county attorney and the public defender screened the arraignment calendar. He would call us and we would get to the court to talk with the families. Recently, we had a turnover in the county attorney's office and the public defender's office – new leadership. [They] know nothing about what to do. The new county attorney is not encouraging. I met with a couple of judges, and the chief judge in the juvenile court is supportive. Judges will in some cases mandate [the case] to go to circle. The problem is to sit with the judge and make sure they understand our criteria [and the caveat that the circle has the right to refuse a case].

Q: You have a unique relationship with the assistant prosecutor and judges, right?

A: We *developed* a personal relationship – worked hard at it – took a whole year before [we] took [the] first case – we had [Judge] Barry [Stuart] do the training around process. Forty of us were trained – twenty from Hennepin County – met every other week for a year, discussing what [we were] going to do. *People in the system also live in the neighborhood.*

For program coordinator Alice Lynch, the answer to the referral problem for community-based programs is focused on building personal relationships, and the 'personal touch.' The challenge is to keep widening the circle of system supporters:

We had the same issue [with some probation screeners] so we recruited some probation officers to join our circle ... The other advantage of having screening done by our circle members is that [system professionals who are also members] get a case assigned to themselves [thus combining system authority and community authority]. Sometimes we struggle with *regular* system folks – [they're] more punitive.

Many sound community-based programs will not be able to emulate the North Minneapolis strategy, however. A persistent problem in getting referrals may have less to do with system trust and power dynamics than with a lack of understanding or, more cynically, a sense that the conferencing program will in some way benefit the person making the referral, e.g. through reducing workload or caseload. Some probation officers may not understand the decision-making role of the conference in contributing to the court disposition, or they (or their judges) may simply not want to take the time for this input prior to the dispositional hearing.

Though programs housed within the referring agency are believed to have an advantage, some professionals in these agencies choose not to refer and thereby diminish the capacity of such conferencing programs. In a Colorado police-based program, for example, the officer who directs the program underscores the importance of personal participation to break down barriers of trust:

> The process is police driven: the cases fall through the cracks because the cops don't feel it is viable, but once they sit in the 'circle' [in this case a family group conference] they see the power. The system sees [their] role as guarding public trust – almost like religious zeal. An early obstacle was judges sending cases [to us] with items [already] ordered to put into the agreement. We tried to educate judges; . . . even refused to take cases. We had one judge overturn the work of the circle – hardest one for me to take – [after] people came in with good faith [to work on the agreement]. This is a huge educational process – the power people wield over others is astounding.

Agreement phase

Getting case referrals is only one aspect of power-sharing and system–community collaboration in restorative justice decision-making. Indeed, some programs receive many referrals, yet are very limited in actual decision-making authority and responsibility. It is not uncommon, for example, to find that the authority of the conference is restricted to assigning community service hours, or simply to deciding where court ordered hours will be served. Here we provide examples of a range of possible arrangements involving shared decision-making discretion.

Scope of authority: community and system discretion
What can go wrong in the relationship between the program and the system once cases get referred? Even in the most advanced restorative justice systems, the scope of authority granted to community vs. formal system agencies may be quite limited. At times the negotiations between program and system seem like a balancing act in which there are no right or wrong answers. While the issue at times is clearly about power and 'turf,' at other times it may simply be about bureaucracy.

A problem in defining the scope of authority between the court and conferencing programs occurred in a jurisdiction with perhaps the highest level of system and community commitment to restorative decision-making in the country. Training in and discussion of restorative justice has been ongoing in this jurisdiction for a number of years, and leaders from each of the key system decision-making agencies have tried to think carefully about how to adapt various components of the system to accomplish restorative objectives. Washington County, Minnesota, which we profile in the next section of this chapter, is an emerging model of system reform and convergence which provides an important lesson in how problems in scope of authority – and the 'fit' between restorative decision-making and traditional juvenile justice priorities – merge even in jurisdictions with strong community programs and supportive system leadership.

One of the first challenges to restorative conferencing in Washington County came from the Deputy Public Defender assigned to juvenile cases. This opposition was something of a surprise given the debatable, but widely shared, assumption that restorative conferencing always yields 'a better deal' for juvenile clients. Following some disagreement about the scope of conferencing vs. court authority in determining outcome requirements for juvenile offenders, this public defender was concerned about the potential for 'double-sanctioning.' Specifically, offenders who were subject to court-imposed dispositional orders, including attending the conference, were then also subject to the conditions of the reparative conferencing agreement. Her personal supportiveness of restorative conferencing, and her ambivalence, was reflected in the following assessment of the process:

> If it were my *daughter*, I would tell her to go to the conference. I think it is a good process. The problem is that I can't advise my *clients* to go to conferencing when I know the result will be expanded punishment.

Sometimes, upon hearing that the court had already ordered restitution and community service, conference participants in Washington County wondered what else was left for them to do. On other occasions, however, the group would develop additional service, restitution, or other requirements for the offender. Although the motivation for these additional requirements is most often a benevolent one, and restorative justice does not require absolute uniformity in sanctions as its measure of 'justice,' there is significant potential for unfairness if one receives additional sanctions by choosing or following a court order to attend a conference.

From the deputy public defender's perspective or that of any youth advocate, overloading a young person with requirements is a predictable path to failure and possible return to court. Indeed, a probation violation that resulted from an uncompleted requirement added by a group of conference participants to the list of required court sanctions became the determining factor for this public defender to stop advising her clients to attend conferences. This concern voiced by the public defender, and worries that attorneys could potentially greatly limit the flow of cases to conferences, led to a series of meetings that eventually changed the way judges made referrals to these programs. Had this problem occurred in a jurisdiction less committed to restorative justice decision-making, the problem might not have been so easily resolved, or would have been addressed by placing additional limits on the scope of the conferencing program's authority to determine where and how the court-ordered disposition should be fulfilled.

The problem of wishing to retain discretion and the reluctance to cede this authority to the conference is of course not limited to judges. A member of the North Minneapolis circle discusses ongoing problems that illustrate how charging authority and control over cases may not be something that is easily ceded to community groups.

> *Q*: How would you describe the relationship between the system and circle now?
>
> *A*: One thing with Northside [the neighborhood circle program] is unique; we have probation, prosecutors, social worker, judges, and the public defender. The relationship is good with what we want to see accomplished. More recently we have an issue at the county attorney's office – has tunnel vision as to what a 'successful' case is – attitude is you do a crime – get punished. In the North Minneapolis circle, if kids go through and do well, the case can be dismissed at the end or charges reduced. This gives the kid more incentive than just to become a better person, which can be hard to grasp for some kids.

Another point of tension between some community-based conferencing programs and system decision-making has been the concern that young people sent to a conference are 'getting away with something' unless a formal charge is filed. For some prosecutors this is viewed as losing control or losing an advantage in future encounters with an offender. For community members who understand the demands of conferencing programs, however, some incentive to participate seems appropriate and perhaps necessary. Many seem to put themselves in the offender's shoes and say that they wouldn't do it either without getting something in return.

> *Q*: How has this affected the circle?
>
> *A*: It almost brought it to a halt in cases where charges were not reduced or dismissed. The system wants the kid to plead guilty and have the court resolve sentencing, and then as part of probation, go to circle. This gives kids no incentive. Circle is *hard* – like having 10 probation officers. We need to resolve this with the new county attorney – in the beginning we were left alone, but now with more attention to RJ, more attention is on the circle. They have people in that department that never come to circle or trainings.

The prosecutor's line of thinking in this case may be more consistent with system attitudes about juvenile offenders. Even among some restorative justice advocates, there is the concern that an incentive to participate somehow weakens the purity of the commitment to the restorative process.[3] As noted in Chapter 5, this circle has also struggled to gain control over determining and monitoring monetary restitution. According to the coordinator the program has not been able to do so because of the view among key system decision-makers that the court must determine restitution.

A final area in which conferencing may threaten formal system authority may be a function of the high visibility of some programs that take cases after court processing, rather than as a diversion option. Commenting on the source of a referral problem faced by circle programs in his county, the director of a police-based diversion program observes:

> I think that is a lot of the problem with circles. [We] had a couple of county attorneys say they would not support circles. You take cases [diversion] and never see them, there is *no threat*. If you come in [post-adjudication], then turn it over to the community and accept whatever they do, *that* is a threat . . . Also, circles are seen as making important sentencing decisions.

Unfamiliar ritual is a problem for some professionals as one circle coordinator observes:

> In the circle, you have candles, holding hands, etc. . . ., it makes people nervous. At [circle] council meetings, system people would stick their head in and want to know what was happening . . . it looks scary, but as long as they do not know about it [i.e. as in diversion cases], it's not a threat.

The 'leveling effect' of these and some other conferencing programs, in which participants generally sit in a circle as equals rather than in front of judges and juries, is also, according to some conferencing coordinators, intimidating to system professionals because:

> When [they] come into the circle, and are judged by the community – they no longer have power. The prosecutor came in with his briefcase – then [he or she was] put into a place with everyone else – you could see the transformation in his or her behavior. Part of it is just not knowing how to act. Even in probation, we get into conflicts with officers who say it has to be done a certain way. There are power conflicts around what is important. There may also be an issue of professional bias in some who wish to play a distant role regarding their cases. They say, 'If I sit in this conference, and then I'm going to go back and supervise this kid, it undermines my authority.'

As a kind of counterpoint that demonstrates how the system can listen more carefully to the voice of the community, and at times may even rely on it, we conclude the section with two anecdotes about engaging the authority of citizens actively involved in conferencing and a sense of the perceived potency of conferencing volunteers to influence criminal justice decision-making and policy. In the first case, the director of a Minnesota circle found herself in court in the role of observer of a dispute between a prosecutor and a public defender before a circuit court judge who was becoming increasingly exasperated and impatient. Interrupting one of the disputing attorneys, the judge addressed the circle coordinator: 'What do *you* think we should do in this case?' Her recommendation became the courts dispositional decision.

In a second example, a newly hired community prosecutor in another Minnesota neighborhood was prepared to address a group of volunteers involved in a conferencing program to outline her agenda for working with them and other groups. She was somewhat taken aback when one of the first questions from the coordinating committee asked her to explain to the group why *they were not consulted* about the need for a community prosecutor in their neighborhood, about the decision to hire her, and about whether funds appropriated for her position were considered for use for other purposes in the neighborhood.

These examples illustrate conferencing program leadership asserting its role as representative of the community. While direct confrontation between community volunteers and system decision-makers has been rare, there appears to be an ongoing struggle in some community-based programs to assert what volunteers view as their obligation to demand more cases and discretion over them, especially when the offenders and victims represented reside or work in these communities. The case studies below represent systemic efforts to implement restorative conferencing and restorative practice generally. The first example is based on the collaborative efforts of all major components of the juvenile justice system and criminal justice in one county. The second describes one conferencing program with systemic implications and impact. The third describes systemic implementation of conferencing in a unique community environment – that of a high school.

Case studies in system transition: changing mission and professional role to support restorative conferencing

Case 1: Washington County, Minnesota: multi-agency leadership

Systemic restorative justice reform is not even on the drawing board in most local juvenile justice systems in the US In a few jurisdictions where there have been efforts to craft new missions and redefine professional roles, generally one individual in one agency (e.g. probation, the judiciary) has taken a leadership role with relatively little participation by other agencies and professionals in these agencies. Washington County, Minnesota provides a rare example of multi-agency leadership in which there appears to be strong and sustained commitment to restorative justice reform from the judiciary, prosecution, community corrections, the public defender's office, victim's advocates, several police departments, and a number of community-based agencies and programs. This vision emphasizes community involvement in decision-making through a wide range of conferencing programs and initiatives, and system leaders appear to have a specific sense of what this vision means for changing the roles that they and their staff play.

Russell Reetz, Director of Court Services, provided much of the initial impetus for piloting and helping to secure funding for a variety of conferencing programs. Beginning in the mid-1990s, court services staff, working closely with a variety of system professionals and community members, began to support various community-based pilot programs. They worked with police departments (including Dave Hines in Woodbury), youth service bureaus, and other agencies to pull together groups of volunteers and community-based groups interested in sponsoring or working with other groups to initiate one or more conferencing programs.

While leaders in each agency were strongly committed to the disciplinary interests associated with their professional roles, each has also tried to model and establish protocols for their colleagues of how their job descriptions might be adapted in support of restorative decision-making. The mission developed by community corrections and court services together is based on restorative justice principles and is now shared by each participating entity. The common ground between these agencies and their leadership is the commitment to community leadership and the credit given to the community for the success of the various restorative justice initiatives in Washington County.

In a small focus group, each leader described the benefits and challenges of restorative decision-making and how their own and their colleague's roles must change to support successful implementation of restorative justice. This leadership group reflects shared understanding of restorative principles and the idea of restorative justice as a systemic approach, which is especially evident in the lack of the usual equivocations whereby many system professionals quickly delineate a rather large group of cases they view as 'not appropriate for restorative justice.' As Chief Judge Gary Schurrer responded when asked what cases would not be appropriate for restorative justice:

> *None!* I have even started talking with court administration about using family group conferencing for dissolution, custody, visitation

cases; then parties are involved in resolving their own problems with help from volunteers ... The court cannot address all issues – community can help work with people. This helps in getting to different layers by building trust, opening up – finally getting to what is important. Cottage Grove just finished two cases [involving incidents of ongoing family violence] that were in circle for two years. We had the family violence network on board from the beginning; without their involvement, we would not have done this.

What is the role of each player in restorative justice?
In contrast to traditional prosecutors, the Washington County Attorney, Doug Johnson, sees his role as

> to stay out of the way ... and to empower my people [prosecuting attorneys] to *trust the circle* ... and make sure the victim has an opportunity for input. This is how we can help in healing; [we also want the] offender to recognize that he has actually hurt someone ... we want to humanize the crime.

Chief Judge Schurrer's view of the role of judges is equally untraditional. He sees power as truly something to be shared:

> We walk a fine line; but we really *need to step back and let the community make decisions.* I do not need to be there as often now that it [restorative conferencing programs] is up and running. Our role is to encourage, invite new volunteers, and increase the number of cases going to conferencing ... The community is trying to do the right thing, and there is agreement about what these things are. There is a focus on values – living values. Oversight? Yes, but you can have the *community* do a lot of that. Also, in circles [which he has been most personally involved in recently] judges are, by definition, sharing power – but we will always have oversight through the sentence.

In a climate of 'best interests' of the child and paternalistic informality where youth advocates have fought in the juvenile court for more than three decades to gain a basic commitment to due process rights, the idea of referral to another informal process that may be viewed as weakening these rights, and removing formal limits on punishment may be received with some apprehension (see Feld, 1999). Deputy Public Defender Pat Zenner clearly feels a strong commitment to her traditional role as well as a desire to accomplish something she believes is truly in the client's best interest:

> My role [in a restorative justice system] is *still* to defend my client, but I am also open to the need to giving them multiple options. RJ

allows for this. 'I want them to get the best deal [but realize that] the best deal is *not necessarily* the easiest deal.' This is where RJ comes in [emphasis ours].

The system leader most responsible for crafting the mission used by the entire system, Russ Reetz, Director of Court Services, echoes the group's general values and personalizes the mission as a community corrections responsibility:

My role is to make sure the offender realizes the severity of what he has done; to help to make the victim whole; to make sure the community supports both.

Common concerns: where do restorative programs fit within the juvenile justice system?
This leadership group is unanimous in their agreement that fitting restorative justice processes into the current system is a bit like fitting a round peg into a square hole. Several specific concerns are cited as inhibiting more effective use of conferencing. First, where legislation defines and gives authority to a court process, it says nothing about the authority and/or limits of alternative informal processes, and hence 'we have restorative processes, but no laws [and procedures] have been changed.' Judge Scherer is also concerned that there is no statewide funding process and that the legislature does not have an understanding of restorative justice. Russ Reetz notes that there is much lobbying going on at the legislature, but they are asking for the wrong things. Referring to the problem of placing 'round pegs in square holes,' he notes that rather than money for more programs, what is needed is legislation 'to create the round holes' for restorative justice. Essentially, in Reetz's view, there should be more concern with teaching the philosophy rather than simply developing the programs.

Second, there are scheduling problems that limit judges' ability to get sufficient information on restorative options in advance of hearings. According to Judge Schurrer and Russ Reetz, this has less to do with judges not being willing to share power and give up sentencing discretion than with case management and scheduling problems. Reetz adds, however, that part of the problem is 'some judges' tunnel vision about scheduling and dispositions.'

Third, as Zenner believes, some judges may resist giving up sentencing authority or are perhaps afraid to deviate from the letter of the law to allow for community input. She suggested that they 'need to be less fearful of challenging the decisions of the circle [the conference] after the fact.' The problem noted is what she called the 'Catch 22' of letting conference participants develop the disposition and then putting the judge in the position of appearing to 'ignore the community's wishes, and making them feel disenfranchised.'

Fourth, everyone agreed that a big training issue for conferencing staff and volunteers is to gain a better understanding of the system, and the legal limits on their authority. According to Russ Reetz, as a result of this lack of understanding, there is simply 'a trust factor between circles and the system.' And County Prosecutor Doug Johnson observes that 'trust goes both ways – my attorneys often do not trust circle.'

From the prosecutor:

Q: Are you really OK with the community taking this ownership?
A: I do have some trouble with circles . . . we need to let them know what their boundaries are.

Finally, the issue of system role change is especially challenging. Prosecutor Doug Johnson added that, 'right now, the law is behind the traditional prosecutor.' This is why he says that, in Minnesota at least, restorative justice works pretty well at the pre-prosecution or diversion stage, but is an uncomfortable fit in the court process itself. And it may only work well at the diversion stage precisely because the Washington County prosecutor has chosen to maximize the discretion granted to local police and the number of cases that will be handled by these decision-makers. In other jurisdictions, prosecutors make it their business to know about, and assume maximum control over, all arrests.

Benefits of restorative conferencing: what is going well?
Each key player has examples of what he or she feels is going well in the restorative justice initiative in Washington County. County Prosecutor Johnson, for example, is especially pleased with the attention victims are receiving through his office and the opportunities offered to victims by restorative conferencing options. While discouraging clients from going to conferencing in the year prior to our study, today Deputy Public Defender Pat Zenner now thinks it might be a good experience for them.

I think it is sometimes better for clients to go through circle than through the court; for some cases, there will be better community monitoring, for example, alcohol offenses. It will be a slower process than court; people who say they want to make some changes in life are best for conferencing. Other benefits are that the victim gets information – e.g. about why they were picked – and school instances: fights between friends – good for V–O conferences. Kids see this as better than going to a school counselor liaison officer – more private.

Judge Schurrer also maintains great optimism as he feels restorative conferencing has increasingly gained acceptance, especially at the police diversion level. Using conferencing as a diversion option has resulted in Washington County having one of the lowest court processing rates in the state and one of the highest diversion rates, which Judge Schurrer attributes in part to extensive use of conferencing (some 300 referrals to conferencing programs were made last year). By comparison, a neighboring county with similar demographics and crime rates, but no commitment to conferencing, had four times the number of court referrals and far fewer diversion cases in the year 2000 as Washington County.

Court Services Director, Reetz, feels that:

Communication is better between conferencing programs and the system. People are listening to each other now ... We are far from perfect, but we are understanding and addressing problems [and] the entire process is more community-driven. There is also evidence of community empowerment and the system's willingness to grant the community more discretion than would have been expected.

His probation staff increasingly view conferencing as a resource; many of these probation officers facilitated conferences themselves before the initiation of new programs, and therefore have direct experience. A benefit for them is that collecting restitution has become less burdensome because they no longer get many calls from victims, and also because conferencing gives the young offender a better sense of who he hurt in committing the crime. They estimate that about half of all probation cases are referred to a conference at intake, although they have some concern about 'circles setting admission standards too high' and about the need for better education of volunteers about system processes and procedures.

Overall, Russ Reetz believes that community corrections has made more movement in the last six months than in the previous four years. Reetz observes a 'big turn around' in the public defenders' office in the last few years, and more 'social consciousness' among the attorneys – making it easier now to 'find common ground.'

Lessons learned
Key system decision-makers, their staff, and the community groups, and citizens whose work is so strongly applauded by system professionals acknowledge that their system has flaws. System decision-makers and community groups continue to struggle over case discretion and defining roles in a formal system that even the most ardent advocates of community involvement do not want to completely abandon.

Community involvement and ownership is key; however, such involvement in restorative decision-making is unlikely to be sustained effectively

265

without a shared vision among multiple organizational components of the system and their respective leaders. While these leaders may continue to have difficult debates about the best strategies to pursue restorative decision-making reforms, moving forward with such reform is made easier when a common vision-makes debate about the goal of community involvement unnecessary.

Case 2: Ceding dispositional power to the community

The second example illustrates the potential for ceding a much greater range of authority and a comprehensive role to community decision-makers if system leaders are willing to do so. In this example, a neighborhood accountability board (NAB) program in Pinal County, Arizona is essentially assigned dispositional authority for virtually all court cases including those involving the most serious offenses. In addition to recommending the usual reparative obligations for making amends such as restitution and community service, community volunteers may, after seeking the advice of a probation officer attending the board hearing, recommend any of a full range of sanctions, including a wide array of supervision and treatment options.

The process works by having all the parties come together, including the offender, the probation officer, and the restorative justice panel, to discuss the offense and various alternative responses. All parties are heard from and the probation officer gathers information to put into the pre-dispositional report to be presented and recommended to the judge. The board can suggest options, ranging from the strictest level of intensive supervision to less intrusive options, and according to the NAB director, '99.9 per cent of the time the judge follows the recommendation of the committee.' The program also refers about one-third of cases with victims to a victim offender mediation program. The following is excerpted from an interview with the director of this program.

Q: Can the community recommend commitment? Does this ever happen?

A: Rarely, since we have had the boards ... it has only happened three times [the judge committed in all three cases].

Q: You mean they could say, just as a judge could, that this one is going to go to ... Have you ever seen the judge say that he can't leave this one to the community?

A: No, I have not seen it happen. He has that ability, but I have not seen a judge go against the recommendation, against the community.

Q: What makes this different if they are just recommending a disposition? What is the advantage over just having the PO do it?

A: They're doing what the judge would do, *but with the ingenuity of the community* . . . The follow-up or post-conference period is of course a time in which the community can exert its authority and role in ensuring that conditions of the agreement are met and that the offender and victim are safely reintegrated.

Q: What happens after the agreement? What role does the board have in monitoring, etc?

A: Then there is a follow up at three-, six-, and nine-month intervals. They come back and the kid, family, and probation officer have to reappear with the restorative justice committee . . . [it is an] update for the committee, a way to acknowledge the kid who is doing good. It is a good way to form that connection [with the community] and allow it to continue and to reinforce the connections [between] the kid, family, and community.

Q: What can they do at this point if things aren't going well? Does it matter if the kid is doing well?

A: On the nine-month review, the committee has the option of directing the probation officer to recommend early release from probation.

Q: What determines the decision to release? Mostly restitution to the victim?

A: Yes . . . I think that's a big incentive to get off probation if they have been fulfilling their restitution [and other requirements] . . . it's really a big thing for the Board members if the community doesn't have to pay to keep them [the juvenile] on probation.

Q: How big is the reduction in supervision time?

A: The average is 14 months [hence, the reduction would be five months].

Q: So it is a significant cut.

A: Yes. Plus, parents [benefit because they] don't have to pay the $50 monthly supervision fee.

As a mini-case study, the Pinal County approach is atypical of most uses of NABs, and other conferencing models for that matter. According to our survey and our examination of other NABs in the qualitative study, most courts do not grant nearly as much authority to boards and panels and most typically use boards only at the diversion level. On the other hand, we do not mean to imply that Pinal boards are necessarily exemplary as a restorative decision-making approach (we have too little first-hand information to draw such conclusions, nor are there clear standards for doing so). What we can suggest, however, is that based on this small example, a much more holistic use of restorative conferencing that places the community on the frontlines of decision-making about important outcomes for offenders, victims, and their families is a possibility.

Case 3: Government/community relationship in the micro-community of the school

An interesting case of change in the community/government relationship is occurring on a small scale within the 'community' of the school. In this micro-community where students, teachers, and staff use classrooms, hallways, playgrounds, parking lots and other areas as essentially streets and neighborhoods, community members must negotiate space. They must also be sensitive to norms of interaction with each other as well as more general rules of conduct that come from principals and ultimately from state agencies and statutes. The latter essentially function in the role of government, enforcing compliance with universal norms of conduct in the state education bureaucracy. Unfortunately, in recent years, zero-tolerance policies have simply moved conflict temporarily out of schools via mandatory expulsion and suspension.

Proponents of restorative decision-making practices in schools have sought to reclaim some of the conflict for victim, offender, and affected community to resolve situations in a healing, and less exclusionary way. In doing so, they may be slowly reversing a trend that provides one of the most vivid examples of the idea of 'stolen conflict' whereby the state claims ownership of a victim–offender conflict and seeks to solve the problem by punishing the offender, leaving victim and community needs unmet and harm unrepaired. The zero-tolerance policies of expulsion and mandatory suspension essentially provide a feeder system into the courts and juvenile justice system, either directly through court referral on criminal charges or indirectly through referral to diversion and other informal programs. Most recently, restorative conferencing programs themselves have been the recipients of cases referred by the schools and have faced a dilemma regarding their own role in removing conflict from its community of origin, while at the same time realizing that the alternative may be court processing. *School-based* conferencing, by contrast, attempts to avoid the zero-tolerance response that fails to deal with broader conflicts in the school community itself (Karp and Breslin, 2001).

According to the Minnesota Department of Education's Nancy Riestenberg, restorative conferencing practices in the school setting seek to respond to trouble and disputes such as fights and arguments by viewing them first as 'violations against the person, rather than violations against the student handbook.' For Riestenberg, school conferencing is based on an ethic of what she says might be called civic spirituality, defined as a 'general concern for the well-being of others.' When there is harm to individual members of the school community and the community itself, the harm needs to be addressed *in* this community, or it will continue and even escalate.

In Riestenberg's view, the problem is not one of lack of rules and aggressive responses to disciplinary infractions. 'Many kids are hurt by others in school, and many kids hurt others. The problem is that neither of these groups hears from others that "this was not OK." Restorative justice processes provide space for empathy to happen . . . kids, teachers, parents [are affected by this].' The approach is premised on inclusion of all parties affected by an incident of harm and on the practical premise, as Riestenberg suggests, that formerly violent and troublesome people are often the best peace-makers.

In presenting examples of restorative programs and practices in school communities, it is important to note that these programs at the time of our study were, to the best of our knowledge, blips on the radar screen of a national zero-tolerance landscape. Additional exceptions to this rule may soon include conferencing programs in a number of school districts in Cook County (Chicago), Illinois and throughout the state of New York where School Resource Officers have recently been trained in family group conferencing. Despite the impressive track record of these conferencing approaches in achieving very tangible outcomes such as reduced suspensions and dramatic reduction in disciplinary infractions (Karp and Breslin, 2001), conferencing as a school community response faces a formidable battle with representatives of a very powerful educational system of rule-driven discipline that is not unlike the battle community conferencing programs face with the criminal justice system. Programs in schools, like those in juvenile justice agencies, are also vulnerable to the loss of strong leaders.

In the course of this project, for example, one of the most effective and apparently institutionalized programs, South St Paul, Minnesota's Kindergarten through High School conferencing program, essentially folded when its director was transferred to a neighboring county. Other programs were begun in one or more classrooms and flourished in other schools – though with little apparent impact on the school as a whole. Regarding our interview with the Arizona principal from which we quote below, the good news is that he has transferred to a school district in the Northwest where he hopes to replicate his school restorative justice approach to discipline and school safety. He believes moreover that he and his staff in Stafford, Arizona have institutionalized this approach and will be able to sustain their accomplishments.

We briefly describe several challenges and accomplishments of school-based conferencing in transforming the community/government role and relationship. In the following section on community-building, in Part 2 of this chapter, the school setting provides some of the most tangible examples of how community-building occurs.

The government/community relationship in a restorative school environment
Another example in a 700-student high school in Stafford, Arizona
suggests that such systemic reform through intensive application of
restorative decision-making is indeed possible and sustainable. Principal
Rex Whipple, after being trained in family group conferencing by
RealJustice, quickly organized training for all the teachers and administrators and began to build consensus around the shared value that, as he
expresses it, 'we are a school, and we want to teach . . . not spend all our
time on student discipline.' The baseline, in terms of the school's discipline
problems, was that in the year prior to implementation of conferencing
(1999), police were called to the school everyday and there were hundreds
of suspensions and expulsions (about 500 short-term expulsions and 40
permanent or long-term three years ago, compared with 75 and 5
respectively in the year following the introduction of conferencing). In this
climate the principal was able to build some consensus that it was time for
experimentation with alternative approaches that might initially take a
significant amount of time to develop and implement. His argument,
however, was that an incredible amount of time was *already* being spent on
discipline – including overtime for teachers due to after-school detention
and in-school suspension responsibilities – hence, conferencing was less a
time commitment, than a time investment.

Changing the role of the school from primary disciplinarian to
supporter/facilitator of restorative processes was demonstrated by such
dramatic steps as doing away with in-school suspension because, as the
school principal believes, this practice simply 'took the stigma away from
removing kids from class,' without solving the problem. In terms of
reliance on the criminal justice system itself, in the year prior to beginning
conferencing, there were more than 300 plus police calls to the school, last
year there were two. The system maintains an important role in the
process, however, by taking on the responsibility for monitoring reparative agreements – a task that would not be possible for teachers and
school personnel in this high school – through the police department.

As a skeptical administrator, the principal 'eased into conferencing' by
testing the process on his most difficult case:

> It was for a kid that I had written off. The kid had a list of offenses
> which included aggravated assault and intent to commit homicide.
> He was on juvenile intensive probation. He called the teacher a
> female dog. After the conference I never saw the kid again. The youth
> had completely changed the path that he was on.

From that beginning, the principal used conferencing a few more times,
most often for 'offenses and infractions such as assaults, truancy, and a
variety of classroom disruptions.' The assaults, Whipple says, were the

cases that 'would have gone to the police, but we kept them here, then, the process became so successful that it just grew from there.'

While we discuss the Stafford High School case in the following section as an example of community-building in the school context, the lesson it provides as illustration of change in the community/government relationship is that community can be strongly encouraged (even pressured) to resolve more of its problems. Such encouragement along with necessary resources seems especially potent when it comes from a system administrator in charge of formal social control in that community. In this school community, the principal simply decided to transfer what had become formal, public social control over community-level incidents of harm and conflict back to the informal process which originally had addressed them as problems with students and teachers rather than problems of juvenile justice.

Part 2: Visions and practice of community and community-building

Part 1 of this chapter focused on the extent to which conferencing programs and system professionals are moving toward a different role and new relationship to the community. In Part 2, we are concerned with the extent to which conferencing can actually be linked to community-building. In addition to documenting the presence and strength of commitment to the community-building vision, we also looked for practical examples of community-building efforts in programs. In this report of descriptive findings based on interviews, observations and focus groups, we are less concerned with judging the 'validity' of the community-building interventions observed and described to us, and we can certainly not attest to their effectiveness. Rather, our goal in this section of the chapter is to classify these interventions and the implied theory guiding their use as emerging examples that may become more refined and intentional. In doing so, we are especially cognizant of interventions pertinent to the three dimensions of community-building – norm affirmation/values clarification, collective ownership, and skill-building – discussed in Chapter 2. In addition, we want to keep in mind the potential salience of various theories associated with these dimensions – social capital/social disorganization, civic engagement, and collective efficacy – for explaining how community-building might enhance, and connect, public, private, and parochial social controls (Hunter, 1985; Bennett, 1998).

General conclusions

Some conferencing practitioners clearly view their role as, in part, building community capacity to carry out restorative responses as a means of exercising informal social control. However, support for this goal as a conferencing objective was not strong either in our survey or in the interviews, focus groups, and observational findings of the qualitative study. Community-building is a difficult transition for many conferencing practitioners, even those with a high level of skill in conflict resolution and reparative work with victim and offenders. Most programs owe primary allegiance to victim and offender, and staff members feel first committed to addressing their needs. For programs that began as mediation processes between victim and offender, moving toward pursuit of more collective goals is especially difficult, and thus the community-building mission is often less fully developed. This focus in itself, however, does not prohibit community-building either as a direct or indirect outcome, and we were able to identify programs that practised community-building in one or more of its forms regardless of program model preference or philosophical orientation.

In addition, in a number of programs, there appears to be a more intentional focus on enhancing local restorative justice skills in a variety of settings including but not limited to conferencing programs. This focus is of course consistent with much national discourse critical of traditional government responses to community problems, and focused on a new emerging vision of a more communitarian response to social problems (Etzioni, 1996) – especially those concerning the socialization of young people – symbolized by the widely used phrase, 'it takes a village' (Schorr, 1988, 1997; McKnight, 1995). While the community remains a relatively weak player in the conferencing process in many programs, and community-building as a goal seems mostly an afterthought in others, some community-based activity has been quite dramatic in its implications for sharing power over cases. There is evidence of community-building on a broader scale as restorative problem-solving has seeped into the larger civic culture in some regions of the country such as Minneapolis/St Paul, the Denver/Boulder area, much of the state of Pennsylvania, and numerous other smaller towns, cities, and rural areas. Symbolic manifestations of this broader cultural impact are in evidence in hundreds of newspaper stories and other media coverage in a few cities like those in the Minneapolis/St Paul area. In some neighborhoods in both of our case study regions, accounts of citizens and neighborhood groups requesting a 'restorative solution' to a local conflict or incident of harm are becoming increasingly common. More concretely, volunteers in restorative justice conferencing projects frequently discuss how they use restorative principles in other arenas of their lives (Pranis, 2001). Schools and faith community groups have adopted many conferencing techniques, and conferencing volunteers told the researchers about how they host meetings to discuss the application of restorative solutions to larger policy issues and problems such as truancy, police/community relations, and the response to substance abuse – often using a restorative process such as a peace-making circle to initiate dialogue.

Although it was not possible to track this spread of restorative justice at all of these levels, more concrete manifestations of community-building impact became apparent in the course of this study focused around the specific activity of conferencing. We recognize that community-building activity around conferencing represents a limited set of the range of such activity that is apparent in the broader context of restorative practice (Pranis and Bazemore, 2000; Maloney and Holcomb, 2001; Braithwaite, 2001b). Certainly, there is tremendous community-building potential around restorative community service (Bazemore and Maloney, 1994; Maloney and Holcomb, 2001; Bazemore and Stinchcomb, 2004). Although outcomes of such efforts may work in tandem with those associated with conferencing, this work is, however, beyond the scope of this book.

In the remainder of this chapter we discuss the three community-building dimensions as strategies employed by conferencing participants in four domains linked to various conceptualizations of community. We describe these domains as 'targets' of community-building after first considering the more general question of the importance of the community role in the response to youth crime, especially as seen through the eyes of conferencing professionals and the community members most involved in restorative conferencing.

Why community and why is it important?

The new community or community justice focus in criminal justice policy and practice (e.g. Clear and Karp, 1999; Bazemore, 2001) is not without controversy. The policy and theoretical emphasis on community has been criticized by criminologists based in part on failures of diversion and alternatives to incarceration movements of previous decades that often had more to do with expanding the reach and control of the formal justice system and its programs than empowering citizens and local institutions (Polk, 1987; Cohen, 1985). Others have expressed concern that the communitarian emphasis in criminal justice policy may simply be a vehicle for justifying government cutbacks as part of a 'responsibilization' strategy (e.g. Crawford, 1997).[4]

The emphasis on community involvement in the justice process, and the focus on community-building as an outcome of restorative processes, is also not universally accepted in the restorative justice movement. Perhaps because of the strong focus on community in numerous justice reform efforts of the past decade in North America (see Cohen, 1985), citizens of the US and Canada are often naturally focused on restorative decision-making programs through the lens of community involvement (e.g. Pranis, 1997; Griffiths and Corrado, 1999; Stuart, 2001). While the community emphasis in restorative justice is not unique to North America (Braithwaite, 1994), and use of volunteers has become a strong feature of the youthful offender panels in the UK (Crawford and Newburn, 2003), it must be noted that the most well-known systemic implementation of family group conferencing in New Zealand does not feature 'community' in any form other than that of the family of the offender, and occasionally the victim. While this can in some cases mean extended family, and the model itself comes from an indigenous practice that views the 'family group' as a clear manifestation of community, it is nonetheless the case that New Zealand conferences are run by paid professionals. Volunteers as facilitators or in other roles are rare. And this is indeed the model of conferencing characteristic of practice in much of Europe (Weitekampe and Kerner, 2002).

Only in the US, Canada, and now the UK, it seems, is there apparent widespread use of citizen volunteers and extensive involvement of community organizations. We do not make an argument for or against a strong community role here, and volunteer involvement is but one manifestation of a community-building focus. Moreover, commitment to the community-building aspects of conferencing is far from a dominant trend in the US, and as suggested in Part 1 of this chapter, the community role in decision-making is for many criminal justice professionals one of the most controversial aspects of conferencing. It is possible, however, to argue from a theoretical, research, and policy perspective that a community-building focus may be essential for sustaining conferencing as something more than another programmatic diversion or probation alternative. As implied in Chapter 2, it is also possible, to envision restorative justice processes as a tool for revitalizing informal social control and social support, and in turn placing limits on the growth of formal juvenile and criminal justice systems (Braithwaite, 1994; White, 2000; Bazemore, 2000, 2001). Practically speaking, the daily existence of many citizens reinforces the disconnect between adult community members and neighborhood children as various forms of informal sanctioning and social support seem to have withered away. With this breakdown has come increased fear and desperation about youth crime and trouble of almost all varieties, despite the official focus on serious and violent crime. The call for a reconnection with community in much literature within and outside of criminal justice has, as mentioned earlier, reflected a widely felt practical need for a more local and value-based grounding to policy that, in particular, affects young people and those who care for them.

Although many system professionals remain leery of sharing decision-making power with citizens and community groups even as a means of engaging their support, others believe the community is a primary source of resistance to crime. For these professionals, breakdowns in informal social control and support are viewed as overwhelming the system's limited capacity to respond (Clear and Karp, 1999), yet communities are nonetheless believed by some to harbor resources needed for a complete and effective response to crime (Pranis, 1997; Earle, 1996). As noted in the previous discussion of Washington County, Minnesota justice system decision-makers, like Judge Scherer and County Attorney Johnson, for example, seem to intuitively recognize the limits of their formal role, to understand the power of community involvement, and to generally trust in the community's decision-making capacity. For their part, citizens who volunteer in restorative conferencing often express strong feelings about the critical importance of the added value of even marginal levels of community involvement independent of the role of juvenile justice professionals. Moreover, these volunteers often seem less concerned about what professionals may describe as the lack of 'readiness' of communities and citizens to move forward (see Karp, Bazemore, and Chesire, 2004). Rather, their motivation and sense of urgency about participating in restorative group conferencing programs is that they feel that the community has not 'been there' for young people and families who look to them for mutual support. Their commitment to community-building is not connected to an academic debate, but is rather seen as a necessity in the neighborhoods where they live and work.

Definitions of community and strategies for community-building

As noted in the theoretical discussion in Chapter 2, community, like community-building, can mean a number of things. Historically, socio-logists have assigned a vital role to the community as a *causal factor* influencing both the ecological distribution of crime, as well as individual propensities toward lawbreaking (Shaw and McKay, 1942; Kornhauser, 1978). Moreover, recent years have brought a notable revitalization of interest in the community/crime relationship and a renewed research emphasis on the role of informal social control in maintaining safe communities (Braithwaite, 1989; Morenoff et al., 2001). Such informal social control, as measured in research by Sampson and his colleagues, includes neighbors' willingness to provide guardianship and to intervene in and respond to the misbehavior of other people's children (e.g. Sampson et al., 1997). Beyond social control, criminologists have also argued that it is important to take account of the impact of differences in the capacity of families and community groups to provide informal 'social support' (Cullen, 1994). For example, community members may look after each other's children, or play roles as 'natural helpers,' advocates, or 'guides' that those in criminal justice and therapeutic professional positions are seldom able to fill effectively (McKnight, 1995; Annie E. Casey Foundation, 2001). Informal volunteer networks such as faith community groups and neighborhood organizations may assist families in crisis, help them locate services and other resources, and counsel or mentor neighborhood children having trouble in school.

'Community' can be defined in a variety of ways that have different implications for how community *building* is understood and engaged. Restorative justice practitioners we spoke with, however, did not appear to spend a lot of time debating definitions, and seemed to conceptualize 'community' in flexible, emergent, and dynamic ways. For the most part, they seemed comfortable with multiple perspectives and a general understanding that 'community is where you find it.' For some, community was often centered at the most micro level around the family, extended family, and supporters of offenders and victims in a conference. For others, community referred instead, or in addition, to a community of volunteers and volunteer groups engaged in restorative justice practices, or to a specific neighborhood. For still others, community meant a neighborhood, or referred to what have been described as 'mediating institutions,' such as schools, churches, small businesses, and neighborhood organizations (Bellah et al., 1991).

Some restorative justice practitioners appeared to have little conceptualization of community-building at all. 'Thin' definitions were those that understood this orientation as activity that amounted to individualized efforts to help offenders appreciate their relationship to their communities, understand the harm their behavior had caused to the community, and essentially fit into their communities. 'Thick' understandings of community building, however, were those in which practitioners emphasized broader consequences of crime, and mutual benefits of responses to what are usually viewed as individual incidents of crime and harm. At the most macro level, one can talk about geographic areas in Minnesota and Colorado where it appears that restorative justice has become relatively common in the language used in considering responses to crime, is widely covered in the media, and in some neighborhoods and community entities such as schools is recognized as an alternative form of dealing with crime and conflict. Although it is possible to describe sweeping cultural changes in which entire cities and regions have been affected by restorative justice values, the context of conferencing programs of most interest in terms of community-building is more middle-range and micro-level. Perhaps least helpful from a community-building perspective are perceptions of community based on the jurisdictional boundaries of local government entities such as an urban county, or on professional bureaus or networks:

Of course, our community is over hundreds of square miles and over 9 million people. Within the neighborhoods there is not much community. On one hand our community is that whole county, in the sense that we want to create awareness of restorative justice. In the

LA Times, on television, that kind of thing, and we try and affect general opinion, but then I think we might have to look at community quite differently . . . so the probation department is our community in a sense, the school district is our community, because the only way that you are going to affect LA county is through the institutions that already exist.

Other definitions seem more focused on manageable units of connected groups and individuals such as this one focused on small towns in Vermont:

What is community? Each town has its own issues and dynamics. We have talked a lot this year about not having it [community] be an institution or a place, but us going there and having it be more sort of paradigm for each town, and that we [conferencing program directors] would fit into that role.

While small towns and neighborhoods have been targeted for a number of restorative justice interventions, the term 'affected community' is a common, somewhat more specific way of signifying that, for purposes of crime and justice, the harm of the offense should define the communities of most importance in the response to crime. At the opposite end of the continuum from the focus on large geographic areas, 'community' for purposes of restorative justice interventions can be, and often is, simply the victim, the offender, and their supporters. In between these extremes of community as entire towns (or urban neighborhoods) and individual victim, offender, and family, Ronnie Earle's definition of a community as 'a *network* of relationships where members share joy and pain' (Earle, 1996, emphasis ours) provides a middle ground. In this definition, relationships can be seen as a step up from individual victims and offenders to the connection between them and their supporters, and the potential connection between these relationships and a larger network of support. At this level, broader networks that link together multiple relationships can be conceptualized and practically viewed as targets for community-building. Such networks are in turn what make up more typically recognized community entities such as neighborhoods.

From another perspective, many conferencing practitioners appear to follow McCold and Wachtel's (1998) insight that community 'is *not* a place' – at least in the sense that community is viewed as *more than* a place. Some might also agree with Warren's (1977) definition that: 'a community is what it does, and much of what it does can be grasped by studying episodes of action' (p. 309). The latter experiential definition also seems relevant to the community-building focus of restorative conferencing in terms of its implied emphasis on skill-building and relationship-building as discussed in Chapter 2 as tools for building networks of informal social support and social control.

What is community-building?

As previously acknowledged, not all conferencing practitioners claim to pursue community-building objectives. In addition, some who claim that they do describe activities that, while perhaps critical to other goals of the conferencing enterprise, would not be considered by most observers as examples of community-building. Simply collaborating with other government agencies and programs, for example, though important for building system support for one's program, does not fit with the goal of building capacity around informal social control and social support. Some conferencing programs we examined, however, do not claim much in the way of community-building as a goal, and/or as in the following comment, see the potential for community change through individual program impacts:

> There isn't much community input in this program. But we tell the offender that he/she is a member of the community, that we want him to be a good neighbor ... we want to enforce how the youth's actions have affected the community and the people around him. I build it on you [the offender] changing to be a part of the community – be a good neighbor, be a good person out in the community, and I reinforce how the community is influenced by your actions.

Even conferencing practitioners who seem to understand and practice community-building may, like many of the rest of us, at times struggle to define the concept. However, when asked the question, 'How do you know community-building when you see it,' several directors of conferencing programs were quite clear both about the concrete practice and the philosophy implied. As the comment below suggests, community-building involves a different way of thinking about a problem or conflict – that is neither about correcting or helping the individuals involved, or even about the less individualized focus on 'problem-solving':

> I think you see it when we are able to *redefine crime* ... not in individual terms, but when we make it a collective issue. [When we think about] first harm to the community, second, tools for the community ... third, where the offender and the community discuss issues of common concern [emphasis ours].

How does community-building happen in the conferencing process? According to some practitioners a lot of community-building emerges organically from conferences, as a leveling process occurs that invites people to step out of professional roles and collectively consider shared problems and responsibilities. This process appears to catch some by surprise:

> Community-building is more subtle – not an explicit goal ... A lot happens very informally. We could be making better use of restorative justice in this area.
>
> Each conference has examples of how there is community-building on a small basis. In general, it's that everybody's role gets blurred and then everybody merges, and it's all just about community – it's [the conference] downright at the end not about the offender, family, victim, its just all community ...

Community-building, at least in the conferencing context, is in the view of these practitioners often a serendipitous activity. Opportunities in conferencing may be elusive windows that can quickly close if practitioners are not attuned to the signs or willing to exploit these opportunities. While most believe the process cannot be forced, some program directors felt that they could be more strategic about 'seizing the moment' and training staff and volunteers to do the same.

From our perspective, understandings of community-building on its highest plane were those that seemed to envision the outcomes of such activity as building community capacity for self-sufficiency and self-governance. One Colorado conferencing practitioner whose job is to train school personnel in conferencing provides a definition of community-building that seems to get at this idea and at the essence of the principle of stakeholder involvement:

> How do we know community-building when we see it? Well, first, our criterion for judging success is different. 'The shift we look for (in contrast to a top-down model of school discipline) is for the principal to offload that responsibility to teachers and students ... the more stakeholders involved, the better – distributive decision-making.' ... One key group is the parents – sometimes they have been so angry for so long – something fundamentally changes for parents [in a conference]. We also involve them as facilitators – they make some of the best facilitators.

The idea of expanding or democratizing the decision-making process, making use of the skills of community members (and allowing them to 'practise' and hone these skills), is from this perspective, the essence of community-building. In addition, at the end of a conference or related conflict resolution process, the parties (in this case the parents) are reengaged as participants in the role of resource to others. Ultimately, this skill-building dimension of community building on its highest plane may include, as Braithwaite and Parker (1999) suggest, opportunities to teach and learn the deliberative skills of democratic citizenship, fostered through restorative justice practice in 'schools, neighborhoods, ethnic communities, and churches – and other non-governmental organizations that deploy restorative justice in their self-regulatory practices' (Braithwaite, 1998: 331).

Community-building targets and strategies

To achieve the general goals of expanding social capital and collective efficacy in the form of enhanced social control and social support in the response to youth crime, it is possible to envision a number of strategic approaches (e.g. Bursik and Grasmick, 1992; Sampson, 1999). Though community-building in restorative group conferencing seemed as often as not unplanned, we observed several specific processes by which conferencing programs in some way appeared to be increasing community capacity. In addition, participants in the research identified several domains or 'targets' of community-building representing different definitions of community.

Community-building strategies

Three distinct, though not mutually exclusive, community-building strategies were apparent in our fieldwork and interviews for this study: (1) connecting community members (including victims and offenders) more closely in new relationships which are then connected to networks; (2) promoting a sense of ownership of the youth crime problem within these networks; and (3) skill-building within these networks. Though these strategies do not occur in linear sequence, developing new relationships based on a sense of shared norms and values is viewed as a first step, to be followed by promoting a sense of group ownership of the problem presented by instances of youth crime and the response to these cases, and then developing community group and citizen competence in the exercise of informal social control and support, repairing harm, and conflict resolution.

Relationship and network-building occurs through values clarification and norm affirmation, as well as through efforts of the conference participants to break down social distance, and connect offenders, victims, and families to support persons and groups. Collective ownership appears to follow on from opportunities provided in the conference process for meaningful civic engagement in decision-making about the response to incidents of crime and harm. Building skills for collective efficacy occurs as community members are allowed to *practise* problem-solving, restorative dialogue, and decision-making about the response to crime in the conferencing process, and to exercise informal social control, social support, and collective action both within and beyond the conference setting.

Targets of community-building intervention
As implied in the theoretical discussion in Chapter 2, conferences may build relationships and networks, promote ownership of the response to crime through civic engagement, and build collective skills in several community domains. Based on our fieldwork in this study, we have identified four such entities that seem susceptible to the influence of restorative conferencing, and which have become potential 'targets' of community-building relevant to the different meanings of community. These targets are loosely associated with different strategies of community-building, but neither the strategies nor the targets are mutually exclusive. Conferencing programs may deliberately or inadvertently, engage in community-building in one or more of these units of community, and utilize multiple strategies in doing so. The community building targets, ranging from the most micro to most macro levels of intervention and analysis, are:

1. *The conference setting.* The community of care around the victim and offender may consist of family and/or extended family, neighbors, teachers, clergy, peers, and so on. As these individuals network with each other and with other conference participants such as volunteers, they expand the group that hopefully develops a shared responsibility for the problems of young people and those they harm.
2. *The community of conferencing volunteers: spillover to other agencies.* It is possible to target community-building efforts toward those networks of volunteers that participate regularly in one or more conferencing programs and, in doing so, seek to build a variety of individual and collective decision-making skills. These volunteers, when asked to assist as facilitators, trainers, and advisors in other agencies, help to build skills, relationships, and networks beyond the program context.
3. *Instrumental communities/mediating institutions.* Between the conference setting and the more macro neighborhood level, skill development and relationship-building in youth conferencing at the middle range are becoming most common in what may be described as 'instrumental communities' where participants learn, work, or temporarily reside. As mediating institutions (Bellah et al., 1991), instrumental communities in educational, residential, workplace, and youth development settings are often among the collectivities most directly affected both by crime and harmful behavior, and by the response to this behavior.
4. *Neighborhoods, community organizations, and small towns.* Though many conferencing programs have been government-funded and tasked by

their sponsoring agency to serve an entire county or judicial circuit, others have arisen from neighborhoods. In the case of NABS, for example, programs have typically been organized by the sponsoring government entity exclusively at the neighborhood level. There is also a track record among restorative justice organizers of working directly with neighborhood groups and associations who wish to utilize other approaches such as circles or FGC (Pranis and Bazemore, 2000).

As might be expected, most of our examples are drawn from the conference setting itself. We first describe these in more detail in categories that depict the specific strategies by which conference practitioners build connections and relationships as social capital, promote collective ownership, and build skills as collective efficacy. Several examples of community building in other entities are described in less detail and with less of an attempt to specifically categorize these strategies. Because the multiple component definition of community-building in the four community entities is one that does not fit easily within the phase and stage discussion, we also consider community-building as something that is either envisioned or not, and if so, may be addressed in some way in every phase of the conference.

Micro-level: the conference setting

At the most micro-level, conferencing may build or strengthen relationships between individual victims and offenders, other citizens and families. At this level, theories discussed in the chapters on the principle of repair and the principle of stakeholder involvement are also related to the idea of community-building. In particular, social support, collective healing, and common ground theories become relevant to building relationships and networks (social capital) as well as skill sets for collective efficacy. Here, we were interested in the extent to which the conferencing process encourages the creation of a new relationship between one or more conferencing participants (e.g. a community member and a young offender, a victim and the family of the offender, a board member and a victim), promotes dialogue that builds trust around common values and norms, encourages collective ownership, and increases the skills and competencies of participants. In doing so, intervention builds upon insights of community-level theories of social capital, civic engagement, and collective efficacy.

Connecting: relationship and network building

Norm affirmation/values clarification
Conferences may build or strengthen relationships, and eventually *networks* of relationships, by helping participants develop a collective

understanding about what behaviors are 'off limits.' Norm affirmation in conferences may also lead to a more general values clarification, when groups identify and reinforce commitments to a core of shared values, while also acknowledging and respecting important diversity of opinion (Pranis, 2001).

This broader clarification seems more likely to occur when conferencing programs give a prominent role to participants from the neighborhoods where conferences take place in addressing harm to the community. While the conference itself often provides a primary forum for such dialogue when facilitators allow it to occur, additional opportunities for norm clarification may then arise subsequent to the conference itself as volunteers begin to encourage such spillover discussion in other contexts.

One of the best examples of how relationships, and eventually a network of relationships, might develop in the conference setting is presented in a Colorado conference involving an incident of rock throwing, fighting, threats, and name-calling at a privately operated skate park after hours (a case presented in more detail at the end of this chapter). The conference had created fear of retaliation among two groups of middle-school youths and their parents, concern among the latter about the kids their children were spending time with, and worries about the level of supervision their parents provided for them. After a two-hour dialogue between the youths and several of their parents resulting in apologies and a positive reparative agreement, parents felt reassured about shared values with other families in a way that seemed to reinforce mutual support for pro-social, consistent childrearing. In the absence of such an encounter, parents may have wondered about what really happened, harbored fear and concern about the other young people and the role of their children in the incident, and been left with concern about other parents who seem to lack standards for their children's behavior. Though not the initial focus of the conference (which was called to address what appeared to be a low-level assault), the encounter presented a unique opportunity for relationship-building between families who benefited most from the opportunities to connect with parents of the other youth involved in this incident and from the recognition of common, shared values that seemed to make resolution of this incident an easy task.

Reducing social distance
Restorative practices are distinct from traditional court processing because they do not promote separation of parties or adversarial relations. Thus, ideally, victims, offenders, their supporters such as family members, friends, or colleagues, and community volunteers are brought together to collectively address the harm of a crime by seeking common ground in a way that both satisfies and meets the needs of these stakeholders.

Establishing a common ground of community membership helps to create trust among strangers and between offenders and victims. As a police lieutenant who coordinates restorative conferences puts it: 'On a case-by-case basis, lots of people come in here who live close by, but do not know each other. In the conference, [they] get to know each other well.' Additionally, stereotyping is diminished as parties come face to face, and a leveling effect and blurring of roles (Pranis, 2001) may also bring about a transformation in social relationships.

As the following example from the Woodbury, MN, program suggests, the dynamics of various communities present unique challenges, but also opportunities when conference participants are open to the possibility of exploiting the community-building opportunities that each conference brings:

> It's a hard community to be a part of. [We're] finding that we are engaging families with very little support in the community. Bringing community members into the conference as volunteers is important because that is a link for them. A case comes in as a crime, but we invite at least four community members into the circle – [it's] about building relationships with families for support. [This means] a longer process is needed and it becomes a 'support circle.' We have this case where circles have been meeting regularly since October [several months have passed since the case began].

The transformation that breaks down social distance is often most surprising when bonds are formed between offenders and victims. A victim–offender dialogue coordinator told us a number of stories about connections that were made in conferences that seemed to lead to future meetings between stakeholders and supporters. In one case, for example:

> ... the victim offered to hire the offender if [the agreement was] completed. Afterwards, he said if the offender pays me back $800 and goes to college, I will pay that money to the college for his books. [We] see the victim and the offender sharing phone numbers to stay in touch. For example, we had a case [in which the victim and offender developed such a close relationship that] ... the victim would say 'come over and have a cup of coffee and tell us how things are going.'

Examples like this are not uncommon in conferences in which an adult victim develops some empathy and affection for a juvenile offender. In addition to the *affective* connection implied here is the possibility for an *instrumental* relationship based on the opportunity for employment. As subsequent examples illustrate, instrumental connections appear more likely to occur when the facilitator is strategic about the human resource makeup of the conference, and is focused on what might be viewed as part of a human capital objective of restorative conferences. The role of resource persons in this mission and the development of social capital are described below.

Strategic identification of support and resource persons
As discussed in Chapter 6, though some restorative models such as family group conferencing give sole or primary emphasis to the participation of intimates of the offender and victim and may discourage involvement of anonymous community members (McDonald et al., 1995), another emerging approach gives emphasis to the role of participants who may often serve as resources or present an important community perspective on the problem. Specifically, proponents of a version of family group conferencing often referred to as 'community conferencing' offer rationales for engaging a larger, more diverse group of neighbors and other participants in the conferencing process in the hope of providing a broader connection to the community.

Taking advantage of opportunities for micro-level community building through relationship building may depend on how well a facilitator identifies stakeholders as resources to conferencing participants and creates opportunities for them to make connection. Other community members may also play this role, and may in addition provide a different kind of emotional/affective support, as well as the practical, instrumental support based on connections to local resources. Both kinds of support and the strategic efforts and assumptions of the facilitator are described in the following account that demonstrates strategic use of service agencies and professionals, as well as volunteer community members:

> ... during a conference most of the support comes from the community – family, friends, and sometimes professionals from 'helping' agencies. We had a conference where a Native American young man at the pre-conference said he wanted to go to college and we managed to get someone from the Native American Center of the local college there to the conference as a potential resource. We are currently planning a conference for a 'homeless' young woman who has had a very minor brush with the law. This 'circle of support' consists of a former female offender who is switched on to resources in the community, members of a church she likes, a friend, and some professionals who hold the resources. We strive to ingrain in the professionals their roles as *supporters* and *resource providers* rather than 'fixers' [emphasis ours].

As suggested, conference participants are capable of moving in a number of directions. If social support is the goal, however, a strategic awareness of this objective, rather than simply giving obligations to offenders and their families, making decisions for them, or making referrals to treatment providers may need to be encouraged and nurtured. The strategic nature of the difficult work in moving from individuals, to one-on-one connections, to relationships is not only not well understood, it has not been described as a sequence of steps when it does occur.

Promoting ownership

Overall, we did not find strong differences by program model or philosophy regarding the definition of, or commitment to, community-building. There does seem to be a certain mindset on the part of the program director however, that is necessary to provide leadership around the idea that community ownership can create a better form of justice.

Reclaiming stolen conflict

As expressed in a letter from a coordinator of a victim–offender dialogue program in Colorado, herself a volunteer, this mindset that communities should take back this responsibility for resolving conflict and repairing harm is about who should be empowered in the response to crime:

> We want to make conflict and justice a community issue. We want the community to take responsibility for justice processes in every possible case . . . offenders and victims live in the community – not in the justice system – and [they] can relate to community-based processes. The long-term goal is to have community members call the program (or volunteers informally outside of the program) *before* calling police for offenses. Much of what used to be taken care of informally in the community is now the domain of the CJS and we want to reverse that trend.

Beyond role restrictions

Ownership is perhaps most apparent when community members seem to take risks to step out of their role and take responsibility for resolving harm or conflict that some might view as the jurisdiction of crime control professionals. As one Colorado conferencing practitioner observes in response to a question about how he defined community building:

> When you see community-building happening – when I've seen [it] – there is a *blurring of boundaries* [and a move away] from 'that's not a part of my job description' . . . the janitor doing conflict resolution in the hall – drawing people toward the larger role. Specialization is shaping our culture – restorative justice helps people see the broader role. Above and beyond what [they're] getting paid for. Count the

number of service providers. If [there's] more there who are not being paid – it's a good sign . . . [emphasis ours].

In this definition and vision, community-building occurs when community members take risks to challenge boundaries, and justice professionals welcome and support this risk-taking. They act in response to crime not because it is part of their requirement of the job they are paid to do, but because they see it as their responsibility and contribution to improve their community. Such initiative seems like the natural thing to do, when – according to the theory of civic engagement – citizens are made to feel they have a stake and responsibility in peace and justice.

Inside the conference, at the micro level, some practitioners recognize ownership as a critical initial step in community-building:

> If I am truly able to sit in the conference with all the active community people and every so often I need to re-direct or remind people because they are always looking to me for the final answer, then I'm not doing so well. But if they are treating me like I'm another community person then that is really good.
>
> Everyone has a direct role in the process. It is *really happening* when the offender acts as another community member. Then the process has been a success. The indicators we look for are signs of shared responsibility.

In the conference environment, community ownership and leadership is often most apparent in the agreement phase when stakeholders are asked to make contributions to the conference agreement. Notably, at this point, recommendations for community service projects that may build community social capital in their own right (e.g. voter registration drives, building playgrounds) can go a long way toward reinforcing the sense of ownership and civic commitment of volunteers as well as offenders and their families (Bazemore and Stinchcomb, 2004). In the most democratized programs everyone in the conference is allowed to contribute ideas to the plan for repairing harm and, in addition, participants are invited to 'step up' to ensure that obligations are met and the offender and family receive the support they need. In the North Minneapolis circle, for example, once a commitment is made (e.g. for a community service obligation; for the offender to no longer be tardy at school), circle volunteers routinely offer to help in some concrete way to ensure the success of the agreement (e.g. by providing transportation, making a 'wake-up call').

Skill-building

According to David Moore, formal justice systems 'deprive people of the opportunity to *practice* skills of apology and forgiveness, or reconciliation, restitution, and reparation [emphasis ours].' The skill-development task for community-building in restorative justice practice is in part aimed at revitalizing these and other capacities related to the responsible exercise of informal social control in democratic societies.

Informal social control
One often unstated theory behind conferences is that they create a space in which community members may feel more comfortable in expressing disapproval of harmful behavior in a respectful way (Bazemore, 2000), while also typically commending pro-social behavior and providing support. As more conferences occur and the word spreads about the value of these events for developing informal sanctions for delinquent youth, supporting youth and their families, and resolving conflict and harm as an alternative to court, more community members may participate and thereby expand the pool of efficacious citizens and community groups.

Conferences can promote the behavior described by Sampson et al. (1997) as *collective efficacy* in which citizens are willing and able, through informal communication and other means, to intervene to prevent and respond effectively to harmful behavior and crime, to provide guardianship, and to intervene in and respond to the misbehavior of other people's children (e.g. Sampson et al., 1997).

Restorative conferences provide a forum to practise these skills of informal social control in a safe forum in a context generally characterized by mutual respect. Consistent with reintegrative shaming theory, participants express strong disapproval of the behavior in question but support for the offender. Generally, the agreement phase of the conference includes a plan to support the offender in pro-social activity and provide for some capable guardianship, often by drawing upon the resources of participants in the conference. Volunteers in the conference, when they are residents of the neighborhood as is the case in NABs and circles, may be able to provide for this informal control by virtue of proximity of the offender.

Most importantly, the most effective conferencing programs offer what is generally viewed as a primary prerequisite for effective informal social control, social support (Cullen, 1994; Braithwaite, 2001b). As described by a volunteer in the North Minneapolis peace-making circle, community-building occurs in the program context through expanding networks of relationships that offer such support often directly, if not apparently, connected with informal social control:

[We are] building relationships within the community. Like [name of foster parent], he calls me and asks about other kids, other issues in the community. One juvenile's mother called me about some trouble her son got into. Kids get to meet people who are right there in the area – seen as neighbors – and see that other people are concerned. One night, two kids did not show up for circle and a couple [of circle volunteers] drove over to their house to find out why. The mother of one juvenile and a volunteer became friends ... [Another circle volunteer] took some kids to [a] camp ... one person stayed on to tutor a kid after circle.

Relationships and connections of support provide a foundation for assisting parents in setting limits with their children, and may even provide the basis for the volunteer, depending of the strength of this connection, to occasionally do so directly. Stories from this circle and some NABs about young offenders who, after going through a conference, felt obliged when they passed volunteers in the street after hours or during school hours to account for their whereabouts provide further evidence of the potential strength of what might otherwise be viewed as rather weak and distant controls.

Social support
The skill set, or 'collective efficacy,' being developed here is group competency in building relationships or networks for marginalized groups that in turn may also reduce social distance, and ultimately increase social integration. In essence, community members – already a part of skill-building networks of relationships in their role of conferencing volunteers – are engaged in this instance in developing new competencies in building networks of support around young offenders and their family (see Christie, 1977, and Chapter 2 regarding the potentially reciprocal relationship between social capital and collective efficacy).

In a police-based conferencing program, an officer and community volunteers had been experimenting with peace-making circles for a particularly troubled family – a single mother who worked evenings and whose three teenage children had been in trouble and in ongoing conflict with neighbors. After numerous police calls to their apartment complex and growing pressure to make arrests and seek court involvement, the group intensified its work with the family and their neighbors. As the officer describes it, the circle process in this case illustrates the perceived inadequacy of traditional therapeutic approaches and the value of an informal restorative process by which participants may move logically and strategically from analysis of individual and family problems, to relationship-building, social support and then networking strategies that begin to address community-level issues:

We worked a long time on building relationships within the family. Suggested counseling – but the daughter said, 'We have gone to counseling and all they do is try to fix us. We like *this* because you listen.' Things are getting better – in April [we] began drawing in neighbors – a better place to begin dealing with neighborhood issues. [There was] benefit in talking about how [we're] treating each other – that empowered them. [Is this a] safe place to talk to each other? Will there be less support over time? Will they need less support from the circle because [they] have [a] better relationship in the family? This spring, the son decided to go out for [the high school] track team. A neighbor that came over was very supportive, and together they are planning a block party. [There] should be more neighbors involved eventually.

Especially important in these comments is the distinction made between restorative problem-solving work and interventions such as counseling which presume an individual 'fix' is possible. Also important is the flexibility in this program director's willingness to adapt processes and resources designed to support what can be a relatively limited intervention (FGC) in terms of its community-building potential. The adaptation of the FGC model typically employed in this program was also driven by the needs at hand, rather than trying to fit the needs into a certain program protocol. The goal was building community support and efficacy rather than building the program.

As suggested in Chapter 2, social disorganization and social capital theory (Putnam, 2000; Bursik and Grasmick, 1993) may be understood to imply that inclusive dialogue in a community context is a primary component of relationship-building that may promote social integration of marginalized groups (see Warner, 2003; Pranis, 2001). Breaking down social distance in this way will not always be sufficient to create community support for offenders and their families. When it is, however, it may also provide a context for informal social control and support (Cullen, 1994), as offenders appreciate the fact that such support is typically being provided by persons not paid to care about them (Pranis, 2001). The process may also build connections as social capital that links the private controls of families with the parochial control of neighborhood groups (Hunter, 1985; see Bazemore, 2001).

This particular circle program, which takes both delinquency and child welfare referrals from the court or social service agencies, has become a vehicle for shoring up family support networks to ensure the supervision and nurturing of youth in trouble at difficult times. Its volunteer members often function as adjunct parents – serving as relatives and friends once did to provide added structure and guidance in the lives of children who find themselves in challenging family situations. Although framed in the following comment as an unrealistic goal, this volunteer perceives the program to be a place that nonetheless offers assistance where the community and public service sector have otherwise failed:

I think our biggest challenge has been networking with people who have no network . . . The resources are out there and the people could benefit from them – be it the victim or the offender that comes into the program – but meeting the qualifications of any particular [social service] program is often very difficult for them . . . The safety net is not there for the people that need it . . . They have no place to go to get this net and no way to integrate it, and we can't be there to do that for everyone; yet they kind of look at us in that way.

Collective action
Working together to achieve collective goals may begin in the conference with the development of a sense of ownership, and then move outward to the community. According to other practitioners a lot of community-building emerges naturally from conferences, but often catches them by surprise:

> Parents were coming out of the meeting (conference) last night and saying they want to meet with the principal to develop a plan to deal with the dispute [about their son and other students] but also deal with some apparent gang activity surrounding the incident. Parents acknowledged their role and responsibility, but then said they wanted to do something so that it wouldn't happen again to other kids. It's an opportunity for the community to establish norms and standards.

In another example that illustrates how circles can be proactive in getting involved in issues of harm precipitated by criminal justice related ultimately to larger issues of social justice, we see how collective action may occur almost as a spur of the moment response. In this case, a circle coordinator who works primarily in Hispanic communities in Salem, Oregon described a difficult conflict resolution intervention involving a drug bust. A Hispanic family in which the parents did not speak English had been the target of a police raid. In this case, the police had the wrong house, yet the officers were unapologetic. As a result of the raid, according to the family, the young daughter lost her baby. After hearing about the incident, circle program volunteers offered to hold a circle for the family and their neighbors. As the volunteer coordinator explains it: 'In the healing circle, community members asked if they could do anything to help. As a result, the family became more connected to the community.' This same program, on another occasion, at the request of a local faith community group, held a circle for concerned neighbors and sex offenders returning from prison to their community that included several of the offenders, clergy, and the neighbors.

Community-building beyond the conference environment: volunteers and spillover

Restorative justice volunteers have assumed two critical roles in conferencing relative to community-building: one involving their participation in the conference itself, and the second involving their role in sowing the seeds of restorative decision-making in other sectors of their community. In Chapter 6, we described the grounded theories volunteers articulate to explain the unique added-value of their impact on offenders, families, and victims in the conference setting. Here we describe the community-building potential of volunteers trained in conflict resolution and problem-solving skills who seek to share their knowledge and apply these skills in other settings. As they do so, in schools, workplaces, faith communities, and other micro-communities, the result is a kind of spillover effect that can spread the skills and values of restorative processes to other community entities.

How might these conferencing volunteers actually build community capacity for exercising informal social control and social support? We suggest that conferencing programs whose volunteers are most likely to infuse other community groups with restorative decision-making skills are those whose leaders understand and encourage this external role of conferencing volunteers and view this sharing as a part of their program mission. In addition, the natural links volunteers have with other community groups are important determinants of the range of impact they may have on community-building.

Some victim–offender mediation program coordinators have traditionally claimed that they involve and build community by virtue of the fact that they use volunteer mediators. While widespread use of volunteers may certainly be said to increase the involvement of at least some sectors of the community in decision-making, such involvement does not easily translate into community-building in programs that, unlike neighborhood boards and circles, are typically not focused on one neighborhood. In fact, as one VOM/D coordinator put it, it may be equally likely that volunteers 'will get the training in mediation – which is really a hot thing now in our county – and then hang up their shingle as private mediators.' Some program directors have managed to integrate community-building and program development, and therefore encourage volunteers to participate in other community groups as yet another way of giving back to their community independent of the positive effects on the program. Carolyn McLeod, a VOM/D coordinator who models this activism for her volunteers and staff, supplies facilitators from her program to community groups on a regular basis for community conflict resolution tasks, public meetings, community research projects, and other functions. When asked why and how she does this, McLeod explains that part of their success in volunteer community-building outside of the conference is due to the connections volunteers have in a variety of community groups:

[Why do you do all of this?] To get the attention of people and just to contribute [the program has become well known in Washington Co., MN as a source of facilitators] ... I do a lot of training. In addition, *I have 58 volunteers that I supervise* – these are the movers and shakers in the community – [they] have pretty high profiles – from all walks of life. Community representatives on the Washington County Board have taken our training. We have county commissioners who are supportive. There is a cumulative effect from involving many in training – Youth Service Bureau, system people, many well-connected with the schools. They are coming from everywhere. In this county, soon it will be that to be elected, the party line will be 'Restorative Justice is the wave of the future – so get on board.' Of course, some of it is just lip service.

Volunteers in collective action

There are of course challenges to volunteerism not unique to conferencing but which can place limits on the role of unpaid 'natural helpers' both within and outside of the conference. As the director of a small-town Colorado program (herself a part-time volunteer) puts it:

The greatest challenge is getting investment from volunteers. We try to 'give' them the power by asking them to take responsibility for teaching each other – both at scheduled continuing education sessions and informally (on their own) (and also through sharing stories in the newsletter). This is not too successful so far. I think part of it is that everyone is so 'busy,' but perhaps this busy-ness masks a subconscious fear of taking responsibility for justice ... and a disempowerment in many realms. I think our new advisory council will make a difference – they will hopefully perceive the program more as theirs if some of their own are involved in decision-making more directly.

Despite such challenges, there are a number of examples of volunteers who get involved outside the conferencing context. While volunteers in conferencing are certainly involved in a variety of relationship and network building activities involving norm and value clarification, reducing social distance and identification of support groups and individuals, most of our examples from this research primarily involve volunteers in skill-building activities. In particular, volunteers were involved in training and assistance to those wishing to learn conferencing skills and were active in social support and efforts to strengthen social control in schools and other community groups. We present examples of collective action and close with an effort that grew from concern about shared norms and values in the conference setting to become a community-wide collective action to affirm these values.

Social distance and community conflict
Volunteers in some well-established programs were notably willing to get involved in broader, sometimes controversial, neighborhood disputes. Such disputes present risks that some programs are not willing to take, but those who do may reap great rewards. Some of these rewards are measured directly in terms of community-building at the neighborhood level using volunteers as their resource, as this example from Beverly Title, Director of Longmont, Colorado's LCJP community conferencing program, suggests in describing what over time was a successful conferencing program intervention to reduce racial and ethnic tension:

> We have a growing minority population – 16 percent Hispanic – [who are] becoming more economically empowered [but are still disenfranchised in many ways]. Recently, this community had one of the messiest neighborhood disputes because a new Hispanic neighbor moved into a predominately white neighborhood. Long-time residents began to make the usual kinds of [stereotypical] complaints – cars jacked up, lots of people coming and going, loud music. Older neighbors began mounting video cameras, decimal recorders. [They were] only interested in 'having the neighborhood back the way it was.' [A neighborhood dispute involved] a Hispanic family – first time [they had] owned property. So much ill will was generated. Coming to the conference, [everyone was] sure the other party was wrong. They were eager to have the conference [which managed to resolve initial tensions and develop a plan for continued work toward finding common ground] ... this is about the reality of changing neighborhoods – having to live together in new ways.

Such community conflict resolution appears to be quite common in programs open to community involvement in collaborative efforts to reduce social distance and promote community peace. Volunteers and staff of conferencing programs may also become involved in community social justice issues.

From cases to advocacy
A direct advocacy role may emerge in programs where volunteers have developed shared values about social justice and public policy issues and frequently discuss broader community problems that they believe lie at the root of these cases. Collective action is also illustrated by one of many

such discussions in the Longmont, Colorado program. Volunteer and trainer Mark Seidler described a point when program volunteers began to take note of the increase in cases involving school truancy, and the not unrelated issue of suspension and zero-tolerance policies. From that point on they began to discuss a number of strategic approaches the group might take to work with principals and the police department to develop better responses (the latter not a difficult task since the police department is the organizational home for the program). Seidler observes that such advocacy is 'primarily about getting beyond the cases to recognize some broader patterns going on in the way the community is dealing with its young people.' It is also about turning the 'bonding social capital' needed to enable the collective to affirm and enforce its norms and values into 'bridging social capital' (Putnam, 2000). Bridging capital may then be used to leverage government resources to support community members as well as to provide a link between families, their neighborhood institutions, and public controls and supports (Hunter, 1985) in a way that may also, as in the current example, at least indirectly engage social justice issues (Braithwaite and Parker, 1999; Pranis, 2001).

Skill-building in other community contexts
Many teachers and students now appreciate spillover efforts of the South St Paul circle in the school system mentioned earlier. According to circle member and former coordinator Barbara Gerten, the clearest indication of this effect, that some claim has changed the culture of the school, is that the students now ask for restorative justice responses when incidents arise. In response to this demand, 7th and 8th grade teachers who had acquired some money for training decided to give it to the elementary school to support continued student training in the circle process. Another community-building focus of this effort – made possible by the work of the circle volunteers – is family-level network building in which the focus is drawing in the parents of younger students with the goal of building volunteer capacity for later involvement and intervention with and support for other youth and families.

In the neighborhood-level discussion later in this chapter, we will consider ways in which volunteers build community within the conference setting and the neighborhoods where they are located. They do so by relying on their problem-solving skills within the conference, and by bringing neighborhood parochial controls into the conference encounter. In addition, as mentioned in the discussion of role-taking in Chapter 6, they bring a neighborhood identity and voice into the program context that can anchor the conference in a way that programs with only a generic case processing focus could not. As Pranis (2001) argues from her circle experience, the network becomes anchored on the one hand by those community leaders in the conventional world and, on the other hand, by those who have experienced and overcome challenges associated with the experience of being offenders, victims, and families of both.

Community-building in instrumental communities

While the geographic neighborhood has been important in restorative justice, it is not the only identifier of community in restorative justice practice. Recently, a variety of 'micro-communities' where people reside temporarily (e.g. treatment or residential programs), work, play, socialize, or worship have been discussed as environments in which community-building efforts have been initiated on some scale. As mediating institutions (Bellah et al., 1991), instrumental communities in educational, residential, workplace and youth development settings are often among the collectivities most directly affected both by crime and harmful behavior, and by the response to this behavior. Our fieldwork provided examples in which restorative practitioners in our case study jurisdictions were beginning to conceptualize these environments as communities in need of enhanced social capital for mobilizing social control and social support. Some residential facilities, for example, utilize conferencing techniques as participatory disciplinary processes, or simply as opportunities for norm affirmation as a means of building resident and staff trust and relationships. Several also reported use of conferencing to: resolve conflict between residents and/or staff and residents; repair harm caused by assaults, threats, or bullying within the facility; and conduct reentry ceremonies to mobilize local support for young offenders returning to their communities.

Because of its special role in youth socialization and discipline, and its new role as a kind of feeder system for the juvenile court (Karp and Breslin, 2001; Bazemore, 2001), we turn now to the micro-community of the school as one of the most significant contexts for community-building that relates to the capacity for delivery of informal social control and social support in the response to youth crime.

Community-building in schools: transforming an educational environment

Conferencing as skill-building for youth development

Community-building may have its most tangible impact in school settings. In the North Minneapolis high school example described earlier, community-building involving teachers and administrators actively in the process has been difficult. Though some are receptive to bringing in an outsider to conduct circles, educational staff seemed unwilling or unable to allow circle trainer Oscar Reed to 'teach them to fish' in order to develop their own internal problem-solving capacity. His youth development strategy therefore has been focused on an attempt to build community around the students themselves.

While youth skill-building is viewed as one possible end-result or secondary goal of some approaches, it is an initial and primary objective of Reed's youth development approach to restorative decision-making in schools (see also Braithwaite, 2001b). He hopes the indirect result will also impact teachers as they 'see kids beginning to solve their own problems.' Moreover, skill-building around conferencing for many young people is a way to, as Reed puts it, 'use the process to get to their own personal issues.' In a reversal of counseling theories that require a professional working with an individual to 'solve' his or her emotional or other problems, this approach suggests that youth, by helping others and helping their community (in this case the school), begin to resolve their own issues (see Riessmann, 1965; Hudson et al., 1996). While this is potentially an educational process for teachers as well, it is one that requires a much larger effort, *or* a more intensive focus on a very limited number of classrooms (the latter has been Mr Reed's approach).

Changing culture

A more systemic community-building strategy in the school context can be seen in those institutions that have attempted a 'whole-school' approach to restorative justice decision-making, generally through the assertive and powerful leadership of a principal or assistant principal. Impact data from the South St Paul elementary, middle and high schools demonstrate the potential of intensive and primary use of circles and other conferencing approaches in response to disciplinary infractions and student conflict.

Initiated by a former teacher who took on a special grant-funded position as Restorative Justice Coordinator, and then became an Assistant Principal, the South St Paul school district Restorative Practices Initiative has demonstrated dramatic results, especially in kindergarten to high school. While this was seen in reductions during the three years of its operation in out-of-school suspensions (from 110 to 55 in junior high and 132 to 95 in the high school), referrals to the principal's office, classroom disruption and discipline, and incidents of physical aggression (773 to 153) (Riestenberg, 2001), it is perhaps best seen in the change in student culture having to do with conflict and its resolution. One illustration of such cultural impact on this 'community' – when kindergarten children tell their teachers that two of their classmates are having a fight or an argument and suggest to her that 'we had better circle them up' – signals a rather profound level of potential long-term transformation. Ultimately, the importance of community-building through conferencing in schools is the potential it illustrates for the use of restorative decision-making as a tool for primary prevention on a large scale in a relatively self-contained learning community.

Changing the structure of school discipline: skill- and network-building
Principal Rex Whipple's use of restorative conferencing at Stafford High School in Stafford, Arizona, has had even more dramatic results as a systemic change catalyst for community-building in a very difficult high-school context. The example from Stafford High is not only about changing the relationship between the disciplinary and governing arm of the school and the community of the school as described earlier. It is also fundamentally about structural change in classroom management. In Stafford, according to Principal Whipple, something important occurred in the course of the approximately 18 months of the school's experimentation with conferencing, initially on a daily basis, that produced an interesting but unexpected result:

Q: How many conferences do you do now in a given week?

A: You know that's a hard one because we haven't done any at all in about three weeks.

Q: Does that mean everyone is slipping back to the old ways of discipline?

A: No, not at all. The fact is, we haven't had a suspension in nine months or seen a police car in more than a year. There just hasn't been a need to have a conference. I don't see kids in my office much anymore . . . things just seem to get worked at in the classroom or in the hall or wherever . . . I never hear about stuff anymore. But in the old days I spent all my time on discipline – and so did most of my teachers. Now they actually focus on what the job is supposed to be – teaching.

Whipple believes that a climate now prevails among teachers and students to 'work things out' using restorative principles. Doing so does not always require a formal conference. Rather, teachers and students, he believes, now 'talk a lot' but in a respectful way and as an alternative to violence and name-calling. Consistent with what David Claussen-Wilson, Director of the Colorado Mediation Forum believes, the climate of conflict resolution and repair works best when students and teachers sit down, however briefly, whenever an incident occurs and go through the inventory of restorative justice questions: what is the harm; what needs to be done to repair it; and who is responsible for this repair. When conferencing can be said to have played a transformative role in changing the nature of school discipline and reducing incidents of crime and harm, community-building in its truest and most holistic sense has been achieved.

One among many of Whipple's strategic approaches to such community-building is the recruitment of a variety of facilitators from various walks of life.

Q: Who facilitates the conferences?

A: Parents, teachers, school administrators, corrections officers, probation officer, police.

Q: Was this strategic?

A: Yes; the one drawback about conferencing is that it is very time-consuming. So the goal was to pass the buck onto other people. It allows for more time to be directed towards teaching as opposed to just disciplining people.

This strategy has also brought a great deal of parental, justice system, and other community involvement into the school, and it seems to have brought collective ownership of, and support for, its new disciplinary practices. This approach is not unlike the strategy employed by other community and system-based conferencing programs that encourage judges, prosecutors, police, and others to participate in their programs in the role of *citizens* rather than professionals. Specific community-building impacts on a small scale include 'good students' and popular students reaching out to develop new relationships with more marginal young people at the school, and parents and community members becoming more involved in all aspects of school activities. In addition, according to Whipple:

> ... the social network of people is growing outside of the school ...
> I can see the parents of students involved talking at the local grocery
> store ... can see kids helping each other in different ways.

His ultimate indicator of community-building, however, is summed up in a basic statement about the current state of the need for any type of disciplinary intervention:

> We have conferenced half as many cases this year as last, and the
> numbers keep going down. Why? The kids are just getting better,
> children in the schools are 'policing' other youth, and kids are also
> building skills, learning that they have to work at it to build up trust.

More qualitatively, the idea of 'kids policing each other' as a form of taking back the conflict from the system and developing new skills is experienced daily when the principal hears kids saying things like: 'do you know how you affected him when you did that?' 'Our kids are the problem-solvers,' he says, 'and I don't want to involve anyone else in this process unless absolutely necessary ... I find I just walk around now and talk to teachers about teaching techniques. I really have a lot of free time on my hands ... that is the best evidence of a safe school community.'

From justice system to schools: keeping cases in schools vs. juvenile justice programs

Perhaps as important as the transformative approach is the 'transplant' strategy (Rosenbaum, 1994) when initiated by juvenile justice and conferencing professionals in a collaborative relationship with schools sensitive to the concerns of teachers and administrators. Transplanting, though arguably more difficult than 'building on' and less holistic than a transformative approach to changing the environment of instrumental communities, can nonetheless have a profound impact on current trends to transfer conflict from the school to the justice system. A small-town, rural example from a conferencing program in Rice Lake, Wisconsin, the largest town (6,000 residents) in a county of 18,000, illustrates how transplanting conferencing from a juvenile justice agency to a school system can change the dynamic of school discipline from one of a pattern of high rates of suspension and referral to the juvenile court or an alternative justice program (in this case the conferencing program) to retaining students and addressing the conflict in the community of origin. Here, the coordinators of a juvenile court conferencing program, after realizing what a high percentage of their cases were coming in as school suspensions or conflicts that might result in suspension, decided to approach school administrators to see if they might be interested in a different approach. Today, they have a working understanding that they will continue to take a minimum number of school referrals, as long as the school agrees to conduct its own conferences as needed and can demonstrate success in dealing with harm internally. The Rice Lake conferencing coordinators have also agreed to provide the training to school staff and school volunteers.

By contrast, conferencing programs at the diversion level that take school referrals of troublesome students without question seem especially vulnerable to becoming what Nils Christie (1977) might call another 'thief of conflict' from its community of origin. Under the expansionist umbrella of juvenile justice systems, such programs may be viewed not as alternatives to court or other formal processes, but as a dumping ground for problems once addressed informally in private and parochial contexts. In stealing the conflict from families, neighbors, and schools, restorative programs would not only potentially widen the justice system net, but also fail to strengthen community nets, and like any other diversion program, would be vulnerable to providing yet another path of entry into the formal system.

The primary objective of the Rice Lake transplant approach, however, is to keep the resolution of conflict in the school and assist staff and students in community-building by developing and enhancing skills in restorative decision-making at all levels. The school and program relationship is of course not the only place where the tension between being a safety valve for community groups and wanting to keep young people out of court arises. It is a complex struggle for the most thoughtful and community-focused practitioners that may create daily dilemmas and tension in the relationship with system decision-makers in some communities, as this comment from a Colorado community-based mediation coordinator suggests:

> Net widening is a tough issue. Dialogue programs like this should never be used by prosecutors to entrap those who cannot be prosecuted for their alleged offenses. This is unethical at best, and should be against the law. Our diversion cases are traditionally marginal. DAs use diversion for cases they can't prosecute successfully, thus in a sense widening the net of criminality. Likewise, police should understand and use the process for genuine problem-solving, not as a sanction for those who cannot be charged.

From another perspective, this same practitioner notes that there is another side to this dilemma:

> However, we can look at this in another way – that is that the community [by sending cases to conferencing programs] is taking conflicts and working them out outside of the justice system. *If the community is governing, running and participating in the program and its processes*, then *I'm all for 'petty' offenses in conference, unless they can be taken care of more informally.* The program's processes must be kept as community-based and informal as possible in order to assure that this is a true community response and not just another mini-judicial process. Much of this can depend upon program director, staff and volunteer understanding of community versus professionalized processes [emphasis ours].

While these distinctions are complex (e.g. is the program part of the system or the community?), as this practitioner suggests, they are based on the ability of conferencing professionals to know a community-driven, and we would add *community-building*, process when they see one.

Residential facilities as instrumental communities

Another use of conferencing with potentially powerful possibilities for community-building in one of the most difficult yet most important contexts is in reintegration of serious offenders housed in correctional facilities. The Connections program at the Red Wing Youth Corrections Center in Minnesota (discussed in Chapter 6) provides an opportunity for residents to meet with their victim(s) in a conference setting in order to make things right with those they have harmed. Transition circles and conferencing are also being used to reintegrate residents back into the community.

At times, community-building is talked about as a kind of spillover effect within agencies or larger programs such as correctional facilities. In essence, this discussion is in part about changing the system. Yet when the focus is on a residential facility as a community, it is appropriately discussed as community-building. The Redwing Minnesota juvenile residential facility which houses some of this state's most serious young offenders is a primary example, as the description of programs and of a general change of focus beginning in 1998–99 indicates:

> The Red Wing Correctional facility here in Minnesota is doing tons of stuff. They have developed a curriculum on Restorative Justice that has been implemented as part of the Social Studies course work that all of the kids take at the high school. They have a Victim Impact class that each cottage group goes through together, they have a Father's Circle for young fathers to discuss parenting, and some of the guards are using circles to deal with conflict, to reintegrate juveniles back into their group after a time in the security lockup unit. They have also started a 'Peace Maker of the Month' award where the residents vote on a peer from each unit to be awarded peace-maker of the month.

In another facility, exposure to restorative conferencing had brought about seemingly small, though in fact profound changes in rules of interaction and discourse between residents that has no doubt challenged traditional correctional protocols:

> [The] facility has community volunteers come in once a week to host a talking circle. The guys thrive on the opportunity to just get real and talk about how they are feeling – confidentiality has been crucial in order for this circle to work! Residents must keep anything shared in the circle in the circle – staff are minimally involved and also must adhere to the expectation of confidentiality [so far this has worked surprisingly well]. This has been quite a challenge for some staff but the group is going great and there are some youth who [after discharge from the program] voluntarily return to the facility each week to participate in the circle.

Discussing the community-building potential when young people in the facility pay visits to their communities, Kelly Prybl, Program Manager at the Redwing facility, observes that:

> It is not often that the resident goes into the community. But when he or she does, that is when the potential for community-building is

at its strongest. This approach [a reentry conference or series of conferences – see Chapter 6] has that potential, because it brings them together – and *they* talk about what they may have done in the community that contributed to delinquency.

Q: Like what?

A: It does not happen often in the metro areas, but usually in the rural areas, that [in the past] the community didn't want to face the fact that they had a problem [and a role in youth crime in their community]. At the end of the reentry conference, they begin to ask, 'What could we have done – what could we have done to help so you wouldn't have done what you did,' and he can give them an honest answer and help them to help him. That's when real community-building occurs.

Neighborhoods and neighborhood organizations and entities

Community-building at the level of entire neighborhoods is often the most difficult, and certainly the hardest to link directly to the work of conferencing programs. Yet a number of the conferencing programs begun in the Minneapolis/St Paul area in the early to mid-1990s grew out of efforts of neighborhood groups to get training and then develop responses that would meet their needs for strengthening local capacity to respond effectively to crime. These efforts led to programs known as the Bemidji Response to Crime, the Central City Neighborhoods Partnership, and a variety of other local responses with names that often reflect a unique neighborhood adaptation of restorative justice principles (Pranis, 1997). Downtown areas and 'merchant accountability boards' have been developed to meet the needs of local businesses and downtown residents and visitors. Boulder, Colorado has now begun a more local focus at the neighborhood level, for example in the University Hill district. States newer to restorative justice such as Illinois are now also planning and developing a neighborhood and city block focus, with the city of Chicago leading the way. Other neighborhood entities such as housing projects and youth development centers in Chicago, Buffalo, Boston, and other cities are now also the target of training and developmental work to begin one or more conferencing programs.

Community-building at the neighborhood level is hard to describe, much less measure and assess its impact. While the link between the conferencing process and the development of new relationships and networks can be effectively documented, 'scaling up' to consider neighborhood level impact is more difficult. Because such community-building goals for conferencing have yet to be formally strategized in most communities, when such an impact does occur it is most likely to be serendipitous, and may even go unnoticed. We describe two such examples in which community building occurred as a direct, though totally unplanned, result of conferencing activity in Woodbury, MN. The first provides an important example of how norm affirmation and values clarification develop in a conference leading to a city-wide follow-up initiative. The second provides a vivid example of citizen efficacy at the neighborhood level and a rather dramatic assumption of ownership for the response to youth crime and local conflict.

Neighborhoods, norms, ownership, and efficacy

From cases to values clarification to action
Some conferencing programs seem to become involved in what could be labeled as clear examples of community norm affirmation, and in effect help citizens identify and clarify shared values as a direct spin-off of conferences. The following example grew out of a Woodbury, MN conference in which the successful resolution did not satisfy some participants' need to address an underlying community problem more strategically and collectively. This community-building effort began after

> ... about the 7th or 8th conference on pot/marijuana at the high school ... parents, PTA began participating as support people. They invited other community people from churches, other stakeholders.

After one such conference, participants came to visit the program director to ask if they could begin to host meetings in their neighborhood to begin to explore shared values, as well as areas where there was disagreement about standards of youth behavior. One participant realized after the conference which had involved his neighbors' children that, as he put it, 'we can't articulate what we want in the community.' As Officer Dave Hines recalls:

> When [the conference] was done they said that [they] needed to do more to establish community norms. They came back with 55 people, formed a community group, up to 105, and polled the city on norms – all businesses, most kids, and the general population. 1,500 surveys were returned. They estimated [among other things] that there were six widely shared community norms about youth behavior and substance abuse. This was a direct result of this conference.

This work, and other conferences since then, has now led to a number of other spin-offs such as neighborhood watch, other youth support groups, circles of support and other discussion groups. Though initially not even remotely a part of the program's objectives as a by-the-book model of family group conferencing, such community-building activity is becoming more common, and Officer Hines now watches carefully for such opportunities and tries to encourage and facilitate wherever he sees interest among citizens and volunteers in taking such action: 'We see this more and more. I actually look forward to burglary cases, because they seem to generate this kind of response.'

Skill-building and collective action in the neighborhood
What has come to be known in Minnesota as the 'Tree House Story' involves the case of an elaborately decorated tree house (with wall-to-wall carpeting, a color TV, and a stereo) in a relatively affluent neighborhood that was damaged by a 12-year-old Native American neighborhood boy. Although the tree house was on the property of one family, it was viewed as the property of the neighborhood, and children ranging in age from 6 to 15 shared this house as a fortress of play away from prying adults.

The boy's mother had been in Michigan at the time and blamed those who had been charged with looking after him for the incident. The family who owned the tree house was in Florida at the time the damage was done. By the time both families returned, the incident had developed into a rather complex neighborhood dispute, and in the period of time subsequent to the incident, the police department reported receiving up to 17 calls a week related to the case. The officer in charge spent two weeks arranging a conference after speaking to numerous individuals and families and hearing, as he put it, 'a whole bunch of sub-plots.'

After the conference had been scheduled, Officer Hines and the colleague who had scheduled the conference were driving through the neighborhood and saw three neighbors they knew to be involved. They stopped and began talking to them about the date for the conference. One of these individuals indicated to the officers that he was a supporter of conferencing because he had participated in one and added that he 'knew how the process worked [he was in a conference with his son].' Officer Hines suggested at that point that they get together and talk about it.

When the facilitator called the victim and offender a week later to make final arrangements, he was told, 'It has already been taken care of.' Working with the man who had been through the earlier conference acting as facilitator, the parties and a number of other neighbors had convened a community conference involving about a dozen neighbors as well as victim, offender, and other families. The conference resulted in an agreement for restitution – including $350 in damages – that, according to the officers following up, was viewed by everyone as successful. In addition, the agreement included having several neighbors donate materials and help in fixing the tree house. Moreover, the participants decided that they needed to get to know each other better as neighbors and planned a picnic for the offender and family, to which they also invited the police officers. The officer's report stated that the encounter was 'a great conference, though I did not attend.'

This case, while certainly not typical, is an example of how the community can assume a lead role when system professionals (though caught by surprise in this case) are willing. Most importantly, it is an example of how conferencing can, if employed frequently enough, even inadvertently, build capacity in participants to apply the process on their own. While this story seems unusual, there is no way of knowing how often participants in a conference may apply the skills they have observed and practised in conferencing in other contexts. We do know, however, that many of the volunteers in conferencing programs report using the processes and principles in other aspects of their lives – e.g. in the workplace, in their church, in their families.

Grounded theory for the impact of neighborhood-based programs and the role of volunteers: the value of parochial control and support

As demonstrated by the impact of the family group conferencing project described in the previous section, programs representing all models have the potential to impact conferencing participants in a way that builds community at a neighborhood level. Yet circles and neighborhood accountability boards appear more likely to focus intervention primarily at this level than other programs and may therefore be more directly poised for neighborhood community-building. NABS are arguably the most neighborhood-based of all conferencing models. While other conferencing models may locate in neighborhoods and specifically serve members of that geographic area, this is relatively rare. It is essentially a structural requirement of NABS (Bazemore and Umbreit, 2001).

Volunteers add immeasurably to the community-building capacity of all conferencing models. But perhaps the most important contribution is the local focus volunteers provide as they literally bring the neighborhood into the conference. Practically, volunteers offer great potential for networking, and for merging public, private and parochial controls (Hunter, 1985; Duffee et al., 2001) at the local level. As we will suggest, they build community in part by virtue of what they bring to conferencing work and by the uniqueness of its impact on conferencing participants.

In an informal focus group with some 20 community volunteers working in NABS in San Jose, California, participants responded to the question: 'Why do neighborhood accountability boards work?' Board members expressed their own theories about why a process in which juvenile offenders meeting with 3–5 neighborhood adults would change behavior, and why this was better than or different from what professionals could do. As they did, several rationales consistent with the focus on norm affirmation and collective efficacy outcomes (as well as social support theory) were in evidence. As the following summary suggests:

- *'We aren't getting paid to do this.'* Several members suggested that young offenders, their families and victims recognize that board members are there because 'they care.' The fact that they are not paid sends a message that these neighbors of the offender and victim represent the 'voice of the community' rather than the agenda of a paid professional. It also is more likely to create a feeling that members expressing a sense of concern and offering support and encouragement really mean it.

- *'We can exercise the authority that parents have lost.'* While there is often ongoing conflict between young people going before NABs and their parents, the fact that other adults seem concerned about youth in trouble and disapprove of their behavior also was said to send an important message.

- *'We live in their community.'* The fact that neighbors are concerned about them and their behavior personalizes the otherwise anonymous behavior of young offenders in a way that court sanctions cannot; it also means that monitoring of agreements and ongoing support is a more likely possibility.

- *'We give them input into the contract.'* Board members said that they typically allow young offenders to propose their own plan for repairing the harm, and always ask for input into proposed conditions that the members develop. This was said to increase commitment to the conditions of the contract in a way that does not occur in more formal processes.

- *'We catch them off guard.'* Board members suggested that often it appears that they are the first adults other than their parents who have expressed concern and support for young people in board hearings. They believe this realization that someone else cares about them is an important factor in motivating offenders to change their behavior.

- *'We have been there, we can relate.'* Several board members revealed that their own children had been in trouble, that they or others in their families had been crime victims, and that they recognized how hard it was for parents by themselves to exercise control over teenage children. Parents have told them that they felt supported and reinforced in their struggles with discipline and other neighborhood influences on their children, because board members often empathized and offered encouragement.

- *'They hear about the harm from real human beings – us and the victims.'* The face-to-face encounter with an affected community member and/or victim was said to personalize the crime in a way formal processes could not.

- *'We follow-up.'* Volunteers expressed the view that the effectiveness of boards was not simply a result of what went on during the hearing. Board members talked about how they monitored and mentored offenders, families, and victims in a variety of ways after the conference.

Conferencing volunteers, regardless of program model, see themselves as distinctly different from the juvenile court and as playing a role no paid professional could easily undertake. Their motivation was, according to one Vermont volunteer, to 'solve a community problem, not to uphold the criminal law. We're there as part of the community – because we care about the community – not because they broke the law.'

In a 'three-strikes-your-out' climate, part of what volunteers bring to the table in dealing with difficult youth and problem families is simply persistence. Some talked about the almost unshakeable commitment to each youth and family, and one panel member described how the group would not give up on one particularly stubborn offender. One volunteer observed: 'This is about building relationships over a long period of time. Maybe [in a conference session] we can only begin to effect change.' Consequently, some volunteers become attached to young offenders as primary support persons, and, as one put it, 'not knowing how they are afterwards is difficult.' Another volunteer described how she participated in community service with the youth, and believed that because of the relationship built there, the youth continued until the service was completed. Not only did they work together, they also talked a lot. This was gratifying for both of them. 'It's really hard to find an end point; you don't want to think that you've failed. We gave one kid so many chances. We refused to fail him. He will come before the panel until he succeeds!'

Because building community, even at a micro level, would seem to logically require more than a one-shot process, this approach (which in a growing number of programs includes multiple follow-up panel meetings with the offender and other stakeholders) appears to have great potential for reinforcing the network of support around the offender and his family. In addition, board and circle volunteers in particular become more aware of problems that arise in these families and neighborhoods by virtue of this deeper and longer-term contact, and they presumably become more skilled at providing even more meaningful assistance.

Community and community involvement is, of course, no 'magic wand' for juvenile justice. Conferencing practitioners most engaged in community-building are those that believe that what drives the movement toward conferencing is a recognition that the community has untapped resources, but also its own deficiencies in how it has responded to the needs of young people and their families. As one program coordinator put it:

> There is a need to create reciprocity ... because support is not there. It [the community] has given them nothing, or very little, in the way of assets – there is this idea about the forty assets that kids need to have to be resilient and successful. The community has deprived them of that by relying so much on the criminal justice system to take care all of the problems. Part of what we do is to try to teach the community about its lack of accountability. This has led the youth to where they are now.

If the neighborhood-level work is the hardest form of community-building, what motivates those that continue to work at it? Although there is no one answer, for many there is a kind of spiritual, though not usually religious, commitment that seems to sustain their efforts. As one circle volunteer put it:

> ... the values and principles of restorative justice is what I am, it embodies who I am, not just what I do ... we want to affect communities, we want to affect the system, if we want to impact on those things, I think people change in the context of relationship and hope. I really think the whole restorative justice thing really has to be internal [commitment] as much as external.

For observers of past informal justice movements, there is an implied problem when the motivation behind a movement is primarily personal self-help (Harrington and Merry, 1988). A cynic observing volunteers who participate in circles night after night may wonder, in fact, to what extent such persons are motivated by personal gratification. The answer seems to be, on the one hand, that restorative justice is *not* a self-help movement. On the other hand, no one could continue a commitment to such difficult work *without* getting something in return. Hence, the energy and spiritual enrichment that comes from this work should probably be viewed as a desirable, if not directly intended, outcome – especially if that enrichment sustains the difficult work of neighborhood community-building.

The challenge as expressed by a VOM/D coordinator who has often struggled in establishing successful neighborhood-based programs in Colorado is to be clear about who the program serves. This is a challenge faced by all practitioners seeking to build community through conferencing, especially in the neighborhood environment:

Our greatest fear is that we become bureaucratic and [therefore] self-defeating. This is an eternal struggle, since we have to be somewhat bureaucratic to even stay in the game and to try to pull people out of the system. We adjust everything from our programmatic structure right down to individual cases as necessary to meet the needs of the stakeholders. However, we try to stick with a basic process structure for conducting conferences, since to do otherwise might open the door to individual volunteers inadvertently pushing their agendas within a dialogue process.

Summary and conclusions

This chapter has addressed questions related to the core restorative justice principle of transformation in the community/government response to crime as it impacts the implementation and operation of conferencing programs. Two reform goals are associated with this principle: (1) systemic change associated with the transformation of the role of justice professionals and of the mission of their programs and organizations; and (2) community-building aimed at increasing the capacity of community groups and citizens to assume responsibility for informal social control and social support.

Our conclusions regarding the system transformation goal are that, in general, little such change has occurred. However, there are examples of initial movement toward change in the role of juvenile justice professionals and in the structure and culture of juvenile justice organizations. Conferencing programs generally attempt to 'model' the new role of juvenile justice professionals and organizations. Yet many struggle to meet goals of transferring decision-making authority to citizens and community groups due to ongoing problems of system resistance. This resistance takes the form of limitations on the number and range of referrals and restrictions on the scope of decision-making authority granted to these programs.

We proposed that 'insider' programs (i.e. those working within an established system agency) could generally resolve these problems and gain discretion over a wider range of cases and case decisions. This is especially likely to occur when referrals are made directly by their parent agency (e.g. a police department) and the program is thereby able to avoid the necessity of managing the discretion surrounding case referral from other agencies (e.g. courts, prosecution). On the other hand, neighborhood-based conferencing programs may struggle to gain the trust of system professionals and to negotiate discretion with the system. Those that manage to thrive develop innovative and sometimes idiosyncratic strategies based primarily on personal relationships with system decision-makers. Such decision-makers may develop strong ties with the program due to residency in or commitment to the neighborhood, and are then essentially 'co-opted' as members of the neighborhood conferencing group. We presented examples of system-based programs that appear to both maximize their discretion and find ways to involve and transfer decision-making to the community, and also described examples of community-based conferencing programs that sustain their efforts through these innovative strategies.

The problems conferencing programs face in sharing decision-making discretion with the community lie ultimately in systemic reform. We considered examples of systemic reform in three contexts: (1) a juvenile justice system in which leaders from four formal system agencies coalesced around a shared vision of maximizing community involvement; (2) a high school which illustrates transformation in government/community roles in a micro-community where students and faculty are given primary responsibility for addressing conflict and harm formerly resolved by the principal and justice system authorities; and (3) a neighborhood-based conferencing program in which judges place most of the discretion over dispositional decision-making in the hands of the program.

If a transfer of authority back to citizens and community groups is at the core of the principle of community/government role transformation, some effort is also required to assist communities in revitalizing their skills in exercising informal social control and social support. We considered the extent to which conferencing program practitioners share a vision of community-building and seek through conferencing work to build relationships and networks as social capital, to encourage community ownership of the response to youth crime, and to build collective skills in mobilizing informal social control and social support. Sound conceptual frameworks in the form of theories of social capital, civic engagement, and collective efficacy provide a logical and empirical basis for pursuing such strategies. Yet they do not necessarily address the level of difficulty in doing so, nor clearly connect restorative processes to community-building efforts.

Though not on the minds of all conferencing practitioners, several participants in our study outlined specific visions of what community-building – as skill development, and relationship/network-building 'looks like.' Others proposed tentative theories about how to create more of each and clearly recognized the necessity of turning over responsibility to community members and groups, while providing skills for sustainability. Clearly, not all restorative group conference programs envision community-building as a goal. However, many practitioners described how this work directly or indirectly sought to increase the capacity of citizens and community groups to respond more effectively to youth crime. Such efforts are often subtle and serendipitous in nature and, as yet, are not well documented. However, some practitioners are becoming more strategic about recognizing and taking advantage of opportunities for community-building before, during, and after the conference.

Community-building seems to have four possible targets and four related outcomes in the conferencing context. We therefore presented examples of community-building, first at the micro level of the conference itself where relationship-building may occur and be connected to other networks of relationships as a form of social capital. Second, community-building may be focused on conferencing volunteers as a target with the goal of increasing their decision-making and conflict-resolution skills and encouraging transfer of these skills into other settings including work, family, school, and neighborhood. Third, community-building can occur in what we called 'instrumental communities' where community members work, learn, temporarily reside, or worship. We described examples of community-building in schools, residential facilities, and other such micro-communities with a focus on how conferencing could be transplanted into such systems or used by system insiders as a transformative tool to restructure disciplinary procedures and generally impact organizational climate. Finally, the most apparent but most difficult target for community-building in the context of conferencing programs may be at the level of neighborhoods or neighborhood organizations and entities (e.g. housing projects), yet even here we are able to trace the initial impacts of community-building efforts.

In summary, theories of professional role change are only partly operationalized in the case studies presented herein. For the most part and with a few notable exceptions it is conference staff rather than traditional juvenile justice professionals that model this new facilitative, community-building role. Conferencing programs are beginning in a tentative and somewhat incidental way to operationalize theories of social capital in cases where relationships and networks appear to emerge from norm affirmative and values clarification within and outside of conference encounters. Skill-building is also apparent, and though not systematically documented, could in the future provide a test of restorative conferencing as an intervention to build collective efficacy.

In the following section, case study examples from two conferences are presented that suggest the potential for exploiting community-building in successful conferencing cases. These cases represent the extremes of serious crime and high-profile incidents vs. low-level and apparently trivial cases. Both suggest that often there is more community-building than meets the eye in the conferencing effort itself, though there is also sometimes *less* than meets the eye in more intentional, well-publicized efforts. These cases provide lessons for the system in the power of community involvement and the need families and citizens have to develop a meaningful and sustainable resolution. They also illustrate what *could be* if system decision-makers were willing to relinquish discretion and engage the community in the response to both low-level and more serious cases.

Observational case studies: more and less than meets the eye – case studies in conferencing and community-building

Earlier in this text we used the phrase 'less than meets the eye' to describe one hypothesis about conferencing programs: that these may well be little more than low-level, trivial diversion programs that have developed reputations for achieving miraculous outcomes not matched by the reality of practice (Bazemore, 2000; Bazemore and Schiff, 2001). Conversely, the phrase 'more than meets they eye' suggests that there may be something more there, something missing at first glance – or that the inadvertent impact of an intervention may be far more profound than the intended result. We want to propose consideration of this latter result and to use it here with reference to community-building specifically. Because we still know so little about community-building and because it is unfamiliar ground, we think scenarios that may indicate community-building can be interpreted in more than one way.

We present two case studies that we believe have implications for community-building; in one case dramatic, in the other more subtle. Both could be critiqued as not really leading to community-building without much additional work (as is true of most examples presented in this chapter). We choose these cases rather than others – some of which are already described in the text – because they represent the upper and lower end of seriousness of the offense incident, and of the direct *potential* for community-building. This potential regardless of the case depends first upon participants having the vision to exploit this potential – as we have emphasized throughout.

Case 1: From circle to community healing

The first case, described in the Introduction to this text, was held in response to an armed robbery in which a 17-year-old African American boy attempted to rob his white neighbor at gun point. For a detailed description of this case, refer to the opening case in the Introduction of this volume.

Case summary

As suggested throughout this chapter, restorative dimensions associated with repairing harm and stakeholder involvement are not easily separated from the community-building features of conferencing, and indeed may be fundamental aspects of skill-building, relationship/network-building, and collective ownership outcomes. This case provides an effective illustration of this insight because in the efforts to respond to the needs of the victim, offender, and family for healing in its various forms, significant community capacity-building was achieved. Victim, community members and the family of the offender clearly had the opportunity to affirm norms and express values, including the value of diversity, and the shared opposition to drug sales and guns. The strong support for the family and the offender, with clear but respectful disapproval of the young man's behavior, empowered the extended family and their supporters as a network now resolved to address the problem at hand.

The circle itself was empowered as a neighborhood program that increased its own collective efficacy and its reputation in the community as a place for conflict resolution and healing which led to a realization among some system decision-makers in attendance that the circle was more powerful than they had realized. The neighborhood impact should also be seen in the context of racial and ethnic relations and white flight as difficult issues in inner-city neighborhoods – even in the absence of serious black on white crime. If some might see a downside, it might be that the circle could have been used to set up an alternative community-based plan for the offender (including close supervision and support from the circle) as an alternative to the residential confinement. While the level of seriousness in the case meant that the system strongly asserted its ownership, it was nonetheless willing to allow the community and the restorative process to come in at various points and play a role that in fact seems to have made the system experience less harmful and bounded on both ends by strong community support.

Regarding neighborhood community-building, beyond the new reputation created for the circle by this case, multiplied by ten, one could imagine tremendous local impact, especially in a self-contained, relatively homogeneous neighborhood, and in a program with so much system involvement. While no one has systematically tried to document this impact, the coordinator believes that it brought in new volunteers and new case referrals. Ultimately, the case as 'story' provides a potent counterpoint to media horror stories about crime (Pranis, 2001) that could be an important heuristic tool in a learning community beginning to recognize the possibilities in restorative processes.

Case 2: Family to family healing

The case described below was referred after arrest to a Colorado police department that is also the organizational home for a family group conferencing program. The program takes primarily diversion and misdemeanor cases and has been in operation for approximately two years. Though one youth was arrested, the conference, conducted and coordinated by a volunteer facilitator, included several young people and their families who had been involved in a group conflict on private property after hours.

Facilitator: 'Thanks for coming. The healing process will begin tonight by understanding what happened. We will focus on the incident at the Skate Park/Boy's and Girls Club. We will focus on Mathew's [fictitious name for actual offender] behavior ... not if he is a good or bad person. We will look for ways to repair the harm ... as Mathew has admitted his part. If Mathew stays he will be taking responsibility for his actions ... Do you want to stay?'

Mathew: 'Yes.'

Facilitator: 'What happened?'

Mathew: 'Me and a friend went to the Skate Park and heard some kids by a tree saying that they were going to break and enter into a building. We told them it was trespassing and then the name calling started and the rock throwing. We went to the Skate Park [starts to cry] I pulled out my screwdriver knife and asked them to leave. I told them if you hit me with that big rock, I'll stab you. They ran away and then stopped and turned around and said "Chase us".'

Facilitator: 'What were you thinking about?'

Mathew: 'Leave us alone.'

[Community Member Enters]

Facilitator: 'This is a community member from the Boys and Girls Club [referring to community member who just entered]. So, Mathew, who all do you think this incident affected?'

Mathew: 'Them' [... silence ...] 'Because, I may have scared them.'

Facilitator: 'I'm going to ask you that later too. Let's go to Samantha [fictitious name for actual victim] now.'

Samantha: 'Before we went to the Skate Park ... the place over by the club ... we decided to knock on the door to see if we could pick up the trash. No one was there ... we wanted to help because the lady that lived there was old ... we threw snow and they started spitting on us. We then went into the Skate Park and Mathew had a scooter and started swinging it. We threw rocks and he pulled out a knife and said that he was going to stab us. He told me he cut up a can. I looked at the can and didn't want to be involved anymore. I don't know if I want to go to the Skate Park anymore ... Mom won't let me go anyway.'

Facilitator: 'What were you thinking and feeling, Louisa [fictitious name for actual second victim]?'

Louisa: 'I don't know what I was thinking about. I was feeling scared. I am still scared and uncomfortable about going to school.'

Facilitator: 'James [fictitious name for actual third victim], why don't you tell us what happened.'

James: 'Me and the girls went to the Skate Park ... We played by the fence and started to pick up trash as we walked over to the door to knock. We were inside the fence which was trespassing. They yelled at us, "Stop trespassing". They started throwing snow and Mathew started spitting. We picked up trash more and they kept throwing snow. We knocked on the front door again and then decided to go the Skate Park. They came over and started to hit me with the scooter. The first time he hit me I told my mom but she told me to, "Go talk to him." I went back and he had a knife and was threatening people.'

Facilitator: 'What were you thinking?'

James: 'That I was going to get hurt.'

Facilitator: 'Any questions?'

Louisa: 'Samantha climbed out of the fence and I was terrified.'

Samantha: 'Mathew's Mom, did you know that he had a knife?'

Mathew's Mother: 'Yes. I teach him walk away. I am not sure why he didn't. Maybe because he is 12.'

James's Mother: 'Words work better than fists. When my son came back, I knew that someone was threatening him with a knife. I confronted Mathew and he pulled out his knife and said, 'You mean this?' I told him it didn't matter how small the knife was. It was still wrong. He said that they "were defending themselves." I didn't want a debate over it ... I wasn't expecting an arrest. It shocked me that he was cuffed. It hurt me as a Mom. I knew it would hurt his Mom. [Mathew crying] This is a teaching moment and I want my son to know that this is why I send him to daycare. It's important to understand why I don't want him out alone. I wonder if he is safe. I hope they have both learned. That's my concern. I want all children to feel safe ... Not on streets with guns and knives. It was hard on me to call the police. I felt I had to. I felt like I wasn't getting through. I felt something bad would happen if I didn't call.'

Facilitator: 'Louisa's Mother.'

Louisa's Mother: 'I was scared. I got a call on my answering machine. I talked to [the police]. I was shocked and scared.'

Facilitator: 'Concerns?'

Louisa's Mother: 'At school ... retaliation ... worried about that. Kids won't stay away from them. I am worried about teasing and taunting. I don't feel comfortable with her going to the Skate Park or really going anywhere. I worry about what she is doing and how she is. I feel a little better now because I feel Mathew has taken the initiative to stay away from her. You showed me how this incident got out of hand. I just want you to be able to pass each other in the hall.'

Facilitator: 'Louisa?'

Louisa: 'I don't feel safe'

Facilitator: 'We will come back to you.'

Samantha's Mother: 'When the officer first called, the call came in as "out of area" and I almost didn't pick it up. The police officer told me that she was involved in throwing rocks with a boy who pulled a knife. I told him that I hoped she learned something because she knows that she shouldn't throw rocks. She knows that I don't allow that. I was angry with her and told her that pulling a knife was wrong too. I waited for 15 minutes for her to come home from the Skate Park and then went to get her when she didn't come home. It really made me mad ... here she is acting like nothing was wrong playing inside the club. I don't get why kids have to be so mean to each other ... you step in and there is a good chance of retaliation.'

Facilitator: 'Community Member?'

Community Member: 'I had come into work and was told that they were arresting kids at the Skate Park for 'pulling a knife.' I was the only one there and knew that there were two police cars. I heard it was Mathew and I couldn't believe it was him being arrested. Stories kept getting bigger and bigger. I hear that he stabbed someone and that Samantha had fallen on the rocks. If kids are skating there are no problems. It's the kids who don't do what the facility was designed for. You can sit and point fingers, but everyone had a part. Don't come crying to me if someone gets hurt out of something little turning big. We need to use this as a learning example.'

Facilitator: 'Mathew's Mother?'

Mathew's Mother: 'I came home to paint the bathroom and the phone rang. The officer said that he had my son. I said, are you kidding? He's never been in trouble. I can't just pick up and leave. I have to go back to work. I went and got him and took him to work. I got the story and told them it's not their job to tell people not to trespass. I heard stories that he stabbed someone. I had to go back home because the girls were scared. I am still scared too. He wanted to be an FBI agent and now he can't. Mathew's sister now hears all this about her brother before I get a chance to tell her ... she hears he's a "cry baby, he stabbed someone." I feel bad that he scared you [looks at victims] but then I hear that you left and then came back. I can't really change his school. I'm not excusing him.

What he did was wrong. It never clicked that the little utility knife would be a problem. It's huge we'll have to see what happens.'

Facilitator: 'Mathew's Sister.'

Mathew's Sister: 'One day after Christmas break, I went to the club. I heard Samantha telling me that my brother went to jail and to court and got expelled from school. I was kind of freaked out.'

Mathew's Mother: 'Mathew's Sister didn't know – she found out everything at the club.' [Mathew's Sister cries] 'I felt really bad about that. I just had no idea that they all went to the same school.'

Samantha's Mother: 'Louisa's Mother told the principal he . . . [Louisa's Mother begins to interrupt]

Louisa's Mother: 'He told me that he would talk to Mathew. I wanted to call and talk to Mathew's Mother to get a feel for what was happening. I wanted to see them together. I felt good when I heard they were leaving each other alone at school. I only brought it up to the school because I didn't know him [Mathew]. Louisa's sister said she hadn't seen Mathew in three days. That made me feel OK. I have no fear now.'

Mathew's Mother: 'I don't think that Mathew will say anything.'

Louisa's Mother: 'Everyone was involved here. All four kids made mistakes.'

Mathew's Mother: 'Better now than later.'

Community Member: 'I had to take Mathew home from the Skate Park a few days after the event. It was hard to do that and see the girls scared. It makes me happy to see that everyone was willing to come together – safety is a concern and it's important they feel safe and that they have a place.'

Facilitator: 'Can we think of ways to repair? So, Mathew, who has been affected after listening to everyone?'

Mathew: 'The parents. I'm sorry for what I did to the kids and the parents.'

Facilitator: 'What do you need?'

Samantha's Mother: 'I think that Mathew needs to apologize to his Mom.'

James's Mother: 'I knew how I would feel as a single Mom if this happened. It's a heart-breaking thing. I was hoping for counseling and anger control help at home. It was a surprise to see him in cuffs and now he has a felony.'

Louisa: 'I am sorry for my part. I was terrified when you were put in the car. It could have been me.'

Samantha: 'I only told one person at the club. I didn't mean for it to happen. I haven't been allowed to go to the club.'

Louisa: 'Mathew, I told one person. I'm glad I did. I had another incident when I tried to hurt myself. I think this is all my fault. I've been pretty depressed.'

Samantha's Mother: 'She wrote a suicide note to a friend at school. It's not all your fault [looks to her daughter].'

Facilitator: 'What do you need to put this behind you?'

Samantha: 'When I heard that Mathew was suspended, I wanted to know for how long.'

Community Member: 'I talked to Mathew; he's not suspended but told him until we come together for a meeting that he should stay away from the club.'

James's Mother: 'For the security of the kids. Mathew is not suspended at this time. It's a time for people to heal . . . There was some worry that the rumors would get worse. Mathew needs to be able to come back into the club and be OK. Maybe setting all the kids straight on what happened.'

Samantha's Mother: 'I agree.'

Samantha: 'I told my friends that Mathew is not a dangerous person and that we all had parts.'

Community Member: 'I want a general consensus from the group on when he can come back.'

Facilitator: 'Community member, you would be willing to meet with staff and kids to set the record straight?'

Community Member: 'Yes.'

Samantha: 'I want him back.'

Louisa: 'I think that I am pretty comfortable now. I won't tell anyone else. I won't make fun of you. I feel a lot better now. I am not afraid.'

Samantha: 'I am sorry for throwing rocks.'

Samantha's Mother: 'This is the first time truth came out. You told me that you were only throwing sticks and snow.'

Facilitator: 'I would hope that after tonight we can all move forward and that the truth has been told.'

Mathew's Mother: 'I think that you are all really courageous, I will say a prayer for forgiveness and peace. I'm going to church right after this. You can choose to learn and grow rather than think "poor me." I would like a promise from Mathew that he won't bother you.'

Samantha's Mother: 'Samantha's biggest upset was not being able to get the birthday cake at the club because of all of this. It was her birthday and because of this incident the club was off limits.'

Louisa: 'I promise not to tease Mathew.'

Mathew: 'I promise not to tease you and I won't threaten you.'

Facilitator: 'Samantha and Louisa . . . do you accept?'

Samantha/Louisa: 'Yes.'

Facilitator: 'Is Monday OK for Mathew to go back?'

Mathew's Mother: 'I feel like I can talk to you know. I'm glad I know who everyone is. I wish Mathew's sister would have been at the club when this happened. She is a great mediator. Even though I am a single Mom I haven't had much conflict.'

Facilitator: 'I think this has been a positive experience.'

Mathew's Mother: 'I think it taught everyone that truth is important.'

Facilitator: 'James's Mother talked about what happened and the possibility of seeing a counselor.'

Mathew's Mother: 'If the court orders it I'll pay.'

Facilitator: 'Mathew, would you agree to see a counselor?'

Mathew's Mother: 'There is a school counselor.'

James's Mother: 'That makes sense. What about baking a cake for Samantha?'

Mathew's Mother: 'He could do that. Right, Mathew?'

Mathew: 'Yes.'

Facilitator: 'OK, let's see what we have. Mathew agrees to talk with counselor, he can go back to the club on Monday, and Community Member will talk with the club members about what happened.'

Samantha's Mother: 'I'd like him to write down what he's learned and address it to Mom.'

James's Mother: 'How about a letter to his Mom and the kids?'

Facilitator: 'The letter needs to come to the police officer. It would be nice to get it done by Thursday ... Bring it to court and hand deliver it to her desk. OK, now we can eat. I'm proud of you kids.'

AGREEMENT:

Conferencing Agreement for: Mathew

Conference Participants agreed to the following contract items:

1. Mathew apologized to each participant. He also promised that he would not tease or threaten again. The other children also apologized and took responsibility for their part in the incident.

2. Mathew agrees to bake a birthday cake for Samantha, because she missed her birthday cake at the club because of the incident.

3. Community Member will talk with the children at the Club tomorrow, Friday, so they will feel comfortable with Mathew returning to the Club on Monday, a date that everyone agrees to.

4. Mathew agrees to write a letter explaining what he's learned and what he would do differently if confronted with the same situation in the future. This letter will be turned into the police officer at the Police Station by Thursday.

5. Mathew will visit with the school counselor about the incident and if they agree that he needs future counseling, he and his mother agree to follow-up with professional counseling.

Case summary

Through the lens of 'less than meets the eye,' this case provides a vivid example of a low-level incident which, like some described in earlier chapters, does not appear to belong in a conference. A minor youth prank, or a misunderstanding between middle-school age youth, the case should have been easily settled by the families and young people without the use of police resources. One may also argue that only by the most literal interpretation of the law did the incident justify arrest when officers might instead have taken the youths home and had a discussion with their parents – though perhaps more detailed information would have supported the arrest decision.

From another perspective, however, it may be said that subsequent to the arrest, the system agency in fact minimized its involvement and use of resources and maximized the use of community resources. While court processing would not have been likely in such a case (though in recent years, with zero-tolerance philosophy exerting its influence in many contexts, such a possibility could not be ruled out), by contrast, another more common system response would have been the likely result. This option would have involved some form of consent decree and subsequent referral of one or more of these youths to a diversion program. Such referral(s) would have likely involved some form of counseling for the offenders as individuals, while bypassing the opportunity for conflict resolution and learning from the incident that occurred in the group dialogue and problem-solving process of the conference. Moreover, diversion program referral risks exposure for extended periods of time, at substantially more cost, of young people to other youth likely more experienced in more serious forms of misbehavior. Instead, the police department made use of its informal alternative process using a volunteer facilitator, and most importantly tapping into the natural resources most capable of addressing the problem at hand, the families. One may argue correctly, we believe, that this process could have occurred, as it often did in different times, without police intervention. Once such an intervention occurred, however, the response provided the least harmful and most potentially productive resolution.

The 'more than meets the eye' aspects of this case are its implications for community-building at an inter-family level, with possible extension to school and neighborhood levels. In contrast to what would have occurred in the typical individually focused diversion program (or if the incident had been ignored), the young people seem likely to have learned important lessons about non-threatening forms of communication and about conflict resolution. Most importantly, the families seem to have benefited most from the opportunities to connect with parents of the other youth involved in this incident and about the shared values that seem to make resolution of this incident an easy task. In the absence of such an encounter, parents may have wondered both about what really happened, harbored fear and concern about the other young people and the role of their children in the incident, and been left with concern about other parents who seemed to lack standards for their children's behavior. The community-building possibilities in this case include the potential for future networking between these parents, for parents to themselves use the process in future incidents (and even for some to become volunteers in the program), and for the parents to recommend the use of conferencing to school personnel.

In summary, when compared to alternative responses and to the option of not addressing the issues involved in this dispute – however minor on the scale of most offenses processed by the system – the conference had a number of advantages. At a minimum, it is likely that it caused less harm at less expense. More optimistically, opportunities for community-building were generated the impact of which will probably not be known. While exploiting such opportunities is the role of the community, program staff and volunteers could be more strategic in making such opportunities available and supporting and creating forums for citizens who wish to follow up. To learn more about whether and how such micro-connections in the context of the conference become relationships, and how such relationships evolve into networks of support and control, researchers studying conferencing will need to begin to track collective changes in participants and others connected to them rather than simply following up with individual offenders and victims.

Notes

1 Canberra, Australia's RISE program, is an international example of a program able to sustain a relatively high level of seriousness and chronicity in referrals, partly due to the prestige associated with being part of an international experiment (Sherman et al., 2000). Another counter example at the police level in our qualitative sample is a popular program in a well-established and highly supportive police department that has nonetheless not created enough confidence in the program to sustain a level of seriousness in referrals beyond minor and/or first offenders. A possible important difference in this program is that it is not directed by a police officer.

2 The same possibilities exist for neighborhoods with political leaders and police who wish to resolve things locally. Such resolution seems possible, especially as restorative justice is introduced into minority communities concerned with disproportionate confinement (Rose and Clear, 1998; Gaines, 2002). We discuss some case examples of such neighborhoods and the added clout they can sometimes mobilize to influence the system response in the following section.

3 Though many early restorative justice programs – including the first one in a Minnesota correctional facility (Heinz, Galaway, and Hudson, 1986; Hudson, 2001) – had incentives in the form of reduced prison time, such incentives for some purists may be viewed as diluting restorative justice as a purely voluntary option. In a similar way, ordering offenders to make restitution or complete community service is viewed by some as inconsistent with restorative justice principles (McCold, 2000; cf. Bazemore and Walgrave, 1999).

4 Stanley Cohen (1985) has observed: 'community is a "magic word" that lacks any negative connotations' (p. 117). '... Almost anything can appear under the heading of "community" and almost anything can be justified if this prefix is used' (p. 116). Weitekamp (1999) has argued that North Americans are obsessed with the idea of community because they have so little of it (see also, Cohen, 1986; Crawford and Clear, 2001).

Chapter 8

Looking back and moving forward: conclusions, implications, and an agenda for future research

Introduction

At the broadest level, the questions addressed by the exploratory research on restorative justice decision-making in this book were designed to answer the question 'What's out there?' More specifically, we wanted to know what participants in restorative conferencing wanted to accomplish, to describe what is new and different about these innovations, and to understand similarities in vision and practice as well as differences.

The primary objective of the current study was to improve understanding and evaluation of restorative justice, with the ultimate goal of improving policy and practice. Our objectives, specifically, were: to develop a useful estimate of the prevalence of conferencing programs; to examine the structural and organizational characteristics of programs and their location within the juvenile justice system; to describe the extent to which conferencing practitioners are committed to the vision of restorative justice with attention to how conferencing practitioners utilize restorative principles in their daily practice; to examine how restorative principles and theories are applied in various stages and phases of the conference; to describe practice and process variation between programs and program models; and to elucidate the complex relationship between theory, outcomes, and practices associated with restorative conferencing.

This final chapter has several objectives. First, we consider the contribution and general implications of our effort to explore a principle-based agenda for evaluation and research on conferencing. Second, we affirm the value of using the grounded intervention theories developed here both to guide research and replicate promising practices. When taken seriously, these practitioner logic frameworks become important tools for improving research that tests theories rather than simply programmatic approaches. Third, we briefly summarize overall findings as they relate to these theoretical concerns and restorative principles. Finally, the bulk of this chapter looks forward to an agenda for future research. To inform this agenda, we consolidate the implications of our findings into three sections: (1) a focus on priority outcomes for conferences; (2) a list of core propositions derived from intervention theories that specify requirements for action if specific conferencing outcomes are to lead to long-term results and provide for specific tests of these theories; and (3) a broad research protocol that proposes three general research designs applicable to the evaluation of (a) individual conferencing practices and programs, (b) programs within a larger multi-modal framework of restorative justice practices not limited to conferencing, and (c) entire agencies, systems, and communities adopting restorative policies and practices in contrast to non-restorative systems and agencies.

Looking back: general implications of this study and the challenge of conferencing policy and research

Restorative justice as a movement and agenda for policy and practice is much larger than the face-to-face decision-making processes we have referred to generically in this book as 'conferencing.' A premise of this study, however, is that conferencing is a central component of a holistic, principle-based framework that provides for a different way of responding to crime and harm of any kind wherever it occurs. There are two general reasons why conferencing as the primary manifestation of restorative decision-making is at the core of the restorative justice vision of reform. First, as a nonadversarial process geared to stakeholder needs, conferencing is generally the most effective way to achieve the goals of repairing harm, and engaging stakeholders in decisions about how to do so. Second, conferencing programs are especially suited to mobilize the resources of communities in decision-making. Third, because it is also a potential 'gateway' to expanding victim, offender, and general citizen input and participation in justice decision-making, conferencing may become a catalyst for change in how other criminal and juvenile justice functions are carried out – e.g. offender rehabilitation, incapacitation, victim services.

It is for all these reasons, and because of its frequently emotional quality and inclusion of non-traditional participants, that restorative decision-making is one of the most controversial, and potentially threatening,

325

innovations in operation in criminal and juvenile justice systems today. Conferencing is therefore clearly difficult to implement and sustain within the confines of adversarial, increasingly bureaucraticized, and more punitive juvenile justice systems. The conferencing movement is therefore fragile; great potential is coupled with dangers that may result in marginalization and irrelevance, if not elimination, of conferencing programs. Although increasingly prominent internationally and highly developed and elaborated as a systemic reform in some parts of the world (Morris and Maxwell, 2001; Braithwaite, 1999), restorative justice decision-making remains in its early stages of development in the US as a program and policy.

To an even greater extent, it is important to acknowledge that research on restorative decision-making must be viewed as in the stages of relative infancy. Although a growing body of research literature now documents the effectiveness of victim–offender mediation or dialogue (see Umbreit, 2001), and newer studies of family group conferencing show promise (e.g. McGarrell, 2001; Sherman, 2003; Hayes and Daly, 2003), these studies do not begin to capture the practical and theoretical distinctions within and between approaches documented in this book. Looking back on the descriptive findings presented here, we believe that evaluation studies and research in general on restorative decision-making, despite method-ological rigor, have been somewhat stifled by conceptual barriers that in turn limit measurement and the possibilities for generalizing findings to theory and policy. Although there are a number of prior and ongoing studies employing sound research designs, two related problems have limited advancement of restorative conferencing research. First, there has been a lack of standards for determining whether and to what extent a decision-making strategy is 'restorative' in nature. Therefore, judgements of the success or failure of a program or strategy may be inappropriately attributed to restorative justice when in fact some other theory and practice, e.g. procedural justice, may be responsible for the result. Second, there has been an absence of guiding theory, or more precisely a lack of clear focus on the theoretical assumptions underlying conferencing practice. Generalization of research results is therefore limited because findings are often relevant to the effectiveness of a programmatic model rather than a general, theoretically informed approach to intervention. With regard to practice, replication is too often limited to 'cookbook' approaches found in program guides, the effectiveness of which may be questionable when such approaches are not contextualized. The apparent lack of transferability (and at times failure to replicate evaluation results) has been often due to a lack of understanding of underlying theoretical principles that have wider implications for intervention, policy, and future theory testing.

Gauging restorativeness: restorative justice principles and a multi-dimensional approach

How do we know restorative justice conferencing when we see it? The first problem is to define the 'independent variable' in conferencing and establish the face and construct validity of relevant measures. In much program evaluation research, this problem is described as determining the 'integrity' of the intervention and in turn its strength (e.g. Andrews and Bonta, 1994). We used the term 'restorativeness' in this study (see also Hayes and Daly, 2002; Braithwaite, 1999; Umbreit, 2001 for different terminology) as a way of referencing a general standard or set of scales for gauging this intervention integrity in restorative policy and practice.

Unfortunately, the idea of restorativeness is at best imprecise, and at worst has been trivialized. In much literature and practice, this distinction is based on what restorative justice is *not* – e.g. it is sometimes viewed as the opposite of retributive justice (Braithwaite, 1999; Zehr, 1990).[1] In many accounts, restorativeness is a dichotomous category in which inclusion is determined apparently by adherence to programmatic criteria, or use of a certain technique – most often, face-to-face meetings between victim and offender (Immarigeon, 1999).

More appropriate criteria we believe are 'yardsticks' or benchmarks for helping observers gauge restorativeness based on scales that acknowledge restorativeness as a relative, rather than an either/or distinction (Zehr, 1990; Zehr and Mika, 1998). Too often, however, uses of such scales in research applications are one-dimensional, or focused on a constricted set of dimensions. Most importantly, it is also typically not clear what empirical, theoretical, or normative considerations go into judgements about the metric which gives higher ratings to one dimension rather than another.

As an alternative, we proposed that standards for gauging restorativeness be derived from core restorative justice principles. The three core restorative justice principles were presented in Chapter 2 as the basis for a normative theory of restorative justice: repairing harm, stakeholder involvement, and transforming community–government roles and relationships in the response to youth crime (Van Ness and Strong, 1997). These general principles resonate with core humanistic values that practitioners have, we think, correctly associated with restorative justice – respect, inclusiveness, problem-solving, and democratic decision-making – to name but a few. Moreover, they are in general consistent with the spirit of restorative justice as a value-driven movement. However, they also offer greater precision in defining the goals of restorative intervention, and most importantly, are restrictive enough to exclude interventions that may be viewed as beneficial and progressive, yet are clearly *not restorative*. More importantly, they provide criteria or standards that potentially allow for measuring the degree of restorativeness across specific encounters, programs, organizations, and systems using standards that are multi-dimensional (for other multi-dimensional statements of criteria for gauging restorativeness using a different frame of reference or more constricted set of principles, see Presser and Van Voorhis, 2002; Hayes and Daly, 2003; Bazemore and Karp, 2002; Van Ness, 2001).

The normative theory based on the three core principles provides a general value-based yardstick for determining whether and to what degree an intervention is restorative. However, to provide testable theories of intervention, it is necessary to link intervention to specific immediate, intermediate, and long-term outcomes by making logical connections in the form of causal propositions. Program evaluation that contrasts the impact of a conferencing program with court or other alternative, assuming standards for determining restorativeness are clear, can establish the relative effectiveness of a program model. However, it is only by articulating and testing such intervention theories that we move beyond programs, and gain the capacity to generalize evaluation findings to a range of settings and related interventions. In doing so, we build and improve theory while also increasing the replicability or robustness of interventions based on principles adaptable to diverse contexts rather than restrictive program models.

Theory for practice and practice for theory

The intervention theories articulated in this study are then theories of practice that use what we call dimensions of restorativeness to create and give priority to specific outcomes to be achieved at the end of the conference. These theories then conceptually link these immediate outcomes to more long-term effects. Some of these theories are more tentative and underdeveloped than others despite their practical application in the field. Together, however, they provide an outline for a multi-dimensional protocol for determining the strength of adherence to principles and for examining the relative utility of various theories of conferencing. To accomplish the latter objective, they provide the basis for developing and testing propositions (see below) and for comparing different theories of intervention in practical evaluation and other research contexts.

The primary purpose of our qualitative research, however, was to examine general consistency and use of core principles to guide practice in the conferencing environment. While we began with an assumption that practitioners of restorative conferencing likely structured their own decisions about alternative responses in the conferencing process around various informal practice theories or theories of intervention, we felt that for the most part these theories would not be fully articulated as identifiable theories of intervention. Hence, rather than ask about these directly, and in order to ground the study in the 'nuts and bolts' or *architecture* of conferences, we focused primary attention on what practitioners wanted to have happen, and what we observed occurring, in what we labeled 'conferencing phases and stages.' We believed that various theories and dimensions that reflect a relative commitment to one or more principles would implicitly guide strategy decisions at this level about who to involve, how to proceed with the process, when to move to the next phase, and so on.

Because practical concerns related to resources and timeframes have much to do with how conferencing staff and volunteers carry out tasks such as preparation activities, conferencing practice does not always line up with outcomes being pursued in a logical fashion. However, many decisions about how to manage the conferencing process were apparently influenced directly by theoretical assumptions about which immediate outcomes would lead to better long-term results and which practices would lead to these results at the conclusion of the conference. Some of these priorities are reflected in the section of this chapter on outcomes that we present below as part of the discussion of a research agenda for the future. The linkage between theory, practice and outcome is made more explicit in the section that lists theoretical propositions for future research.

Summary of findings

General findings

The national scene

At the most general level, our national inventory established for the first time a baseline count of some 773 programs nationally and suggested that conferencing programs exist in almost every state, though only a relative handful of communities have access to such programs. While all of the basic models are represented, victim–offender mediation and dialogue remains the dominant model, followed closely by neighborhood accountability boards. Circles are by contrast quite rare, although over the course of the study we found examples of the use of circle processes in many contexts – residential programs, youth service agencies, schools – regardless of whether they were part of a formal circle program.

Chapter 3 provided prevalence data establishing the existence of restorative conferencing in one form or another as a national phenomenon, though there is not one uniformly implemented approach across the US. These data also confirmed the existence of four model types and what appeared to be a number of hybrids, and indicated that some models –

notably VOM/D and NABs – were in more common use than others. Based on a sample of known programs, we described a number of organizational characteristics that distinguished programs from each other and from formal decision-making approaches. Programs in general are relatively small, non-profit entities that serve primarily minor, non-chronic and non-violent offenders and their victims. A number of procedural indicators (e.g. victim involvement, face-to-face dialogue) established these as *restorative* programs with practice emphases distinct from those in the court or other formal decision-making processes (e.g. plea bargaining). Most importantly, a series of questions in the survey established strong commitment to the general principle and goal of repairing harm, to the principle and goal of stakeholder involvement, and to the principle and goal of transformation of the community/government relationship in the response to crime. This part of the study also documented wide variation in organizational location, referral sources, and caseload. Consistency of program vision with restorative principles was generally strong and, for the most part, these respondents felt that they were able to accomplish goals consistent with this vision. The area of greatest ambivalence for conferencing programs in this study was their commitment to and capacity for community-building.

Conferencing programs in depth and in context

Consistent with our attempt to develop a model for principle-based evaluation, we summarize basic findings of this study of restorative decision-making in the US primarily with reference to commitment to, and application of, the three core principles of restorative justice. While we have focused on distinctions between principles throughout this book, in this summary we minimize these distinctions in favor of more integrative statements and with the general concern with principle conflict and the need to achieve balance in the conferencing environment. Overall, the quantitative and qualitative studies established a general commitment of conferencing programs to restorative principles at the level of program vision, and most programs we encountered demonstrated efforts to incorporate principles into practice.

Consistent with national survey findings, among the 25 programs included in our qualitative purposive sample there was, if anything, a stronger focus on the normative theory of restorative justice relative to the values and theories more common to traditional juvenile justice policy models such as crime control, best interests/individual treatment, just desserts, or libertarian orientations. There is also at times evidence of some deviation from principles and a leaning toward offender support and rehabilitative concerns rather than a focus on the three principles. There was, however, little or no indication of 'get tough' or punitive sentiments, with most program staff and volunteers leaning heavily toward offender support in addition to a high priority given to victim satisfaction and generally addressing victim needs.

While commitment to all principles is strong, repairing harm receives the greatest focus among our group of programs in the qualitative study. This appears to be in part due to the fact that the restorative agreement almost by definition requires emphasis on making things better than they were, or 'healing' in the broadest sense of this term. Regarding the various dimensions or intermediate outcomes associated with repairing harm, when we examined conferencing agreements and observed participants involved in making those agreements, the dominant focus was on the obligation to make amends. This focus was followed closely by a focus on repair as building or rebuilding relationships.

There is also strong commitment to stakeholder involvement. However, conferences vary in the extent to which they prioritize and devote resources to ensuring victim and community participation. Programs, as well as program models, also vary in their adherence to various dimensions of involvement such as inclusion, communication, and management of stakeholder roles in the conference. The victim is of primary concern in most programs, although often the most difficult party to engage. As reported in the program profile section of Chapter 4, victim participation is quite high in the programs in our qualitative sample. There are also differences between conferencing programs in their commitment to different process outcomes associated with the stakeholder involvement principle such as victim–offender exchange, respectful disapproval of offender behavior or collective transformation. These process outcomes are important in part because they relate directly to objectives focused on repair, but also because they are associated with theories about the importance of the offender experiencing respectful disapproval, the importance of victim and offender well-being (with more or less attention to underlying dimensions of satisfaction such as reduced fear, vindication, and respectful treatment), and the mutual transformation of victims, offenders, and community members toward shared understanding and common ground. The relative amount of focus on these outcomes is related to adherence to theories of reintegrative shaming, healing dialogue, and common ground respectively.

Finally, commitment to the third core principle of restorative justice, community/government role transformation, is least consistent according to both quantitative and qualitative data. In the national survey, for example, respondents gave lower priority to community-building as a goal and in general appeared to be more practically focused on victim and offender outcomes. In the qualitative data, the reason for this is made obvious: most conferencing programs were designed primarily to meet the needs of individual offenders and victims rather than those associated with community-building; the role of their program as a catalyst for system change may therefore seem to many of these small operations to be far-fetched. Between the two broad goals of principle three, most practitioners attached primary importance to the system change dimension, as described in Chapter 7, apparently because system agencies were still unwilling to refer a great number and wide array of cases, or to share discretion with the program over more than a narrow range of decisions.

Looking forward: toward a research agenda for restorative decision-making

Perhaps the most important contribution of the current research and this book are the questions raised for future studies of restorative justice and informal decision-making. We suggest that such questions may contribute to a research agenda for restorative conferencing in three ways, which are considered in detail in three following subsections of this chapter. First, we consolidate information from our case study programs about conferencing priorities that suggest dominant practitioner concerns linked directly to core restorative principles and the theories they reflect. Second, having considered these principles and theories in the practical context of conferencing stages and phases in our qualitative study (Chapters 5–7), we are now prepared to catalogue relevant propositions for future research. We categorize these propositions into groups based on the three core principles, their relevance to the theoretical linkage between conference practice and short-term outcomes, and their implications for the linkage between these outcomes and long-term impacts. Third, we suggest general research designs needed to study the impact of restorative conferencing at various levels of analysis in future process and outcome studies.

Defining 'success' in conferencing: outcome priorities and the connection to theory

What is success in conferencing? We have argued that decision-making processes that are referred to as 'restorative' are necessarily multi-dimensional in their focus on outcomes. Yet theories employed by practitioners to guide decision-making necessarily presume that certain outcomes will receive priority. For example, if a program coordinator believes strongly that offenders must above all first make amends to their victims, they are likely to give primary emphasis to ensuring that offenders make restitution or other forms of reparation to victims and the community (e.g. by making sure that a workable agreement is developed, that follow-up and support are provided, etc.). They may in turn be less concerned with whether offenders feel shame or build new relationships, or with whether victims feel vindicated.

In the real world of conferencing, practitioners can and do pursue multiple outcomes, are likely at different times to employ more than one theory, and may have difficultly setting priorities. The data from our qualitative studies reveal that practitioners do rank relative conferencing priorities based on a belief that they will lead to better immediate and long-term outcomes for one or more conference participants. Though implicit, these beliefs are grounded in both commitment to one or more principles and one or more theories of intervention. To better understand the relative priority these practitioners might attach to theoretically based outcomes, we contacted by telephone a group of previously interviewed program coordinators (see description of these in Chapter 4) for exit interviews in the final month of our study (March, 2002) (see Appendix for Exit Interview Protocol).[2]

Respondents were asked to prioritize the immediate and long-term results they felt were most important to achieve in the conferencing process. As shown in Table 8.1, the first and second highest ranked average priorities for results to be achieved at the conclusion of the conference were victim satisfaction and victim safety, both clearly related to the stakeholder involvement principle and, possibly, to a commitment to victim–offender exchange and the theory of healing dialogue.[3] These were followed by 'the offender feels more empathy for the victim' (related to the victim–offender exchange and/or mutual transformation dimension) and getting a 'clear agreement about how the offender will "make amends," ' related to theories of earned redemption and making amends. Of less short-term importance to conferencing practitioners was the offender's expression of shame, perhaps because use of the word shame was a negative factor for some of these practitioners. Additionally, consistent with our survey findings in Chapter 3, the community-building outcomes were not high priorities for most of these programs.

Regarding long-term vs. immediate outcomes, Table 8.2 suggests that victim satisfaction was again ranked first as a long-term outcome, although a goal more associated with making amends (or possibly relationship-building) and earned redemption, 'offenders completing all reparative requirements,' was ranked second. Making sure that 'offenders did not recidivate' ranked third in priority among long-term objectives, and 'offenders make new positive connections and/or strengthen relationships' (the building relationships dimension of repairing harm) ranked fourth, suggesting a focus on social support theory that, in turn, might *lead* to decreased recidivism.[4] In contrast to more immediate objectives, long-term goals also reflected attention to community-building and to the changes in the roles and responsibilities of justice system agencies and programs themselves needed to build this capacity (see Table 8.2).

Table 8.1 Conferencing practitioners priority ranking for immediate conferencing goals

Conferencing practioners' immediate desired outcomes	Relative priority rank order
The victim says he or she is satisfied.	1
The victim feels safer, relieved, less apprehensive about the future.	2
The offender feels more empathy for the victim.	3
There is a clear agreement that specifies how the offender will 'make amends' to the victim and community.	4
The offender's relationships with other positive, supportive adults and/or peers has been strengthened, or new positive connections have been made in the conference.	5
Offender and victim gain a shared understanding of the problem, or find some common ground.	6
The victim gains an understanding and appreciation of the offender's situation.	7
The offender says he or she is satisfied.	8
Participants leave the conference with new skills for resolving conflict and responding effectively to crime and harm in the future.	9
Participants in the conference affirm community standards and clarify norms.	10
The victim feels vindicated (believes that others appreciate what he or she has been through and that he or she is not the one responsible for the crime).	11
The group has considered a variety of past harms to victim and/or offender as possible causes of the current problem (e.g. family problems, prior abuse, substance abuse, community deficits) and included ways to respond to these in its plan for follow-up.	12
The victim's relationships with supporters has been strengthened, or new positive connections have been made in the conference.	13
The offender feels safer, relieved, less apprehensive about the future.	14
Offender and community gain a shared understanding of the problem, or find some common ground.	15
The offender indicates through emotional expression that he or she has experienced shame as a result of participants' disapproval of his or her behavior.	16
Victim and community gain a shared understanding of the problem, or find some common ground.	17

Table 8.2 Conferencing practitioners priority ranking for long-term conferencing goals

Conferencing practioners' long-term desired outcomes	Relative priority rank order
Victims are satisfied and experience healing and reintegration.	1
Offenders complete all reparative requirements.	2
Offenders do not recidivate.	3
Offenders make new positive connections and/or strengthen positive relationships.	4
Schools, neighborhoods and other community groups and organizations become more capable of responding effectively to crime, harm, and conflict.	5
System professionals – police, judges, prosecutors, and others – begin to define their job in terms of supporting community involvement in the response to crime and harm.	6
Victims make new connections and/or strengthen supportive relationships.	7
Neighbors and community members become more capable of discussing common values and behavioral standards.	8
Community adults become more willing to provide support and guidance to young people in the neighborhood.	9
Conferencing volunteers become more skilled.	10
Your program grows and increases its referrals.	11
Community adults become more willing to exercise informal control and informal sanctioning with young people in the neighborhood.	12
Your program gets more discretion over decisions about the kinds of cases you can conference.	13
Your program gets more discretion over decisions about the contents of the agreement.	14

In summary, at the conclusion of the conference, practitioners in our case study programs want to be sure that above all they have satisfied and reassured victims as primary stakeholders in the decision-making process. They also seek offender empathy and repair in the form of making amends and relationship-building. For the long term, they want some of the same goals as top priorities along with reduced recidivism and a variety of community-building options to ensure that they and others will be able to live in safe communities. How other immediate and longer-term outcomes might fit together logically, and how they relate to conferencing practice, is the topic of the next section of this chapter. There we present propositions and theoretical statements about how immediate conferencing outcomes may relate to long-term healing and community peace and safety, and what practices according to each theory must receive priority.

Principles to practice and practice to outcomes: theory and data-based propositions for future research

The assumption of conferencing is that positive outcomes are generally more likely to be achieved by participation in the conferencing process than in court or other formal proceedings. Hence, a general proposition is that outcomes associated with the three core principles of restorative justice are more likely to be achieved in conferencing than from formal decision-making processes. Our study and report on principle-based evaluation has been focused throughout on three core principles that together define the normative theory of restorative justice. Three overarching propositions about conferencing can be derived directly from the three core principles of restorative justice. These general propositions link core dimensions and related outcomes associated with each principle to the conferencing process as follows:

- *Repairing harm.* Outcomes associated with making amends and building relationships are more likely to be achieved in conferencing than through court or other formal decision-making approaches.
- *Stakeholder involvement.* Outcomes associated with victim–offender exchange, collective transformation, and respectful disapproval are more likely to be achieved in conferencing than through court or other formal decision-making approaches.
- *Transforming community/government roles and relationships.* Outcomes associated with changes in professional roles and organizational mandates, collective efficacy, and norm affirmation are more likely to be achieved in conferencing than through court or other formal decision-making approaches.

Beyond these general statements of a hypothesized relationship between conferencing and these general outcomes, Chapter 2 discussed specific outcomes and dimensions associated with several intervention theories. We group these outcomes and dimensions here first under the heading of the relevant core principle. Then, within each principle category, we articulate and group relevant propositions under each theory of intervention.

Repairing harm

Two key dimensions of repairing harm, by their linkage to outcomes through three intervention theories, suggest testable propositions about how goals related to repairing harm can be accomplished. The first set of propositions under each theory listed below are statements about the long-term impacts expected to result from achieving immediate and intermediate outcomes associated with making amends and relationship-building. The second set of propositions under each theoretical category is more directly related to the conference tasks required to produce these theoretically important outcomes.

Theory 1: Earned redemption (Dimension: Making amends)
Based on the core assumptions of the need for reciprocity in earned redemption theory, we suggest the following propositions regarding the connection between the intermediate outcome of making amends and longer-term intermediate change in the behavior of the offender and the well-being of the victim.

- *Proposition 1.* Offenders who complete, or make credible attempts to complete their obligation to make amends to the satisfaction of victims and community members essentially 'earn their redemption' and are more likely to gain support and acceptance than those who do not and will therefore be less likely to reoffend.
- *Proposition 2.* Offenders who take on an active helping role in making amends are more likely to undergo cognitive and behavioral changes leading to a decrease in recidivism than those who complete reparative activities more as a routine requirement or as punishment.
- *Proposition 3.* Victims whose offenders acknowledge responsibility for the harm to them and make amends will feel vindicated and more likely experience well-being.

Propositions linking practice to the immediate conferencing outcome of amends include:

- *Proposition 1 (A).* When the purpose of the conference is clearly presented as repairing harm (vs. open dialogue or discussion of other issues), amends will be more likely to result.
- *Proposition 2 (B).* Offenders who accept responsibility for the crime in the conference will be more likely to make amends and their subsequent behavior will be more likely to be positively affected by this act than those who do not.
- *Proposition 3 (C).* When offenders, victims, and other participants have direct input and take ownership of the agreement, rather than the juvenile justice system representatives, amends are more likely.

Theory 2: Social Support (Dimension: Relationship-building)
Propositions relevant to the linkage between relationship-building as a conferencing outcome and victim and offender reintegration are concerned with the type, duration, and diversity of relationships that emerge from the conferencing experience. These can be stated as follows.

- *Proposition 1.* Offenders in ongoing relationships of informal support who have access to roles that create a legitimate identity and help the offender build new relationships that commit them to conforming behavior will be less likely to reoffend.
- *Proposition 2.* Victims in ongoing relationships of informal support will be more likely to move forward with a healing process than those who do not have access to such relationships.
- *Proposition 3.* Multiple relationships formed between offenders and victims, and between offenders, victims, and community members – as well as family and intimates – will make reoffending less likely and victim movement toward well-being more likely.

Though relationship-building generally occurs organically, it seems more likely to occur in the conference if the facilitator and participants envision it as a primary goal and are open to allowing/encouraging discussion that facilitates such connections. Propositions linking practice to the immediate outcome of relationship building include:

- *Proposition 1.* The more participants in the conference, the greater the likelihood that social support will emerge and relationship-building will occur.
- *Proposition 2.* The greater the extent to which participants who are either important in the lives or the offender, or bring special resources to the agenda, the greater the likelihood that social support will emerge and relationship-building will occur.
- *Proposition 3.* When facilitators restate and build upon supportive comments about the offender or victim, especially in the agreement phase, the greater the likelihood that social support will emerge and relationship-building will occur.
- *Proposition 4.* When participants are assigned a specific role to work with the offender and others in carrying out and monitoring the reparative agreement, relationship-building and social support is more likely.

Stakeholder involvement

Three key dimensions associated with the principle of stakeholder involvement, and the three theories with which they are associated, suggest testable propositions about how goals related to this principle can be accomplished. The first set of propositions under each theory listed below are statements about the long-term impacts expected to result from achieving immediate and intermediate outcomes associated with the dimensions of stakeholder satisfaction, respectful disapproval, and mutual transformation, or in some cases about the nature or quality of the action taken to achieve these. The second set of propositions under each theoretical category is more directly related to the conference tasks required to produce these theoretically important outcomes.

Theory 1: Healing dialogue (Dimension 1: Victim/offender exchange)
Based on the healing dialogue theory of intervention, we suggest the following three propositions about the connection between immediate and intermediate conferencing outcomes related to victim and offender well-being:

- *Proposition 1.* When victims report less fear of the offender and of revictimization at the conclusion of a conference, healing and well-being are more likely to be achieved.
- *Proposition 2.* When victims and offenders gain more understanding of the situation of the other, intermediate and long-term outcomes regarding healing and well-being are more likely to be achieved. When offenders reduce apprehensions and are relieved at having met with victim and others, intermediate and long-term adjustment will be more likely to be achieved. When victims feel vindicated by the dialogue of the conferencing process, intermediate and long-term outcomes regarding healing and well-being are more likely to be achieved.
- Proposition 3. When offenders and victims feel they have worked with others to develop a plan for meeting needs and obligations in the aftermath of the crime, intermediate and long-term outcomes regarding healing and well-being are more likely to be achieved.

Propositions linking practice to the immediate conferencing outcome of stakeholder satisfaction include:

- *Proposition 1 (A).* When facilitators maximize the time given to the victim and offender story and to the dialogue between them, relative to the time spent on the agreement, the level of satisfaction will be higher; when facilitators maximize their own silence and minimize interference with the discussion between victim and offender, the level of satisfaction will be higher; when facilitators do not rush to get to the agreement, the level of satisfaction will be higher.

Theory 2: Reintegrative shaming (Dimension: Respectful disapproval)
Given the need in reintegrative shaming theory for respectful disapproval coupled with support as an immediate outcome of the conference, and the caution against stigmatizing shame, it is possible to theoretically connect these immediate conferencing outcomes to intermediate and long-term offender reintegration and reductions in reoffending. Based on this theory of intervention, we therefore suggest the following propositions about the

connection between immediate and intermediate conferencing outcomes related to shame/respectful disapproval:

- *Proposition 1.* When the offender is concerned that loss of status and affection will result from continuation of such behavior, reoffending will be less likely.
- *Proposition 2.* When the offender experiences empathetic engagement and support and a collective resolve to stop the harmful behavior, reoffending will be less likely.

Propositions linking practice to the immediate conferencing outcome of respectful disapproval and victim affirmation include:

- *Proposition 1(A).* Respectful disapproval is more likely to occur when the offender has understood the harm caused and can articulate and express his feelings about this.
- *Proposition 1(B).* Respectful disapproval is more likely to occur when the victim's voice is heard, when ample time for discussion of harm is allowed that is not diminished by expressions of support for the offender.
- *Proposition 1(C).* Respectful disapproval is more likely to occur when those whose opinions matter to the offender are present in the conference and respectfully express their disapproval.
- *Proposition 1(D).* Victims in conferences based on reintegrative shaming will gain the most benefit when they hear the expression of disapproval from others as a confirmation of their vindication and sense of community support, when they are allowed to tell their story and participate actively in all phases of the process, and when the offender expresses remorse for the harm to the victim. (Conversely, victims may be harmed when support expressed for the offender diminishes the harm, and when concern with the offender's behavior overshadows concern with the victim's needs.)

Theory 3: Common ground (Dimension: Collective transformation)
Conferences concerned with achieving mutual or collective transformation are based on the assumption that overall stakeholder healing is dependent in part on developing joint understandings that may transform conflict and allow for productive resolution. Based on the theory of common ground, we therefore suggest the following three propositions about the connection between immediate and intermediate conferencing outcomes relating this transformation to the long-term behavior and well-being of stakeholders:

- *Proposition 1.* Offenders who have the experience of gaining a shared understanding of the harm they have caused and of the views of others will become more empathetic and therefore more likely to avoid confrontations and encounters that lead to crime in the future.

- *Proposition 2.* Offenders who have opportunities to give active input into the agreement are more likely to honor these agreements and are more likely to avoid confrontations and encounters that lead to crime in the future.
- *Proposition 3.* Offenders who have opportunities for reinforcement of the experience of finding common ground and for practising skills in conflict resolution/transformation will be more likely to avoid confrontations and encounters that lead to crime in the future.
- *Proposition 4.* Offenders who have support from conference participants which reinforces commitment to agreements will be more likely to avoid confrontations and encounters that lead to crime in the future.
- *Proposition 5.* Community groups who practise consensus decision-making in the form of shared leadership in pursuit of common ground will become more effective in resolving conflict and addressing harm and conflict.

Propositions linking practice to the immediate conferencing outcome of mutual transformation include:

- *Proposition 1(A).* The objective of mutual transformation is more likely to be achieved in the conference when the facilitator and others build upon small points of common understanding after careful listening to victim and offender stories and the necessary exchange and clarification regarding these stories, and are encouraged to reframe and reinforce areas of common understanding.
- *Proposition 2(B).* The objective of mutual transformation is more likely to be achieved in the conference when the facilitator does not move toward agreement until there are signs from the group of some shared ownership of the conflict and willingness to participate in its resolution and follow-up activities.

Community/government role transformation

There are four key dimensions associated with the principle of community/government role transformation that, by their linkage to outcomes related to *systemic change* and *community-building*, suggest testable propositions about how these outcomes can be accomplished. The first set of propositions listed below are statements about the long-term systemic change expected to result from achieving immediate and intermediate outcomes associated with changing the role of justice professionals. Similarly, propositions related to the theories associated with dimensions of norm affirmation, community ownership, and skill-building as community-building objectives provide statements about the long-term impacts expected to result from these immediate and intermediate outcomes.

1. Systemic change

Theory: Street-level bureaucracy (Dimension: Transforming professional roles)
Missions and visions not supported by organizational realignment of incentives for system professionals are likely to fail at the 'street level' of implementation. Ultimately, system and organizational outcomes drive practice because value statements, such as those favoring the use of restorative justice decision-making, have little practical value when incentives for performance are not consistent with these values.

- *Proposition 1.* Conferencing programs are more likely to win professional support and receive greater numbers and diversity of cases when system professionals are in roles that provide incentives (and minimize disincentives) for referring cases to conferencing.
- *Proposition 2.* Conferencing programs are more likely to win ongoing professional support and receive greater numbers and diversity of cases when one or more system professionals act as a champion for the program.
- *Proposition 3.* Conferencing programs are more likely to win ongoing professional support and receive greater numbers and diversity of cases when professionals gain trust through direct participation in the conferencing process.
- *Proposition 4.* Conferencing programs are more likely to win ongoing professional support and receive greater numbers and diversity of cases when only one or a minimum number of decision-making agencies have discretion over referrals.
- *Proposition 5.* Conferencing programs are more likely to win ongoing professional support and receive greater numbers and diversity of cases when the program has clout with one or more community groups who are able to influence system decision-makers.

2. Community-building

Theory 1: Social disorganization/social capital (Dimension: Norm affirmation/values clarification)
The concern with norm affirmation is based on the premise that communities in which citizens have no forum for dialogue about norms and values will often be unaware of differences in standards of conduct. They will also be unaware of common beliefs and shared norms that could

form the basis for collective action, and therefore feel incapable of setting or reinforcing tolerance limits on behavior, become fearful of doing so, and perhaps are inclined to retreat into isolation from their neighbors. Where conferences serve as a forum for clarification of shared and conflicting values and allow for norm affirmation about the harmful impacts of offense behaviors (and perhaps of prior harms), they address an important ingredient in building a 'learning community' (Senge, 1990) that can begin to develop common standards of conduct.

Based on these assumptions, we can state the following propositions with regard to the potential of conferencing to build community by encouraging norm affirmation:

- *Proposition 1.* Conferencing programs are more likely to promote norm affirmation/values clarification when they invite discussion of values and encourage respectful debate about tolerance limits.
- *Proposition 2.* Conferencing programs are more likely to become a forum for norm affirmation/values clarification when this is an accepted part of their vision and mission.
- *Proposition 3.* Conferencing programs are more likely to become a forum for norm affirmation/values clarification when they are neighborhood based and make maximum use of neighborhood volunteers in the conferencing process.

Theory 2: Stolen conflict/civic engagement (Dimension: Collective ownership)

According to the theory of *stolen conflict*, citizens and community groups who no longer have responsibility for exercising informal social control and social support begin to lose their capacities for carrying out these tasks (Christie, 1977; Moore, 1994). This creates a need to redevelop these skills by maximizing citizen involvement in decision-making, in this instance using conferencing as the primary vehicle for this involvement.

The theory of civic engagement (Uggen et al., 2003; Bazemore and Stinchcomb, 2004), however, suggests that civic participation builds a sense of ownership which in turn nurtures a sense of personal responsibility. Propositions related to the developing of collective ownership in the context of restorative conferencing are as follows:

- *Proposition 1.* Conferencing programs that encourage shared leadership of the decision-making process by assigning responsibilities to participants will be more likely to promote collective ownership.
- *Proposition 2.* Juvenile justice and conferencing professionals who invite community participation at all levels will be more likely to promote a sense of ownership for the response to problems of youth crime.

343

- *Proposition 3.* Offenders, victims, and community members given direct input into conference agreements and responsibility for follow-up will build closer civic connections to their communities.

Theory 3: Collective efficacy (Dimension: Skill building)
Based on the assumptions that collective efficacy in the response to crime requires that citizens are willing and able to exercise informal sanctioning and social control, we can state the following propositions about the ability of conferencing programs to build efficacy:

- *Proposition 1.* Conferencing programs are more likely to strengthen collective efficacy when they focus more on community-building than program-building and are encouraged to support skill-building efforts in other neighborhood entities.
- *Proposition 2.* Conferencing programs are more likely to build collective efficacy when they promote collective ownership of crime problems confronted by conference participants.
- *Proposition 3.* Conferencing programs are more likely to build collective efficacy when they target smaller community entities with clear boundaries.
- *Proposition 4.* Conferencing programs are more likely to build collective efficacy when they build on existing institutions and traditions of community support and informal control rather than introducing completely new techniques and strategies.

Research design and comparative protocols

Preferred designs for testing the above propositions will maximize internal validity and facilitate generalizability. For testing causal proposi-tions, experimental or at least quasi-experimental designs are of course preferable when feasible. While we take these assumptions as a given, the discussion below is a general one focused on the types of comparisons that are most urgently needed at present, knowing that design and statistical procedures for ensuring internal validity will need to be adapted to the research context.

Hayes and Daly (2003) suggest that evaluation studies of conferencing are of two basic types: (1) comparative studies that contrast conferencing with courts or other decision-making process; and (2) those focused on procedural, practice, and impact variation within conferencing programs (e.g. variation across conferencing encounters, facilitators, number of participants, etc.). They view both as important but argue that the former approaches have sometimes missed important theoretical variation within conferencing programs. We agree, but suggest that the key to capturing this variation is essential attention to intervention integrity and strength based on clear and hopefully theoretically derived standards. Only then can we know *what theory* of intervention is actually being operationalized and tested regardless of whether the study is comparative or internally focused.

In general, we wish to suggest that research relevant to conferencing in the context of normative theory and principles is needed at the micro-, middle-range and macro-levels. In the remainder of this section, we discuss four conferencing research contexts that provide an opportunity for testing some of the propositions outlined in the previous section. The micro-level agenda is primarily concerned with individual conferences as suggested by Hayes and Daly (2002), as well as with program variation in individual conferencing encounters over time, and comparisons on specified practice variations with other conferencing programs. At the mid-range level, we suggest that it is important to examine the impact of conferencing as a component of a holistic restorative approach or part of a range of restorative interventions rather than as a single stand-alone program.

At the macro-level, more broadly conceived studies are needed which examine the influence of restorative conferencing programs as a key decision-making component within a system and community committed to a restorative justice vision in a range of policies and programs. A second macro-level study focused on the community-building agenda of restorative conferencing would contrast clearly bounded and easily identifiable community entities actively making use of restorative conferencing with similar entities not doing so (e.g. defined communities such as schools or institutions, or clearly bounded neighborhoods or cities).

The micro-level: the impact of programs and alternative practices

The value of micro-level, internally focused research designs can be best realized when practitioners are willing to test theoretical premises underlying their commitment to one or more practice preferences. The practical value for the program of such tests is broadened when the preference and premise are also related to a theory of intervention. For example, at the most basic practice level, comparing the impact of having the victim speak first in programs informed by the healing dialogue theory with having the offender speak first as advocated by reintegrative shaming proponents on various outcomes could provide empirical support for one preference or another.

The qualitative data presented in this book, and the propositions outlined in the section above, provide the basis for numerous practice-level empirical tests of conferencing strategies that are often based on deeply felt, though not empirically validated, commitments to specific approaches. With sufficient referrals, programs could randomly select cases that would receive a different form of intervention than that used in their typical program protocol. A facilitator might, for example, alter the approach to developing agreements in the conferencing process. Programs could also track the extent to which young offenders and victims who make connections with other conference participants in fact develop long-term relationships, monitor completion rates of restitution obligations for offenders in conferences with crime victims present vs. those without, or monitor young people who came to conferencing as part of an ongoing conflict to assess the extent to which they continue to utilize skills of finding common ground learned in the conferencing process. Programs could also follow-up with victims with high and low levels of initial satisfaction with the dialogue and exchange with the offender to determine the relationship of these immediate outcomes to long term well-being and satisfaction of those expressing reduced fear or new insights as a result of the conferencing experience.

For comparisons *between* programs, the most important prerequisite is to develop ways of documenting consistent implementation of alternative theories of intervention, e.g. reintegrative shaming vs. the theory of common ground. Programs informed by very different theories of intervention and accompanying protocols for stakeholder involvement could also be compared on achievement of intermediate and long-term outcomes. Programs that strategically recruit participants who bring either affective or instrumental resources to the conference, for example, could be compared on various outcomes with those that leave these decisions strictly to the preferences of victim and offender. Assuming sufficient variation between facilitators and use of different protocols, any and all such comparisons could be also made within the same program.

Restorative justice conferencing outcomes in a multi-modal model

As noted previously, conferencing is only one comprehensive component of a holistic restorative justice approach. Though the decision-making component is often perceived to be the equivalent of restorative justice, isolating it for comparison with comprehensive intervention programs does a disservice to restorative conferencing. This is because evaluations of treatment programs, for example, are often focused on multi-modal, more long-term and comprehensive interventions. Indeed, one of the criteria for being considered an effective treatment program is that the program not limit its focus to one form of intervention, i.e. represent a multi-modal approach (Andrews and Bonta, 1994).

While we suggested in Chapter 2 that conferencing is most appropriately compared with other decision-making approaches such as court, this kind of research is unsatisfying in part because it has already been empirically demonstrated that conferencing works better than court (e.g.

Braithwaite, 1999; Umbreit, 2001). Moreover, as this study and the propositions outlined in the previous section suggest, conferencing is believed (and has to some degree been demonstrated) to have a wide range of long-term impacts on offenders, victims, and communities that would never be expected for court. We suggest therefore that the best solution is to identify and/or develop multi-modal restorative interventions that can be meaningfully contrasted with other comprehensive interventions including multi-modal treatment programs, comprehensive victim service approaches, or other interventions emphasizing offender surveillance, sanctioning, or community-building.

While multi-modal restorative approaches exist, they remain rare. However, one could conceivably design an intervention for victims, for example, that featured a range of experiences and supports grounded in restorative principles (Achilles and Zehr, 2001). For offenders, various combinations of conferencing with restorative forms of community service (Bazemore and Maloney, 1994), restitution, victim awareness education, and more relationship-focused reintegrative/rehabilitative approaches would provide a good basis for comparison with one or more multi-modal treatment programs (Bazemore, 1999b; Bazemore and O'Brian, 2002). Indeed, the often comprehensive, ongoing work of circles with offenders and their families (Pranis, 2001; Boyes-Watson, 2004) could be compared in terms of various outcomes with comprehensive treatment programs. In this case, the primary variable of theoretical interest is the role of community-based natural helpers in offender transformation. Finally, restorative forms of community-building featuring a focus on mobilizing informal social control and support could be compared with other forms of prevention and capacity building. Another feature of this strategy would involve the fairly straightforward assessment of the 'added value' of the conferencing experience to the accomplishment of goals associated with other components of the restorative model. For example, what is the added contribution of conferencing to the completion of restitution contracts over and above the completion rate of a restitution program? To what extent is victim awareness and sensitivity increased by the conference over and above the level achieved from a victim impact panel? What is the impact, if any, on offender success in a drug and alcohol treatment program when the recommendation is made by a conference rather than by a court or therapeutic professional?

The impact of restorative justice conferencing in restorative systems and communities

As suggested in our profile of Washington County, Minnesota in Chapter 7, restorative conferencing appears to be more likely to thrive in systems and agencies that share the restorative vision and provide support. The

agenda for comparative research here is straightforward in conceptualization, though complex in operationalization. The unit of analysis would
be a juvenile justice system, with a possible fallback approach focused on
a single agency. The community as a whole would necessarily be an
important sub-unit of this study.

For the system comparison, the goal would be to contrast a jurisdiction
in which some combination of prosecution, police, courts, and corrections
agencies shared a common restorative justice mission that included
multiple conferencing program options with a comparison jurisdiction on
a variety of shared outcomes. The latter might be a community with one
or more conferencing programs without such commitment, and/or a
similar jurisdiction with no conferencing programs. Such a contrast would
offer an opportunity for in-depth process evaluation and ethnographic
study to determine how and to what extent conferencing or alternative
decision-making is utilized. The research design could also consider a
number of traditionally measured impacts such as the rate of diversion,
recidivism, and court workload, as well as a variety of impacts important
in restorative research (yet relevant to mainstream systems) such as victim
satisfaction, community involvement and satisfaction, and community-
building efforts.

Again, the added-value comparison mentioned previously would also
be relevant at the system level. Where conferencing was the primary
decision-making process, cases going into other intervention programs
could be compared on success rates as well as satisfaction with the entire
process and the system. At the agency level, this comparison in two or
more communities in which a corrections or police agency, for example,
is committed to restorative policies and practices would allow for a more
rigorous contrast with greater potential for strong internal validity due to
a focus on inter-agency vs. system-wide outcomes.

Assessing community-building and conferencing in micro-environments

The discussion of the community-building possibilities of conferencing
presented in Chapter 7 will be for some both encouraging and provocative
in its implications for restorative justice. Yet, as noted, much of this
important impact appears to be serendipitous and random, with little
systematic documentation and virtually no rigorous measurement of
outcomes. We suggest, however, that a more strategic and systematic effort
will make assessment of impact possible, and eventually quite rigorous.

Building upon the last set of propositions in the previous section, we
suggest that one of the most fruitful avenues for future research is to
conduct systematic comparisons of the impact of conferencing on collective efficacy and norm affirmation, or more generally, informal social
control and support in the response to youth crime. Methodologically, the

key to validity and overall rigorousness in such research is dependent upon the clarity of boundaries in micro-communities. Such bounded micro-communities include the units of analysis, or targets, for community-building discussed in Chapter 7: schools, residential settings, housing projects, and neighborhood blocks, to name a few.

School and residential facilities, though they may be classified as 'total institutions,' are also communities of a sort. As such they are especially useful units for intensive observation and tracking of the development and spread of restorative responses to incidents of harm, as well as use of restorative practices by adults and young people as tools for promoting informal social control and social support. Using comparison schools and facilities matched to the greatest extent possible to resident, student, and staff populations should allow for valid contrasts and for trend measurement of a variety of outcomes including crimes, incidents of violence, student/student and student/teacher conflict, and disciplinary actions – including school suspensions and expulsions, as well as visits to the principal's office.

Though not as tightly controlled as the total communities of schools and residential settings, neighborhoods and housing projects provide, on the other hand, a more naturalistic setting for observing the impact of one or more conferencing programs on the social capital of informal control and support in a clearly demarcated space. Multiple city blocks and housing projects with and without access to conferencing programs would increase the generalizability of the findings and could be pursued as a strategy following a more intensive look at one community entity and a comparison entity in depth using a design that would include ethnographic observation. In the multiple unit design we could also hope to increase validity using trend data to gauge changes in crime and other incidents of harm over time.

While research using any and all of the above designs and comparative approaches is greatly needed at this time, we submit that the community-level comparisons are most salient for a number of reasons. Most importantly, such comparisons allow for an examination of restorative conferencing in its most contextualized and least artificial application. It is at this level that conferencing will succeed or fail in accomplishing what may be its most important goal, community-building. It is also at this level that restorative decision-making holds the most promise for accomplishing other principle-based goals.

Epilogue

There is nothing so practical as a good utopia. (Lode Walgrave)

You can observe a whole lot just by watching. (Yogi Berra)

In training sessions on restorative justice, a colleague of ours (Dennis Maloney) sometimes begins by asking the group to think of terms that come to mind when they hear the word 'justice.' Time and again, he says trainees come up with the same list: fairness, equality, peace, harmony, democratic, community. Then he asks the group what they think of when they hear that someone was 'brought to justice.' Invariably, a different and more limited set of terms is listed: 'punishment, retribution, incarceration.'

There is, in the US at least, an apparently unbridgeable chasm between our everyday sense of what 'justice' and 'criminal justice' is about. Increasingly, this disconnect is troubling to many citizens, and it of course underlies some of the most challenging issues facing criminal and juvenile justice systems today, most notably chronic levels of overrepresentation of persons of color in prisons and jails (Mauer, 2004).

Restorative justice advocates clearly seek what Mark Moore in another context has called a 'more ambitious form of justice.' This is a justice that is bigger than punishment and indeed bigger than the criminal justice system itself. It is a justice that would merge the concerns with peace, fairness, safety, democracy, and community harmony with those of justice systems and justice professionals. Yet this is not a justice that is 'ambitious' in the sense of assigning new and expanded responsibilities to professionals and criminal justice or juvenile justice agencies. Those who, as Yogi Berra might suggest, have 'watched' the evolution of juvenile justice in particular in the past three decades cannot not help but have 'observed' that the system has taken on ever increasing responsibilities for problems once handled by the community in its various manifestations. And it is this professionalization and expansionism in justice systems that have gradually removed social control and social support functions from their communities of origin. We have suggested in several chapters of this book that this transfer of authority and the accompanying decline in skill sets that should be viewed as a vital part of the social capital of communities is at the heart of the frustration many feel today with their justice systems. The frustration may also be the catalyst behind the willingness of many citizens to experiment with restorative decision-making – especially as a response to youth crime.

In contrast to this expansionist response, restorative justice, by contrast, is ambitious in the 'practically utopian' sense by virtue of its commitment to the difficult task of reengaging citizens and community groups in the justice process. The restorative conferencing movement has direct implications for supporting this task in part because of its very focus on decision-making. As strongly demonstrated by the empirical work on procedural justice, as well as findings from research on restorative processes, the decision-making process itself is fundamental to citizens' sense of justice, and thereby to their confidence in justice processes. But restorative decision-making also promises to add a distinctive new dimension to the quest for fairness and uniformity of procedural justice. This dimension is community participation and its implications for a revival of a sense of democratization of sanctioning and social control. This more democratized, deliberative decision-making seeks to mobilize what John Braithwaite (2001a) has called the 'collective resolve' to deal with what can no longer be viewed simply as individual problems of offenders or victims. Perhaps more than any other factor, it holds promise for opening the door for a merger of ideas of peace, harmony, and community with notions of justice.

Indeed, the collective nature of conferencing has been an underlying theme throughout this report that we can now underscore as perhaps the most important distinguishing characteristic of restorative processes. Despite the slower progress of conferencing programs toward the community-building goal documented in this research, the good news from this perspective is that the convergence and hybridization of conferencing approaches appears to be in large measure primarily about expanding the number and diversity of participants included in conferencing encounters. In this sense, this trend may indicate a realization of the need to engage broader segments of community in conferencing programs. This convergence, along with a healthy tension between theories that provide the research agenda needed to refine what has become rather complex practice, may well be the key to the future success of the conferencing movement.

Through the 'half-empty' lens we have concluded in various parts of this text that in much of restorative conferencing there is less than meets the eye. Yet where conferencing processes seem trivialized or lackluster in their performance, we suggest that this is due in part to inappropriate use of these approaches for minor offenses that do not require such an intensive mobilization of human resources. In addition, conferencing in the US is, relative to much of the world, underutilized in more serious and complex cases where it is most needed. Indeed, in the former minor cases, other less intensive, albeit restorative, resolutions could be applied. Moreover, we suggest that use of such lower-level responses could become more likely if restorative decision-making is viewed as something other than a process that can only be accessed by referral from a juvenile or criminal justice agency to a restorative program. In this case, restorative decision-making would become more a part of the culture of institutions and communities.

For now, we can also be cautiously optimistic in noting that restorative conferencing may represent much *more* than meets the eye. This optimistic account seems especially justified when the collective implications of the vision and practice are fully taken into account. If we may imagine the impact of 500 conferences per year, rather than 50, in some of the small communities examined in this study, and consider the fact that each conference has the potential to impact not only an offender, but also their families, victims and their families, and a variety of other community participants, more optimism seems justified. The principle-based agenda for research that takes seriously what is claimed by the restorative vision can ensure that interventions called 'restorative' are true to the collective emphasis of the restorative normative theory. In doing so, this agenda may ensure that practitioners are indeed following the path toward the practical utopia envisioned.

Notes

1 Howard Zehr (2000) has recently noted that his original distinction between retributive justice and restorative justice, though heuristically useful, exaggerates differences and ignores commonalities between retributive and restorative paradigms. What he calls the 'currency' of intervention, punishment on the one hand, and repair on the other, constitutes the primary distinction (Zehr, 1990). Similarly, in much discourse among practitioners, the idea of restorativeness appears at times to be presented as the opposite of all things not humanitarian or progressive values – e.g. not being disrespectful, not being rigid or dictatorial, not acting in a punitive way with offenders (as in the now common phrase, 'that wasn't a very restorative way of dealing with him/her').

2 In these telephone interviews we asked respondents to rank 10 of a set of 17 possible immediate conferencing outcomes, and 10 of a set of 15 possible long-term outcomes, based on a list we sent them several days prior to the interview. While such priorities had been discussed earlier in other forums including focus groups and interviews, we had until that time not 'forced' practitioners to choose between priorities. As will be clear from our discussion of various outcomes associated with intervention theories outlined in Chapter 2, these priorities also implicitly reflect an emphasis on specific dimensions tied to specific restorative principles, as well as a commitment to a theory of intervention.

3 Of the top ranked items for short-term or immediate outcomes, the first priority to victim satisfaction and reduced fear is not necessarily surprising, though the strength of support for this goal was stronger than expected. While this does not mean these goals are prioritized in practice, they have been adopted or ingrained in practitioners through restorative justice training or literature that emphasizes the need for more attention to victim needs and literature critical of conferencing for this reason. Although there may be some degree of political correctness in these victim-focused goals as stated priorities, these advanced practitioners seem to recognize the central importance of crime victims to the viability of the process itself vis-à-vis other objectives. Increased empathy and commitment to the agreement as a plan for increasing the likelihood of amends are also not surprising, and indeed a lower rank for the latter might have suggested that the concern with healing dialogue had overshadowed the basic focus on ensuring that harm was repaired.

4 Relationship-building has become a positive goal that cuts across two or more theoretical perspectives on conferencing, e.g. social support, and reintegrative shaming. Indeed, more than one practitioner said something like 'this is what it's all about,' or 'this is what keeps them out of trouble,' or 'this is why we want to include community members in the conference.'

Appendix

Follow-up questionnaire: case study programs

I. Case flow update

Past year: 1–2001 to 1–2002

Please provide actual percentage, or best estimate, for each question below for the past one-month period.

In the past year:

1. How many cases on average have you conferenced *per month?* _____
   (Check whether: Estimate _____ or _____ Exact)?

2. Percentage of all cases during the 12-month period that involved first offenders?
   (Check whether: Estimate _____ or _____ Exact)?

3. Percentage of all cases that were *felonies* during the 12-month period?
   (Check whether: Estimate _____ or _____ Exact)?

4. Percentage of all cases referred as diversion cases during the 12-month period?
   (Check whether: Estimate _____ or _____ Exact)?

5. Percentage of all cases referred post-adjudication during the 12-month period?
   (Check whether: Estimate _____ or _____ Exact)?

6. Percentage of all conferences where the crime victim(s) was present during the 12-month period?
   (Check whether: Estimate _____ or _____ Exact)?

7. Percentage of all conferences where *surrogate* victim was present during the 12-month period?
   (Check whether: Estimate _____ or _____ Exact)?

II. Issues addressed in conferences

For cases conferenced in the past 12 months

Which of the following issues is usually addressed *in the conference* vs. by the court or other criminal justice agency?

1. Restitution amount (*check one*):
   ____ Conference; ____ Court; ____ Other agency (*specify* ____)
2. Restitution schedule (*check one*):
   ____ Conference; ____ Court; ____ Other agency (*specify* ____)
3. Community service hours (*check one*):
   ____ Conference; ____ Court; ____ Other agency (*specify* ____)
4. Community service type (*check one*):
   ____ Conference; ____ Court; ____ Other agency (*specify* ____)
5. Community service schedule (*check one*):
   ____ Conference; ____ Court; ____ Other agency (*specify* ____)

III. Follow-up responsibilities

Who does follow-up?

You or your program staff ____ Police ____ Probation ____ Other

Volunteers?

Police?

Probation?

What does follow-up look like?

Number of contacts: ____

For what purpose?

IV. Conference outcome priorities

The following list includes a wide range of outcomes that may or may not result from the conferencing process in some situations. Think of these outcomes as things you would most like to say are true *at the conclusion of the conference* – **independent of whether this outcome is a common occurrence.** Then, please **rank** the *relative importance* of the following conferencing outcomes, according to your own preferences for your program.

The list may reflect different priorities, but there are no right or wrong, correct or politically correct, rankings. Base rankings **on your own preferences for your program**.

While you may value and attach high priority to achieving most or all of these outcomes, we ask you to make *a forced rank* of each compared to the priority given to other outcomes. Rank your top ten in descending order, where 1 is your *most important* priority – if you had to choose – and 10 is the *least important*. (You can include two ties.) For example, if item 3 below is your most essential outcome, you would score it a 1; if 6 is your tenth most essential give it a 10. If items 7, 6, 10, 8, 9, 11 and 13 are your seven least essential outcomes, don't rank them. Or you may rank two of these if you choose to rank any two items the same.

Outcomes at the conclusion of the conference

1. There is a clear agreement that specifies how the offender will 'make amends' to the victim and community.
    [Rank relative to all other items in this section = ____]

2. The group has considered a variety of *past harms* to victim and/or offender as possible causes of the current problem (e.g. family problems, prior abuse, substance abuse, community deficits) and included ways to respond to these in its plan for follow-up.
    [Rank relative to all other items in this section = ____]

3. The offender's relationships with other positive, supportive adults and/or peers has been strengthened, or new positive connections have been made in the conference.
    [Rank relative to all other items in this section = ____]

4. The victim's relationships with supporters have been strengthened, or new positive connections have been made in the conference.
    [Rank relative to all other items in this section = ____]

5. The victim says s/he is satisfied.
    [Rank relative to all other items in this section = ____]

6. The offender says s/he is satisfied.
    [Rank relative to all other items in this section = ____]

7. The victim feels safer, relieved, less apprehensive about the future.
    [Rank relative to all other items in this section = ____]

8. The offender feels safer, relieved, less apprehensive about the future.
    [Rank relative to all other items in this section = ____]

9. The offender feels more empathy for the victim.
    [Rank relative to all other items in this section = ____]

10. The victim gains an understanding and appreciation of the offender's situation.
[Rank relative to all other items in this section =____]

11. The victim feels vindicated (believes that others appreciate what s/he has been through *and* that she/he is not the one responsible for the crime).
[Rank relative to all other items in this section =____]

12. Offender and victim gain a shared understanding of the problem, or find some common ground.
[Rank relative to all other items in this section =____]

13. Victim and community gain a shared understanding of the problem, or find some common ground.
[Rank relative to all other items in this section =____]

14. Offender and community gain a shared understanding of the problem, or find some common ground.
[Rank relative to all other items in this section =____]

15. The offender indicates through emotional expression that he/she has experienced shame as a result of participants' disapproval of his/her behavior.
[Rank relative to all other items in this section =____]

16. Participants in the conference affirm community standards and clarify norms.
[Rank relative to all other items in this section =____]

17. Participants leave the conference with new skills for resolving conflict and responding effectively to crime and harm in the future.
[Rank relative to all other items in this section =____]

V. Long-term conference program goals

Rank the following using the same procedures and assumptions as above comparing each item only to others in this section with your personal preferences for your program in mind. Rank only 10, excluding two ties.

1. Offenders complete all reparative requirements.
[Rank relative to all other items in this section =____]

2. Victims are satisfied and experience healing and reintegration.
[Rank relative to all other items in this section =____]

3. Offenders do not recidivate.
[Rank relative to all other items in this section =____]

4. Offenders make new positive connections and/or strengthen positive relationships.
   [Rank relative to all other items in this section = ____]

5. Victims make new connections and/or strengthen supportive relationships.
   [Rank relative to all other items in this section = ____]

6. Conferencing volunteers become more skilled.
   [Rank relative to all other items in this section = ____]

7. Schools, neighborhoods and other community groups and organizations become more capable of responding effectively to crime, harm, and conflict.
   [Rank relative to all other items in this section = ____]

8. Citizens become more capable of responding effectively to youth crime.
   [Rank relative to all other items in this section = ____]

9. Neighbors and community members become more capable of discussing common values and behavioral standards.
   [Rank relative to all other items in this section = ____]

10. System professionals – police, judges, prosecutors and others – begin to define their job in terms of supporting community involvement in the response to crime and harm.
    [Rank relative to all other items in this section = ____]

11. Your program grows and increases its referrals.
    [Rank relative to all other items in this section = ____]

12. Your program gets more discretion over decisions about the contents of the agreement.
    [Rank relative to all other items in this section = ____]

13. Your program gets more discretion over decisions about the kinds of cases you can conference.
    [Rank relative to all other items in this section = ____]

14. Community adults become more willing to exercise informal control and informal sanctioning with young people in the neighborhood.
    [Rank relative to all other items in this section = ____]

15. Community adults become more willing to provide support and guidance to young people in the neighborhood.
    [Rank relative to all other items in this section = ____]

References

Abel, R. L. (1982) 'Introduction,' in R. Abel (ed.), *The Politics of Informal Justice: Comparative Studies*, Vol. 2: Studies on Law and Social Control. New York: Academic Press.

Achilles, M. and Zehr, H. (2001) 'Restorative Justice for Crime Victims: The Promise, the Challenge,' in G. Bazemore and M. Schiff (eds), *Restorative Community Justice: Repairing Harm and Transforming Communities*. Cincinnati, OH: Anderson Publishing.

Ahmed, E., Harris, N., Braithwaite, J., and Braithwaite, V. (2001) *Shame Management through Reintegration*. Cambridge: Cambridge University Press.

Alreck, P. and Settle, R. (1995) *The Survey Research Handbook*, 2nd edn. Wisconsin: Irwin, McGraw-Hill. *American Sociological Review*, 61(1): 1–12.

Anderson, J. E. (1984) *Public Policy-Making*. New York: Holt, Rinehart & Winston.

Andrews, D. and Bonta, J. (1994) *The Psychology of Criminal Conduct*. Cincinnati, OH: Anderson Publishing.

Annie E. Casey Foundation (2001) *Walking Our Talk in the Neighborhood: Partnerships Between Professionals and Natural Helpers*. Baltimore, MD: Annie E. Casey Foundation.

Argyris, C. and Schön, D. (1974) *Theory in Practice: Increasing Professional Effectiveness*. San Francisco, CA: Jossey-Bass.

Balanced And Restorative Justice (BARJ) Curriculum (2000) Office of Juvenile Justice and Delinquency Prevention, Washington, DC.

Barajas, E. (1998) 'Community Justice: An Emerging Concept and Practice,' in *Community Justice Concepts and Strategies*. Lexington, KY: American Correctional Association.

Bazemore, G. (1997) 'The Community in Community Justice: Issues, Themes and Questions for the New Neighborhood Sanctioning Models,' *Justice System Journal*, 19(2): 193–228.

Bazemore, G. (1998) 'Restorative Justice and Earned Redemption: Communities, Victims and Offender Reintegration,' *American Behavioral Scientist*, 41(6): 768–813.

Bazemore, G. (1999a) 'After the Shaming, Whither Reintegration: Restorative Justice and Relational Rehabilitation,' in G. Bazemore and L. Walgrave (eds), *Restoring Juvenile Justice*. Monsey, NY: Criminal Justice Press.

Bazemore, G. (1999b) 'The Fork in the Road to Juvenile Court Reform,' *Annals of the American Academy of Political Social Science* (July), 564(7): 81–108.

Bazemore, G. (2000) 'Community Justice and a Vision of Collective Efficacy: The Case of Restorative Conferencing,' in National Institute of Justice (ed.), *Policies, Processes and Decisions of the Criminal Justice System*, Criminal Justice 2000, Vol. 3. Washington, DC: US Department of Justice.

Bazemore, G. (2001) 'Young People, Trouble, and Crime: Restorative Justice as a Normative Theory of Informal Social Control and Social Support,' *Youth and Society* (December), 33(2): 199–226.

Bazemore, G. and Maloney, D. (1994) 'Rehabilitating Community Service: Toward Restorative Service in a Lanced Justice System,' *Federal Probation*, 58: 24–35.

Bazemore, G. and Umbreit, M. (1995) 'Rethinking the Sanctioning Function in Juvenile Court: Retributive or Restorative Responses to Youth Crime,' *Crime & Delinquency*, 41(3): 296–316.

Bazemore, G. and Washington, C. (1995) 'Charting the Future of the Juvenile Justice System: Reinventing Mission and Management,' *Spectrum: The Journal of State Government*, 68(2): 51–66.

Bazemore, G. and Day, S. (1996) 'Restoring the Balance: Juvenile and Community Justice,' *Juvenile Justice*, 3(1): 3–14.

Bazemore, G. and Griffiths, C. (1997) 'Conferences, Circles, Boards, and Mediation: The New Wave in Community Justice Decisionmaking,' *Federal Probation*, 59(2): 25–37.

Bazemore, G. and Terry, C. (1997) 'Developing Delinquent Youth: A Reintegrative Model for Rehabilitation and a New Role for the Juvenile Justice System,' *Child Welfare*, 74(5): 665–716.

Bazemore, G. and Umbreit, M. (1999) *Conferences, Circles, Boards, and Mediations: Restorative Justice and Citizen Involvement in the Response to Youth Crime*. Washington, DC: US Department of Justice, Office of Juvenile Justice and Delinquency Prevention.

Bazemore, G. and Walgrave, L. (1999) 'Restorative Juvenile Justice: In Search of Fundamentals and an Outline for Systemic Reform,' in G. Bazemore and L. Walgrave (eds), *Restorative Juvenile Justice: Repairing the Harm of Youth Crime*. Monsey, NY: Criminal Justice Press.

Bazemore, G., Nissen, L. and Dooley, M. (2000) 'Mobilizing Social Support and Building Relationships: Broadening Correctional and Rehabilitative Agendas,' *Corrections Management Quarterly*, 4(4): 10–21.

Bazemore, G. and Stinchcomb, J. (2000) 'Restorative Conferencing and Theory-Based Evaluation,' in G. Burford and J. Hudson (eds), *Family Group Conferencing: New Directions in Community-Centered Child and Family Practice*. New York: Aldine De Gruyter.

Bazemore, G. and Schiff, M. (eds) (2001) *Restorative and Community Justice: Repairing Harm and Transforming Communities*. Cincinnati, OH: Anderson Publishing.

Bazemore, G. and Umbreit, M. (2001) 'Comparison of Four Restorative Conferencing Models,' *Juvenile Justice Bulletin* (February) Office of Juvenile Justice and Delinquency Prevention, Office of Justice Programs, US Department of Justice.

Bazemore, G. and Earl, T. (2002) 'Balance in the Response to Family Violence: Challenging Restorative Principles,' in J. Braithwaite and H. Strang (eds), *Restorative Justice and Family Violence*. London: Cambridge University Press.

Bazemore, G. and Karp, D. (2002) 'Community Justice Sanctioning Models: Assessing Program Integrity,' in J. Perry (ed.), *Repairing Communities Through*

Restorative Justice. Lanham, MD: American Correctional Association Press, pp. 185–212.

Bazemore, G. and McLeod, C. (2002) 'Restorative Justice and the Future of Diversion and Informal Social Control,' in E. Weitekamp and H.-J. Kerner (eds), *Restorative Justice: Theoretical Foundations*. Cullompton, UK: Willan Publishing.

Bazemore, G. and O'Brien, S. (2002) 'The Quest for a Restorative Model of Rehabilitation: Theory-for-Practice and Practice-for-Theory,' in L. Walgrave (ed.), *Restorative Justice and the Law*. Cullompton, UK: Willan Publishing.

Bazemore, G. and Schiff, M. (2002) *Final Report on Understanding the Community Role in Restorative Conferencing for Youthful Offenders*. Princeton, NJ: Robert Wood Johnson Foundation.

Bazemore, G. and Griffiths, C. (2003) 'Police Reform, Restorative Justice and Restorative Policing,' *Police Practice and Research: An International Journal*, 4(4): 335–46.

Bazemore, G. and Stinchcomb, J. (2004) 'Civic Engagement and Reintegration: Toward a Community-Focused Theory and Practice,' *Columbia Human Rights Law Review*, 36, forthcoming.

Becker, H. (1960) *Studies in Sociology of Deviance*. New York: Free Press.

Bellah, R., Madsen, R., Tipton, S., Sullivan, W., and Swidler, A. (1991) *Good Society*. New York: Alfred A. Knopf.

Bennett, S. (1998) 'Community Organizations and Crime,' in D. Karp (ed.), *Community Justice*. Lanham, MD: Rowman & Littlefield.

Bennett, T. (1994) 'Community Policing on the Ground: Developments in Britain,' in D. P. Rosenbaum (ed.), *The Challenge of Community Policing: Testing the Promises*. Thousand Oaks, CA: Sage.

Benson, P. (1997) *All Kids Are Our Kids*. San Francisco, CA: Jossey-Bass.

Black, D. (1976) *The Behavior of Law*. New York: Academic Press.

Bluehouse, P. and Zion, J. (1993) 'Hozhooji Naaliannii: The Navajo Justice and Harmony Ceremony,' 10 *Mediation Q.* 327.

Boland, B. (1998) 'Community Prosecution: Portland's Experience,' in D. Karp (ed.), *Community Justice: An Emerging Field*. Lanham, MD: Rowman & Littlefield.

Bowman, C. G. (1994) 'The Arrest Experiments: A Feminist Critique,' in R. Monk (ed.), *Taking Sides: Clashing Views on Controversial Issues in Crime and Criminology*. Gilford, CT: Dushkin Publishing Group.

Boyes-Watson, C. (2004) What Are the Implications of Growing State Involvement in Restorative Justice?' in H. Zehr and B. Toews-Shenk (eds), *Critical Issues in Restorative Justice*. Monsey, NY: Criminal Justice Press, pp. 215–26.

Bradshaw, W. and Umbreit, M. S. (2003) 'Assessing Satisfaction with Victim Services: The Development and Use of the Victim Satisfaction with Offender Dialogue Scale,' *International Review of Victimology*.

Braithwaite, J. (1989) *Crime, Shame, and Reintegration*. New York: Cambridge University Press.

Braithwaite, J. (1994) 'Thinking Harder about Democratizing Social Control,' in C. Alder and J. Wundersitz (eds), *Family Group Conferencing in Juvenile Justice: The Way Forward or Misplaced Optimism?* Canberra: Australian Institute of Criminology.

Braithwaite, J. (1998) 'Restorative Justice,' in M. Tonry (ed.), *The Handbook of Crime and Punishment*. New York: Oxford University Press.

Braithwaite, J. (1999) 'Restorative Justice; Assessing Optimistic and Pessimistic Accounts,' in M. Tonry (ed.), *Crime and Justice: A Review of Research*, 25. Chicago: University of Chicago Press.

Braithwaite, J. (2001a) 'Restorative Justice and a New Criminal Law of Substance Abuse,' *Youth and Society*, 33: 227–48.

Braithwaite, J. (2001b) 'Youth Development Circles,' *Oxford Review of Education*, 27(2): 23–52.

Braithwaite, J. (2002) *Restorative Justice and Responsive Regulation*. New York: Oxford University Press.

Braithwaite, J. and Petit, P. (1990) *Not Just Desserts: A Republican Theory of Criminal Justice*. Oxford: Oxford University Press.

Braithwaite, J. and Mugford, S. (1994) 'Conditions of Successful Reintegration Ceremonies: Dealing with Juvenile Offenders,' *British Journal of Criminology*, 34(2): 139–71.

Braithwaite, J. and Parker, C. (1999) 'Restorative Justice is Republican Justice,' in G. Bazemore and L. Walgrave (eds), *Restorative Juvenile Justice: Repairing the Harm of Youth Crime*. Monsey, NY: Criminal Justice Press.

Braithwaite, D. and Roche, D. (2001) 'Responsibility and Restorative Justice,' in G. Bazemore and M. Schiff (eds), *Restorative and Community Justice: Repairing Harm and Transforming Communities*. Cincinnati. OH: Anderson Publishing.

Brooks, D. (2000) *Evaluating Restorative Justice Programs*. Paper presented to the United Nations Crime Congress: Ancillary Meeting, Vienna, Austria.

Burford, G. and Hudson, J. (eds) (2001) *Family Group Conferencing: New Directions in Community-Centered Child and Family Practice*. New York: Aldine De Gruyter.

Bursik, R. J. and Grasmick, G. (1993) *Neighborhoods and Crime: The Dimension of Effective Community Control*. New York: Lexington Books.

Bushie, B. (1999) *Community Holistic Circle Healing: A Community Approach*. Proceedings of Building Strong Partnerships for Restorative Practices Conference, Burlington, VT. Pipersville, PA: RealJustice.

Butts, J. and Mears, D. (2001) 'Reviving Juvenile Justice in a Get-Tough Era,' *Youth and Society*, 33(2): 169–98.

Carey, M. (1998) 'Building Hope Through Community Justice,' *Community Justice Concepts and Strategies*. Lexington, KY: American Correctional Association.

Carey, M. (2001) 'Infancy, Adolescence, and Restorative Justice: Strategies for Promoting Organizational Reform,' in G. Bazemore and M. Schiff (eds), *Restorative Community Justice: Repairing Harm and Transforming Communities*. Cincinnati, OH: Anderson Publishing.

Castellano, T. (1986) 'The Justice Model in the Juvenile Justice System: Washington State's Experience,' *Law and Policy*, 8: 479–506.

Chavis, D. (1998), 'Building Community Capacity to Prevent Violence through Coalitions and Partnerships,' in D. Karp (ed.), *Community Justice: An Emerging Field*. Lanham, MD: Rowman & Littlefield.

Chen, H. (1990) *Theory-Driven Evaluations*. Newbury Park, CA: Sage.

Christie, N. (1977) 'Conflict as Property,' *British Journal of Criminology*, 17(1): 1–15.

Clear, T. and Karp, D. (1998) 'The Community Justice Movement,' in D. Karp (ed.), *Community Justice: An Emerging Field*. Lanham, MD: Rowman & Littlefield.

Clear, T. and Karp, D. (1999) *The Community Justice Ideal: Preventing Crime and Achieving Justice*. Boulder, CO: Westview Press.

Clear, T. R. and Karp, D. R. (2000) 'Toward the Ideal of Community Justice,' *National Institute of Justice Journal*, 245: 21–7.

Coates, R., Umbreit, M., and Vos, B. (2000) *Restorative Justice Circles in South Saint Paul, Minnesota*. St Paul, MN: Center for Restorative Justice and Peacemaking, University of Minnesota.

Cohen, S. (1985) *Visions of Social Control, Crime, Punishment and Classification*. Oxford: Polity Press.

Coker, D. (2000) 'Shifting Power for Battered Women: Law, Material Resources, and Poor Women of Color,' *UC Davis Law Review*, 33: 109–1055.

Crawford, A. (1997) *The Local Governance of Crime: Appeals to Community and Partnerships*. New York: Oxford University Press.

Crawford, A. and Clear, T. (2001) 'Community Justice: Transforming Communities Through Restorative Justice?' in G. Bazemore and M. Schiff (eds), *Restorative Community Justice: Repairing Harm and Transforming Communities*. Cincinnati, OH: Anderson Publishing.

Crawford, A. and Newborn, T. (2003) *Youth Offending and Restorative Justice: Implementing Reform in Youth Justice*. Portland, OR: Willan Publishing.

Cullen, F. T. (1994) 'Social Support as an Organizing Concept for Criminology: Residential Address to the Academy of Criminal Justice Sciences,' *Justice Quarterly*, 11: 527–59.

Daly, K. (2000) *Ideals Meet Reality: Research Results on Youth Justice Conferences in South Australia*. Paper prepared for the Fourth International Conference on Restorative Justice for Juveniles, Tübingen, Germany, October.

Daly, K. (2001) 'Restorative Justice in Australia and New Zealand: Variations, Research Findings, and Prospects,' in A. Morris and G. Maxwell (eds), *Restoring Justice for Juveniles: Conferencing, Mediation and Circles*. Oxford: Hart Publishing.

Daly, K. and Kitcher, J. (1999) 'The Revolution of Restorative Justice through Researcher-Practitioner Partnerships,' *Ethics and Justice*, 2(1): 14–20.

Delgado, R. (2000) 'Goodbye to Hammerabi: Concerns about Restorative Justice,' *Stanford Law Review*, 52(4): 751.

Dignan, J. and Marsh, P. (2001) 'Restorative Justice and Family Group Conferences in England: Current State and Future Prospects,' in A. Morris and G. Maxwell (eds), *Restorative Justice for Juveniles: Conferencing, Mediation and Circles*. Oxford: Hart Publishing.

Doble, J. and Immerwahr, S. (1997) 'Delawareans Favor Prison Alternatives,' in M. Tonry and K. Hatlestad (eds), *Sentencing Reform in Overcrowded Times*. New York: Oxford University Press.

Dooley, M. (1998) 'The New Role of Probation and Parole: Community Justice Liaison,' in American Probation and Parole Association, *Community Justice: Concepts and Strategies*. American Probation and Parole Association.

Duffee, D., Renauer, B., Scott, J., Chermak, S., and McGarrell, E. (2001) 'Measuring Community Building Involving the Police,' *The Final Research Report of the Police–Community Interaction Project*. Albany, NY: University at Albany Hindelang Criminal Justice Research Center.

Durkheim, E. (1961) *Moral Education: A Study in the Theory and Application of the Sociology of Education*, trans. E. K Wilson and H. Schnuter. New York: Free Press.

Earle, R. (1996) 'Community Justice: The Austin Experience,' *Texas Probation*, 11: 6–11.

Elliott, D. (1994) *Serious Violent Offenders: Onset, Developmental Course, and Termination*, The American Society of Criminology, 1993 Presidential Address. Reprinted from *Criminology*, 31(1).

Erickson, E. (1968) *Identity, Youth and Crisis*. New York: Norton.

Fader, J., Harris, P., Jones, P., and Poulin, M. (2001) 'Factors Involved in Decisions on Commitment to Delinquency Programs for First-Time Juveniles Offenders,' *Justice Quarterly*, 18(2): 323–41.

Feld, B. (1999) 'Rehabilitation, Retribution and Restorative Justice: Alternative Conceptions of Juvenile Justice,' in G. Bazemore and L. Walgrave (eds), *Restorative Juvenile Justice: Repairing the Harm of Youth Crime*. Monsey, NY: Criminal Justice Press.

Fishman, D. B. (1999) *The Case for Pragmatic Psychology*. New York: New York University Press.

Fowler, F. (1988) *Survey Research Methods*, revised edn. Newbury Park, CA: Sage .

Gaines, P. (2002) 'The Restorative Justice Movement Seeks to Repair Those Harmed by Crime,' *The Crisis*, July/August.

Gerten, B. (2001) Personal communication. St Paul, MN, March.

Gilligan, J. (1996) *Violence: Our Deadly Epidemic and Its Causes*. New York: Vintage Books.

Gilligan, J. (1996) *Violence: Reflections on a National Epidemic*. New York: Random House.

Gilligan, J. and Lee, B. (2001) *The Resolve to Stop the Violence Project: Effectiveness of a Jail-Based Intervention on Reducing Violent Behavior During Incarceration and After Return to the Community*. Cambridge, MA: Harvard Center for the Study of Violence.

Godwin, T. (2001) *The Role of Restorative Justice in Teen Courts: A Preliminary Look*. Monograph, National Youth Court Center, American Probation and Parole Association, Louisville, KY.

Goffman, E. (1963) *Stigma. On the Management of Spoiled Identity*. Englewood Cliffs, NJ: Prentice Hall.

Griffiths, C. T. and Corrado, R. (1999) 'Implementing Restorative Youth Justice: A Case Study in Community Justice and the Dynamics of Reform,' in G. Bazemore and L. Walgrave (eds), *Restorative Juvenile Justice: Repairing the Harm of Youth Crime*. Monsey, NY: Criminal Justice Press, pp. 237–63.

Guarino-Ghezzi, S. and Loughran, N. (1995) *Balancing Juvenile Justice*. New Brunswick, NJ: Transaction Press.

Harrington, C. and Merry, S. (1988) 'Ideological Production: The Making of Community Mediation,' *Law and Society Review*, 22(4): 709–33.

Harris, N. and Buriel, R. (1990) 'Family Ecologies of Ethnic Minority Children,' *Child Development*, 61: 347–62.

Hayes, H. and Daly, K. (2003) 'Youth Justice Conferencing and Re-Offending,' *Justice Quarterly*, 20: 725–64.

Heinz, J., Galaway, B., and Hudson, J. (1986) 'Restitution or Parole: A Follow-up Study of Adult Offenders,' *Social Service Review*, 50: 148–56.

Herman, S. (1999) *The Search for Parallel Justice*. Paper presented to the Restoration for Victims of Crime Conferences, AIC, Melbourne, September.

Herman, S. and Wasserman, C. (2001) 'A Role for Victims in Offender Reentry,' *Crime and Delinquency*, 47(3): 428–45.

Hirschi, T. (1969) *Causes of Delinquency*. Berkeley, CA: University of California Press.

Hudson, J. (2001) Personal communication, September.

Hudson, J. and Galaway, B. (1990) 'Introduction: Towards Restorative Justice,' in B. Galaway and J. Hudson (eds), *Criminal Justice, Restitution, and Reconciliation*. Monsey, NY: Willow Tree Press.

Hudson, J., Galaway, B., Morris, A., and Maxwell, G. (1996) 'Introduction,' in J. Hudson, J. Galaway, A. Morris, and G. Maxwell (eds), *Family Group Conferences: Perspectives on Policy and Practice*. Monsey, NY: Criminal Justice Press.

Hunter, A. J. (1985) 'Private, Parochial and Public Social Orders: The Problem of Crime and Incivility in Urban Communities,' in G. D. Suttles and M. N. Zald (eds), *The Challenge of Social Control: Citizenship and Institution Building in Modern Society*. Norwood, NJ: Aldex Publishing.

Immarigeon, R. (1999) 'Restorative Justice, Juvenile Offenders and Crime Victims: A Review of the Literature,' in G. Bazemore and L. Walgrave (eds), *Restorative Juvenile Justice: Repairing the Harm of Youth Crime*. Monsey, NJ: Criminal Justice Press.

Ingram, H. and Schneider, A. (1991) 'The Social Construction of Target Populations,' *Administration and Society*, 23(3): 353–1.

International Conference on Restorative Justice and Family Violence (2000) Aboriginal Justice and Family Violence Panel, Center for Restorative Justice, Research School of Social Sciences, Australian National University, ACT, 17 July.

Jensen, G. F. and Rojek, D. G. (1998) *Delinquency and Youth Crime*. Prospect Heights, IL: Waveland Press.

Juvenile Court (1996) Pinal County Arizona Mission Statement.

Kahan, D. M. (1996) 'What Do Alternative Sanctions Mean?' *University of Chicago Law Review*, 63: 591–653.

Karmen, A. (2001) *Crime Victims: An Introduction to Victimology*. Belmont, CA: Wadsworth.

Karp, D. (1999) 'Harm and Repair: Observing Restorative Justice in Vermont,' *Justice Quarterly*, 18, 727–57.

Karp, D. (2001) 'The Offender/Community Encounter: Stakeholder Involvement in the Vermont Reparative Boards,' in D. Karp and T. Clear (eds), *What Is Community Justice? Case Studies of Restorative Justice and Community Supervision*. Thousand Oaks, CA: Pine Forge Press.

Karp, D. (2002) *What Is Community Justice? Case Studies of Restorative Justice and Community Supervision*. Thousand Oaks, CA: Pine Forge Press.

Karp, D. and Breslin, B. (2001) 'Restorative Justice in School Communities,' *Youth and Society*, 33: 249–72.

Karp, D. and Walther, L. (2001) 'Community Reparative Boards in Vermont,' in G. Bazemore and M. Schiff (eds), *Restorative Community Justice: Repairing Harm and Transforming Communities*. Cincinnati, OH: Anderson Publishing.

Karp, D., Bazemore, G., and Chesire, J. (2004) *Volunteer Satisfaction in Community Justice Initiatives: A Survey of Vermont Reparative Probation Board Members*. Paper presented at the American Society of Criminology, Atlanta, Georgia.

Karp, D. and Drakulich, K. (2004) 'Minor Crime in a Quaint Setting: An Evaluation of Vermont Reparative Probation,' *Criminology and Public Policy*, forthcoming.

Knot, J. H. and Miller, G. J. (1987) *Reforming Bureaucracy: The Politics of Institutional Choice*. Englewood Cliffs, NJ: Prentice Hall.

Kornhauser, R. R. (1978) *Social Sources of Delinquency*. Chicago: University of Chicago Press.

Krisberg, B. and Patino, V. (2004) *Juvenile Justice in Florida: What Kind of Future?* Monograph, National Council on Crime and Delinquency, Oakland, CA 94612.

Kurki, L. (1999) 'Incorporating Restorative and Community Justice into American Sentencing and Corrections,' *Sentencing and Corrections: Issues for the 21st Century*, National Institute of Justice, Research in Brief Series. Washington, DC.

Kurki, L (2003) 'Evaluating Restorative Practices,' in A. von Hirsch, J. Roberts, A. Bottoms, K. Roach, and M. Schiff (eds), *Restorative Justice and Criminal Justice: Competing or Reconcilable Paradigms?* Oxford: Hart, pp. 293–314.

Lehman, J., Maloney, D., Seymour, A., Gregorie, T. Russell, S., and Shapiro, C. (2002) *The Three R's of Reentry*. Monograph, Justice Solutions, Washington, DC.

Lemert, E. M. (1971) *Instead of Court: Diversion in Juvenile Justice*. Rockville MD: National Institute of Mental Health.

Levrant, S., Cullen, F., Fulton, B., and Wozniak, J. (1999) 'Reconsidering Restorative Justice: The Corruption of Benevolence Revisited?' *Crime and Delinquency*, 45(1): 3–27.

Lipsky, M. (1980) *Street Level Bureaucracy: Dilemmas of the Individual in Public Services*. New York: Russell Sage Foundation.

Lofland, J. and Lofland, L. (1995) *Analyzing Social Settings: A Guide to Qualitative Observation and Analysis*, 3rd edn. London: Wadsworth.

Males, M. (1996) *The Scapegoat Generation*. Monroe, ME: Common Courage Press.

Maloney, D. (1998) *The Challenge of Restorative Community Justice*. Address at the Annual Meeting of the Juvenile Justice Coalition, Washington DC, February.

Maloney, D., Bazemore, G., and Hudson, J. (2001) 'The End of Probation and the Beginning of Community Corrections,' *Perspectives*, Summer: 23–30.

Maloney, D. and Holcomb, D. (2001) 'In Pursuit of Community Justice,' *Youth and Society* (December), 33(2): 296–313.

Marshall, T. F. (1996) 'The Evolution of Restorative Justice in Britain,' *European Journal on Criminal Policy and Research*, 4: 21–43.

Maruna, S. (2001) *Making Good: How Ex-Convicts Reform and Rebuild Their Lives*. Washington, DC: American Psychological Association.

Maruna, S., LeBel, T., and Lanier, C. (2002) 'Generativity Behind Bars: Some "Redemptive Truth" about Prison Society.' Draft Paper, State University of New York at Albany.

Maruna, S., LeBel, T., Burnett, R., Bushway, S., and Kierkus, C. (2003) 'The Dynamics of Desistance and Prisoner Reentry: Findings From a 10-Year Follow-Up of the Oxford University "Dynamics of Recidivism" Study.'.

Mauer, M. (2004) 'Race, Class, and the Development of Criminal Justice Policy,' *Review of Policy Research*, 21(1): 79.

Maxwell, G. and Morris, A. (1993) *Family Participation, Cultural Diversity and Victim Involvement in Youth Justice: A New Zealand Experiment*. Wellington, New Zealand: Victoria University.

Maxwell, G. and Morris, A. (1999) *Understanding Re-offending*. New Zealand Institute of Criminology.

McCold, P. (1996) 'Restorative Justice and the Role of the Community,' in B. Galoway and J. Hudson (eds), *Restorative Justice: International Perspectives*. Monsey, NY: Criminal Justice Press, pp. 85–102.

McCold, P. (2000) 'Toward a Holistic Vision of Restorative Juvenile Justice: A Reply to the Maximalist Model,' *Contemporary Justice Review*, 3(4): 357–72.

McCold, P. and Wachtel, T. (1998) *Restorative Policing Experiment: The Bethlehem Pennsylvania Police Family Group Conferencing Project*. Pipersville, PA: Community Service Foundation.

McCold, P. and Wachtel, T. (2002) 'Restorative Justice Theory Validation,' in E. Weitekamp and H.-J. Kerner (eds), *Restorative Justice: Theoretical Foundations*. Collompton, UK: Willan Publishing, pp. 110–42.

McCold, P. and Wachtel, T. (2003) *In Pursuit of Paradigm: A Theory of Restorative Justice*. Paper presented at the XIII World Congress of Criminology, 10–15 August, Rio de Janeiro.

McDonald, J., Moore, D., O'Connel, T., and Thorsborne, M. (1995) *Real Justice Training Manual: Coordinating Family Group Conferences*. Pipersville, PA: Piper's Press.

McDonald, J. and Moore, D. (2001) 'Community Conferencing as a Special Case of Conflict Transformation,' in K. H. Strang and J. Braithwaite (eds), *Restorative Justice and Civil Society*. Cambridge: Cambridge University Press.

McGarrell, E. (2001) *Restorative Justice Conferences as an Early Response to Young Offenders*. Washington, DC: Office of Juvenile Justice and Delinquency Prevention.

McGillis, D. (1997) *Community Mediation Programs: Developments and Challenges*. Washington, DC: US Department of Justice, National Institute of Justice.

McKnight, J. (1995) *The Careless Society: Community and Its Counterfeits*. New York: Basicbooks.

Melton, A. (1995) 'Indigenous Justice Systems and Tribal Society,' *Judicature*, 70: 126–33.

Miethe, T. (1995) 'Fear and Withdrawal from Urban Life,' *Annals of the American Academy of Political and Social Science*, 539: 14–27.

Miller, W. (1993) *Humiliation*. Ithaca, NY: Cornell University Press.

Molm, L. and Cook, K. (1995) 'Social Exchange and Exchange Networks,' in K. Cook, G. Fine, and J. House (eds), *Sociological Perspectives on Social Psychology*. Boston: Allyn & Bacon.

Moon, M., Sundt, J., Cullen, F., and Wright, J. (2000) 'Is Child Saving Dead? Public Support for Rehabilitation,' *Crime and Delinquency*, 46: 38–60.

Moore, D. (1994) *Illegal Action-Official Reaction*. Paper prepared for the Australian Institute of Criminology.

Moore, D. and McDonald, J. (2000) *Transforming Conflict in Workplaces and Other Communities*. Sydney: Transformative Justice Australia.

Morenoff, J. D., Sampson, R. J., and Raudenbush, S. W. (2001) 'Neighborhood Inequality, Collective Efficacy, and the Spatial Dynamics of Urban Violence,' *Criminology*, 39(3): 517–59.

Morris, A. and Maxwell, G. (2001) 'Restorative Conferencing,' in G. Bazemore and M. Schiff (eds), *Restorative and Community Justice: Repairing Harm and Transforming Communities*. Cincinnati, OH: Anderson Publishing.

Morris, A. and Maxwell, G. (2003) 'Restorative Justice in New Zealand,' in A. Hirsch, J. Roberts, A. Bottoms, K. Roach and M. Schiff (eds), *Restorative Justice and Criminal Justice*. Oxford: Hart Publishing.

Morrison, B. (2001) 'The School System: Developing Its Capacity in the Regulation of a Civilized Society,' in J. Braithwaite and H. Strang (eds), *Restorative Justice and Civil Society*. Cambridge: Cambridge University Press.

Nathanson, D. (1992) *Shame and Pride: Affect, Sex and the Birth of the Self*. New York: Norton.

National Association of Counties (2001) *About Counties: United States Counties*. Washington, DC. Retrieved 12 March 2001 from the World Wide Web: New Zealand Institute of Criminology.

Nugent, W., Williams, M., and Umbreit, M. S. (2003) 'Participation in Victim-Offender Mediation and the Prevalence of Subsequent Delinquent Behavior: A Meta-analysis,' *Utah Law Review*.

O'Brien, S. (1998) *Restorative Juvenile Justice Policy Development and Implementation Assessment: A National Survey of States*. Washington, DC: US Department of Justice, Office of Juvenile Justice and Delinquency Prevention, Balanced and Restorative Justice Project.

O'Brien, S. (1999) *Restorative Justice in the States: A National Survey of Policy and Practices*. Paper presented at the annual conference of the Academy for Criminal Justice Sciences, Orlando, Florida, March.

O'Brien, S. (2000) *Restorative Juvenile Justice Policy Development and Implementation Assessment: A National Survey of States*, Doctoral Dissertation. Florida: Florida Atlantic University.

Oregon State University Information Services (2001) *Government Information Sharing Project: USA Counties*, Oregon 1998. Retrieved 12 March 2001 from the World Wide Web: http://govinfo.kerr.orst.edu/usaco-stateis.html.

Osborne, D. and Gaebler, T. (1992) *Reinventing Government: How the Entrepreneurial Spirit is Transforming the Public Sector*. Reading, MA: Addison-Wesley.

Packer, H. (1967) *The Limits of the Criminal Sanction*. Palo Alto, CA: Stanford University Press.

Patton, M. (1990) *Qualitative Evaluation and Research* Methods, 2nd edn. Newbury, CA: Sage.

Pennel, J. and Burford, G. (2000) 'Family Group Decision Making: Protecting Children and Women,' *Child Welfare*, 79(2): 131–58.

Perry, J. and Gorczyk, J. (1997) 'Restructuring Corrections: Using Market Research in Vermont,' *Corrections Management Quarterly*, 3: 2–35.

Polk, K. (1987) 'When Less Means More: An Analysis of Destructuring in Criminal Justice,' *Crime and Delinquency*, 33: 358–78.

Polk, K. (2001) 'Positive Youth Development, Restorative Justice and the Crisis of Abandoned Youth,' in G. Bazemore and M. Schiff (eds), *Restorative Community Justice: Repairing Harm and Transforming Communities*. Cincinnati, OH: Anderson Publishing.

Polk, K. and Kobrin, S. (1972) *Delinquency Prevention Through Youth Development*. Washington, DC: Office of Youth Development.

Pranis, K. (1996) *Communities and the Justice System – Turning the Relationship Upside Down*. Paper presented to the Office of Justice Programs, US Department of Justice.

Pranis, K. (1997) 'From Vision to Action: Church and Society,' *Presbyterian Church Journal of Just Thoughts*, 87(4): 32–42.

Pranis, K. (1998) *Restorative Justice: Principles, Practices and Implementation, Section 6, Building Community*, National Institute of Corrections Curriculum. Washington, DC: US Department of Justice, Federal Bureau of Prisons, National Institute of Corrections.

Pranis, K. (2001) 'Restorative Justice, Social Justice, and the Empowerment of Marginalized Populations,' in G. Bazemore and M. Schiff (eds), *Restorative Community Justice: Repairing Harm and Transforming Communities*. Cincinnati, OH: Anderson Publishing.

Pranis, K. and Umbreit, M. (1992) *Public Opinion Research Challenges Perception of Widespread Public Demand for Harsher Punishment*. Minneapolis, MN: Minnesota Citizens Council on Crime and Justice.

Pranis, K. and Bazemore, G. (2000) *Engaging Community in the Response to Youth Crime: A Restorative Justice Approach*, Monograph. Washington, DC: Department of Justice, Office of Juvenile Justice and Delinquency Prevention, Balanced and Restorative Justice Project.

Pranis, K. and Stuart, B. (2000) 'Establishing Shared Responsibility for Child Welfare through Peacemaking Circles,' in G. Burford and J. Hudson (eds), *Family Group Conferencing: New Directions in Community-Centered Child and Family Practice*. New York: Aldine De Gruyter.

Presser, L. and Van Voorhis, P. (2002) 'Values and Evaluation: Assessing Processes and Outcomes of Restorative Justice Programs,' *Crime and Delinquency*, 48(1): 162–88.

Pressman, J. L. and Wildavsky, A. (1973) *Implementation*. Berkeley, CA: University of California Press.

Putnam, R. (2000) *Bowling Alone: The Collapse and Revival of American Community*. New York: Simon & Schuster.

Regnery, A. (1985) 'Getting Away with Murder: Why the Juvenile Justice System Needs an Overhaul,' *Policy Review*, 34: 65–8.

Retzinger, S. M. and Scheff, T. J. (1996) 'Strategy for Community Conferences: Emotions and Social Bonds,' in B. Galaway and J. Hudson (eds), *Restorative Justice: International Perspectives*. Monsey, NY: Criminal Justice Press.

Riessman, F. (1965) 'The "Helper Therapy" Principle,' *Social Work*, 10: 27–32.

Riestenberg, N. (1996) *Restorative Measures in the Schools*. Roseville, MN: Minnesota Department of Children, Families and Learning.

Riestenberg, N. (2001) *In-School Behavior Intervention Grants: A Three-Year Evaluation of Alternative Approaches to Suspensions and Expulsions*, Monograph. Roseville, MN: Minnesota Department of Children, Families, and Learning.

Roberts, A. W. and Masters, G. (1999) *Group Conferencing: Restorative Justice in Practice.* Minnesota: The Center for Restorative Justice and Mediation.

Roche, D. (2003) *Accountability in Restorative Justice.* New York: Oxford University Press.

Rojek, D. (1982) 'Juvenile Diversion: A Study of Community Cooptation,' in D. Rojek and G. Jensen (eds), *Reading in Juvenile Delinquency*. Lexington, MA: DC Heath.

Rose, D. and Clear, T. (1998) 'Incarceration, Social Capital and Crime: Implications for Social Disorganization Theory,' *Criminology*, 36(3): 471–9.

Rosenbaum, D. (ed.) (1994) *The Challenge of Community Policing: Testing the Promises.* Thousand Oaks, CA: Sage.

Rosenbaum, D., Lurigio, A., and Davis, R. (1998) *The Prevention of Crime: Social and Situational Strategies.* New York: International Thompson.

Ross, R. (1996) *Returning to the Teachings: Exploring Aboriginal Justice.* London: Penguin Books.

Ross, R. (2000) 'Searching for the Roots of Conferencing,' in G. Burford and J. Hudson (eds), *Family Group Conferencing: New Directions in Community-Centered Child and Family Practice.* New York: Aldine de Gruyter.

Rothman, D. (1980) *Conscience and Convenience: The Asylum and Its Alternatives in Progressive America.* New York: HarperCollins.

Sadd, S. and Grinc, R. (1994) *Innovative Neighborhood-Oriented Policing: Descriptions of Programs in Eight Cities.* New York: Vera Institute of Justice.

Sampson, R. (1999) 'What "Community" Supplies,' in W. J. Dickens and W. T. Dickens (eds), *Urban Problems and Community Development.* Washington, DC: Bookings Institution Press, pp. 241–92.

Sampson, R. and Groves, W. (1989) 'Community Structure and Crime: Testing Social-Disorganization Theory,' *American Journal of Sociology*, 94: 774–802.

Sampson, R. and Laub, J. (1993) *Crime in the Making: Pathways and Turning Points Through Life.* Cambridge, MA: Harvard University Press.

Sampson, R. and Wilson, J. (1995) 'Toward a Theory of Race,' in J. Hagan and R. D. Peterson (eds), *Crime and Urban Inequality.* Stanford, CA: Stanford University Press.

Sampson, R., Raudenbush, S., and Earls, F. (1997) 'Neighborhoods and Violent Crime: A Multi-level Study of Collective Efficacy,' *Science Magazine* (August), 277(4): 918–24.

Sampson, R. J. and Raudenbush, S. W. (2001) *Disorder in Urban Neighborhoods – Does it Lead to Crime?* Washington, DC: National Institute of Justice, Research in Brief.

Scheff, T. J. (1990) *Microsociology: Discourse, Emotion, and Social Structure.* Chicago: University of Chicago Press.

Schiff, M. (1998) 'Restorative Justice Interventions for Juvenile Offenders: A Research Agenda for the Next Decade,' *Western Criminology Review*, 1(1). Available online at: http://wcr.sonoma.edu/v1n1/schiff.html.

Schiff, M. (1999) 'The Impact of Restorative Interventions on Juvenile Offenders,' in G. Bazemore and L. Walgrave (eds), *Restorative Juvenile Justice: Repairing the Harm of Youth Crimes*. Monsey, NY: Criminal Justice Press.

Schiff, M. and Bazemore, G. (2001) 'Exploring and Shaping the Future,' in G. Bazemore and M. Schiff (eds), *Restorative and Community Justice: Repairing Harm and Transforming Communities*. Cincinnati, OH: Anderson Publishing.

Schiff, M., Bazemore, G., and Erbe, C. (2001) *Understanding Restorative Justice: A Study of Youth Conferencing Models in the United States*. Paper presented at the Annual Meeting of the American Society of Criminology. San Francisco, California. November.

Schneider, A. (1986) 'Restitution and Recidivism Rates of Juvenile Offenders: Results from Four Experimental Studies,' *Criminology*, 24: 533–52.

Schneider, A. (1990) *Deterrence and Juvenile Crime: Results from a National Policy Experiment*. New York: Springer Verlag.

Schorr, L . (1988) *Within Our Reach: Breaking the Cycle of Disadvantage*. New York: Doubleday.

Schorr, L. (1997) *Common Purpose: Strengthening Families and Neighborhoods to Rebuild America*. New York: Anchor.

Schur, E. (1973) *Radical Nonintervention: Rethinking the Delinquency Problem*. Englewood Cliffs, NJ: Prentice Hall.

Schwartz, I. (1989) *(In)justice for Juveniles: Rethinking the Best Interests of the Child*. Lexington, MA: Lexington Books.

Schwartz, I. (1992) 'Public Attitudes toward Juvenile Crime and Juvenile Justice: Implications for Public Policy,' in I. Schwartz (ed.), *Juvenile Justice Policy*. Lexington, MA: Lexington Books.

See, C. (1996) 'Interview with Reverend Charles See,' in *Restoring Justice* [video]. Louisville, KY: Presbyterian Church (USA).

Senge, P. (1990) *The Fifth Discipline*. New York: Doubleday Currency.

Seymour, A. and Bazemore, G. (1999) *Victims, Judges and Partnerships for Juvenile Court Reform Project*. Office for Victims of Crime Final Report.

Shaw, C. and McKay, M. (1942) *Juvenile Delinquency in Urban Areas*. Chicago: University of Chicago Press.

Shaw, M. and Jane, F. (1998) *Restorative Justice and Policing in Canada: Bringing the Community into Focus*, Monograph. Montreal: Concordia University, Department of Sociology and Anthropology.

Shennan, L., Strang, H., and Woods, D. J. (2000) *Recidivism Patterns in the Canberra Reintegrative Shaming Experiments*. Canberra: Australian National University.

Sherman, L. (2000) *Repeat Offending in the Canberra RISE Project: An Overview*. Paper presented at the Annual Meeting of the American Society of Criminology, November, San Francisco.

Sherman, L. (2003) 'Reason for Emotion: Reinventing Justice with Theories, Innovations, and Research: The American Society of Criminology Presidential Address,' *Criminology*, 41(1): 1–38.

Sherman, L., Strang, H., and Woods, D. J. (2000) *Recidivism Patterns in the Canberra Reintegrative Shaming Experiments*. Canberra: Australian National University.

Shonholz, R. (1983) *New Justice Theories and Practice*, Community Board Program, 149 Ninth Street, San Francisco, CA 94103.

Skiba, R. and Peterson, R. (1999) 'Zap Zero Tolerance,' *Education Digest*, 64(8): 24–31.

Skogan, W. (1990) *Disorder and Decline: Crime and the Spiral of Decay in American Neighborhood.* New York: Free Press.

Sparrow, M. K., Moore, M. H., and Kennedy, D. M. (1990) *Beyond 911: A New Era for Policing.* New York: Basic Books.

Strang, H. (2003) *Repair or Revenge: Victims and Restorative Justice.* Oxford: Oxford University Press.

Stuart, B. (1996) 'Circle Sentencing-Turning Swords into Ploughshares,' in B. Galaway and J. Hudson (eds), *Restorative Justice: International Perspectives.* Monsey, NY: Criminal Justice Press.

Stuart, B. (2001) 'Guiding Principles for Designing Peacemaking Circles,' in G. Bazemore and M. Schiff (eds), *Restorative and Community Justice: Repairing Harm and Transforming Communities.* Cincinnati, OH: Anderson Publishing.

Tocqueville, A. (1956) *Democracy in America.* New York: Mentor (original work published in 1835).

Toews-Shenk, B. and Zehr, H. (2001) 'Restorative Justice and Substance Abuse: The Path Ahead,' *Youth and Society* (December), 33(2): 314–28.

Tomasic, R. and Feeley, M. (1982) *Neighborhood Justice: An Assessment of an Emerging Idea.* New York: Longman.

Tomkins, S. S. (1962) *Affect Imagery Consciousness: Volume I, The Positive Affects.* New York: Springer.

Tontodonato, P. and Erez, E. (1994) 'Crime, Punishment and Victim Distress,' *International Review of Victimology*, 3: 33–55.

Torbet, P., Gable, R., Hurst, H., Montgomery, I., Szymanski, L., and Thomas, D. (1996) *State Responses to Serious and Violent Juvenile Crime.* Pittsburgh: Office of Juvenile Justice and Delinquency Prevention Research Report, National Center for Juvenile Justice.

Trojanowicz, R. (1993) *Community Policing Survey of Jurisdictions over 50,000 People.* East Lansing, MI: Michigan State University.

Tyler, T. (1999) *Why People Obey the Law.* London: Yale University Press.

Uggen, C. and Janikula, J. (1999) 'Volunteerism and Arrest in the Transition to Adulthood,' *Social Forces*, 78: 331–62.

Uggen, C. and Manza, J. (2003) 'Lost Voices: The Civic and Political Views of Disfranchised Felons,' in Mary Pattillo, David Weiman, and Bruce Western (eds), The Impact of Incarceration on Families and Communities. New York: Russell Sage Foundation.

Uggen, C., Manza, J., and Behrens, A. (2003) 'Less than the Average Citizen': Stigma, Role Transition, and the Civic Reintegration of Convicted Felons, Working Paper, University of Minnesota Department of Sociology.

Umbreit, M. (1993) 'Crime Victims and Offenders in Mediation: An Emerging Area of Social Work Practice,' *Social Work*, 38(1): 69–73.

Umbreit, M. (1996) 'Restorative Justice Through Mediation: The Impact of Programmes in Four Canadian Provinces,' in B. Galaway and J. Hudson (eds), *Restorative Justice: International Perspectives.* Monsey, NY: Criminal Justice Press.

Umbreit, M. (1998) *Victim Offender Mediation Continuum: From Least to Most Restorative Impact*. St Paul, MN: Center for Restorative Justice and Peacemaking, University of Minnesota.

Umbreit, M. (1999) 'Avoiding the Marginalization and McDonaldization of Victim Offender Mediation: A Case Study in Moving Toward the Mainstream,' in G. Bazemore and L. Walgrave (eds), *Restorative Juvenile Justice: Repairing the Harm of Youth Crime*. Monsey, NY: Criminal Justice Press.

Umbreit, M. (2000) *Restorative Justice Conferencing: Guidelines for Victim Sensitive Practice*. Centre for Restorative Justice and peacemaking, University of Minnesota.

Umbreit, M. (2001) *The Handbook of Victim–Offender Mediation*. San Francisco: Jossey-Bass.

Umbreit, M. S. and Coates, R. B. (1992) *Victim Offender Mediation: An Analysis of Programs in Four States of the US*. St Paul, MN: Center for Restorative Justice and Peacemaking, University of Minnesota.

Umbreit, M. and Stacey, S. (1996) Family Group Conferencing Comes to the US: A Comparison with Victim Offender Mediation,' *Juvenile and Family Court Journal*, 47: 29–38.

Umbreit, M. S. and Fercello, C. (1997) *Interim Report: Client Evaluation of the Victim/Offender Conferencing Program in Washington County (MN)*. St Paul, MN: Center for Restorative Justice and Peacemaking, University of Minnesota.

Umbreit, M. and Greenwood, J. (1997) *Criteria for Victim Sensitive Mediation and Dialogue with Offenders*. St Paul: University of Minnesota, Center for Restorative Justice and Peacemaking.

Umbreit, M. and Greenwood, J. (1999) 'National Survey of Victim Offender Mediation Programs in the US,' *Mediation Quarterly*, 16: 235–51.

Umbreit, M., Greenwood, J., Umbreit, J., and Fercello, C. (2003) *Directory of Victim–Offender Mediation in the US*. St Paul, MN: Center for Restorative Justice and Peacemaking.

Van Ness, D. (2001) *The Shape of Things to Come: A Framework for Thinking about a Restorative Justice System*. Paper presented at the Balanced and Restorative Justice Train the Trainers Seminar, 19 May, Jupiter, Florida.

Van Ness, D. and Strong, K. H. (1997) *Restoring Justice*. Cincinnati, OH: Anderson.

Van Ness, D. and Schiff, M. (2001) 'Satisfaction Guaranteed? The Meaning of Satisfaction in Restorative Justice,' in G. Bazemore and M. Schiff (eds), *Restorative and Community Justice: Repairing Harm and Transforming Communities*. Cincinnati, OH: Anderson Publishing.

Van Ness, D. and Strong, K. H. (2001) *Restoring Justice*, 2nd edn. Cincinnati, OH: Anderson Publishing.

Van Voorhis, P. (1985) 'Restitution Outcomes and Probationers Assessment of Restitution: The Effects of Moral Development,' *Criminal Justice and Behavior*, 12: 259–87.

Warner, B. (2003) 'The Role of Attenuated Culture in Social Disorganization Theory,' *Criminology*, 41: 73–98.

Warren, R. (1977) *Social Change and Human Purpose: Toward Understanding and Action*. Chicago: Rand McNally College Publishing.

Weiss, C. (1997) 'How Can Theory-Based Evaluation Make Greater Headway?' *Evaluation Review*, 21(4): 501–24.

Weitekamp, E. (1999) 'The History of Restorative Justice,' in G. Bazemore and L. Walgrave (eds), *Restorative Juvenile Justice: Repairing the Harm of Youth Crime*. Monsey, NY: Criminal Justice Press.

Weitekamp, E. and Kerner, H.-J. (eds) (2002) *Restorative Justice: Theoretical Foundations*. Cullompton, UK: Willan Publishing.

White, R. (1998) Public Spaces for Young Persons: A Guide to Creative Projects and Public Spaces. Melbourne: Australian Youth Foundation, Commonwealth of Australia.

White, R. (2000) *Restorative Community Justice: Community Building Approaches in Juvenile Justice*. Paper presented at the 4th National Outlook Symposium on Crime, Australia Institute of Criminology, Canberra, Australia, June.

Whitehead, J. T. and Lab, S. P. (1996) *Juvenile Justice: An Introduction*. Cincinnati, OH, Anderson Publishing.

Wright, M. (1991) *Justice for Victims and Offenders*. Buckingham, UK: Open University Press.

Yin, R. (1994) *Case Study Research: Design and Methods*. Sage.

Young, M. (1995) *Restorative Community Justice: A Call to Action*. Washington, DC: National Organization for Victim Assistance.

Young, R. and Hoyle, C. (2002) 'New, Improved Police Led Restorative Justice? Action-Research and the Thames Valley Police Initiative,' in A. von Hirsch, A. Bottoms, J. Roberts, K. Roach, and M. Schiff (eds), *Restorative Justice and Criminal Justice: Competing or Reconcilable Paradigms*. Oxford: Hart Publishing.

Zehr, H. (1990) *Changing Lenses: A New Focus for Crime and Justice*. Scottsdale, PA: Herald Press.

Zehr, H. (2000) *Journey to Belonging*. Paper presented at the Fourth International Conference on Restorative Justice for Juveniles, Tübingen, Germany, September.

Zehr, H. (2001) *Transcending: Reflections of Crime Victims*. Intercourse, PA: Good Books.

Zehr, H. and Mika, H. (1998) 'Fundamental Concepts of Restorative Justice,' *Contemporary Justice Review*, 1: 47–55.

Index

Added to the page number, 'f' denotes a figure and 't' denotes a table.